THE COMPLETE
ENCYCLOPEDIA OF THE

SAS

THE COMPLETE ENCYCLOPEDIA OF THE SAS

BARRY DAVIES B.E.M.

Dedication

I dedicate this book to all members of the Special Air Service family, both past and present. More specifically to those SAS soldiers who fought in World War II, who operated without the high-tech military hardware available today, and without the luxury of helicopter extraction; men whose names I cannot find, whose deeds may never be told – but who will always be remembered.

Barry Davies

This edition first published in 2001 by
Virgin Books Ltd
Thames Wharf Studios
Rainville Road
London W6 9HA

First published in Great Britain in 1998 by Virgin Publishing

Reprinted 2003

ISBN 07535 0534 7

Typeset by TW Typsetting, Plymouth, Devon
Printed and bound by Mackays of Chatham PLC

Introduction

It is now almost 57 years since the Special Air Service came into being, during which time many special men have given their lives or suffered great hardships, but through it all have won outstanding victories which have given them supremacy within the armies of the world. Yet from the very beginning such men have remained hidden, often shrouded in myths and half-truths. Their story is deserving and long overdue, but now is told.

The Complete Encyclopedia of the SAS categorizes the outstanding deeds, not just of the British Special Air Service but of the whole Special Air Service family. I served for eighteen years in the SAS, yet if I am honest, my knowledge of the regiment's founders and their daring raids in the empty deserts of North Africa was minimal to say the least. Unlike their present-day counterparts in 22 SAS, they had no high-tech equipment, little state-of-the-art weaponry; all they had was courage to dare and to win. Likewise, although I knew of the existence of the Rhodesian, Australian and New Zealand SAS units, I had scant knowledge of their history. So I endeavoured to research their acts of personal bravery, and tell of their operations, many of which equal any in the British SAS.

Research for this book has taken many forms and required the reading of over 30 books about the SAS family. By far the best information was gleaned from a complete collection of war-time magazines, *The War Illustrated*, that were published throughout World War II and which I found sitting in a damp, dark corner in a bookshop in Hay-on-Wye.

Many operations and individuals are mentioned more than once in this volume, but where possible I have tried to keep the repetition of stories to a minimum. While tales of bravery and unselfish effort abound, one snippet did catch my eye, which, considering it was sent from the battlefront, highlights the British sense of humour. It is a message sent back to GHQ by a member of the 'Phantoms', which I quote from *Phantom*, by Philip Warner:

11 April 1945: We are now in Leek, east of Weser, opposite Niemberg. Division now advancing north of Bremen. Technique! Dedication on a girl's photograph found amongst the papers of PoW Obergefreiter Karl Schagg of 115 Panzer Battalion: '*Du kannst es so nett und so lange*' (You can do it so lovely and so long).

Unlike the previous books, I have written *The Complete Encyclopedia of the SAS* in a clinical, matter-of-fact style; inevitably, however, a number of personal opinions have crept into the text. Should you find these, please accept them as my personal opinions, as they do not reflect the official opinions or policies of any Special Air Service unit. Neither should the reader take the word 'Complete' too literally, for few military units in modern times can lay claim to the numerous actions undertaken by the Special Air Service units, and even this book has limitations. Yet herein lies the truth, for I have tried to paint a fair and honest picture, one that will dispel the myths and misunderstandings that conceal the Special Air Service. I have written about the SAS family as it truly is, a brotherhood of special men. For when men of the right calibre accept a common philosophy based on the individual spirit acting in tune with his brother soldier to form a whole, then excellence can be the only result.

Finally, on the subject of Special Air Service soldiers past or present divulging information, I can only state that I was trusted implicitly for eighteen years while serving in 22 SAS, and for me personally that loyalty still remains unquestionable. Real secrets remain secret, but this does not bind us to some blind compulsion for secrecy for secrecy's sake. If it did, why then have so many men died maintaining our liberty of free speech? The Special Air Service I know has nothing to hide; if anything their tight-lipped approach to their work is often due to their non-boastful shyness, something which is often found in a true professional.

Barry Davies

A

AAA OR TRIPLE A The name given to anti-aircraft artillery mainly in reference to actions into the Gulf War.

ABBOTS, SERGEANT RAYMOND 'GROWLER' A member of G Squadron, Sergeant Abbots was the first and only member of the SAS to die in the Hereford-based training facility known as the 'Killing House'. The accident happened on 15 January 1985, during assault team training. Despite instant expert medical assistance, Sergeant Abbots died within a few minutes. Known affectionately as 'Growler', so called for his likeness to the cartoon character Mutley, and his dry humour, Ray Abbots originally joined the SAS in January 1973, after serving with 4 Royal Tank Regiment.

'ABEL', OPERATION An SAS operation undertaken around Doubs in eastern France, between 27 August and 22 September 1944. Operation 'Abel', under the command of Captain Sicand, comprised 82 soldiers of 3 French Parachute Battalion (3 SAS). One company successfully carried out several blocking actions and hit-and-run raids, in a combined effort with Maquis (French underground) units, and troops of the advancing French First Army and the US Seventh Army. The aim was to capture a strategic pass between the Vosges and Jura mountains known as the Belfort Gap. Tragically, between 16 July and 7 October, 3 SAS lost much of its effective strength when 96 men were killed, wounded or captured. By contrast the battalion succeeded in killing 2,340 Germans, wounding a further 2,976 and taking 1,090 prisoners, in addition to causing the enemy enormous material damage.

ABSEILING The SAS use abseiling in two main ways: descending a rock face during mountain training or operations, and as an entry method in anti-terrorist work.

Abseil equipment comprises the following: an abseil harness; abseil ropes and karabiners. The abseil harness is a full-body harness, permitting a team member to be suspended for protracted periods of time (ie outside a window). It consists of a waist belt and chest harness connected by a combi-sling. Abseil ropes are 11mm (.42in) in diameter, non-stretch, black polyester rope. This is available in differing pre-cut lengths of 50 (54), 100 (109), 150 (163), and 200m (218yds). Various descenders are used. The ANKA descender is a horned 'figure 8' abseil descender with the lower ring set at 90 degrees to the upper one, eliminating any tendency to twist during a descent. The STOP descender works on the 'fail safe' principle in that it requires the user to apply pressure on its handle for the rope to move through it. Release of the handle causes descent to be halted immediately. Karabiners, with locking screwgates and with a breaking strain of 3,000kg (1,350lbs), join the separate abseiling units. Rope bags are used during anti-terrorist work to facilitate smooth deployment of a rope during a descent.

ACCURACY INTERNATIONAL L96A1 PM 7.62 SNIPER RIFLE *Specification* Calibre: 7.62mm × 51 NATO standard; Weight: 2.9kg (6.5lbs) with sight; Muzzle velocity: 850m (926yds) per second; Magazine capacity: 10-round, box.

The current favoured sniper rifle of the SAS. The PM is designed and manufactured by Accuracy International and has a reputation for great accuracy in any conditions, achieving head shots at 300–600m (327–654yds). The rifle can be fitted with different sights, according to what is required. There are also various versions of the model, including one that can be used in Arctic conditions without freezing up. The PM is a bolt-action 7.62 rifle with a stainless steel barrel. The rifle is very comfortable to fire, and the sniper's head need not be moved during bolt operation, allowing for continuous observation through the sight. It has a bipod and a retractable spike beneath the rear of the butt for stability. It is also available in a covert model which is fitted with a silencing suppressor, and a Super Magnum version which fires either .338 Lapua Magnum, .300 Winchester Magnum or 7mm Remington Magnum rounds.

ACTIVE SERVICE UNIT An operational cell of the Irish Republican Army (IRA). Such cells usually consist of three to four people but this number may increase to ten in certain circumstances. Their purpose is to carry out bombings, mortar attacks, assassinations and strikes against the security services, prestige targets and individuals, both in Northern Ireland, the British mainland and Europe. Each unit operates independently thus cutting the risk of any disloyalty or double-dealing, which would affect the whole organization. Weapons and explosives will be supplied by the member designated to be quartermaster, and a set of trusted go-betweens will normally ferry such equipment around. Cell members are normally well known to the security forces and they are constantly stopped and searched. If a member of the cell is killed or arrested then the next most trusted go-between is usually moved into his place.

ADAT (ARMY DEPENDANT'S ASSURANCE TRUST) ADAT is a type of military insurance in the British Army. Soldiers are encouraged to buy shares in the scheme – the greater the number of shares the larger the pay out. Although ADAT is not compulsory in the British Army, it is actively encouraged within the SAS due to the nature of their work. Upon the death of a soldier the next of kin will receive an interim payout within 24 hours with the bulk of the claim following in a few weeks.

ADEN Aden was under British rule from 1839 to 1967. By 1963 it had joined with the British-governed Federation of South Arabia (FSA), originally set up in 1959 as an amalgamation of several small states, emirates and sultanates. It had joined the FSA on the stipulation that Britain would maintain a presence there after full independence, scheduled for 1968 or before. In 1962 the Soviet Union backed unrest in neighbouring Yemen which led to the overthrow of the ruling imam. The deposed ruler escaped and raised an opposition army, which was secretly aided by the British and French governments and contained several former SAS soldiers. This was based in the Aden Protectorate. Yemen claimed territory in the lands held by the FSA and supported two resistance groups in the Aden Protectorate: the National Liberation Front (NLF) and the Front for the Liberation of Occupied South Yemen (FLOSY). In 1963, in response to calls for assistance, Britain intervened with military aid. The inhabitants of the mountainous Radfan area, armed and trained by the Egyptians and Yemenis, were preparing to make war on British and Federal forces. The British assembled a task force to deal with the uprising. Known as Radforce, it included an SAS detachment from A Squadron.

A Squadron's base was located at Thumier, 100km (62 miles) north of Aden. One of its first missions was to take an important enemy position code-named 'Cap Badge'. Once secured, this area would be used as a drop-zone for units of the Parachute Regiment. The mission was compromised when they were spotted by a goatherd and the SAS were forced to fight their way out, making their way back to their camp. The plan to drop the paras into the area had to be abandoned and the SAS were forced to rethink their operations along less ambitious lines.

Subsequent SAS operations tended to concentrate on establishing covert observation posts (OPs) and gathering intelligence about the enemy. This was carried out by members of A, B and D Squadrons, who were rotated from operations in Borneo. As the date for British withdrawal neared, enemy activity intensified and the SAS became increasingly worried about their base at Thumier being attacked.

Meanwhile, a different kind of war was being fought in the port of Aden itself. The terrorists of the NLF operated within the town and the SAS found themselves caught up in counter-terrorist activity. From their base at Ballycastle House a group of twenty men, who could pass themselves off as Arabs, were busy infiltrating the Crater and Sheikh Othman districts.

Despite the manpower, time, hardship and lives invested in Aden, it was a lost cause. On 26 June 1967, Radfan was handed over to the Federal Regular Army and the British Army pulled out without anything being gained. However, the SAS had at least developed some new and important skills in the art of counter-insurgency. Once the British withdrawal had been completed in November 1967, Aden became governed by the communist-backed People's Democratic Republic of Yemen. It was this regime that backed the overthrow of the sultan of its neighbour, Oman, a conflict in which the SAS were also to find themselves involved.

ADOO The Arabic word for 'enemy' and a term used by the SAS in Oman for the guerrilla forces of the People's Front for the Liberation of the Occupied Arabian Gulf (PFLOAG) and the Dhofar Liberation Front (DLF). Most Adoo dressed in a similar way to the Firqat, the local 'irregulars', but some of their leaders were better dressed than the SAS, with khaki shorts and shirt, ammunitions belt, water and AK-47. This would all be topped off with a blue beret complete with red star and a copy of the *Thoughts of Chairman Mao*. Captured Adoo would normally be handed to the Omani authorities who, after interrogation, would try to persuade them to join the Firqat.

AEGEAN SEA The Aegean features the Dodecanese, a large group of islands which were the scene of operations in World War II by the Special Boat Section (SBS), commanded by Major the Earl George Jellicoe. These were carried out against German forces in occupation on a number of islands including Crete, Karpathos, Leros, Kos, Simi, Tilos, Astipalaia and several smaller ones, these forming part of a defensive perimeter against Allied operations in the eastern Mediterranean.

In January 1944, the SBS established 40 heavily camouflaged anchorages which served as bases for operations among the Dodecanese Islands. A schooner, the *Tewfik*, acted as a forward headquarters for Major Jellicoe while a fleet of armed caïques, motor launches and other small craft, under the command of Lieutenant-Commander Adrian Seligmann RN, was employed to ferry the SBS squadrons around the islands. Overall control of raiding operations in the Aegean was the responsibility of Headquarters Raiding Forces, based in Cairo, which was formed in late October 1943 under the command of Colonel (later Brigadier) Douglas Turnbull.

AGEDABIA On 21 December 1941 the airfield at Agedabia, on the coast of Libya south of Benghazi (see Raid on), was raided by a force of five members of L Detachment SAS, comprising Sergeants Bob Tait and DuVivier and Privates Byrne and Phillips, under the command of Lieutenant Bill Fraser. Having been dropped off by a Long Range Desert Group (LRDG) patrol 16km (10 miles) south of their objective, they marched throughout the night and reached a lying-up position (LUP) from which they were able to observe the airfield throughout the following day. Each man carried a water bottle, compass, revolver, eight Lewes bombs, a tin of chocolate, plus other rations consisting of raisins, cheese and broken biscuits. After nightfall on the following day, Fraser and his men succeeded in penetrating the defences of the airfield, which was heavily wired and well guarded, placing Lewes bombs on 37 aircraft. The raid was a great success; all the bombs went off resulting in 37 Italian CR42 fighter-bombers being destroyed. During the explosions, the patrol withdrew in the subsequent confusion without loss, and made its way to a rendezvous with an LRDG patrol which was waiting for them. Though no casualties were suffered during the raid itself, two members of the unit were killed when two Allied Blenheim aircraft strafed their vehicles, despite the fact that the correct air recognition signals had been displayed. The remainder reached the LRDG and SAS base at Jab Oasis on 23 December.

AGHEILA An ineffectual raid carried out in December 1941 led by Captain John Lewes. The Agheila airfield on the Gulf of Sirte, North Africa proved to be abandoned. Some success was achieved when the frustrated raiding party came across a large number of Italian vehicles near a roadhouse at Mersa Brega, which they destroyed. 'Jock' Lewes used a captured Italian truck complete with machine gun mounted on the back to shoot up the roadhouse.

AH HOI A Communist Terrorist (CT) notorious during the Malayan Emergency campaign (1948–60), Ah Hoi was nicknamed the 'Baby Killer' after murdering the pregnant wife of a man suspected of being an informer for the security force. This brutal act was carried out as a warning to all local people in the area of Kuala Tengi and Kuala Selangor. Ah Hoi was reported to be in hiding in the Telok Anson swamp which covers an area of 450sq km (180 sq miles) in the state of Selangor, and D Squadron 22 SAS, commanded by Major Harry Thompson MC, was given the task of dealing with him. In February 1958 a force of 37 men from the squadron was dropped by parachute into the area. Unfortunately one man, Trooper Jerry Mulcahy, broke his back after his parachute canopy failed to snag in the trees – using the technique known as tree-jumping, this is crucial – and he had to be evacuated by helicopter.

Thereafter the search began with 6 Troop, commanded by Captain Peter de la Billière, following the river line of the Sungei Tengi. As the troop progressed upriver, it came across a number of abandoned terrorist camps. After seven days, just as dusk was falling, a troop commanded by Sergeant 'Bosun' Sandilands was informed by a native that the latter had seen two CTs, a man and a woman, by the river. Accompanied by Corporal Finn, Sergeant Sandilands moved up and shortly afterwards spotted the two terrorists. Working their way to within 45m (50yds), Sandilands and Finn opened fire, killing the man but missing the woman who disappeared into the jungle. The troop followed up and soon afterwards found two camps showing signs of having been hastily abondoned.

A cordon of troops and police was established around the area while B Squadron closed in on its quarry. Two days later a female terrorist, named Ah Niet, approached a police post with a message from Ah Hoi, who offered to surrender in exchange for a sum of money for himself and each of his men, as well as an amnesty for all previously captured terrorists languishing in prison. Not surprisingly, this offer was refused and Ah Niet was despatched back to the jungle with a message which made it clear to Ah Hoi that he should surrender within 24 hours or face being hunted down and killed. That evening, Ah Hoi and some of his men appeared and surrendered. The remainder gave themselves up 48 hours later. Ah Hoi himself was subsequently despatched to China in exile.

AH MING During the Malayan Emergency, Ah Ming was the leader of a small but active Communist Terrorist (CT) group operating under the name of the Asian States Liberation Army (ASAL) which dominated the area around the fortified base of Fort Brooke on the border between the two states of Perak and Kelantan. Such was ASAL's influence, exerted initially by somewhat brutal means, that all the indigenous people in the area had been cowed into submission. It was decided that Ah Ming and his group had to be neutralized and the task was given to the New Zealand SAS (NZSAS) squadron, under Major Frank Rennie, which was operating from Fort Brooke. The operation was to prove a lengthy one, lasting three months.

The squadron's 3 Troop was deployed a few days before the start of the main operation with the task of making contact with a group of ten natives who had approached the Royal Malay Police Special Branch after defecting from the CT cause. The rendezvous was made one evening in the jungle and the aborigines joined forces with the troop who were soon on the trail of Ah Ming.

A few days later a patrol under the troop commander, Lieutenant Ian Burrows, carried out a dawn attack on a CT camp and killed two terrorists, one of whom was identified. Thereafter, the fortunes of ASLA continued to decline: another contact with the NZSAS squadron resulted in the death of Ah Ming's second-in-command, Kam Chen, in whose possession was found a letter addressed to another CT group, operating in the north of Malaya, asking for help. Unfortunately, the NZSAS did not escape unscathed: Trooper 'Charlie' Thomas was wounded during a contact and died before he could be evacuated.

AH POY Ah Poy, a Communist Terrorist (CT) district committee secretary in Malaya, was killed in 1954 by members of A Squadron 22 SAS, commanded by Captain Johnny Cooper. The squadron had been tasked with Operation 'Ginger', designed to flush out the terrorists from the south of Ipoh.

AH TUK Ah Tuk was a well-known Communist Terrorist (CT) who led a small group operating east of Taiping, on the east coast of Malaya. He enjoyed good relations with the indigenous people in the area who supported the terrorists, and who gave warning of the presence of security forces units. In January 1957 D Squadron 22 SAS returned to the area, having operated there previously and thus being very familiar with it. Shortly afterwards, a patrol was inserted into the area and while moving through the jungle the lead scout, Sergeant Bob Turnbull, a man with legendary skill as a tracker, spotted a man's head at a range of 18m (20yds). Firing three rounds rapid, Turnbull brought down his target who was subsequently identified as Ah Tuk. A subsequent search of the terrorist's possessions revealed diaries and documents which provided much useful information.

AIRBORNE CORPS Commanded by Lieutenant General Sir Frederick 'Boy' Browning, 1st Airborne Corps was the higher command formation for the SAS Brigade during operations in Europe in World War II. Although the brigade co-ordinated with other Special Forces, such as SOE (Special Operations Executive), and 'Jedburgh' teams via Special Forces Headquarters (SFHQ), which in turn came under the direct command of Supreme Headquarters Allied Expeditionary Force (SHAEF), the Airborne Corps headquarters included its own SAS cell which comprised General Serving Officer (GSO) 1, GSO 2, GS03 and two intelligence officers.

AIR STRIKE All members of the SAS are instructed in how to call in an air strike. The system is not difficult and at times, such as at the Battle of Mirbat in 1972, it can make the difference between success and failure. In the past air strikes were directed by a simple radio call to the pilot, giving him a call-sign and indicating the positions of friendly forces and that of the enemy.

High visibility air-marker panels are carried by the SAS and normally laid in a 'T' configuration, the top surface indicating which way to the target. The marker panels, which measure 50cm × 2m (19in × 2.1yds), are orange dayglo, making them an easy feature for the pilot to observe. Once voice contact with the pilot has been established, a simple: 'See my Tango; 300m; enemy behind large tree', will get the caller results.

Modern technology allows for a more sophisticated method of air strike using Laser Target Marking (LTM). This enables an SAS patrol to distance itself from the target, simply illuminating it with a laser beam. An inbound aircraft will then fire its missile, again from a safe distance, knowing that the laser will 'lock-on' and guide it faithfully to the target.

AIR TROOP   Air Troop is the 'free-fall' troop within each squadron, whose normal role is that of pathfinder or, when operational necessity demands, covert parachute entry. They specialize in both High Altitude Low Opening (HALO) and High Altitude High Opening (HAHO).

Depending on the tactical circumstances, aircraft deploying free-fall troops are able to fly at heights up to 10,640m (35,000ft). At this altitude oxygen is required and is administered from a central console when in flight, and by an individual supply during the drop. Each parachutist usually carries his equipment in a bergen which is attached, upside down, to the back of the thighs until it is released once the canopy is deployed. Weapons are also carried, usually the AR-15 M16/203, depending on the operation. Most free-fallers will hold the bergen with their feet until they are some 15m (50ft) from the ground, despite it being attached to the parachute harness by a 4.5m (15ft) line, as releasing the bergen incorrectly can result in serious injury.

Ram-air parachutes are normally used by free-fall troops since the rectangular box-like design of the canopy allows for improved manoeuvrability and control, as well as an adjustable rate of descent. The front of the parachute is open to the driving air, whilst holes in the internal sections allow for cross venting of the currents, causing the parachute to inflate like a wing. Direction and descent of the canopy is controlled by two lines attached to the outer, rear corners of the wing. Pulling both control lines down fully literally stalls the canopy to a complete stop on landing. The glide ratio on a ram-air parachute is about 4:1.

Air Troop also participate in various other methods of flying, one of which has included the use of a small motor-powered trike attached to a ram-air parachute. The vehicle was relatively easy to fly, with a range of up to 288km (180 miles), despite being particularly frightening at take-off and landing.

The first free-fall operation carried out by the SAS was in the north of Oman in December 1970, when two Air Troops entered the Wadi Rawdah under cover of darkness. Unfortunately, due to the nature of the terrain and the heavy amount of equipment carried, there was one fatality.

AK-47 ASSAULT RIFLE *Specification* Calibre: 7.62mm × 39 Soviet standard; Weight: 4.3kg (9.46lbs); Muzzle velocity: 710m (776yds) per second; Magazine capacity: 30-round, box; Rate of fire: 600rpm.

The Avtomat Kalashnikova was developed by the Soviets in the late 1940s and was designed for close-range combat. Robust, easy to mend and reliable, with a fully automatic capacity, it became the standard infantry weapon in the Warsaw Pact countries. By 1959 it had been largely replaced by the AKM, and later the AK-74. However, the AK-47 has remained one of the most widely used weapons in the world and is often found in the hands of conscripts in Third World armies and guerrilla forces.

AK-74 ASSAULT RIFLE *Specification* Calibre: 5.45mm × 39 Soviet standard; Weight: 3.6kg (8lbs); Muzzle velocity: 900m (984yds) per second; Magazine capacity: 30-round, box; Rate of fire: 650rpm.

The Russian-made successor to the AK-47 and the AKM. This assault rifle, however, uses a smaller calibre round which is designed to deform when it hits a target. Introduced in 1979, this weapon is in use mainly within former Soviet republics and some previous Warsaw Pact forces.

AKACHE, ZOHAIR A Palestinian terrorist first identified as a member of the Popular Front for the Liberation of Palestine (PFLP) while he was studying in Britain. He is thought to have been responsible for the assassination of the former Prime Minister of North Yemen, al-Qadi Abdulla al-Hajri, who was in London for talks. The diplomat, his wife and the chauffeur were gunned down outside the Lancaster Hotel in Westbourne Street, at 11:00 on Sunday 10 April 1977. Akache fled the country, returning to the Middle East, where in October he commanded a PFLP team which hijacked a German Lufthansa 737 airliner. Five days into the hijack, the aircraft, now in the Somali capital Mogadishu, was stormed by German GSG9 aided by two SAS specialists. Akache was killed during the attack.

AKEHURST, BRIGADIER JOHN Operational Commander of the SAF (Sultan's Armed Forces) of Oman between the years of 1974 and 1976. The use of Firqats, or local 'irregulars', greatly contributed to the success of the final stage of the war. Indeed, the brigadier later gave an unclassified lecture to describe their techniques. Working closely in conjunction with the SAS to win the support of the civilians, these troops were able to gather intelligence and establish settlements with essential facilities such as water, thereby diminishing support for the guerrillas. Firqat and the SAS also fought alongside each other, creating strong defensive lines.

In the last major battle of the Oman War, on Akehurst's approval of Major Alan Trant's plan to mount an attack on the Shirshitti caves, on

4 January 1975 the SAF Jebel Regiment, Firqats and the SAS together fought a hard and bloody fight in a successful assault on the caves.

ALBINEA The village of Albinea in Italy's Po Valley was the location of the headquarters of the German LI Corps, which was quartered in two houses, called the Villa Calvi and Villa Rossi, and whose staff numbered about 300 personnel. After an overnight approach march down from the Apennine mountains, on 24 March 1945, an attack was carried out on the following night by elements of 3 Squadron 2 SAS, under the command of Major Roy Farran, supported by a force of 170 Italian and Russian partisans, the latter being escapees from German prison camps. Two groups, each of ten SAS and twenty partisans, attacked the villas while the remainder of the partisans formed a screen to the south of the objective to block any enemy reinforcements approaching the area. There was fierce fighting at both houses; enemy casualties were heavy and included a number of staff officers killed, among them the headquarters' Chief-of-Staff, Oberst Lemelson. It later transpired that the corps commander, Generalleutnant Hauk, was away from his headquarters at the time. The SAS suffered three fatal casualties, Lieutenant Riccomini, Sergeant Guscott and Corporal Bolden, and two wounded, Corporal Layburn and Parachutist Mulvey. The partisans suffered five wounded and six captured. Also wounded was Major Michael Lees, an SOE (Special Operations Executive) liaison officer working with the partisans who had attached himself to the SAS. Nevertheless, Farran's force succeeded in withdrawing and, having avoided German forces searching the valley plain, made its way back to its base in the mountains.

'ALBUMEN', OPERATION 'Albumen' was a Special Boat Section (SBS) operation carried out on 22 June 1943 when S Squadron SBS was landed on the south coast of Crete near Cape Kochinoxos. The mission was the destruction of enemy aircraft on airfields at Heraklion, Timbakion and Kastelli and these were the targets of patrols led by Lieutenants Kenneth Lamonby, Ronnie Rowe and Anders Lassen respectively. Lamonby found no aircraft but destroyed a large fuel dump and Rowe found his objective deserted. Lassen's patrol was engaged in a firefight with alert sentries, but nevertheless succeeded in destroying four Stuka aircraft, an armoured vehicle and a fuel dump. Despite being betrayed by a Cretan villager, Lassen and one of his men succeeded in evading capture and returned safely to the squadron base where he met the rest of his patrol.

ALDERSHOT Home of the British Army, in particular the various parachute units from which the SAS draws many of its soldiers.

ALIMNIA The island of Alimnia was the scene of the capture of a Special Boat Section (SBS) patrol on 9 April 1944, when Captain Hugh

Blyth and his patrol of S Squadron was captured on board the caïque commanded by Sub-Lieutenant Allan Tuckey, RNVR. Blyth and his men, together with Tuckey and his crew, were taken to Salonika where they were interrogated by Wehrmacht intelligence officers. Blyth was, for some inexplicable reason, sent to a PoW camp in Germany while the remainder were handed over to the Sicherheitsdienst, the SS Security Service. They were subsequently executed under the terms of Hitler's Commando Order of October 1942 which stipulated that all members of Allied Commando and Special Forces were to be executed after capture.

AL JOUF AIR BASE   A coalition air base in north west Saudi Arabia where the SAS established a forward operating base during the 1990–91 Gulf War. The men, who had been formed into fighting columns and foot patrols at the training camp code-named 'Victor' were eventually launched into Iraq from Al Jouf.

ALLAN, WO1 (RSM) PETER   WO1 Peter Allan was regimental sergeant-major of the Rhodesian 1st Special Air Service Regiment (RhSAS). In addition to his duties as RSM, he took part in a number of actions in which he and teams of the regiment's mortars provided fire support and diversions for RhSAS squadrons and patrols deployed on operations. These included Operation 'Bastille', in April 1979, when C Squadron carried out an attack on the house of Joshua Nkomo, the president of the ZAPU/ZIPRA (Zimbabwe African People's Union/Zimbabwe Independent People's Republican Party) terrorist organization, in the Zambian capital of Lusaka. The objective of the raid was to assassinate Nkomo, but this was not achieved as he was attending the opening session of the Afro-Asian People's Solidarity Organization elsewhere.

Previously, on 4 September 1978, RSM Allan had been one of twenty members of 1 RhSAS who parachuted into the area of the Urungwe Tribal Trust Land, to provide paramedic assistance for the passengers of an Air Rhodesia Viscount airliner shot down the previous day by ZIPRA terrorists armed with a SAM-7 missile. Of the 58 passengers and crew, eighteen survived the crash but ten were subsequently massacred by the terrorists. When the SAS came across the remaining eight survivors, RSM Allan spotted a close friend of his among them.

ALLOT, CAPTAIN K.   An early member of the Special Boat Section (SBS), he and Lieutenant Duncan Ritchie made a coastal recce paddling their canvas canoe some 240km (150 miles) through rough waters and enemy patrolled seas. Their journey from Ras-el-Tin headland to the Gazala inlet, which began 22 May 1943, took over a week to complete. Allot later commanded several successful beach-landing type raids against the Germans.

ALMONDS, LIEUTENANT JIM   Tall and somewhat reserved, Lieutenant 'Gentleman' Jim Almonds was one of the original members of L Detachment who went on many early SAS missions in North Africa. He was captured during a disastrous raid on Benghazi (see Raid on) in September 1942, but later escaped and went on to serve with the SAS in Europe, receiving a commission. After the war, in typical SAS style, he built a boat and sailed it across the Atlantic.

ALPHA   Alpha was an elite KGB unit, whose main functions included counter-terrorism, VIP protection and Special Forces operations, roles bearing more than a little similarity to those of the British SAS, with a structure that was almost identical. Little was known about Alpha prior to the coup against President Gorbachev in 1991, during which they reversed the direction of the coup by standing alongside Boris Yeltsin rather than attacking him in the White House of the Russian Parliament, as they had been requested to do by the coup directors. As a consequence of their actions they gained a very high level of access and the unit itself was removed from KGB control.

A private organization known as Alpha A was established in 1991 and officially registered with the approval of the Russian Government. Its directors are drawn from former professional security and anti-terrorist officers of Government Special Security, and the anti-terrorist forces unit, Alpha. Alpha A is a unique company in the Russian marketplace, where they face little or no competition in expertise, capabilities and personnel. Alpha A actively employs a varied group of professional experts in consultancy and support, giving the company the ability to respond effectively to any demand for security, nationally or internationally.

'AMHERST', OPERATION   In early 1945 the SAS Brigade, commanded by Brigadier Mike Calvert, was tasked by First Canadian Army with Operation 'Amherst', which involved the landing of SAS units behind enemy lines in northeast Holland. Their mission involved harassing German forces and preventing them from forming a defensive line against the advance of Canadian II Corps, thereby preventing the demolition of eighteen bridges over the canals or, where bridges had already been blown, reconnoitring alternative routes for Canadian Corps; securing Steejnwijk airfield for the RAF; reporting back on enemy movements and dispositions; providing guides for leading ground force units, and supporting Dutch Resistance operations in the area.

The operation was carried out by a total of 700, all ranks of 3 and 4 French Parachute Battalions, which had by then been redesignated 2 and 3 Regiments de Chasseurs Parachutists (2 RCP and 3 RCP). On the night of 7/8 April 1945 a total of 50 patrols were dropped in bad weather by Stirling bombers of 38 Group RAF on to nineteen dropping zones in the area of Gröningen, Emmen and Meppel. A subsequent drop of armed jeeps an hour later had to be cancelled because of cloud which was obscuring the lights marking the dropping zone.

The French parachutists carried out all their tasks with skill and aggression, on several occasions attacking enemy-held villages with only small arms. During the following seven days, assisted by the Dutch Resistance, they succeeded in tying down enemy units, intercepting their movements and preventing them from forming any cohesive defence until the arrival of the forward elements of Canadian II Corps, which thereafter continued its advance to the North Sea. Casualties suffered by both French battalions were 29 killed, 35 wounded and 29 missing. Enemy losses totalled 270 killed, 220 wounded, 187 captured and 29 vehicles destroyed.

AMMUNITION   In addition to the standard British Army 5.56mm and 7.62mm ammunition, the SAS uses a variety of specialist ammunition, particularly in counter-terrorist and hostage rescue. In these scenarios the most important point is to neutralize any opposition quickly, with the least risk to hostages or other SAS members. In counter-terrorism strikes 9mm calibre weapons are used, but normal 9mm bullets do not always stop when they hit a target; they will pass on through the body and may hit an innocent party.

To reduce this risk, a number of different rounds have been developed, which stop when they hit the body. There are two main types of rounds which have this property: accelerated energy transfer (AET) rounds, which flatten on hitting their mark, and frangible rounds which break up in the target's body.

AET rounds can be divided into three types. The 'equalloy' is a bullet made from an aluminium alloy, making it relatively light. The 'Geco' is a hollow bullet with a plastic core. On firing, the bullet and core separate. When it enters the target's body the hollow bullet then tumbles, causing massive tissue damage. The 'THV', a French bullet, has a concave front which also causes massive tissue damage on impact.

Frangible rounds include the British 'Spartan', which is made up of polymer mix and lead dust and breaks up on impact. A further development of the 'Spartan' is the 'Splat' where the lead dust is replaced by a non-lead metal. This has the same effect as the 'Spartan', but will also go through a certain amount of cover first, without breaking up, until it reaches the target's body. A more deadly, although more costly, frangible round is the US Glaser Safety Slug. This is basically a plastic cap fitted to the front of a small shotgun cartridge. When it hits its target, the impact causes the shot to fly out of the cartridge causing death, mainly through shock. Because of the risk to hostages, lest they be inadvertantly hit, it is used with great caution.

As shotguns are also used by the SAS counter-terrorist team, various shotgun rounds are also employed, especially buck-shot, armour piercing and high explosive rounds. Solid Hatton rounds are used to blow hinges and locks off doors.

ANAK KAYAN   The name of a tribesman of the Iban, a headhunting people from Borneo who did much to assist the SAS in Malaya in 1950–51. Anak Kayan taught jungle tracking skills to the Malayan Scouts. His techniques were the basis for a book produced in the late 1960s by the SAS called *Visual Tracking*.

ANCONA   The last operation carried out by 2 SAS in Italy in 1943 was an attack on the railway line between Ancona and Giulianova. In November a small force of sixteen men, under the command of Major Roy Farran, embarked in an Italian MTB commanded by a Royal Navy officer. Despite the presence of an enemy U-boat charging its batteries on the surface, Farran and his men disembarked from the motor torpedo boat (MTB) in pitch darkness at the mouth of the River Tronto, some 56km (35 miles) north of Pescara, and paddled ashore in rubber boats. Moving separately inshore in four-man patrols, commanded respectively by Major Farran, Captain Grant Hibbert, Sergeant Rawes and Sergeant Seddon, they marched until just before dawn when they stayed for the rest of the day. On the following evening a reconnaissance of the railway line, which lay about 457m (500yds) away, was carried out and two enemy sentries were spotted on a bridge. During the night three of the patrols reached a pre-determined RV (rendezvous) but there was no sign of Sergeant Rawes and his men. Major Farran decided to postpone the attack because of the appalling weather and the three patrols dispersed once more.

On the following night, Sergeant Rawes and his men succeeded in making the RV and Major Farran went ahead with the attack. Three of the patrols laid charges on the line and blew it in over sixteen places, while Sergeant Seddon's patrol laid Hawkins mines on roads in the area and demolished seven telegraph poles. Sergeant Rawes' patrol also destroyed three enemy trucks. Having completed their tasks, the patrols set out on a long exfiltration of 112km (70 miles) towards the coast where they would be picked up by the MTB. The weather closed in and the terrain over which the patrols travelled soon deteriorated, making movement very difficult. Furthermore, one of the members of Major Farran's patrol was suffering severely from malaria. Moving by night, the patrols lay-up each day seeking help from local Italians who provided shelter and food. Eventually, however, Farran's patrol was forced to march during daylight in order to make the RV with the MTB. On arriving at the appointed beach Farran met Captain Grant Hibbert, who was signalling out to sea with his torch, but there was no sign of the vessel, and so the patrols dispersed back inland to lie up. On the following night the boat appeared and Farran and his men were taken off. Two of their number, Sergeant Seddon and a member of his patrol, were, however, missing as they had been captured. Nevertheless, the operation had been successful, as all objectives had been achieved.

ANDARTES Andartes was the name given to Greek partisans who were armed and trained by the British during World War II. Numbers of them worked in Crete and mainland Greece with the Special Boat Section (SBS). They were frequently more concerned with internal political power struggles than fighting the enemy.

ANDERSON, Captain M. E. – SPECIAL BOAT SECTION (SBS) Captain Mike Anderson, a South African, was a new member of the SBS when he led the first raid by L Squadron on the island of Stampalia. Departing from Castelrosso on 27 January 1944 on an armed motor launch, he and his men endured Force 6 gales and rough seas before they were landed in a bay. On the following night, Anderson and one of his men, Lance-Corporal Nixon, proceeded by canoe along the coast to the island's harbour with the purpose of attacking some caïques which the Germans had chartered from their Greek owners. Bad weather prevented that attack, but another, mounted overland by the rest of Anderson's patrol under the command of Corporal Asbery, proved successful with one seaplane and two caïques being sunk with explosive charges. Not to be outdone, however, Anderson returned to the harbour on the following night and succeeded in sinking two further caïques.

A few weeks later, in March, Captain Anderson led a force of two SBS patrols, commanded by Lieutenants David Clark and John Harden, in an attack on the island of Kalymnos. Having captured two German soldiers and extracted the password for that night, Anderson led his men into the area of the enemy barracks, located on the outskirts of the town of Calino, which they promptly attacked, killing a number of troops and setting buildings ablaze. Lieutenant Harden's patrol took up positions between the barracks and the town, engaging and killing German troops as they withdrew. Meanwhile, Lieutenant Clark's patrol had entered the town centre and blew up a fuel dump and a large caïque under construction. An enemy observation post was also attacked, its six occupants being killed in the process. Anderson's force subsequently withdrew without loss.

ANDRAWS, SUHAILA, A member of the Popular Front for the Liberation of Palestine (PFLP), Suhaila Andraws was one of four Palestinians who hijacked a German Lufthansa 737 aircraft on 4 October 1977. The aircraft was stormed by German GSG9 anti-terrorist police assisted by two SAS men. All four hijackers were shot, but Andraws, despite being wounded seven times, managed to survive. She was jailed in Mogadishu for over a year before being released and taken first to Baghdad, and then to Czechoslovakia where she received much-needed medical treatment.

In 1993 she was discovered living in Norway, and after a hard legal battle was eventually extradited to Germany for trial. She received a twelve-year sentence in 1996.

ANTI-PERSONNEL MINES The SAS use a variety of anti-personnel mines, mostly as a form of protection. These mines are set out as a perimeter defensive measure and are collected before departing from the location. The application of mines is dealt with during the Demolition Course run internally by the SAS. The American 'Claymore' mine has been used by the regiment for many years, and remains a staunch favourite for ambush and perimeter defence.

ANTI-TERRORIST TEAM Following the massacre of eleven Israeli athletes by Palestinian terrorists at the Munich Olympic Games in 1972, world governments became determined to combat a new breed of terrorism. At the G7 summit talks the following year, the heads of government made an agreement to establish dedicated forces capable of dealing with any terrorist situation. In Britain the SAS were tasked with equipping and training for the new force, known by a variety of names including the anti-terrorist team, SP Team (Special Patrol) and the Pagoda Team. New equipment was purchased and the SAS responded to the training with unmatched keenness.

Today the SAS anti-terrorist team is housed in a purpose-built building which is manned by two teams, Red and Blue, 24 hours a day. Each team member is issued with an alert device and his movements are restricted to allow for a quick response. On call-out the vehicles are loaded with a vast array of weapons and equipment, before a briefing is given on the operational requirement. The anti-terrorist team will only move into position when requested by the Home Office. The two teams are capable of working independently or together, as the task dictates. The SAS anti-terrorist team is regarded by most of its peers to be the best in the world.

ANTONOVITCH, TROOPER GRAEME – AUSTRALIAN SAS REGIMENT (SASR) Trooper Graeme Antonovitch was a member of a 1 Squadron SASR patrol, commanded by Sergeant Lawrie Fraser, which was inserted south east of Nui May Tao, on the border between the provinces of Binh Tuy and Long Khanh, in South Vietnam, on 5 January 1971. Six days later, the patrol was in its lying-up position (LUP) when Trooper Antonovitch moved away a short distance of 20m (21yds) to carry out his morning ablutions. While doing so, he spotted three Vietcong (VC) approaching the LUP and without further ado, with his trousers still around his ankles, opened fire, killing two VC and wounding the third, who escaped. The patrol followed up, tracking the blood trail left by the wounded guerrilla, and shortly afterwards found a hastily abandoned enemy camp. Later in the day a bunker complex was discovered some 100m (109yds) away, and this was destroyed by the patrol with helicopter gunship support.

ANTRIM ROAD SHOOTING   Belfast. It was discovered that a number of IRA weapons, which had previously been under observation by the security forces, had been moved. Among these weapons was a 7.62mm M60 machine gun, which had originally been stolen in America. Despite the use of sophisticated surveillance devices, the weapons' new home remained a mystery. However, they were later found to be located amid terraced houses in the Antrim Road, although the exact location could not be identified. After an intelligence check by the Royal Ulster Constabulary (RUC) Special Branch, it became known that the IRA had previously used one of three houses close to where the weapons had been re-housed. On the afternoon of 2 May 1980 two cars containing SAS soldiers headed down the Antrim Road and, screeching to a halt outside Number 369, another vehicle containing three SAS men secured the rear. For security reasons, there had been no cordon or military activity prior to the raid, and the SAS team stormed straight into the house. Unknown to them, the IRA had mounted the stolen American M60 in the upstairs window of the adjoining house. Captain Richard Westmacott, who had been sitting in the middle of the rear seat and so was last to move, caught the full blast as the M60 opened fire, killing him instantly. Realizing what had happened the whole assault was quickly switched, but by this time the IRA man had surrendered. The sound of gun fire quickly brought the Army and RUC to the scene. At the same time a Catholic priest had also suddenly materialized to see that the IRA man was allowed to give himself up.

'APOSTLE', OPERATION   At the end of World War II, a mission undertaken by HQ SAS Brigade, 1 and 2 SAS, all under the command of Brigadier Mike Calvert, to disarm the 300,000 German soldiers remaining in Norway. The two regiments were shipped from Ostend to Tilbury, and in England they were issued with new jeeps, new clothing and equipment.

An advance party made up of representatives from both regiments and a detachment from brigade staff arrived at Stavanger on 12 May 1945, and by the end of the month a total of 760 troops, 17 motorcycles, 68 trailers and 150 jeeps were in the country. The SAS Brigade was based at Bergen to administer the operation. The four months which the SAS soldiers spent in Norway were hardly taxing, and most of the men regarded the time as a sort of holiday. The Germans gave no trouble (although there were clashes with Quislings – Norwegian collaborators), the locals were largely friendly and the weather was warm. The SAS returned to England at the end of August. An amusing footnote to the operation is the so-called Battle of Bergen. The young ladies of the town were quite fond of the daring British soldiers in their midst, a fact resented by many young Norwegian males and members of the local police force. This culminated in a large-scale brawl in the town's centre which the SAS won hands down. The 'victory' resulted in British diplomats in Norway urgently requesting the War Office to withdraw the SAS back to England.

APPLEYARD, MAJOR GEOFFREY Commenced his career in Special Forces with the Small Scale Raiding Force (SSRF). This unit also had the designation 62 Commando, a unit which carried out raids on the coast of France and on the Channel Islands under the joint direction of the Chief of Combined Operations and the Special Operations Executive. At the end of 1942 SSRF (62 Commando) was disbanded and Appleyard joined his commanding officer, Lieutenant-Colonel William 'Bill' Stirling, as the latter formed 2 SAS Regiment at Philippeville, Algeria. Appleyard was given command of a squadron but his tenure was short-lived. On 12 July 1943 he was aboard an aircraft carrying a patrol of ten men of his squadron, code-named 'Pink' and under command of Captain Phillip Pinckney, on Operation 'Chestnut' which involved parachuting patrols from 2 SAS into northeast Sicily prior to landings by 15th Army Group. The drop took place, but the aircraft, with Appleyard still aboard as he had accompanied his men to supervise the drop, disappeared on the return flight. This was a serious blow to 2 SAS which, as a newly formed unit, could ill afford to lose such an experienced officer.

AR-15/M16 ASSAULT RIFLE *Specification* Calibre: 5.56mm × 45 NATO standard; Weight: 3.18kg (7lbs); Muzzle velocity: 1,000m (1,090yds) per second; Magazine capacity: 20- or 30-round, box.

The AR-15 was designed in the United States by the Armalite Company in the late 1950s. When it was adopted by the US Air Force in the mid-1960s, however, it was renamed the M16. The US Army called it the M16A1 and it became the standard rifle in the Vietnam War. However, it had been used in combat before Vietnam, by the British fighting in Borneo. The M16 was among the first of the modern-style rifles, firing the smaller 5.56mm ammunition, as opposed to the standard NATO 7.62mm round. Its construction of pressed steel and plastic made it prone to damage and there was an initial problem with reliability, but its successor the M16A2 has overcome these, and is the current model in use with the US armed forces. The M16 is also the preferred combat rifle of the SAS, especially when combined with the M203 grenade launcher.

'ARCHWAY', OPERATION At the close of World War II in Europe, Operation 'Archway' was carried out by a composite force comprising elements of A and D Squadrons 1 SAS, under the command of Major Harry Poat, and A Squadron 2 SAS commanded by Major Peter Power.

The latter would subsequently be joined later in the operation by another 2 SAS squadron under Major Grant Hibbert. The entire force, commanded by Lieutenant-Colonel Brian Franks, the commanding officer of 2 SAS, was christened 'Frankforce' and numbered 430 all ranks. It was mounted in 75 armed jeeps, some carrying 3-inch mortars, and a number of 15-cwt and 3-ton trucks which transported the administrative tail. The 1 SAS element was divided into three large troops commanded respectively by Majors Bill Fraser, Alec Muirhead and John Tonkin. A Squadron 2 SAS was organized in two troops under the command of Captains Mackie and Miller.

Frankforce departed from England on 18 March 1945 and, having landed at Ostend, made its way to a concentration area west of the Rhine to prepare for operations after the main assault crossing of the river, code-named 'Varsity', which would be carried out by the 2nd British and Ninth US Armies. On 24 March, its two squadrons crossed the Rhine in 'Buffalo' tracked amphibious vehicles and thereafter pushed forward through the area held by 6th Airborne Division to take up its main role of reconnaissance. Thereafter it operated under command of 6th Airborne Division, 11th Armoured Division and 15th (Scottish) Division.

Confronted by a variety of enemy units, including Fallschirmjager (paratroopers) of the German First Parachute Army, Hitler Youth and Volkssturm home defence units, Frankforce experienced hard fighting during the advance into Germany. On 8 April, a section of one of the 1 SAS troops, commanded by Captain Johnny Cooper, was ambushed by an enemy force supported by three armoured vehicles while reconnoitring an area of woodland in advance of an armoured car squadron of the Inns of Court Regiment. Three men were killed and five wounded, the latter including Lieutenant Ian Wellsted.

A week later, on 14/15 April, 1 SAS elements of Frankforce arrived at Belsen concentration camp where they found some 50,000 to 60,000 inmates living in conditions so appalling as to be beyond description. Four days later, several patrols were deployed in support of the Field Security Police, who were hunting down known Nazi war criminals, and carried out a number of arrests.

Subsequently, Frankforce rejoined the advance through Germany. At the crossing of the River Elbe at the end of April, it was joined by Major Grant Hibbert's squadron of 2 SAS which had earlier been deployed on Operation 'Keystone' involving the capture of bridges north of Arnhem, which had subsequently been cancelled. Thereafter, it continued its advance through Germany, heading through Schleswig-Holstein and eventually reaching Kiel on the Baltic coast. Shortly afterwards, it was withdrawn to Belgium and on 10 May departed for England. Its losses during Operation 'Archway' had been light: seven killed and twenty-two wounded.

ARGENTINA   On 2 April 1982 Argentina invaded the Falkland Islands and the island of South Georgia, both of which were militarily dependent on Britain. Argentina claimed they were liberating territory known to them as Las Malvinas. When diplomacy failed the British Government despatched a large force to make the 12,800km (8,000 mile) journey and retake the islands. It was the move which began the Falklands War.

ARMSTRONG, TROOPER RAYMOND   Armstrong joined the SAS in 1979 and was posted to D Squadron. Despite having served only a short time in the regiment, when the SAS were sent into the Falklands War he showed exceptional talent. During the raid on Pebble Island in May 1982, whilst the troops were getting ready to extract, it was discovered that several Pucara aircraft were still intact. Armstrong, together with Captain Hamilton, returned to destroy the remaining aircraft, earning him the nickname 'Pucara Paddy'. Sadly Trooper Armstrong died shortly after, when the helicopter in which he was travelling crashed during a ship-to-ship cross-decking operation.

ARMY AIR CORPS (AAC)   The SAS has had its own AAC flight since the early 1960s. The helicopters are mainly used for surveillance, reconnaissance and VIP transportation. In the event of a terrorist incident, the SAS will dispatch the commanding officer, along with the team commander, in order to assess the situation first hand.

Elements of the AAC provide support for Special Forces within the United Kingdom. These include 8 Flight of 9 Regiment AAC which is located at the 22 SAS base at Hereford, and which operates four Augusta 109 helicopters. There is also 657 Squadron AAC, located at Disforth, which is equipped with twelve Westland Lynx Mk.7 helicopters which can be armed with pintle-mounted .50 calibre heavy machine guns when necessary. In Northern Ireland, the AAC special operations-dedicated unit is the 'Bat Flight' which operates AH-1 Gazelle light helicopters equipped with surveillance and forward-looking infra-red (FLIR) systems.

ARNOTT, TROOPER ROBERT P.   Arnott joined the British Army in 1973 and served with the Royal Engineers before passing Selection in January 1986. He was assigned to D Squadron Mountain Troop and shortly after was sent to France on a climbing course. He was killed while climbing Aiguille du Chardonnet in the Mont Blanc range.

ARTHY, SERGEANT JOHN LESLIE   Arthy originally joined the Welsh Guards. On passing SAS Selection in 1975 he was posted to D Squadron Mobility Troop but, having a keen interest in climbing, was transferred to Mountain Troop a couple of years later. On completing the one-year Mountain Guides course in Germany, 'Lofty', as he was known, set out on a series of climbing expeditions.

During the Falklands War, on the 22 April he was leading a patrol on the island of South Georgia that became trapped in bad weather on top of the Fortuna Glacier. His expertise is said to have saved the patrol, whose extraction cost two Wessex helicopters, both of which crashed due to the weather. A third chopper, over-laden and in blind conditions, finally managed to lift them off. 'Lofty' later took part in the raid on Pebble Island, but died a few days later, when the helicopter in which he was flying crashed during a ship-to-ship cross-decking operation.

ARTISTS RIFLES The Artists Rifles were formed in 1859 as a volunteer corps. Set against the background of the Crimean War, the unit was initiated by an artist named Edward Stirling, and was to be a reserve of some 12,000 volunteers, made up from musicians, actors and similar talents, all of whom had a distinguished fighting record. It is purely coincidental that the founder of today's SAS was also called Stirling. As well as designing their own uniform, they also produced a cap badge depicting Mars and Minerva, from which is derived the name of the regimental magazine. In 1863 they became part of the British Army. During World War II the unit served as an Officer Cadet Training unit, until it was disbanded in 1946. The government at the time reconstituted the Artists Rifles as a territorial unit on the 1 January 1947, at which time 21 SAS came into being.

ARWEN The Arwen is a 37mm gas, smoke and baton round launcher. It is basically an anti-riot weapon that has been adapted for hostage rescue. It has a five-round rotating magazine, which is part of the weapon and works in a similar way to the cylinder on a revolver. The baton round will cause immobilizing damage up to 100m (109yds), although the accuracy is not all that good. The CS gas rounds vary; some are capable of penetration through either light wooden doors or glass before discharging.

ASBERY, CORPORAL – SPECIAL BOAT SECTION Corporal (later Sergeant) Asbery was a member of a patrol of L Squadron SBS, commanded by Captain Mike Anderson, which carried out a raid on the Dodecanese island of Stampalia at the end of January 1944. The patrol landed in bad weather, and on the following night, while Anderson and Lance-Corporal Nixon paddled a canoe along the coast to the island's harbour, to attack some caïques being used by the Germans, Corporal Asbery led the rest of the patrol overland to raid the harbour from the landward side. Explosive charges were planted on an enemy seaplane moored near the shore. Asbery and three others then swam out to two caïques lying offshore and laid charges in their engine rooms. Shortly afterwards, as Corporal Asbery and his men made good their escape, all the charges exploded and the seaplane and both caïques were sunk successfully.

ASCENSION ISLAND British-owned island in the Atlantic Ocean, with an area of some 85sq km (34 sq miles) and a population of just over 1,000 people. During the Falklands War in 1982, Ascension Island became the staging post for British shipping and aircraft. At the start of the Falklands offensive the airport on Ascension became the busiest in the world.

ASKAR The native term for an armed Arab tribesman, loyal to the Sultan of Oman. Thirty or so of these men fought beside the SAS at the Battle of Mirbat in July 1972.

ASSAULT BELT RIG The assault belt rig is designed for the SAS anti-terrorist team, and carries members' personal weapons and ammunition. Manufactured in top quality black bridle leather, it comprises a heavy-duty fully lined belt, a pistol holster and two magazine carriers, a grenade carrier holding two stun grenades, and a three-magazine carrier for the Heckler & Koch MP-5 sub-machine gun. Canvas versions of the same style rig are also used.

ASSAULT EQUIPMENT The range of assault equipment used by the SAS is vast. Most items have been designed to fulfil a specific task: either protection or speed entry. Products range from body armour and stun grenades to special cartridges that can rip off a door hinge without causing damage to anyone inside the room.

The SAS have spent many years perfecting their assault equipment. The closer and swifter the SAS can get to the terrorists, the better the chances are of saving the hostages. Techniques and equipment used to tackle hijack situations are constantly worked on to ensure that the SAS remain one step ahead of the terrorist. Assault teams can gain access to buildings or board any major airliner in seconds from an assault platform mounted on the roof of a vehicle. The double ladder allows one man to open the aircraft door while the following man can immediately enter, maintaining that all-important element of surprise. See also Anti-terrorist Team; Assault Ladders; Hooligan Bar; Iranian Embassy Siege.

ASSAULT LADDERS The SAS use an extensive range of assault ladders of differing widths to cater for the majority of operational requirements in a siege situation. These include single section, multi-sectional and extending types in single width, double width and triple stile designs. All ladders are manufactured from structural grade aluminium alloy with deeply serrated rung sections and heavy-duty rectangular sections. All are built to order and thus non-standard designs and lengths are available. All ladders are fitted as standard with non-slip rubber feet, noise-reducing buffers on all exposed faces, and are finished in black polyester powder coating with etch primer.

1. Single Section Ladders
These ladders are available to the SAS in single and double widths and triple stile designs up to 4m (4yds) in length. They offer silent climbing and are ideally suited for gaining rapid access to public transport vehicles, ships, aircraft, or for scaling walls. Wall hooks and sniper platforms can be fitted to all sizes.

2. Multi-Sectional Ladders
Manufactured mainly in double width or triple stile configurations, these ladders range in length from 1m (1yds) up to 4m (4yds) and can be quickly assembled to give finished lengths of up to 8m (8.5yd). They can be transported easily in vans or estate cars and provide team capability for two to four personnel, depending on length and conditions. They are fitted as standard with heavy-duty channel connectors complete with nylon slides and locking pins. Sniper platforms are also available for use with these ladders.

3. Extension Ladders (Multi-Level)
These give the SAS a choice of widths including a triple stile, with single and double sliding sections both available. Standard fittings include full-length nylon slides, quadruple section restraining brackets, over-extension stops and an auto-swing safety clutch.

ASSAULT SUIT The assault suit is designed to provide maximum protection against injury from heat and flame when worn with the assault undersuit. A one-piece garment worn under the assault body armour, the suit is manufactured in Arvex SNX 574 flame-resistant, anti-static, liquid-repellent black 210gsm fabric. A full-length two-way zip fastener, protected by a storm flap, fastens the suit and Panotex knitted cuffing is fitted at the collar, cuffs and ankles. Patch pockets are fitted to the chest (for use when body armour is not being worn), and pouch pockets to the thighs. Identification patch holders are fitted to both upper arms. The areas of the forearms, knees and shins are reinforced with quilted Arvex fabric containing Panotex flame-resistant felt, which provides additional protection against heat conduction should the wearer come into contact with extremely hot surfaces. Fitted with a drag-handle, the suit permits the wearer, when unconscious or incapable of movement, to be dragged out of the line of fire to safety.

ASSAULT TEAM Assault teams focus mainly on assault entry, concentrating primarily on all methods of getting into an aircraft, train or building and closing with the enemy. They work in pairs, so that if one man is shot the other will immediately replace him. All members of the SAS anti-terrorist team spend hundreds of hours in the now famous 'Killing House', where drills and shooting techniques are honed to a fine edge.

All assault team members wear a black, one-piece fire-retarding suit, on top of which goes the body armour and weaponry. The weapon is normally a Heckler & Koch MP5 sub-machine gun, which clips flush across the chest. Additionally, a low-slung Browning Hi-Power pistol is strapped to the leg for backup, or for use in confined spaces. In the past few years the SAS has evaluated many hand weapons, the current model being the SIG-Sauer P226. Respirators are carried in their container strapped to the back, but more likely during the actual assault, the pack is discarded and the respirator is shoved up the left arm and kept for immediate use. Most actions now involve wearing the respirator: it not only protects against gas, but also presents a threatening face to the terrorists. Boots are non-slip, similar to professional climbing boots.

The assault teams have unlimited access to aircraft, buildings, trains, ships and oil rigs during their training. Scenarios of terrorist-type sieges and hijacks are constantly played out in exercises where police and government officials take an active part.

ASTOR, MAJOR THE HONOURABLE 'JAKIE' The commander of several patrols of F Squadron 'Phantom' attached to both 1 and 2 SAS during the European offensives of 1944–45. As always, the expertise of the Phantom personnel, officially designated GHQ Reconnaissance Regiment, greatly assisted the SAS units, especially in the area of communications.

ASTROLITE LIQUID EXPLOSIVE Astrolite is a liquid high explosive that can be sprayed from aircraft and soaks into topsoil to a depth of a few centimetres. With a life of only four days, it is reputedly undetectable, except by chemical agent sensors, and can subsequently be detonated remotely by personnel equipped with the necessary initiation device.

ATHENS In early December 1944, civil war broke out in the newly liberated Greek capital of Athens. Major Ian Patterson's L Squadron SBS, which was at that time based at the nearby airport, was ordered to assist in quelling the disorder in the city. Athens was largely under the control of ELAS (Hellenic People's Army of Liberation), the military element of the Communist EAM (Greek National Liberation Front) organization, and initially, the SBS co-operated with the ELAS troops in keeping order, but this relationship was terminated abruptly after the disarming and abduction of an SBS patrol whose members were kept prisoner for almost a month. They were later released when ELAS forces were driven out of Athens by British troops in the following month. Shortly afterwards, tragedy struck when Major Patterson, who had left Athens on a flight for Brindisi in Italy, was killed when the Dakota aircraft in which he was travelling crashed in bad weather.

ATHLIT Athlit, in Palestine, was the initial base location of the Special Boat Section (SBS) on its birth after the reorganization of 1 SAS into the

Special Raiding Squadron (SRS) and SBS in April 1943. The latter underwent thorough training in its new role in Athlit, prior to deploying on operations in the Aegean. Thereafter, new recruits for the SBS underwent Selection and training there before joining one of the unit's three squadrons. Featuring a castle built during the Crusades, Athlit was an ideal location as its beaches lent themselves to training in canoes and other small craft.

ATKINSON, MALCOLM Atkinson, or 'Akker' as he was known to most, passed Selection in 1966 and was posted to G Squadron's Boat Troop. His career progressed well and he became a strong character within the squadron, rising to the position of Squadron Quartermaster. He was killed during the Falklands War when the helicopter in which he was travelling crashed during a cross-decking operation.

A-TYPE AMBUSH An A-Type ambush is made up of a series of unmanned explosive devices that are set up and left for the enemy to walk into. The explosive could vary from WP (white phosphorus) to grenades and Claymore mines, all linked by detonating cord into a single triggering device. They are mainly planted on set routes used by the enemy for ferrying weapons. A-Type ambushes were laid during Borneo operations in the 1960s and during the Oman War. The explosives were always clearly recorded and removed if not triggered.

AUCHINLECK, GENERAL SIR CLAUDE General Auchinleck was commander-in-chief of British forces in the Middle East, when in 1941 David Stirling first proposed his plan to form the SAS. Having managed to gain access to the headquarters, Stirling found himself face to face with the objections of Auchinleck's second-in-command, General Ritchie. However, it suited Auchinleck's purpose to allow Stirling to form the unit. The title 'Special Air Service' was to fool the Germans into thinking there was some form of elite troops in the area.

AUCTIONS In the late sixties and early seventies it was common for the SAS Regiment to hold auctions, selling personal kit and equipment of those who had died. These auctions would raise money that would be given to the deceased's next of kin. It was also a way of expressing feelings and holding on to a small piece of a personal friend or colleague. The auctions have since ceased.

AUGUSTA Augusta, on the east coast of Sicily, was the scene of a daylight attack by the Special Raiding Squadron (SRS) on the evening of 12 July 1943. Supported by gunfire from a Royal Navy cruiser and two destroyers, the squadron disembarked in landing craft from the troop transport HMS *Ulster Monarch*, which was being shelled by enemy artillery. Having landed, the squadron encountered strong opposition from units of the Hermann Goering Division sited in the town and on the heights above. After some hard fighting, the town was eventually cleared by dusk, but enemy artillery and snipers continued to harass the SRS throughout the night. On the following day troops of 17th Infantry Division, who had advanced overland, linked up with the squadron which re-embarked on the *Ulster Monarch* shortly afterwards.

AUSTRALIAN SAS   The Australian Special Air Service Regiment (SASR) was formed on 4 September 1964 with an establishment of 15 officers and 209 other ranks. Initially it comprised a headquarters, consisting of 3 officers and 37 other ranks, and two Sabre Squadrons (designated 1 and 2 respectively), each of which comprised 6 officers and 86 other ranks. Each squadron would consist of a headquarters and three troops, each of the latter numbering 21 all ranks. In December 1964, a headquarters squadron was added to the regiment's establishment and the strength of each squadron was increased by one troop. Shortly afterwards, authorization was given for the raising of two further squadrons, to be formed by December 1965 and June 1966 respectively.

During the period from February 1965 to July 1966, 1, 2 and 3 Squadrons saw action in Borneo, where they took part in the Borneo Confrontation against Indonesia under command of 22 SAS, including participation in cross-border operations, code-named 'Claret'.

In June 1966, 3 Squadron was deployed to South Vietnam as part of the 1st Australian Task Force, where it served until March 1967 when 1 Squadron relieved it. Thereafter, SASR squadrons served twelve-month tours on rotation until Australian forces withdrew from Vietnam in 1971.

Today SASR comprises a regimental headquarters, Base Squadron, Signals Squadron, three Sabre Squadrons and a Training Squadron. Base Squadron provides all the administrative and logistical support for the regiment while 152 Signals Squadron provides HF radio communications support for squadrons on operations and for the regimental headquarters.

At any one time, two of the Sabre Squadrons are in the war role, each being organized as a headquarters, a free-fall parachute troop, water operations troop and vehicle-mounted troop. The third squadron is in the counter-terrorist role, this being rotated on an annual basis. The training squadron comprises the following wings which provides instruction in: climbing/survival; guerrilla warfare; water operations; air (airborne operations); vehicle-mobility; demolitions, and reinforcement (which is responsible for conducting Selection courses).

AUTUN   In August 1944, as part of Operation 'Houndsworth' in eastern France, an attack was carried out on a German synthetic petrol plant by a mortar section of A Squadron 1 SAS. The target was well guarded and strong anti-aircraft defences were sited there to protect against air attack. Led by Lieutenant Alec Muirhead, the section approached their target without incident and set up their 3-inch mortars in dead ground. At 01:30 hours in bright moonlight they opened fire on the plant, discharging a total of 40 high explosive and incendiary bombs in rapid succession. Within seconds, the fuel storage tanks and plant buildings were ablaze and continued to burn for three days. The mortar section was subsequently able to withdraw unhindered as the enemy thought it was an air raid and had taken to air raid shelters.

AWACS – E-3 SENTRY The AWACS (Airborne Warning And Control System) aircraft provides all-weather surveillance, command, control and communications. The E-3 Sentry is a modified Boeing 707/320 commercial airframe, with a rotating radar dome attached to the upper body. It contains a radar subsystem and an identification friend or foe (IFF) subsystem, which permits surveillance from the Earth's surface up into the stratosphere, over land or water. The radar has a range of more than 320km (200 miles) for low-flying targets, and even greater range for airborne targets flying at medium to high altitudes. The AWACS can look down to detect, identify and track enemy and friendly low-flying aircraft by eliminating ground clutter returns which confuse other radars. The AWACS was much used during Operation 'Desert Storm', controlling the vast number of Coalition aircraft flying in and out of Iraq. The ill-fated SAS patrol 'Bravo Two Zero' had problems with their TACBE (Tactical Beacon) radios when they tried to contact the AWACS for help; it was later discovered that the TACBEs were assigned to the wrong frequency.

AYER HITAM RIVER During the Borneo Confrontation, cross-border operations were restricted to a distance of 2,750m (3,000yds). By September 1965 this distance was increased to 9,140m (10,000yds). This allowed the SAS to ambush the Ayer Hitam River which the Indonesian troops frequently used. At this stage, the SAS started using sixteen-man patrols, one of which laid an ambush on the river and took out two long boats, each carrying eight soldiers. Both were shot up and the patrol retreated back to the border under heavy mortar fire from the Indonesians.

AYLING, PRIVATE F.J. – AUSTRALIAN SAS REGIMENT (SASR) During the Borneo Confrontation, Private Frank Ayling was a member of a four-man patrol of 2 Squadron SASR, commanded by Lieutenant Ken Hudson, which was inserted in the Bungo Range area of the First Division of Sarawak on 21 March 1966. The two other members were Privates Bob Moncrieff and Bruce Gabriel. The patrol's task was to carry out a close reconnaissance of an Indonesian base believed to be in the area of a village called Entabang, which the patrol had kept under observation during the previous two days. At 03:00 hours, having established an emergency rendezvous (RV), the patrol moved off from its observation post (OP) in pitch darkness and after 30 minutes reached the Sekayan River which lay between them and their objective. The river was in spate because of heavy rain and it was not long before all four members of the patrol found themselves in difficulty. Private Ayling was swept away, but, retaining a grip on his rifle and equipment, a few seconds later he encountered a log and succeeded in clambering onto it. Shortly afterwards he managed to catch hold of Private Bruce Gabriel, who had seen Ayling's luminous watch, and haul him on to the log. After several minutes, both men reached the river bank, where they listened for any sound from Lieutenant Hudson and Private Moncrieff and waited for daylight.

Realizing they were some 540m (500yds) downstream from where they had entered the river, Ayling and Gabriel made their way back to the patrol OP location before heading for the emergency RV. While waiting for the two missing men, they attempted to establish radio contact with the squadron base but without success. Thereafter they headed for the border RV, which they reached at 17:30 hours on 22 March, and attempted again to establish contact, but were again unsuccessful. On the morning of the following day, however, they established radio contact and were extracted by helicopter at 12:45 hours.

A patrol, commanded by Corporal Jeff Ayles, was inserted into the area the following day to search for Lieutenant Hudson and Private Moncrieff. They were never found, however, and were subsequently reported missing presumed dead. Privates Ayling and Gabriel were commended for their actions and the former received a Mention In Dispatches.

AZZIB   After the reorganization of 1 SAS on 1 April 1943, the Special Raiding Squadron (SRS) moved to a new base at Azzib in Palestine. There the squadron underwent a tough training programme in preparation for its part in the invasion of Sicily. The SRS remained in Azzib until 6 June 1943 when it left by rail for Suez, its ultimate destination being Port Said from which it would embark for Sicily a month later.

B

BADGED Once a soldier has successfully passed all Selection tests and Continuation training, he is granted the prestigious beige beret with its winged dagger badge. This is known as being 'badged' and is a memorable moment for every SAS recruit. He will then go on to complete the twelve-month probationary period which started with his Continuation training.

BAGNARA A port in southern Italy seized by the Special Raiding Squadron (SRS) on the night of 3 September 1943, during Operation 'Baytown'. The fighting lasted for about three days before the SRS met up with Allied troops, at which stage the SRS were withdrawn.

BAGOUSH AIRFIELD On the North African coast, Bagoush was an Axis airfield which was first attacked by L Detachment SAS on 16 November 1941. It was also the scene of a raid on the night of 7 July 1942 led by Major David Stirling and Captain Paddy Mayne. After an overland approach in vehicles, the initial attack on the airfield was carried out by a group of four men under Captain Mayne, while Major Stirling established a roadblock nearby to attack any enemy vehicles. Lewes bombs were placed on a total of 40 aircraft but only twenty exploded because of faulty primers. Fourteen more aircraft were then attacked and destroyed by the whole force mounted in three jeeps, each vehicle being armed with twin Vickers K machine guns. Stirling and his men then withdrew without loss.

BA KELALAN On the 4 May 1963 a helicopter took off from Ba Kelalan in Kalimantan, Borneo. On board were a number of SAS men including Major Ronald Norman, second-in-command of the regiment, and Major Harry Thompson, the operations officer, who were intent on visiting all the SAS jungle locations. Unfortunately the helicopter crashed and all were killed. Corporal Frank Williams, who strangely had been turned off the helicopter at the last moment, led a search party to locate the crash site.

BAKER, CORPORAL (LATER COLONEL) PADDY Corporal Paddy Baker was one of the ill-fated members of a patrol lead by Captain Robin Edwards during the Radfan campaign in South Yemen, 1960–67. The patrol was spotted and confronted by rebels near the village of Shi'b Taym, and came under heavy fire. During the extraction Captain Edwards and his signaller were killed, leaving command to Corporal Baker, himself shot and seriously injured in the leg. In a well-directed withdrawal, Baker managed to extract the remaining patrol members to safety, until they were picked up by a search party. Corporal Baker received the Military Medal for his part in the operation. He was later commissioned into 22 SAS where he served amid other appointments as Training Wing OC (officer commanding). Upon leaving the regiment he became commanding officer of the Hereford TA Centre.

BALACLAVAS Manufactured in Panotex double jersey knitted black fabric, balaclavas are available in standard closed-face configuration with apertures for the eyes and mouth, and provide protection against flame to the face when a respirator is not used. The SAS anti-terrorist team and members of the counter revolutionary warfare (CRW) unit wear balaclavas, in many cases, to protect their identity during public exposure during operations, such as seen during the Iranian Embassy Siege in 1980.

BALCOMBE STREET SIEGE On 6 December 1975, after attacking a restaurant, a four-man Active Service Unit of the IRA took a middle-aged couple hostage in a flat in Balcombe Street, in central London. Armed police were on the scene almost immediately and Scotland Yard were able to monitor the proceedings in the flat using fibre optics. However, the gunmen held their ground and the siege, moving into its eighth day, looked as if it was going to continue indefinitely. Inside the flat, the terrorists were able to listen to a transistor radio and heard a report from the BBC suggesting that an SAS unit was preparing to intervene and take over the building. Hearing this, the terrorists immediately surrendered to the police.

BALL, MAJOR TONY Tony Ball joined the SAS as a trooper, having initially joined the Parachute Regiment. He was commissioned and given the task of organizing the Northern Ireland (NI) Cell that was to become the basis of 14 Intelligence and Security Unit. He did much to establish the undercover work carried out by the regiment in Northern Ireland. He left the SAS in 1976 to serve with the Sultan's Special Forces in Oman; tragically he died in a road accident in 1978.

BALLYCASTLE HOUSE In Aden in the early 1960s, two blocks of flats known as Ballycastle House, which had served as married quarters, were turned over to the SAS for use as their accommodation HQ. The front block housed administration personnel, stores and an operations room, whilst the second block served as accommodation for the men. There was no cookhouse and the men preferred to fend for themselves, utilizing the appliances left behind as part of the married quarters. The complex was close to Khormaksar airport and Aden could be reached in a little over ten minutes by vehicle. Operations up-country were mounted from here, as was the relief force when rebel mobs took over the district of Crater. Keeni-Meeni counter-terrorist squads also operated from Ballycastle House, working the back streets of Sheikh Othman.

BALLYSILLAN POST OFFICE In June 1978, intelligence indicated that an IRA team was to fire-bomb the Post Office depot in Belfast. An SAS team was inserted, comprising a reaction group in a parked van and an observation post (OP) in a nearby house. The OP had a clear view of the small alley that ran to the side of the Post Office compound where vehicles and utilities were housed. The compound was protected by a high fence, and it was thought that the IRA might try to climb this in order to gain access.

After several days, the reaction group was moved from the van to a small clump of bushes close to the small alley, with several cut-off groups secreted around the compound. On the night of 21 June the SAS soldier in the observation house, together with a member of Special Branch, observed several men enter the alley and stop. Almost immediately one of the men threw a small satchel over the compound fence, at which time the ambush jumped in front of them. Two of the IRA members were about to throw more satchel bombs over the compound fence, whereupon the SAS opened fire. Two were killed instantly, as was the third as he tried to run back down the alley. The men were later named as Jacki Mealy, Jim Mulnenna and Dennis Brown.

At that moment another two men walked into the alley and again the SAS called out a challenge. One man obeyed and thrust his hands into the air, the other made a run for it. He was killed by a single bullet. As the situation cleared, it turned out that the two men were just returning from the pub and had accidentally walked straight into the firefight. Had the man, a Protestant by the name of William Hanna, remained still after the challenge he would be alive today.

BALSILLIE, LIEUTENANT KEITH – SPECIAL BOAT SECTION (SBS) The commander of a patrol of S Squadron SBS tasked with carrying out a reconnaissance of the island of Patmos and neighbouring islands of the Dodecanese during early November 1943. He and his men returned to their base on the British-held island of Leros at dawn on 12 November to find German forces landing on the island's beaches. Fortunately, they avoided detection and succeeded in reaching the squadron headquarters in time to take part in the battle for the island. The fighting continued for four days until the surrender of the British garrison less the elements of S Squadron, which had quietly withdrawn to the nearby island of Lisso before sailing for the SBS base on the Turkish coast.

Later, in April 1944, Lieutenant Balsillie found himself on the island of Piscopi where he made contact with the mayor, who offered to help in a plan to capture the officer commanding the local German garrison. Lured to the main town by the offer of a large pig to feed his men, the German officer, escorted by his quartermaster, two men and a pack mule, were walking to the town when they were ambushed by Balsillie and his patrol. The mule was the only survivor.

Later that month, on the night of 22/23 April, Lieutenant Balsillie's patrol was one of two S Squadron patrols, under the overall command of Captain Anders Lassen, which were landed on the island of Santorin. Lieutenant Balsillie and his patrol were ordered to carry out an attack on an enemy radio station and outpost located in three houses in the village of Meravigli, the island's highest point.

Having captured the German signallers in their beds, Balsillie and his men placed explosive charges which subsequently destroyed the station and outpost as the raiders withdrew.

During the first week of October that same year, L Squadron SBS were part of 'Bucketforce' which was formed for the landings on the Peloponnese and the subsequent advance on Athens. Lieutenant Balsillie and his patrol were deployed by caïque into the Bay of Salamis where they were landed at Scaramanga. Making their way to Piraeus, they were the first uniformed Allied troops to enter the city since its occupation by the Germans in 1941.

BALUCHIS People of Baluchistan, an area now part of Iran and Pakistan, but once part of Oman. Baluchi soldiers were traditionally used by the Sultanate of Oman and Muscat, usually in preference to local tribes-people, whom the Sultan distrusted. They made good soldiers, but due to their inability to speak Arabic were unpopular with the local civilians. This friction between the two groups caused many problems for the SAS during operations in Oman, because part of their strategy was to try and instil a 'hearts and minds' campaign to win the support of the civilians for the sultan's cause.

Most of the Baluchi units had British officers, some of whom did not understand the Baluchi customs and traditions. As fighting soldiers the Baluchis were excellent; many of their NCOs were trained in mortar control, and discipline was good. That said, the Baluchi unit stationed at Point 825 in 1975 rebelled after two of their soldiers were killed by an inaccurate mortar fire order called down by their company commander. The soldiers mutinied to the point of shooting the white officer, who they claimed had also caused the death of a brother soldier some time previously. SAS soldiers at the location defused the insurrection by diplomacy, backed up by heavy firepower.

BANDIT COUNTRY The name adopted by the British Army for the countryside of South Armagh in Northern Ireland. This was mainly due to the high incidence of IRA activity there between 1969 and 1985. It is an area of traditional importance to the IRA because of its closeness to the border with the Irish Republic. Many of the first SAS actions were conducted in the area, all with great success.

'BAOBAB', OPERATION At the end of January 1944, 2 SAS mounted Operation 'Baobab' which was one of a number of operations tasked with cutting strategically important railway lines on the northern coast of Italy prior to the Allied landings at Anzio. The target for 'Baobab' was a railway bridge between the towns of Pesaro and Fano. On the night of 30 January, Lieutenant Laws and a signaller were landed near Pesaro to reconnoitre the area and secure a landing beach prior to the arrival of the raiding party on the following night. On doing so the following day, they discovered a group of Italian Carabinieri billeted in a house near the objective. That evening, before signalling the rest of their group to come ashore, the two men blocked the single door of the house, trapping the Italians inside the building. Meanwhile at the railway, explosive charges were laid by Captain Miller, and the party was withdrawing to the beach when the Carabinieri escaped and subsequently opened fire. The SAS, however, succeeded in embarking in the boats waiting to take them off and shortly afterwards the charges exploded, cutting the railway line as intended.

BARCE Axis airfield in North Africa, which was raided by the SAS, on the night of 8 March 1942. In vehicles of the Long Range Desert Group (LRDG), Major Bill Fraser led his party to the target, which turned out to be only one aircraft and a number of trucks. Although these were destroyed by the SAS, it was a rather poor return for the effort.

'BARCLAYCARD' A method-of-entry tool that works particularly well in gaining quick access into a building.

'BARKER', OPERATION Together with 'Harrod' and 'Jockworth', Operation 'Barker' was mounted by a force of 7 officers and 95 other ranks of 3 French Parachute Battalion (3 SAS), in the area north of Lyons in France.

The purpose of the operation was to establish, in co-operation with the Maquis in the area, a series of bases from which the withdrawing German forces could be harassed and, as one of a number of missions conducted throughout August and September 1944, to protect the open right flank of General Patton's US Third Army as it advanced through France to the River Rhine and the German border.

On 13 August, 27 men from 3 SAS, under the command of Lieutenant Rouhan, jumped into the Saône-et-Loire area of the Massif Central. A large amount of weapons and equipment was dropped by the RAF in support of this operation, which proved very successful. Operation 'Barker' was over by 19 September, following almost continuous attacks on the Germans. These attacks accounted for 3,000 enemy casualties with 500 prisoners taken.

BARKER, SERGEANT 'GEORDIE' Barker joined the SAS from the Royal Engineers, passing Selection in 1968. He was posted to G Squadron's Air Troop where he became a free-fall expert. 'Geordie', as he was known, was one of the most popular men in the SAS: a brilliant soldier to work with and one who could always raise people's spirits. Sadly, after surviving many operations, he was killed during a parachute accident in Oman.

BARKWORTH, MAJOR ERIC 'BILL' The intelligence officer of 2 SAS Regiment. In May 1945, he was despatched by his commanding officer, Lieutenant-Colonel Brian Franks, with a small party of 2 SAS to investigate reports of discoveries of bodies of British troops at Gaggenau in Germany. Barkworth's group, designated the SAS War Crimes Investigation Team, identified the bodies as those of members of 2 SAS deployed on Operation 'Loyton' in August 1944. Captured by the Germans, they had been taken to a concentration camp at Rotenfels, in Germany, summarily executed and buried. Barkworth and his men continued their investigations, travelling to Moussey, in the Vosges mountains of northeastern France, where they uncovered further bodies of members of 2 SAS. Despite the disbandment of the SAS in 1946, the group carried on with its work in investigating the deaths of men from both SAS regiments, whose fates were unknown, until 1949. Several men were identified as being responsible for the atrocities, they were tried by military courts sitting at Wuppertal and hanged.

BARRETT, LIEUTENANT-COLONEL GARTH – RHODESIAN 1ST SAS REGIMENT (RhSAS) In January 1973, as second-in-command of C Squadron Rhodesian SAS, Captain Barrett took part in the first operational free-fall parachute insertion by the unit. Two four-man pathfinder patrols, commanded by Barrett and Lieutenant Chris Schollenberg, were dropped on the evening of 19 January into Mozambique from a Royal Rhodesian Air Force Dakota at a height of 3,340m (11,000ft). Their task was to find and mark two dropping zones for an RhSAS main force, which would drop two hours later from two Dakotas, to cut off infiltration routes used by terrorists crossing from Mozambique into Rhodesia. The drop was marred by the death of

Trooper Frank Wilmot, the fourth man in Schollenberg's patrol, whose parachute failed to open. Difficulties were encountered after landing as both patrols found that the terrain was highly unsuitable for use as drop-zones. But subsequently Barrett located a usable area, and Schollenberg's patrol was ordered to join him. The main drop went ahead and, apart from a broken ankle, there were no further accidents. Thereafter the RhSAS split up into patrols, one of which was commanded by Barrett during the rest of the operation which lasted almost a month.

In April 1974, Barrett assumed the appointment of acting commander of the squadron in the absence of the OC, Major Brian Robinson, who had contracted hepatitis. In October of that year he led Operation 'Big Bang', a raid on a newly built Zimbabwe Independent People's Republican Army (ZIPRA) camp and underground arms dump located in Zambia. The operation was successful, resulting in a huge haul of arms and ammunition, but was marred by an attack on the forward base party, who were surprised in their position by two terrorists opening fire at close range and wounding three of the party.

Four years later Major Garth Barrett was commanding 1st SAS Regiment when, on Sunday 3 September 1978, he received a request from Combined Operations, known as 'ComOps', for RhSAS assistance in providing tracker and paramedic support for an operation searching for a missing Air Rhodesia Viscount airliner. This had disappeared en route to the Rhodesian capital of Salisbury from the lakeside holiday resort of Kariba. Barrett assembled a force of twenty men, including two doctors and a patrol medic, equipped with five containers of medical equipment. On the morning of the following day, he and his men emplaned in a Dakota and, having found the wreckage of the missing airliner in enemy-held territory, dropped nearby. Shortly afterwards, they encountered the first of eight survivors who had managed to crawl into the bush before ZIPRA/ZANLA guerrillas arrived. The remaining fifty passengers and crew had either died when the aircraft crash-landed or were murdered shortly afterwards.

Subsequently promoted to the rank of lieutenant-colonel, Garth Barrett continued to command 1st SAS Regiment until its disbandment in 1980. During his tenure of command, a large number of operations were mounted by the regiment against the ZANLA and ZAPU/ZIPRA terrorist organizations of Robert Mugabe and Joshua Nkomo, resulting in a large number of terrorists killed and considerable amounts of weapons and equipment seized.

'BASHA' A well-used word within the SAS meaning any form of shelter, both permanent or temporary. This can include anything from a bed space in the old buildings of Bradbury Lines to a shelter sheet covering a pole bed in the jungle.

BATEMAN, LIEUTENANT LESLIE   A patrol commander in D Squadron 1 SAS during operations in France in June 1944. His squadron commander, Major Ian Fenwick, had decided to disperse his force for added security, and so Bateman and his patrol were despatched to link up with a large group of several hundred Maquis at Thimory, under the command of a Captain Albert, who was preparing for an attack on Orleans. Shortly after their arrival, however, the Maquis base was attacked by a large enemy force equipped with armoured vehicles and flame-throwers. The resistance fighters scattered and the SAS patrol, which was travelling in civilian cars, came under heavy fire as it made its escape. The vehicle carrying Lieutenant Bateman, Corporal Wilson, Lance-Corporal Essex and a downed US Air Force officer who had earlier been sheltered by the Maquis, was hit. Bateman was wounded but succeeded in leaving the vehicle and gaining the cover of the woods, unlike the American who was killed as he attempted to crawl under the vehicle. Corporal Wilson received a head wound and was initially knocked unconscious; on coming round inside the vehicle, however, he drew his Colt .45 pistol and opened fire on four Germans as they approached, killing or wounding three of them. He was subsequently taken prisoner and, after interrogation, was sent to a hospital in Orleans where he was released by American forces which arrived in the city two days later.

Lieutenant Bateman, meanwhile, had met two of his patrol who had also been wounded in the ambush. The three men remained in hiding until they linked up with the Maquis and eventually made their way to an area in the forest where they met their commanding officer, Lieutenant-Colonel Paddy Mayne. Bateman remained with the Maquis while his men accompanied Lieutenant-Colonel Mayne to a rendezvous with C Squadron at Le Mans.

BATT (BRITISH ARMY TRAINING TEAM)   Name attributed to the first SAS units to enter the war in Oman in the early 1970s. The war was kept secret from the general public, hence the designation British Army Training Team, or BATT as it was commonly known. SAS detachments were first sent to Oman in July 1970, directly after Sultan Qaboos had deposed his father in a coup. As well as supporting the new regime in a military sense, the BATT teams also engaged in a 'hearts and minds' campaign to establish support for the new sultan amongst his people. The group of SAS men who held the town of Mirbat against incredible odds were a BATT team.

BATT HOUSE   Generally used during the Oman War. In the early years the SAS would move permanently into a village from where they would conduct patrols and ambushes. Having chosen a house in the village, and given that the SAS were officially known as British Army

Training Team, the building would become the BATT House. It was customary to use the BATT House as a form of HQ for the individual Firqats (local militias) and a place for issuing kit and equipment, and for briefing the commanders.

BAXTER, SERGEANT ANDY   Baxter was a first-rate soldier who joined the SAS in 1969 after serving with the Guards Independent Parachute Company. On passing Selection he was posted to G Squadron's Mountain Troop, where over the next few years he proved himself an excellent climber. Having completed the Mountain Guides course in Germany, he became a member of the second SAS team attempting to climb Mount Everest. During the ascent an avalanche swept Baxter down the mountainside. He survived and returned to Hereford but died of a brain tumour on the 12 August 1985.

'BAYTOWN', OPERATION   On 4 September 1943 the Special Raiding Squadron (SRS) landed at Bagnara – situated to the north of the Straits of Messina which the Eighth Army had crossed from Sicily on the previous day, prior to landing in the area of Reggio. The SRS had been tasked with cutting lines of communication in the enemy's rear.

The squadron met little opposition in the area of Bagnara itself, but soon came under artillery and mortar fire from German units in the surrounding hills. It took up positions to block any enemy counter-attack, and held the town for three days until the arrival of the leading elements of the Eighth Army which had advanced from Reggio. Casualties suffered were five killed and seventeen wounded. Shortly after being relieved by the Green Howards, the squadron withdrew to Sicily.

'BEAST'   A word used to describe punishing physical exercise during SAS Selection. The word has also been used as a code-name for a situation when SAS soldiers are in dire trouble. The request 'Send the Beast' normally indicated that the situation was extremely desperate, requiring every available SAS soldier to assist. This happened during the relief at Mirbat in 1972, when members of G Squadron arrived carrying enough firepower to start a small war.

'BEAT THE CLOCK'   This uniquely SAS expression means to stay alive. At the Stirling Lines base in Hereford stands the Regimental Clock Tower. Before the new barracks was built, plaques were inscribed with the names of men who had died, which also included members of the Rhodesian SAS. Names of those who failed to 'beat the clock' were fixed to the base of the Tower. Although the Clock Tower still remains, the plaques have now been removed to a position outside the Regimental Chapel.

The Clock Tower also carries the following inscription from James Elroy Flecker:

We are the pilgrims, master. We shall go
Always a little further: it may be
Beyond that last blue mountain barred with snow,
Across that angry or that glimmering sea.

BECKWITH, COLONEL CHARLES US Special Forces officer who trained with the SAS and saw action in Malaya. He later developed a reputation for ruthlessness and bravery in the Vietnam War, where he commanded a unit known as Project Delta. Later, in 1977, he was given the task of setting up the US's first counter-terrorist unit, which became known as Delta Force. Beckwith based his new unit on the SAS and, indeed, the first Delta recruits trained at Hereford.

BEEHIVE The Beehive demolition device is a 155mm diameter cylinder containing an inverted stand-off hollow charge which is filled with 3.1kg (7lbs) of RDX/TNT high explosive. The Beehive is primed with a RDX wax booster unit, and comes complete with three legs, which are used to obtain the stand-off. The Beehive was extensively used by the SAS during the Oman War for smashing holes through rock.

'BEERCAN' Name given to the mountain objective during the 1959 Jebel Akhdar operation in northern Oman, whereby two squadrons of SAS (A and D) raced to the top of a large mountain plateau in Northern Oman, outwitting the rebels who had taken refuge there.

BEESLEY, COLONEL REG – AUSTRALIAN SAS REGIMENT (SASR) Reg Beesley was commissioned into the Royal Australian Regiment (RAR) from the Royal Military College Duntroon in 1959, and subsequently served with 3 RAR until 1961 when he joined the 1st SAS Company RAR. During the next four years he served as reconnaissance officer, platoon commander, adjutant, second-in-command and, after the formation of SASR in 1964, as commander of 2 Squadron, before departing in 1964 for a staff appointment with 28th Commonwealth Brigade. Four years later he was commanding 3 Squadron in South Vietnam until January 1970, when he left SASR to attend courses in Britain. In October 1977 he returned to the regiment as commanding officer, a post he held until December 1979. During the period 1981 to 1983 he held the appointment of Director Special Action Forces (DSAF).

BEGLEY, CORPORAL 'BILL' Begley arrived at Hereford in 1978 after being posted as part of the Royal Corps of Transport section. Some two years later he tried for Selection and passed, when he was posted to G Squadron. An excellent soldier with an assured future, he was tragically killed in the Falklands War when the helicopter in which he was travelling crashed during a cross-decking operation.

'BEGONIA', OPERATION   Carried out jointly by elements of 1st Airborne Division and 2 SAS. On 2 October 1943 five patrols, one of them comprising a troop of B Squadron 2 SAS under Lieutenant Alastair McGregor, parachuted into Italy with the task of collecting together large numbers of Allied PoWs, released after the Italian surrender, and guiding them to the coastline between Ancona and Pescara, where they would be evacuated by Special Operations Executive (SOE) fishing craft. Hundreds of PoWs were assembled and led to the coast where the remainder of B Squadron and the regiment's French squadron, which had landed between 4 and 6 October as Operation 'Jonquil', were waiting for them. In the event, however, only 50 PoWs were taken off due to the lack of co-ordination between the SOE craft and the SAS patrols, this being exacerbated by the latter not being equipped with radio sets. Furthermore, German aircraft and patrols were active along the coast. The PoWs were forced to return to the hills and the SAS troops made their way back either overland or by boat, the operation having been a failure caused largely by poor planning and preparation.

BEHM, SECOND-LIEUTENANT LLOYD – AUSTRALIAN SAS REGIMENT (SASR)   Behm joined SASR direct from the Officer Cadet School at Portsea in July 1968 and was posted to 1 Squadron as a troop commander. During a tour of duty in South Vietnam on 29 May 1970 he was leading a five-man patrol, which had been inserted five days earlier into Long Khanh from the north west corner of the province with the task of reporting on any Vietcong (VC) movement in the area. During the morning the patrol established an ambush on a recently cut track and at 15:30 hours three VC entered the killing area. The ambush was duly sprung but, as they searched the bodies, the members of the patrol heard another group of enemy approaching their position. After withdrawing, the patrol was extracted and two companies of the 8th Battalion Royal Australian Regiment were deployed into the area, subsequently killing another VC.

A month later, on 29 June, Second-Lieutenant Behm's patrol was inserted into an area 11km (7 miles) west of Xuyen Moc near the Song Rai River. As they were disembarking from their helicopter, he and his men came under automatic fire from a group of ten VC. The aircraft took off immediately with two members of the patrol still aboard. The three on the ground returned the enemy fire, supported by a helicopter gunship, until their helicopter returned to extract them ten minutes later.

BEIHAN   Name of a safe house used in 1962 by the SAS during covert operations against the Yemenis in the interior of Aden.

BELGIAN 1ST PARA-COMMANDO BATTALION   In recognition of their origins as part of the SAS Brigade in World War II, the unit wears the SAS wings.

BELGIAN SAS REGIMENT The first Belgian unit of parachutists was formed on 8 May 1942, under the command of Captain (later Major) Blondeel, from a company of the 2nd Battalion Belgian Fusiliers. Following completion of parachute training in October, it was incorporated into the British 3 Parachute Battalion, but in January of the following year it was redesignated the Belgian Independent Parachute Company, and then in August became part of the British 8 Parachute Battalion. In January 1944, having undergone training at the Special Allied Training Centre at Inverlochry in Scotland, it became part of the newly formed Special Air Service Brigade.

After D-Day, elements of the company were dropped in the areas of Le Mans and Chartres on Operations 'Chaucer', 'Shakespeare' and 'Bunyan'. On 16 August, Major Blondeel and forty of his men, together with some jeeps, were parachuted into the Ardennes on Operation 'Noah'. On 2 September, patrols of the company were dropped into Belgium on Operation 'Brutus', their task being to link up with the Belgian Resistance. Three days later, on 5 September, a small force from the company was inadvertently dropped into Germany as reinforcements for Operation 'Berbang', thus becoming the first SAS troops to enter the country.

In early 1945 the company was expanded and redesignated the Belgian SAS Regiment, subsequently serving in Denmark and Germany in a counter-intelligence role. Later that year the regiment was handed over to the Belgian Army and redesignated the 1er Regiment Parachutiste-SAS. Initially, it was based at Westmalle but subsequently, from April 1946 onwards, at Poulseur with a training school located at Schaffen.

Members of the regiment served in the Korean War as part of the Corps Volontaires Corea (CVC), which saw a considerable amount of action until its withdrawal from Korea in 1954. During that period, in February 1952, the 1er Regiment Parachutiste-SAS and the Belgian Commando Regiment, which had been formed from the wartime Belgian commando units, were absorbed with other elements of the CVC into the newly formed Belgian Para-Commando Regiment. The SAS regiment was redesignated 1er Bataillon Parachutiste (SAS) and retained its maroon beret and SAS badge. The other battalions were designated 2ème, 3ème and 4ème Bataillons de Commandos, 5ème Bataillon de Para-Commandos and 6ème Bataillon de Commandos. In addition, the regiment at that time also possessed six independent commando companies numbered 11 to 16 respectively. In 1962 the 3ème, 4ème, 5ème and 6ème Bataillons were disbanded.

In November 1964 civil war broke out in the Congo. On 17 November, 320 men of 1er Bn Para (SAS), reinforced by a company of the 2ème Bataillon de Commandos and logistics elements, were airlifted to Ascension Island by the US Air Force. Four days later, on 21 November, they were deployed on Operation 'Red Dragon', when they parachuted on to Stanleyville airport and advanced on the town to rescue hostages held by Simba rebels. On 26 November, they carried out a similar hostage rescue operation, 'Black Dragon', at Paulis. In both instances, the operations were successful.

Fourteen years later, in 1978, the 1er Bn Para (SAS) was once again in action after a rebellion broke out in the Belgian colony of Zaire, where rebels had invaded the provinces of Shaba and South Kasai from bases in Angola. On 20 May 1978, in an operation code-named 'Red Bean', the battalion was airlifted into the airfield at the mining town of Kolwezi, which had been secured on the previous day by French Foreign Legion troops of the 2ème Regiment Etranger de Parachutistes. Thereafter the battalion participated in clearing the area and rescuing Belgian civilians caught up in fighting between government forces and the rebels.

The SAS element of the Belgian Para-Commando Regiment still survives in the form of the 1er Bataillon de Parachutistes, the other battalions being the 2ème Bataillon de Commandos and the 3ème Bataillon de Parachutistes. Together with its headquarters and training centre, the regiment also possesses a long range reconnaissance company (Equipes Speciales de Reconnaissance), a swimmer/canoeist unit and a mountain leader cadre, as well as light-armoured reconnaissance and anti-tank companies and a parachute light artillery battery.

BELIZE Formerly British Honduras, the official name of the territory was changed to Belize in June 1973, and granted full independence on 21 September 1981. Even so, the British Army remained responsible for the protection of Belize, and a British garrison remained there, primarily to stave off military advances from neighbouring Guatemala, who laid claim to Belize. From time to time Guatemala would rattle its sabres and prepare to take Belize by force. Fortunately, Britain has managed to prevent any incursions by show of force or by diplomatic means.

The last major incident occurred in 1975 when Guatemala threatened to invade. G Squadron, 22 SAS, were flown out with orders to observe any Guatemalan troop movements crossing the border. The arrival of six heavily armed Harriers zipping up and down the border was enough to curtail any real action and the Guatemalan threat fizzled out. Although British gunboat diplomacy worked, and Belize was returned to normal, the SAS patrols remained in the jungle for several weeks carrying out a 'hearts and minds' campaign, before extracting to Belize and finally home to the UK.

BELL, CAPTAIN RODERICK Spanish-speaking Royal Marine officer who aided Colonel Mike Rose in persuading the Argentinians to discuss surrender during the Falklands War. On 14 June both men flew into Port Stanley where they started talks with General Menendez, which led to the signing of a surrender document.

BELT KIT   The belt kit is one of the most important items an SAS soldier has. Each man is responsible for constructing his own belt kit and for packing the contents. The basic assembly will include a belt, which can be anything from a rigging strap from a heavy-drop pallet, to a standard issue belt which has been adapted to take the pouches, and sometimes a supporting yoke. There are no hard and fast rules, but the belt must carry the following: two ammunition pouches, each capable of holding four magazines; two water bottles – one with a metal brewing mug; two large mess tin-sized pouches – one for permanent use, ie survival kit, emergency rations, flares, medical kit etc, and one for daily use, mess tins and consumable rations for that day. The belt should also have a knife or golok (broad-bladed jungle knife), and several First Field dressings attached to it.

'Grab your belt kit' is a common cry within the SAS, and this sums up its importance. Even while in Stirling Lines the belt kit, with the exclusion of ammunition, always remains ready to go at a moment's notice. In the field, unless he is sleeping, it remains around the soldier's waist at all times. During an operational contact, the bergen rucksack may be dropped, but the belt kit remains with the soldier to the bitter end.

BELUM VALLEY   The isolated Belum Valley in northern Malaya, near the border with Thailand, was the location of one of the headquarters of the Communist Terrorist (CT) organizations during the Malayan Emergency. The number of terrorists in the valley was estimated at 100, and in February 1952 an operation was mounted to remove them with a force comprising 22 SAS, a troop of Royal Marine Commandos, and elements of the Police Field Force (PFF).

A and C (Rhodesian) Squadrons, the Commandos and the PFF approached the area on foot, moving along steep mountain tracks, climbing slippery, muddy slopes and crossing rivers. B Squadron, numbering 54 in total, was inserted into the area by parachute. This was the regiment's pioneering attempt to use the technique of parachuting into trees in action. There were only three casualties, and none of the injuries proved to be serious. The operation, however, proved inconclusive.

BENINA   In North Africa in World War II Benina was the location of a major enemy aircraft repair base and was the target of three attacks by L Detachment SAS. On each occasion these were led by Major David Stirling, accompanied by Sergeants Johnny Cooper and Reg Seekings. On the first two occasions, they found the base deserted, but in June 1942 they achieved success. During an RAF bombing raid on nearby Benghazi (see Raid on), they once again made their way past the enemy sentries and succeeded in placing Lewes bombs on a number of aircraft, some new aircraft engines in crates and some machinery. As a coup de grâce, Stirling attacked the enemy guardroom with grenades as he and his men withdrew. On reaching the rendezvous with the Long Range Desert Group (LRDG), he met the patrols of Captain Paddy Mayne and Lieutenant Andre Zirnheld, who had attacked Berka Satellite and Berka Main airfields respectively.

Not content with these results, Stirling decided to mount a further raid on the area, and on the following night, accompanied by Captain Mayne's patrol and a number of other individuals, drove down the escarpment in a borrowed LRDG vehicle towards Benina. Having bluffed their way through a German check-point, Stirling and his party encountered a number of Italian troops who opened fire but were unsuccessful in halting the SAS vehicle as it sped on. Shortly afterwards, a number of enemy vehicles were spotted at a petrol-station and these soon had Lewes bombs planted on them. By now the entire area was alive with enemy troops and Stirling decided to withdraw. Heading across the desert, successfully avoiding enemy patrols despatched to intercept them, the SAS succeeded in reaching the Jebel Akhdar. As they reached the top of the wadi which led up the escarpment, however, Corporal Bob Lilley spotted that the time pencil fuse of one of the remaining Lewes bombs was burning. Thanks to his split-second warning, all the occupants of the vehicle succeeded in baling out from the vehicle which was blown to bits a few seconds later. Stirling and his men thus had to complete the journey to the rendezvous with the LRDG on foot.

BENNETT, REGIMENTAL SERGEANT-MAJOR BOB, MM
One of the original members of the SAS, Bennett, was an ex-Grenadier Guardsman serving with the Brigade of Guards and No. 8 Commando. A cockney, he joined the SAS to get away from the stuffy atmosphere of the Guards. On joining 1 SAS he served with them for most of World War II. After 1 SAS had been given regimental status, he served with B Squadron of the Malayan Scouts. He was the regimental sergeant-major of the SAS before his retirement in 1962 and was awarded both the British Empire Medal and the Military Medal.

'BENSON', OPERATION
Was carried out by one officer and five other ranks of the Belgian Independent Parachute Company during the period 28 August to 1 September 1944. The patrol was dropped northeast of Paris tasked with the mission of reporting on enemy dispositions and movements. The operation was highly successful, not least because the patrol captured a copy of the German order of battle

for formations deployed along the River Seine. The speed of the Allied advance north to the Seine, however, resulted in this operation being somewhat short-lived.

BERET, SAS The original SAS beret was white and not appreciated by the men, who rapidly changed it to beige. In 1944 the SAS came under 1st Airborne Division and the beige beret was changed to red. The beige beret was restored in 1957 and remains to this day. When G Squadron was first formed in 1965, it was decided that a Guards blue and red flash would be placed behind the SAS badge. This instantly caused resentment and the idea was discarded.

'BERGBANG', OPERATION This unsuccessful mission took place between 2 and 12 September 1944, conducted by 41 members of the Belgian SAS, commanded by Captain Courtoy, in the Liège-Aachen-Maastricht area. The aim was to aid the local Resistance and sever German communications east of the River Meuse. However, the men were dropped too far from the operational area and bad weather dispersed the group over a wide range. One group of men was actually dropped in Germany.

BERGE, COMMANDANT GEORGES – L DETACHMENT SAS The commander of the group of Free French parachutists which joined L Detachment SAS at the beginning of 1942. A regular French army officer, he had previously been a member of an independent Free French parachute company trained by the Special Operations Executive (SOE) for coups de main operations in German-occupied France. In March 1941, he had led a five-man group which dropped near Vannes, in southern Brittany, tasked with ambushing and killing the pilots of Kampfgeschwader 100, a Luftwaffe pathfinder unit based at an airfield at Meucon near Vannes. The operation had proved unsuccessful and Berge and his men made their way to the Bay of Biscay from where they were eventually extracted by submarine.

In June 1942, Berge led a raid on the island of Crete, accompanied by three of his French troop, Captain the Earl Jellicoe, who was a newcomer to the SAS, and a Greek guide named Lieutenant Costi. After landing at night from the Greek Navy submarine *Triton* by inflatable boats, the party marched for two nights over the mountains to the enemy airfield at Heraklion, where it was known there were 60 Junkers 88s and a number of Stuka dive bombers. Having moved on to the airfield with some difficulty because of the wire defences and numerous guards, Berge and his men succeeded in placing Lewes bombs on 21 aircraft, a number of vehicles and a fuel dump before withdrawing. They were unwittingly assisted by an RAF aircraft which happened to bomb the airfield at the same time, causing confusion which the raiders used to good effect.

After travelling for the next two nights, and lying-up during the day, Berge's group was within a few miles of the beach where they were due to rendezvous with the submarine on the following night. While Berge and the three other Frenchmen hid in a cave, Captain Jellicoe and Lieutenant Costi went off to a nearby village to make contact with a Cretan who would signal the submarine to confirm the pick-up. Unfortunately, during their absence, Berge and his companions were accidentally discovered by some local people who betrayed them to the Germans. The result was that the four Frenchmen found themselves facing three enemy patrols who heavily outnumbered them. Berge decided to stand and fight, intending to hold out until he and his men could slip away under cover of darkness. Unfortunately, however, the Frenchmen ran out of ammunition and had no option other than to surrender. He and his men were captured and taken to Heraklion, where they were tortured before being executed. When Captain Jellicoe and Lieutenant Costi returned to the cave, they discovered their companions' fate. Three days later, accompanied by twenty Cretan refugees, they were taken off by the submarine.

BERGEN (RUCKSACK) The bergen rucksack first came to be associated with the SAS during the first Malayan campaign in the 1950s, and has remained ever since. The old jungle bergen used by the SAS had a metal 'A' frame which was very uncomfortable. This was replaced in the mid-1970s with an upgraded waterproof version which was equally as hard to carry. The advent of the newer 'Cyclops' and 'Crusader' soft carry rucksacks replaced the obsolete metalled framed bergens around the time of the Falklands War.

The SAS bergen contains everything the soldier needs to survive: ammunition; shelter; sleeping bag; clothes; food and water. It is the equivalent of carrying a home around on one's back and, like a well-kept home, everything should be serviceable, clean, and in its place. The SAS have one tried and tested method that works, and it is based on the principle that you should always be able to get to your equipment with the minimum of effort. Waterproof inner bags seal all clothes and porous items, protecting them from heavy rain and water whilst river crossing.

BERJONGKONG-BRUANG The Berjongkong-Bruang area of Indonesia was the scene of 'Claret' operations carried out by 2 Squadron Australian SAS Regiment, commanded by Major Jim Hughes, during the Borneo Confrontation. On 16 May 1966 a four-man patrol, commanded by Sergeant Barry Young, infiltrated the Berjongkong-Bruang area of Indonesia, across the border from Sarawak, and headed south. Its task was to discover whether the Indonesians were using the Poeteh River and, at the same time, to try and locate the baseplate position of a mortar which had attempted to engage one of the squadron's other patrols during the previous month, and which Sergeant Young and his men could hear firing occasionally.

Five days later, the patrol headed north, parallel to the river, through swamps towards Berjongkong. On the morning of 23 May, while reconnoitring the river, Sergeant Young and Private Easthorpe suddenly encountered five Indonesians in a canoe. Young engaged them with his AR-15 at a range of 25m (27yds), hitting three of them and knocking them out of the canoe. Private Easthorpe killed the other two with his SLR1A1.

Rapidly withdrawing from the area, the patrol headed north and shortly afterwards heard a mortar open fire to the rear. After moving 1,500m (1,600yds) Sergeant Young changed direction eastwards but at 15:00 hours detected enemy troops on a spur to the front. At 18:30 hours the patrol established a lying-up position (LUP) and shortly afterwards heard signal shots fired by Indonesians to the east and west at a range of approximately 800m (870yds).

Aware that the Indonesians were searching for them, the patrol moved off before first light the next morning and headed east. Crossing back across the border into Sarawak, it established a lying-up position and was extracted by helicopter around noon on 25 May.

BERKA AIRFIELDS The Berka Main and Satellite airfields were the targets of L Detachment SAS on more than one occasion. In March 1942 Captain Paddy Mayne mounted an operation involving a number of attacks on Benghazi (see Raid on) and the airfields in the area, with Berka Satellite being the main objective of a four-man patrol which also comprised Corporals Bennett and Rose, and Private Byrne. Travelling with a Long Range Desert Group (LRDG) patrol via the Siwa Oasis, Mayne and his men arrived at the Jebel Akhdar from which they could observe the area of coastal plain on which Benghazi and the airfields were located. Under cover of darkness on the following night, they left the wadi in which they had been lying-up and made their way down the escarpment to their target. Moving on to the airfield, they placed Lewes bombs on fifteen aircraft, a number of fuel dumps and twelve large bombs, before withdrawing and making their way during the rest of the night to a rendezvous where they were collected by the LRDG.

Another raid on the Berka airfields took place on 13 June 1942. This coincided with a raid on Berka Satellite by the RAF, whose bombers arrived overhead as Mayne, accompanied by Corporals Lilley and Warburton and Private Storey, was moving across the airfield towards some aircraft. There was little they could do but seek what scant cover there was on the airfield until the raid was over. With the enemy on full alert, Mayne withdrew after planting some bombs on a fuel dump and, avoiding enemy patrols already scouring the area, led his men to the rendezvous with the LRDG where he also met Major David Stirling, who had attacked a nearby aircraft repair base at Benina. Also at the rendezvous was Lieutenant Zirnheld and a patrol of L Detachment's Free French troop which had attacked Berka Main, destroying eleven aircraft.

'BERME' During the Gulf War Iraqi engineers constructed massive bank and ditch systems which were referred to as 'Bermes'. Many such constructions were over 4.5 (15ft) high and 6m (20ft) thick, offering a major obstacle to the vehicles of the SAS fighting columns.

BESSBROOK MILL Bessbrook Mill in South Armagh was used by the SAS at the start of the Troubles in Northern Ireland. The large disused mill had been taken over by the British Army, and housed the regular battalion during its tour of duty. SAS patrols would operate from here into the border countryside of Crossmaglen and Forkhill. While covert cars were sometimes used for drop-offs and pick-ups, RAF or Army Air Corps would airlift most patrols. Although the SAS shared the Mill with the regular battalion, for security they retained their own accommodation and facilities.

BEVERLEY An aircraft built by the Blackburn Company, which saw service from 1955 to 1967. This robust transport plane supported SAS operations in Malaya, Oman and the Radfan. Its large capacity meant that it could carry helicopters and vehicles, or alternatively 94 troops or 70 paratroopers. It also had the invaluable ability to take-off and land on small airstrips, such as those in the jungle. The Beverley was powered by four Bristol Centaurus engines and had a top speed of 238km/h (142mph) and a range of 2,100km (1,260 miles).

BFT Battle Fitness Test is an annual fitness test undertaken by all soldiers in the British Army. The first part consists of running 2.5km (1.5 miles) in a group in 13 minutes. The second part is a solo run, over the same distance, in 11.5 minutes. Most SAS soldiers carry out their own fitness routine far in excess of the BFT; however, the test is used by the Directing Staff (DS) during SAS Selection.

BIEN HOA PROVINCE One of four areas in South Vietnam in which operations were carried out, during the period 1966-71, by squadrons of the Australian SAS Regiment, which were based from 1967 onwards at Nui Dat in neighbouring Phuoc Tuy Province.

'BIG FOUR' Used to describe the four answers a prisoner may give to his captors during interrogation: number; rank; date of birth; and name.

'BIG TIME' A frequently used phrase that has many meanings in the SAS, but normally relates to some excessive measure. Soldiers who show off or do something dramatic are said to be 'big time' while the same phrase is used to describe hitting the enemy hard. 'We hit them "big time".'

'BIN' Those who fail the SAS Selection test are often referred to as being 'binned'. To 'bin' means to reject something or someone that is not working as it should.

BINH TUY PROVINCE Lies to the east of Phuoc Tuy Province in South Vietnam. Like the other provinces in which the Australian SAS Regiment operated during the period 1966-71, the areas around the towns and villages were cultivated, comprising padi fields or rubber plantations, while the mountains and border areas with Cambodia were covered in jungle.

BIRDSTRIKE A potentially lethal occurrence when birds hit and damage a vital part of an aircraft or helicopter. If they become sucked into the engine's air intakes it may cause immediate power failure, and the aircraft will crash. This is the most likely reason for the loss of a Sea King helicopter in the 1982 Falklands War, while it was cross-decking from HMS *Hermes* to HMS *Intrepid*.

BIR FASCIA An area to the north of the Siwa Oasis in North Africa, and the base location of the newly formed B Squadron 1 SAS, which installed itself there on 13 December 1942. Commanded by Major Vivian Street, the squadron mounted raids on an allocated stretch of road between Bouerat and Tripoli, attacking enemy transport by night and thus forcing it to use the road by day when it would be vulnerable to air attack by the RAF. Unfortunately, however, it suffered heavy casualties in the process, most of its patrols being killed or captured. Bir Fascia eventually fell to the enemy. Only a few survivors, notably four officers and a small number of the more experienced other ranks, succeeded in making their way back to British lines.

BIR ZALTEN The wadi at Bir Zalten, 96km (60 miles) south of enemy positions at Agheila, and south of Benghazi (see Raid on), was the base location of A Squadron 1 SAS, commanded by Major Paddy Mayne. The squadron established itself there on 29 November 1942 and its task was to attack enemy transport on the road between Agheila and Bouerat and it proceeded to do so, mounting some sixteen raids a week at night and thus forcing the enemy to use the road by day. Vehicles were attacked, telegraph poles blown down and the road mined or cratered. Such was the effect of these operations that the Germans were forced to divert troops to carry out operations against the SAS.

BIVI-BAG Slang for a waterproof sack which is normally made from a 'breathing' material such as Gore Tex or Aquatex. The bivi-bag comes in a variety of shapes, some of which simply cover the sleeping bag, whilst others offer the benefits of a small tent. During the Falklands War, bivi-bags allowed the SAS to remain in their observation positions for many weeks. Since that time, the British Army in general have adopted the bivi-bag as standard issue equipment.

BLACK SEPTEMBER The Palestine Liberation Organization (PLO) had constantly raided Israel from bases in Jordan, and as a result this brought retaliation on Jordan. Matters came to a head when the People's Front for the Liberation of Palestine (PFLP) hijacked four airlines between 6 and 9 of September, forcing three of them to land at an old British airfield 32km (20 miles) from King Hussein's palace in Amman. Hussein capitulated to ensure the safety of the passengers, but once they had been released, the planes were blown up, and although none of the passengers was harmed, he turned on the Palestinians. On 16 September he released his vicious Bedouin troops to confront the Palestinian forces, and at the same time his artillery pounded the Palestinian refugee camps. Over 3,000 were killed and 11,000 wounded. The majority of the people in the camps were civilians. The conflict ended on 25 September. It is from this action that the terrorist group Black September took their name.

'BLIMEY', OPERATION One of four operations, one large and three small, mounted by 3 Squadron 2 SAS under Major Roy Farran in Italy in 1945. A patrol of 25 men under Captain Scott was dropped between Genoa and La Spezia on the Italian Riviera with the task of operating with partisans in support of American ground operations in the area. Unfortunately, the operation only achieved limited success and most of the members of the patrol were taken prisoner.

BLITZ BUGGY The Blitz Buggy was Major David Stirling's personal vehicle and consisted of a Ford V-8 staff car modified for SAS desert operations with the roof and windows removed. Armed with a Vickers K machine gun in the front, and twin guns in the rear, it was equipped for desert operations with a long-range fuel tank, sun compass and radiator condenser. Painted in the olive drab field grey of the Afrika Korps, it always sported the current air recognition decal on the bonnet. The vehicle was used on several operations, including two forays into Benghazi (see Raid on). Unfortunately, however, it met an untimely end in the aftermath of an attack by L Detachment SAS on Bagoush airfield in July 1942. During the raid itself the Blitz Buggy, accompanied by two jeeps, had led the way over the airfield, its Vickers guns and those of the jeeps setting aircraft ablaze. On the morning after, however, as the SAS were withdrawing to a rendezvous, the three vehicles were spotted by two Italian aircraft which attacked, destroying the Blitz Buggy and one of the jeeps.

BLOOD CHIT   The blood chit is basically a piece of paper that an escaping soldier will show to any civilian that may help him. Each blood chit has a unique number at the top, and any civilian that has aided a soldier may approach any British Embassy or consulate and claim his reward. The blood chits issued during the Gulf War were in English, Arabic and Farsi.

BLOOD MONEY   Gold half sovereigns are issued to SAS soldiers who operate behind the enemy lines. The purpose of such money is to back up the blood chit, since not everyone can read. Additionally, gold is recognized the world over for its value. All SAS soldiers in the Gulf War were issued with 20 gold half sovereigns, and many were used in order to effect the safe return of soldiers to their own lines after getting separated from their unit. In some parts of the world American dollars are used in the same way.

BLOWPIPE MISSILE   Man-portable surface-to-air missile. *Specification* Weight: 2.8kg (6.2lbs); Length: 153cm (5ft); Warhead diameter: 76mm (3in); Warhead weight: 2.2kg (4.8lbs); Maximum range: 3,500m (3,815yds); Velocity: Mach 1.

The Blowpipe is the first anti-aircraft missile of its type to be developed and used by the British Army. It differs from other anti-aircraft missiles in that it is controlled from launcher to target by the operator, which makes it an outstanding weapon. The SAS trialed the Blowpipe but found it cumbersome to operate and much prefer to use the US-made Stinger, which they have had access to since the Falklands War.

BLUEY   A single-sheet air-mail letter used by soldiers. They are issued free of charge and used because of their lightness. All British Forces mail is directed through the British Forces Post Office (BFPO).

BLYTH, CAPTAIN HUGH – SPECIAL BOAT SECTION (SBS)
On 4 April 1944, Captain Hugh Blyth and his patrol of S Squadron, comprising Sergeant Miller, Privates Rice and Evans, and Gunner Jones, were despatched on a reconnaissance mission to the island of Calchi on board a caïque of the Levant Schooner Flotilla, commanded by Sub-Lieutenant Allan Tuckey RNVR. Having completed their task, the patrol was in the process of re-embarking when four German heavily armed 'P' class lighters appeared in the bay where the caïque was moored, and a brief battle ensued. Blyth and his men swam ashore and succeeded in evading the enemy search parties which subsequently combed the island.

Once the enemy had departed, Captain Blyth succeeded in persuading a local fisherman to take the patrol to the island of Rhodes which was only some 6km (4 miles) away. On 9 April, while halfway across the channel, the fishing boat was unfortunately stopped and searched by a German patrol boat. Despite being concealed in the bilge, Blyth and his men were found and taken prisoner. They were taken to Salonika where they joined Sub-Lieutenant Tuckey and his crew and were interrogated by Wehrmacht intelligence officers. Blyth was, for some inexplicable reason, sent to a PoW camp in Germany while Tuckey, his Greek crewmen and the remainder of the SBS patrol, were handed over to the Sicherheitsdienst, the SS Security Service. They were subsequently executed under the terms of Hitler's Commando Order of October 1942 which stipulated that all members of Allied commando and Special Forces were to be executed after capture.

BOAT TROOP   The Boat Troop of an SAS Sabre Squadron is responsible for all forms of water insertion methods including diving and canoe work right down to swimming ashore on surf boards. In recent years, members of the Special Boat Section (SBS) have been stationed at Hereford, and cross training between the two units and several operations have been jointly carried out.

Boat Troop members are required to be proficient in handling Klepper canoes, Gemini inflatables and other small raiding craft. Infiltration techniques have even covered the firing of SAS soldiers from submarine torpedo tubes. The men are given a small breathing apparatus before being loaded three to a tube, one behind the other, in place of the torpedo. The inner hatch is then closed and the forward hatch opened, thus flooding the tube, at which time the men are pushed out into the open sea by compressed air.

BODY ARMOUR   Specifically designed for the assault role, body armour is available in differing grades of ballistic protection, according to clients' operational requirements, and can incorporate a groin protector and pockets in front and rear for the insertion of ceramic plates. A ballistic collar can also be fitted if required.

The outer cover of the assault body armour is manufactured in Arvex SNX 574 flame-resistant fabric. Based on Nomex Delta C fibre and with a weight of 210gsm, this fabric is also anti-static and liquid repellent. The body armour is designed to accommodate the CT400 radio communications harness and can be fitted with a radio pouch and magazine carriers or utility pouches if so required.

When worn with body armour, the Level III Plus ceramic plate provides protection against high velocity ballistic threats up to and including 7.62mm × 51 US M61 ball armour piercing and 7.62mm × 54 Soviet heavy ball (steel core) ammunition. Weighing 1.12kg (2.5lbs) and measuring 250mm × 300mm (10in × 12in), the plate can be worn in the front and rear of the assault body armour.

BODY GUARDING   Since the end of the campaign in Aden in 1967, the SAS has become increasingly involved in body-guarding duties. SAS soldiers, trained in close protection, often act as bodyguards to the British prime minister, senior members of government and the royal family, as well as foreign diplomats considered important to British interests. They have been used in unique international situations, such as in the guarding of the safety of Sultan Qaboos of Oman in 1970 after he deposed his father, Sultan Said bin Taimur. They stayed until local bodyguards could be found and trained.

They are also responsible for the training of other clients, such as the Metropolitan Police's VIP protection squads, in the same skills. Some of the training takes place in the Close Quarter Battle House, or the 'Killing House', at Hereford, where many of the techniques used in counter-terrorism are also put to use in close protection.

The SAS body-guarding skills and techniques cover every aspect of VIP protection, from one-on-one to four- and six-man teams. Many SAS soldiers use their bodyguard skills to seek employment once they have left the regiment, and they now protect many of the world's most prominent people.

BOMBAY The Bristol Bombay was developed in 1935 but did not come into service until 1939. Two Bristol Pegasus engines gave it a maximum speed of 307km/h (192mph) and a cruising speed of 256km/h (160mph). It had a crew of three and could carry 24 troops when used for transport (some were converted to be used as bombers). It had a maximum range of 4,000km (2,230 nautical miles) when fitted with extra fuel tanks, which most were. During its service in World War II, it was fitted with Vickers K machine guns fore and aft.

BOND, MAJOR DICK Major Bond was a member of 1 SAS who, under Lieutenant-Colonel Mayne, commanded B Squadron. He died during the advance towards Oldenburg in North Germany in April 1945. The two squadrons (Mayne commanded C Squadron) were part of Operation 'Howard', supporting the advance of the Canadian 4th Armoured Division. The operation, which meant confronting stiff German resistance with jeeps head-on, was not a normal task, and several times they ran into serious trouble. Major Bond and his driver Trooper Lewis were both killed attacking a German position near Borgerwald. The main problem arose from the speed with which the SAS jeeps could move forward in advance of the Canadian Sherman tanks, which gave them little protection from fortified German positions. The problem was resolved when Mayne halted and waited for the Canadian armour to catch up.

'BONE' SAS word used to describe someone who is stupid, meaning they have a thick skull.

BONNINGTON, LIEUTENANT CHARLES   Commander of one of the teams that took off from Bagoush airfield, North Africa, in five Bristol Bombay transports during the SAS's first, disastrous operation in November 1941. High winds, poor visibility and hits from anti-aircraft fire forced the aircraft carrying Bonnington's command to make an emergency landing (the pilot had a defective engine, no instruments and was low on fuel). Later, after taking off and heading back to Tobruk, they were hit again by anti-aircraft fire, which set fire to the aircraft's internal long range fuel tank, and were pursued by an enemy fighter. The two crew and one SAS man died when the Bombay crash-landed; the remainder, including Bonnington himself, were captured.

BORDER SCOUTS   Between 1963 and 1966 Major-General Walter Walker, Director of Operations Borneo, recruited irregular troops from the native population there during the campaign in Borneo. With their primary role being one of intelligence gathering, they helped to defend the Malaysian border with the Kalimantan region of Indonesia. These forces became known as the Border Scouts.

The Scouts were recruited from local tribesmen and were trained by SAS soldiers in a number of jungle camps, becoming the 'eyes and ears' of the British forces, as well as liaison officers with the local people. These jungle-training camps were all alike in layout, consisting of a simple long house for the Scouts and a smaller one for the instructors. The SAS soldiers were responsible for all aspects of training, discipline and administration before handing over the training programme to the Gurkha Independent Parachute Company.

Although the Scouts could not be described as a true militia, they were used to patrol and act as guides for regular infantry. Walker employed helicopters to move companies of infantry to trouble spots from their positions at fortified posts close to the border. In September 1963, a Scout post at Long Jawi, 44km (28 miles) from the border, was almost totally destroyed by a substantial group of well-equipped Indonesians. As a result, Walker restricted the role of the Scouts to one of intelligence gathering only. It was in this capacity that they really proved their worth to the SAS, frequently complementing individual SAS patrols by enabling communication between Commonwealth forces and the native inhabitants.

BORNEO   In the early 1960s, Malaya sought to bring together Singapore, and the Bornean states of Sabah, Sarawak, Brunei and itself under the Federation of Malaysia, an idea fully supported by Britain. The Indonesian President Sukarno, however, vehemently opposed the move as it threatened his own designs on the rest of Borneo. The first sign of trouble came in 1962 in the Sultanate of Brunei, when a small Indonesian-backed, anti-Malaysian element rebelled. The British forces, however, quickly ended this revolt.

By early 1963, the situation had worsened, with well-trained Indonesian insurgents infiltrating over the border from the Kalimantan region. In response, Britain raised a force of Malaysian, Commonwealth and British troops, including the SAS, to deal with the situation. Unfortunately, the force was only a small one and the border stretched for 1,120km (700 miles) through thick jungle. Not only did they face a threat from the Indonesians, but also from an internal terrorist element, the Clandestine Communist Organization (CCO), who were made up mainly of Chinese settlers from Sarawak.

The British commander in Borneo, Major-General Walter Walker, initially wanted the SAS to parachute into the jungle, as they had in Malaya, and recapture any helicopter landing areas that had fallen into rebel hands. The commander of 22 SAS at the time, Lieutenant-Colonel John Woodhouse, remembering the high casualty rate of tree-jumping, persuaded Walker that the SAS would be better suited to patrolling the border instead.

A Squadron consisted of only 70 men, a small number to patrol such a long stretch of border, especially in such hostile jungle conditions. However, by operating in 21 patrols of two to three men, and staying in the jungle for long periods of time, they were able to provide early warning of any Indonesian military or Communist incursions. As well as patrolling the border, the SAS took on another very important task – that of winning the 'hearts and minds' of the native people. By gaining an understanding of their lifestyle and language, by living with them and dispensing medical aid when necessary, the SAS gained important allies in intelligence gathering. The local people, who still crossed the border freely into Kalimantan to trade their goods, often brought back valuable information on Indonesian troop movements.

The SAS also recruited some of the local people as Border Scouts. Their role was primarily one of gathering intelligence as they proved to be unsuited to conventional combat roles. Another group recruited and trained by the SAS from 1964 onwards, however, was known as the Cross-Border Scouts and they took part in raids across the border into Kalimantan. So, when the Indonesian incursions started in earnest in 1963, A Squadron were already prepared to repel them. They knew the best ambush sites and helicopter landing zones, and the 'hearts and minds' campaign was working well.

By 1964, attacks by the Indonesian military were becoming more frequent, and Walker authorized the first top-secret 'Claret' raids across the border into Kalimantan. B Squadron reformed in January 1964 (G Squadron would be formed in 1966 from guardsmen who had been undertaking SAS-type patrols with the Guards Independent Parachute Company on the central Sarawak border) and, together with A Squadron, conducted a number of 'Claret' missions.

During late 1964, patrols from B Squadron were concentrated in the Pueh range of hills of western Sarawak, a favourite route for CCO agents making their way to Lundu where a number of Communist cells were located. After a short break, D Squadron returned in May 1965, commanded by Major Peter de la Billière. He continued the cross-border raids with the aid of the Gurkhas, but the enemy often proved elusive. The patrols established likely ambush sites and potential helicopter landing zones. They made notes of all the likely places the Indonesians would try to infiltrate, and charted a previously unexplored region known as 'The Gap'. All intelligence collected was relayed back to SAS headquarters on high-frequency radios, where it could be acted upon immediately.

In August, working closely with the Gurkhas, the SAS launched a series of cross-border raids which met with varying success. The search for an elusive foe often ended in frustration; in September 1965, for example, twelve four-man patrols from A Squadron conducted a three-week search for a CCO camp in the area between the headwaters of the Sempayang and Bemban Rivers, but nothing was found.

SAS activity, which continued into 1966 did, however, convince the Indonesians that Britain would continue to support Malaysia. The Indonesian military leadership began to lose faith in their president and, in March, Sukamo was overthrown in a coup. Five months later Indonesia made peace with Malaysia.

The campaign in Borneo is an outstanding example of the tenacity, resourcefulness and skill of the individual SAS soldier, and illustrates that a small number of properly trained and motivated men can achieve results out of all proportion to their numbers. Walker himself stated, 'I regard seventy troopers of the SAS as being as valuable to me as 700 infantry in the role of "hearts and minds", border surveillance, early warning, stay behind, and eyes and ears with a sting.' See also **Border Scouts; de la Billière; Gurkhas; Jungle Warfare; Kalimantan; Sarawak; Tree-jumping; Walker; Woodhouse.**

BOSNIA The first public involvement in Bosnia by the SAS came with Major-General Mike **Rose**, who officially took over from the Belgian, Lieutenant-General Briquemont, on 24 January 1994, two days after a mortar shell had killed six children in Sarajevo. Rose's first task was to improve his HQ's intelligence of Serb intentions by having all information fed directly to him. Secondly, he made it clear that the aid convoys would no longer negotiate for passage. Days later, British soldiers fired back on the snipers that sought to prevent free passage of the convoys. Rose's attitude to the Bosnian Serb leaders was clear: back off or we will hit you hard. It was a policy that would have worked, had it not been for the weakness of the UN and the indecisiveness of NATO. Agreements with the Serbs were full of lies, deception and intimidation, tactics designed to win time and ground against the disadvantaged Bosnian Muslims. These stop-go tactics angered Rose and, although he had employed the correct tactics in reply, the politicians failed to back his response, thus the key element of force was lost to him.

Towards the end of March the Serbs started shelling the eastern enclave of Gorazde, and it was at this stage that Rose asked for, and got, a small team of SAS soldiers. Once it became clear that the Serbs were intent on capturing the city, Rose tried every means to arrange air-cover. His main problem was the handful of British soldiers stationed there. The air-support was not sanctioned, but a local cease-fire was arranged while all casualties were evacuated. Two of them died. The role of the SAS was to act as independent observers for Major-General Rose – this they did by positioning themselves in close proximity to Serbian forces. It is rumoured that two members of the regiment were spotted and fired upon, and that as a result one was killed and the other badly wounded.

On 10 July 1997, the SAS initiated Operation 'Tango', whereby they would arrest two wanted Serb war criminals in Prijedor. During a shoot-out one of the men was killed by the SAS, but the other was arrested and handed over to the Criminal Tribunal authorities in the Hague.

'BOSS' The term used instead of 'sir' by SAS troopers and NCOs when addressing officers. 'Sir' is usually only used when speaking to officers of other regiments. Despite the high standards of professionalism and the strict self-discipline within the regiment, there is a close working relationship between officers and the men, and over the years a certain amount of informality has been allowed to develop. Many SAS soldiers, who start out as troopers, finish up as officers themselves.

BOUERAT Port on the North African coast. In January 1942 Benghazi (see Raid on) fell to the British, an event which led David Stirling to believe that Bouerat, 480km (300 miles) to the west, would become the new supply centre for the Afrika Korps. He therefore decided to mount a raid against the port to blow up shipping in the harbour.

Stirling and twelve SAS men, accompanied by two Special Boat Section (SBS) personnel and transported by the Long Range Desert Group (LRDG), set off on 17 January. The navigator was Mike Sadler and the LRDG commander Captain Hunter. Their equipment included a collapsible canoe, which they intended to use to plant bombs on the ships. The first stage of the journey involved a trip to the Wadi Tamit. All the vehicles were overloaded with supplies, and once at the wadi the trucks had to be manhandled down the rock-strewn defile. However, they were spotted by an Italian aircraft and the convoy dispersed to lessen the risk of losses when enemy fighter-bombers appeared. The wireless truck and its crew disappeared, but Stirling decided to carry on with the mission. When they were 96km (60 miles) from Bouerat, the raiding party loaded into just one truck – sixteen SAS and SBS, and four LRDG personnel – and headed off for the target. However, the truck carrying the party ran into a gully during the journey and the canoe, which was wedged between the soldiers, was damaged. Undeterred, they carried on and entered the port on the night of 23 January. They split into small groups and moved cautiously towards the waterfront.

To their surprise they found there were no enemy sentries around the town and, unfortunately, no shipping in the harbour. However, the SAS did manage to blow up a number of warehouses, petrol tankers and the harbour radio station before retreating with no loss.

By this time Rommel had launched an offensive that would push the Eighth Army back to the Egyptian border. This meant that the base at Jalo had to be evacuated, which meant Stirling's party had to strike for Siwa, another oasis but 320km (200 miles) further to the east. This was reached without too much difficulty.

BOURGOIN, COMMANDANT One-armed commander of 4 French Parachute Battalion (4 SAS), who took part in Operations 'Dingson' (June 1944) and 'Spenser' (August–September 1944) in northwest Europe.

BOYES ANTI-TANK RIFLE An anti-tank rifle developed in 1938. It was not a popular piece of equipment due to its size and the powerful recoil when fired. Early SAS units toyed with the weapon, but it was not extensively used.

BRADBURY LINES The original name given to the SAS barracks at Hereford when the site, which had formerly been an Artillery barracks, was taken over as the headquarters of 22 SAS in 1960. The buildings, known as 'spiders', made of wood and erected during World War II, were rather second rate and in dire need of repair. By 1980 a new barracks had been built and the whole site was renamed Stirling Lines in honour of David Stirling, the regiment's founder.

BRADSHAW, CORPORAL ROBERT, MM One of the men of 22 SAS involved in the Battle of Mirbat on 19 July 1972. A member of B Squadron, he helped to direct the jet strikes by the Omani air force which helped to turn the battle against the enemy. For his role in defending the port he was awarded the Military Medal.

BRAMMER, SGT GRAHAM – AUSTRALIAN SAS REGIMENT (SASR) The commander of a five-man patrol of 2 Squadron SASR deployed in South Vietnam during May 1971 in the area 6km (4 miles) southwest of the Allied operational base Black Horse, situated in the southern part of Long Khanh Province some 5km (3 miles) from the border with Phuoc Tuy Province. The patrol was one of a total of seventeen tasked with reconnoitring the areas east and west of the Courtenay rubber plantation and locating Vietcong (VC) bases.

On 26 May, Sergeant Brammer's patrol located an enemy bunker and heard digging, but was unable to carry out a close reconnaissance because of the dry undergrowth and areas of open ground. On the following afternoon they directed helicopter gunships on to the area of the enemy positions, and shortly afterwards were joined by another patrol under Lieutenant Andrew Freemantle, which was inserted by helicopter. The two patrols then commenced an attack on the VC position but came under very heavy fire from AK-47 assault rifles, an RPD light machine gun and RPG-7 grenade launchers. The engagement continued for some twenty minutes, during which one patrol member, Trooper Crane, was wounded in the left shoulder and right ankle by grenades thrown by the enemy. The patrol then broke contact with the enemy and withdrew, and were extracted shortly afterwards by helicopter.

BRATHWAITE, COLONEL BILL – AUSTRALIAN SAS REGI-MENT (SASR) Assumed command of Headquarters SAS Regiment on the formation of the regiment on 4 September 1964, and was promoted to lieutenant-colonel in April of the following year. In World War II, he had served with the 2nd/3rd Independent Company during the Salamaua campaign in New Guinea in 1943. Commissioned in 1944, he subsequently served with the Z Special Unit, and was dropped behind Japanese lines on 23 July 1945 into the area of the Mahakam Lakes in Dutch Borneo as a member of a five-man patrol. After the war he had served in the Citizen's Military Force until 1951, when he rejoined the Regular Army. He attended the Staff College in 1955, and then held various appointments on the staff in Australia. Overseas, he served in Thailand on the staff of the South East Asia Treaty Organization (SEATO) in the early 1960s. He returned to Australia in 1963, and was subsequently appointed Deputy Assistant Quartermaster General (DAQMG) of Headquarters Western Command.

Brathwaite's wartime experience and knowledge of special operations were of undoubted value to him in his new post, but he was faced with problems over manpower and lack of resources while having to oversee the expansion of the new regiment to four squadrons. These problems were made none the easier by the deployment of 1 Squadron to Borneo in February 1965, the requirement to bring 2 Squadron up to strength and train it to a state of operational readiness as quickly as possible, and the raising of 3 and 4 Squadrons by December 1965 and mid-1966 respectively. Nevertheless, Brathwaite managed to overcome these difficulties and the three years of his tenure of command saw his squadrons deployed on operations in Borneo during the period 1965–66 and thereafter in Vietnam from June 1966 until he relinquished command of SASR in 1967.

'BRAVO TWO ZERO'   On the evening 22 January 1991, eight members of a patrol using the call-sign 'Bravo Two Zero' were infiltrated into Iraq by Chinook helicopter. Their task was to observe the main supply route (MSR) and to sever underground communications cables which ran between Baghdad and Jordan. In addition they were to seek and destroy any Scud missiles in the area. Each member of the patrol was overloaded with huge bergens and additional stores needed to sustain them during the time in Iraq. Once the helicopter had left them, the patrol moved some 20km (12 miles), where they found a small cave in which to hide. The cave was about 5m (5.5yds) high, and cut into rock with an overhang which would conceal them from view and provide cover from fire. The patrol commander Sergeant Andy McNab (real name withheld) soon realized that the radio they had was not working. This meant returning to the landing site the following night to rendezvous with a helicopter and exchange radios. The patrol soon found themselves in a difficult position and decided to move, during which they made contact with the enemy. A ferocious firefight ensued and the patrol were forced to withdraw, heading for the Syrian border some 120km (72 miles) to the west. The journey was hard and dangerous added to which the area was experiencing the worst weather in its history.

Through hypothermia and injury the patrol became separated and as a result four were captured, three died and one managed to escape. Those that were captured by the Iraqis faced weeks of beatings and horrendous torture. In the end they were released and returned to the regiment. The patrol commander wrote a book about the incident called *Bravo Two Zero*, and the man who escaped also told his story in an equally compelling book, *The One That Got Away*.

BRECON BEACONS   Located in South Wales, the area in which most of the SAS Selection courses take place. The mountains are not high, but adverse and changeable weather conditions can make them extremely dangerous. The rough terrain is ideal for testing soldiers' endurance, survival and navigation skills. Exposure and hypothermia are constant threats and some undertaking Selection, as well as badged SAS soldiers, have been known to die on the Beacons. The area is covered by Ordnance Survey map No. 160 of their 'Landranger' series. The Story Arms is the focal point for many of the routes over the Brecon Beacons.

BREN L4A4 LIGHT MACHINE GUN   *Specification* Calibre: 7.62mm × 51 NATO standard; Weight: 4kg (8.68lbs); Muzzle velocity: 840m (915yds) per second; Magazine capacity: 30-round, box.

First produced by the Skoda company, this is a Czechoslovakian-designed weapon which was taken up by the British Army in the 1930s. First models were chambered at .303 but converted to NATO standard 7.62mm in 1950. Royal Enfield produced them in great numbers and it became the standard section support weapon for the infantry. Attracted by its reliability and rugged nature, combined with its light weight, many SAS soldiers used it as an individual weapon during the 1960s. The weapon is still in service with many Third World armies.

'BREW'   One of the most popular words in SAS jargon, meaning to have a brew of tea.

'BRIGGS PLAN'   Name given to a strategy developed by Lieutenant-General Sir Harold Briggs, Director of Operations in the Malayan Emergency (1948–60), to protect isolated Chinese villages from extortion by the Communist Terrorists (CTs). Major Mike Calvert (later commander of the Malayan Scouts), had written an in-depth report in 1950 on how to defeat enemy terrorists, and it was this which formed the basis for the 'Briggs Plan'. The Chinese were relocated to fortified villages or other protected areas, which denied the terrorists an important source of supplies and money. The plan resulted in the successful resettlement of 600,000 people over a period of two years. The 'Briggs Plan' also formed part of a subsequent strategy to deny food to the terrorists.

BROOKE, LIEUTENANT-COLONEL OLIVER   Commanded 22 SAS Regiment from 1953 to 1955, replacing Lieutenant-Colonel Tod Sloane. Like his predecessor, Brooke had no previous Special Forces experience and was a firm disciplinarian: some members of B Squadron soon found this out when they set off a small explosive charge outside the Officers' Mess where he was attending a dinner held to welcome him. Brooke studiously ignored the explosion and the destruction of the wall beside him, but the following morning discovered the culprits and had them returned to their parent units.

Brooke's tenure of command in Malaya saw the departure of C (Rhodesian) Squadron and the formation of D Squadron from volunteers from units in Malaya. During that time, 22 SAS was heavily engaged in a 'hearts and minds' programme to win the trust and support of the local people. They also constructed a number of forts in the jungle, including Fort Brooke, built towards the end of 1953 on the border of Perak and Kelantan. In addition, the regiment's four squadrons were actively patrolling in an effort to locate Communist Terrorists (CTs) and their camps. Tours of operation in the jungle were lengthy, a good example being one of 122 days carried out by D Squadron during the period from October 1953 to 7 February 1954.

In 1955, Lieutenant-Colonel Brooke unfortunately suffered a severe injury to one of his ankles while parachuting, and was invalided back to Britain. He was replaced briefly by Lieutenant-Colonel Mike Osborne, and then by Lieutenant-Colonel George Lea. Brooke was also instrumental in designing the 7–14 day ration pack, essential to the survival of Special Forces troops on operations.

BROWNING 50 M2HB HEAVY MACHINE GUN *Specification* Calibre: 50 cal M2 ball (12.7mm × 99); Weight: 17kg (38lbs) with tripod; Muzzle velocity: 930m (1,000yds) per second; Magazine capacity: belt-fed.

The M2HB is a hard-barrelled development of the original M2 produced in the 1920s. Despite the fact that the design has not changed much since then, it is still in use with armies all over the world, and was used with great success in both the Falklands and the Gulf Wars. The secret of its popularity is the stopping power of the .50 round. With the development of armour piercing, incendiary and explosive rounds, the power of this heavy machine gun is being increased all the time. The SAS still use the .50 Browning.

BROWNING 9MM HI-POWER PISTOL *Specification* Calibre: 9mm Parabellum; Weight: 882g (2lbs); Muzzle velocity: 350m (381yds) per second; Magazine capacity: 13 rounds.

Designed in the 1920s by John Browning and produced by Fabrique National in Belgium, the Browning 9mm Hi-Power has proved to be one of the most successful pistols used by the SAS. Despite being quite a large pistol as the result of the 13-round magazine, it was found to be extremely reliable. Although the SAS turned to the SIG-Sauer pistol in the 1990s, it is still in service.

BRUNEI A country tucked away in the northwest corner of Borneo, between the Malaysian states of Sarawak and Sabah. A former British Protectorate, Brunei's Sheikh Azahari staged a revolt there in 1962. His plan was to become prime minister over what he wanted to be known as North Kalimantan, an area containing Brunei, Sarawak and Sabah. The revolt did not last long, crushed within eight days by British troops brought in from Singapore. The SAS arrived too late to become involved in that particular conflict. However, some of the guerrilla forces that escaped later joined up with the Clandestine Communist Organization (CCO), a group which the SAS were to become familiar with in Borneo.

Today Brunei is a tranquil nation, populated by a warm and friendly people. Most of the 277,000 inhabitants are of Malay origin, but the country is also home to Chinese, Indian, and Europeans. Most of the inhabitants are Muslim, but they co-exist happily with those of other religions, which are openly practised. While Malay is the national language, English is spoken by the majority of inhabitants. The SAS and SBS still visit and train with the Brunei forces, and students from SAS Selection attend the Jungle Training School at Tutong. Experts from several nations, including instructors from SAS Hereford, staff this school. The six-week training periods take place in March and September, depending on the Selection course attended.

'BRUTUS', OPERATION   Carried out by a group of twenty all ranks of the Belgian Independent Parachute Company, dropped into the area south east of Namur, Belgium, on 2 September 1944. Their task was to link up with Operation 'Noah', on which another group of the squadron was engaged in the same area. The objective of 'Brutus' was to join 'Noah' and pass on orders for future operations to the latter's commander and to the commander of the Belgian Resistance's No. 5 Zone.

BUCKETFORCE   In September 1944 the Germans were withdrawing north from southern Greece and the Peloponnese in order to meet the threat from the Red Army as it advanced through Bulgaria, Rumania and Poland and to avoid the risk of their forces, notably XXI Mountain Corps, being cut off. At the same time, the decision was made by the British War Cabinet to make every effort to liberate Greece at the earliest opportunity and prevent the Communists there taking power. It was recognized in turn that any liberating force would need air support, which would require airfields from which to operate.

An ad hoc force, code-named 'Bucketforce' and commanded by Lieutenant-Colonel the Earl Jellicoe, was rapidly assembled for the task. The force consisted of L Squadron, Special Boat Section (SBS) under Major Ian Patterson; two companies of the 2nd Battalion Highland Light Infantry; 2908 Squadron Royal Air Force Regiment; a patrol of the Long Range Desert Group (LRDG); a section of 40 Commando Royal Marines; a Royal Navy Combined Operations Pilotage Party and a number of RAF ground staff.

The first element of Bucketforce to land in Greece was an SBS patrol under Captain Charles Bimrose, which was dropped in the hills to the south of Araxos airfield. Bimrose reported that the airfield was clear of the enemy but that the port of Patras to the east was still held by the Germans. On the morning of 23 September the rest of L Squadron was dropped on the airfield, and shortly afterwards Major Patterson despatched patrols to the port of Katakolon to the south to reconnoitre it for use by the sea-borne element of Bucketforce. On the following day, Lieutenant-Colonel Jellicoe and his headquarters flew in by Dakota transport and landed at Araxos.

Advancing eastwards towards Corinth, resistance was first encountered at the town of Patras which was occupied by a German garrison and a battalion of Greek Fascists. After negotiations with Major Patterson, the Greeks decided that discretion was the better part of valour and disappeared. A combination of the SBS armed jeeps and the RAF Regiment's armoured cars produced sufficiently heavy firepower to persuade the German garrison to withdraw by ferry.

During the following week Bucketforce succeeded in reaching Co-rinth. Heading north thereafter, SBS patrols encountered a force of some 700 Germans who were fighting a determined rearguard action. Shortly afterwards they reached Megara, 64km (40 miles) west of Athens, where they secured an airfield to be used for the arrival of reinforcements in the form of 2nd Independent Parachute Brigade Group. On 12 October the SBS were relieved by C Company 4th Parachute Battalion, plus supporting elements, which was dropped in very high winds on the airfield. On 14 October 5th Parachute Battalion was also dropped on Megara and three days later, on 15 October, the SBS and 2nd Independent Parachute Brigade entered Athens shortly after the withdrawal of the last German troops from the city.

'BUCKSHEE' Old Indian word cried out by the poor when asking for alms. Used by the SAS to indicate that something is free, surplus or without charge.

BUDDY-BUDDY SYSTEM SAS soldiers are highly individualistic, but on occasions it is beneficial to team up with a partner in order to survive or guarantee operational results. Members of the anti-terrorist team, both assault and sniper, are paired off to guarantee that their missions have the best possible chance of success, ensuring that if one is injured the second man can continue. In the Arctic it is advisable to have a 'buddy' who can watch out for the first signs of hypothermia and frostbite.

BUG-OUT A word used by the SAS to describe a quick exit. If an observation post (OP) or hide is located, or in danger of being located by the enemy, the patrol will 'bug-out'. Depending on the circumstances and the patrol commander's orders, the 'bug-out' may be with full equipment or in belt order leaving the bergens behind.

BUKIT TAPAH The scene of the first operation carried out by the 1st New Zealand SAS Squadron after its deployment to Malaya in December 1955. The squadron was deployed to track down a body of some 40 Communist Terrorists (CTs) known as 31 Platoon, led by an individual called Siu Mah. On 6 October 1951, he had ambushed and murdered the High Commissioner of Malaya, Sir Henry Gurney, while he was travelling by road between Kuala Lumpur and Fraser's Hill, a resort to the northeast of the capital. The task was a difficult one as the CTs had gone to ground deep in the jungle. The squadron carried out lengthy and thorough patrolling of the area but was unsuccessful in locating 31 Platoon. It did, however, find a considerable amount of information in the form of documents and maps, which not only indicated that 31 Platoon was no longer active, but also that the entire CT organization was finding it increasingly difficult to continue its campaign of terror. Siu Mah survived in the jungle until March 1959 when he was betrayed by two of his own men and subsequently shot after being found hiding in a cave near Ipoh.

'BULLBASKET', OPERATION   Carried out in central France in 1944 by a troop of B Squadron 1 SAS commanded by Captain John Tonkin and 3 Patrol of F Squadron Phantom under Captain R.J. McSadoine during the period from 6 June to 7 August 1944. At 01:37 hours on D-Day, Tonkin and one of his officers, Lieutenant Crisp, were dropped without forward reconnaissance into the area ahead of the rest of the troop and shortly afterwards made contact with 'Samuel', a local Special Operations Executive (SOE) agent who advised them that the area was too dangerous and that they should move to a safer location. Tonkin's primary mission was to reconnoitre the area of the Vienne and determine whether it was suitable for use as an SAS base area. In addition, he was also to gauge the strength of enemy forces and to investigate the organization and strength of the Maquis in the area.

The following night an advance party of nine men, led by Lieutenant Tom Stephens, was dropped successfully to link up with Tonkin and Crisp. The rest of the troop and the Phantom patrol was dropped on the night of 11 June. One aircraft succeeded in locating the drop-zone (DZ), dropping twelve men and a number of equipment containers. A second aircraft, having spotted the lights of an enemy division on a main road close to the DZ, turned away and dropped eight members of the troop and the Phantom patrol 48km (30 miles) away.

The rest of the troop had been dropped in four small groups tasked with attacking railway targets in the area, before making their way to rendezvous with the rest of the troop. Lieutenant Morris and his patrol dropped near the main line linking Poitiers and Tours and successfully cut the line, as did Sergeant Holmes and his men. Similarly, Lieutenant Weaver's patrol succeeded in derailing a train on the line between Bordeaux and Saumur. The fourth patrol under Corporal Kinnevane, however, suffered misfortune when it was dropped well away from its intended DZ, into the small town of Airvault. One man was captured and two others lost their weapons and equipment while making good their escape. Despite the loss of one of their number, all four patrols succeeded in rejoining the rest of the troop.

Meanwhile, the rest of the troop was active. The railway line between Limoges and Poitiers was cut on twelve occasions, a train destroyed, another derailed and roads in the area mined. In addition, information on rail targets for air attack was transmitted back to England and this resulted in eleven fuel trains and thirty-five locomotives being destroyed. In answer to all this, there was, inevitably, considerable activity by enemy forces in the area and Tonkin was forced to move his base on a number of occasions, which was difficult due to his force's lack of mobility. Furthermore, the Phantom patrol had still not joined him and thus his rear link communications with the SAS base in England were hampered. Nevertheless, he succeeded in requesting four armed jeeps, which were dropped to him successfully on the night of 17 June.

During the following weeks Tonkin's troop mounted repeated raids on the local rail network despite increased enemy activity in the area. On 25 June he moved his force to a new base in the forest near the small town of Verrieres. A week later, on the morning of 3 July, the base was attacked by a large force of enemy who, because of lax security and other lapses on the part of the SAS, achieved almost total surprise. During the ensuing action 30 members of the troop, together with a downed American airman, were captured and subsequently taken to Poitiers. On the night of 6 July they were transported in trucks to the forest near Saint Sauvan where they were executed by firing squad, under the terms of Hitler's Commando Order of October 1942, and were buried nearby.

Captain Tonkin and fourteen of his men, three of whom had been away from the base in a jeep at the time of the attack, escaped and linked up with Captain McSadoine's Phantom patrol. They carried out a small number of attacks on rail targets thereafter but, having lost three of the jeeps (destroyed by Captain Tonkin before he escaped), they were limited in their mobility. During the first week of August, Tonkin and his men were relieved by elements of 3 French Parachute Battalion and together with the Phantom patrol were subsequently evacuated by air to England.

BULLIED, DAVID An ex-member of the SAS, Major Bullied was seconded to the Dubai Defence Force, where he was in charge of the Palace Guard. In October 1977 he greatly assisted the two SAS men sent by the British prime minister to help the West Germans with the aircraft hijacked and flown to Dubai's airport.

'BUMPED' Slang term used by the SAS when a patrol has unexpectedly been attacked, or when it has inadvertently 'bumped' into enemy forces.

BUNGEES A thick elasticised strand about 1m (1yd) long with a metal wire hook at each end. Designed to secure a shelter sheet, the bungee has a multitude of other uses from securing equipment to a rucksack to fixing explosive charges. Most SAS soldiers carry six to eight bungees as standard.

'BUNYAN', OPERATION   Together with Operations 'Chaucer' and 'Shakespeare', Operation 'Bunyan' was carried out by a force of 31 all ranks of the Belgian Independent Parachute Company during the period 3–15 August 1944. The force was dropped behind German lines north of the River Loire and to the west of Paris, with the task of causing as much mayhem and confusion as possible among enemy forces, which were withdrawing to the east. A number of attacks were mounted, resulting in 30 enemy killed and a number of vehicles destroyed. The Belgian parachutists suffered four wounded.

BURNS AND MOONEY ARREST INCIDENT   At Flurry Bridge in County Louth on the border with Northern Ireland, the SAS arrested two men who they suspected might have been part of an IRA active service unit. The two men, Kevin Burns and Patrick Mooney, were taken by helicopter to Bessbrook Mill for questioning. In fact the two men were completely innocent and also claimed that they had been picked up inside the border of the Irish Republic. Whatever the facts, after three hours of interrogation, the men were released, but the incident had caused great embarrassment to the Army. Official reports claimed that the 3 Para, rather than the SAS, had been involved.

BURY, LIEUTENANT BOB – SPECIAL BOAT SECTION (SBS)   A patrol commander in M Squadron SBS, commanded by Major Ian 'Jock' Lapraik, when on 20 November 1943 he led his men on a raid on the Dodecanese island of Simi, which was garrisoned by German and Italian troops totalling 100 in all. Having landed, he and his men advanced into the town of Castello and reached the Governor's house. Entering the building, Bury came upon the quarters of a light machine gun detachment whose members were swiftly eliminated when he threw a grenade into their room. Immediately afterwards, Sergeant 'Tanky' Geary, who had been covering the main entrance to the house, killed eight Germans who appeared outside on the quayside by the building and Bury shot another before detonating an explosive charge in the building next door, which demolished it and part of the Governor's house. Having planted a booby trap in the street, which was set off soon afterwards by the enemy, Bury and his men withdrew.

On the night of 13 July 1944 Lieutenant Bury returned to Simi as a member of a combined force of some 220 men of M Squadron SBS and the Greek Sacred Squadron, which landed on the island unobserved by the enemy. At dawn on the following day the castle on Simi was subjected to heavy fire by machine guns and mortars. Bury's patrol was part of a force which attacked enemy positions in the monastery and eventually forced their occupants down a promontory at one end of the island, where they were subsequently persuaded to surrender.

In late October 1944 Lieutenant Bury was given the task of carrying out a reconnaissance in a caïque along the coastline of the island of Spetsia. They approached a bay occupied by monarchist partisans who were awaiting an attack by ELAS Communist guerrillas. On seeing the vessel, which they assumed to be that of ELAS, they opened fire and hit the helmsman. Recognizing that the vessel was not under fire from German weapons, Lieutenant Bury leapt up to take over the tiller and steered the vessel nearer to the shore in attempt to land, while at the same time trying to make his identity known to the partisans. In doing so, however, he was fatally wounded and died shortly afterwards. His men and the partisans buried him on Spetsia the following day.

C

C-130 HERCULES *Specification* Manufacturer: Lockheed; Engines: 4 Allison T56-A-15 turboprops, 4,508 static horsepower; Wingspan: 40.41m (44yds); Take-off weight: 70,310kg (69 tons); Max speed at 9,100m: 614km/h (30,000 ft: 384mph); Range: 7,840km (4,900miles).

The American C-130 Hercules first came into production on 7 April 1955, and remains in service to this day. It is one of the world's most popular transport aircraft, capable of most medium lifting roles. It has been used extensively in both war and peace, from delivering troops to air-dropping vital humanitarian aid to the Third World. Paratroopers, including the SAS, use them for static, HALO (High Altitude Low Opening) and HAHO (High Altitude High Opening) type jumps. It is known affectionately as the 'Herc Bird' and the 'Benzene Budgie'. The RAF operates 60 Hercules, mostly from the RAF Lyneham Transport wing. The SAS will normally use their own Special Forces Flight that is also stationed at RAF Lyneham.

CACHE A hidden store of supplies which can contain anything from weapons and ammunition to food and water. Those who build the cache and then bury it make out a report and file it with headquarters upon their return. By tradition, SAS cache reports are notoriously poor, and even when well documented, the cache usually remains undiscovered by the seeker. Special containers were developed by the regiment's Operations Research unit which are used to protect long-term caches.

CAD (COMPUTER AIDED DESIGN) A new development in the operational planning of anti-terrorist work, this highly advanced CAD-based software allows a trained operator to feed in a 3D visualization of the target and surrounding area. This image, be it a building, aircraft or ship, can be generated in a matter of hours and updated as new intelligence comes in. The image may show floor plan, positions of windows and door, routes to and from the building, adjacent buildings, video, stills photographs and so on.

The system is a tremendous aid in assault team planning. It is now possible to visualize the image of a person in an adjoining building, or look through a window and assess the view from that point without ever leaving the control room. The system allows the commander a 'fly on the wall' interpretation without compromising people on the ground. Data from one work station can be relayed from even a small lap top so that assault teams can be instantly updated. The CAD system is currently being evaluated by members of the anti-terrorist planning team.

CADS (CONTROLLED AERIAL DELIVERY SYSTEM) Used to supply payloads of vital equipment with great accuracy. The system is basically a remotely-controlled radio-guided parachute, which activates on exit from the aircraft, and responds to a guidance transmitter on the ground. A skilled operator can guide a payload to within a 100m (109yd) drop-zone.

'CALIBAN', OPERATION Code-name for a mission undertaken by 26 troopers of the Belgian Independent Parachute Company (5 SAS), led by Lieutenant Limbosch, between 6 and 11 September 1944. They were dropped southeast of Bourg Leopold, northeast Belgium, to sever German communications west of the River Meuse. However, the men were widely dispersed, resulting in only limited activity. 'Caliban' came to a premature end when the Belgians were reached by advancing British troops.

CALL-SIGN Signals designation for an individual or unit. Call-signs identify the caller, as in the Gulf War where 'Bravo Two Zero' was the call-sign for the now famous ill-fated foot patrol infiltrated into Iraq in January 1991, led by Sergeant Andy McNab.

CALVERT, BRIGADIER MIKE A key figure in the post-World War II history of the SAS. Calvert, nicknamed 'Mad Mike', joined the Royal Engineers in 1933 and, after a spell in China, as an observer during the latter part of the decade. With the outbreak of war he held a post in Military Intelligence Research where he helped organize guerrilla units that were to be used if Britain was invaded. Other duties included training commandos from New Zealand and Australia, and guerrilla groups for China. Calvert was next posted to Burma where he met the legendary Major-General Orde Wingate. Together they raised the Chindits, a force created to operate deep behind Japanese lines on sabotage and interdiction missions. In 1944 Calvert, now commanding the Chindits' 77th Indian Infantry Brigade, was awarded the DSO and bar, and the US Silver Star. Returning to Europe towards the end of the war, Calvert was given command of the SAS Brigade in March 1945, a position he would hold until the unit was disbanded in October.

In 1950 Calvert, then a staff officer in Hong Kong, was asked by General Sir John Harding, Commander-in-Chief Far East Land Forces, to make a threat analysis of the Malayan Emergency and suggest means of defeating the Communist Terrorists (CTs). Several months later, after extensive and exhausting field research, Calvert presented his paper. He drew two main conclusions: first, Malaya's Chinese villagers should be moved into fortified settlements to keep them out of the clutches of the CTs; second, a special military force should be raised and trained to operate in the jungle for long periods.

Both suggestions were accepted and Calvert was ordered to raise his special military force, which was to be named the Malayan Scouts. Recruits came from three main sources: from the thousands of military personnel dotted about the Far East, particularly ex-members of the Special Operations Executive, Force 136 and Ferret Force; from a body of Rhodesians that Calvert had helped select, and from a territorial unit that was organizing a detachment for service in Korea, 21 SAS.

Calvert also devised the new unit's operational procedure. A detachment of up to 14 men would be despatched into the jungle and establish a defendable base, from where small patrols of three to four men would be sent out into the jungle to gather intelligence, spring ambushes and destroy enemy bases. A key part of Calvert's method was the waging of a 'hearts and minds' campaign designed to gain the confidence of the indigenous population who would in turn aid the Malayan Scouts' patrols. Calvert's methods gradually began to pay dividends, although he was invalided home in 1952. The success of his theories had done much to aid the return of the SAS to the Regular Army's order of battle. In 1952, the Malayan Scouts became 22 SAS.

CAMPBELL, SERGEANT GRAHAM – AUSTRALIAN SAS REGIMENT (SASR) During the Vietnam War in January 1970 Sergeant Graham Campbell of 3 Squadron SASR was the commander of a five-man patrol of 4 Troop New Zealand Special Air Service (NZSAS) operating 12km (7.5 miles) southeast of Nui May Tao, in Binh Tuy Province. On the second day of the patrol, 14 January, he and his lead scout were moving up to observe a track seen on the previous night when they were engaged at a range of 10m (11yds) by five Vietcong (VC). Campbell was hit in the head but the scout returned the enemy's fire while the rest of the patrol came forward in support. Under the covering fire of a helicopter light fire team, the patrol withdrew and was extracted at 10:40 hours. Unfortunately Sergeant Campbell, who was considered to be one of 3 Squadron's best patrol commanders, died during the return flight.

'CANDYTUFT', OPERATION On the east Italian coast two operations, 'Saxifrage' and 'Candytuft', were run together to cut the railway line that ran between Ancona and Pescara. Four small detachments from 2 SAS landed on the coast on the night of 27 October 1943, led by

Major Roy Farran together with Lieutenant Grant Hibbert. The next six days were spent behind enemy lines in such dreadful conditions that one of the SAS soldiers contracted malaria before being taken in and cared for by a local farmer. The railway line was successfully blown up in several places, and the main coast road mined before the patrol, less two troopers who had been captured, was extracted by motor torpedo boat. As an interesting footnote, the men were issued exceptionally poor quality clothing for the operation, most notably boots that leaked continually

'CANUCK', OPERATION In early 1945 Canadian Captain Buck McDonald led a party from 2 SAS into northern Italy. His task was to break up enemy communications between the Italian Riviera and northern Italy. McDonald and his team managed to equip and organize a group of partisans who, aided by a 75mm howitzer, successfully overcame the garrison of Alba, a small town near Turin.

'CAP BADGE' During the Aden conflict in the 1960s, the name given to a feature in the Radfan mountains where an SAS patrol were tasked to observe a potential drop-zone for the Parachute Regiment. The eight-man patrol, led by Captain Robin Edwards, was spotted by a goatherd, and became surrounded by rebel tribesmen. As a result of the ensuing fight, both Edwards and his signaller Trooper Warburton where killed.

CAPE, CORPORAL PETER – AUSTRALIAN SAS REGIMENT (SASR) A member of the SASR team which took part in July 1988 in the Great Australian Camel Race from Ayers Rock to the Gold Coast of Queensland, a distance of 2,400km (1,488 miles). He was, however, hampered by the fact that his camel was totally untamed. Nevertheless, in the best traditions of the regiment, he persevered and succeeded in persuading the animal to let him ride it, albeit for only a few hours at a time. By the time he reached Longreach, having travelled some 1,900km (1,178 miles), he estimated that he had covered approximately 900km (558 miles) on foot while leading the beast. He finished in second place, though beaten by an entrant from Queensland who had spent the previous year training his camel.

CARL GUSTAV 84MM M2 RECOILLESS ANTI-TANK GUN
Specification Warhead diameter: 84mm (3in); Warhead weight: 1kg (2.6lb); Launcher weight: 6kg (14.2lbs); Muzzle velocity: 310m (337yds) per second; Effective range: moving targets 300m (327yds); bunkers 500m (545yds); exposed troops 1,000m (1,090yds); smoke 1,300m (1,417yds); illumination 2,300m (2,500yds).

This recoilless anti-tank gun is one of the most popular of its type in the world. Designed in Sweden, it can be used for destroying tanks, bunkers, or as an anti-personnel weapon. The weapon, although heavy in comparison with many similar other anti-tank guns, is extremely accurate. A lighter version, the M3 Carl-Gustav, is in use with British and American Special Forces.

'CARPET', OPERATION In June 1979, C Squadron of the Rhodesian 1st SAS Regiment (RhSAS) was tasked with a deep penetration operation which would take it 198km (124 miles) into Zambia. Its mission was to capture the head of ZIPRA's Russian-trained department of National Security & Order (NSO), Dumiso Dabengwa, together with his Assistant Director of Intelligence, Victor Mlambo, and the Assistant Director of Counter-Intelligence & Security, Gordon Butshe. At the same time, the squadron was to destroy the NSO headquarters, known as 'the Vatican', which was located in Roma Township, a residential suburb of the Zambian capital of Lusaka.

Twenty-four men of C Squadron, under its commander Captain Martin Pearse, were selected for the operation and organized into three assault groups, the second and third under Lieutenants Rich Stannard and Mike Barlow respectively. A four-man command group, comprising Lieutenant-Colonel Garth Barrett, Lieutenant Stan Hornby and two medics, would accompany them. Rehearsals were carried out on an old farm in a game reserve some 50km (31 miles) from the Rhodesian capital of Salisbury. Full details of the layout and interior of the NSO headquarters were supplied by a former member of ZIPRA who had been captured in April by the SAS during Operation 'Bastille', the raid to kill Joshua Nkomo.

Just before 05:00 hours on 26 June, the assault force took off in four Bell 205 helicopters of 8 Squadron Royal Rhodesian Air Force (RRAF). Flying low to keep below radar coverage level, the aircraft took one hour and forty-five minutes to fly to the target area, which they reached at first light. Meanwhile, an RhSAS/RRAF command team, comprising the second-in-command of 1st SAS Regiment, Major Dave Dodson, and Air Commodore Norman Walsh, was airborne in a Dakota. The latter had on call four RRAF Hawker Hunter ground attack aircraft ready to carry out a diversionary air strike on a nearby ZIPRA camp known as FC. Two more Hunters would provide defence against any attempt at interception by the Zambian Air Force.

Five minutes after the Hunters carried out their air strike, the helicopters came in low over the NSO headquarters compound, the door gunners mowing down the ZIPRA guard force as it ran to its positions. One terrorist succeeded in opening fire on the helicopter carrying Lieutenant-Colonel Garth Barrett and his command element, but was quickly dealt with as he ran for cover. As their aircraft landed on vacant ground adjacent to the buildings, the assault groups disembarked and placed 5kg (2lb) breaching charges against a stone wall surrounding the buildings. Two of these failed to explode but Lieutenant Rich Stannard and his team succeeded in blowing in the main gate of the compound, while Lieutenant Mike Barlow and his men followed Captain Martin Pearse's team.

Resistance inside the compound was quickly overcome and the assault force turned its attention to the buildings. Captain Pearse inserted his 'bunker bomb' through the window of the four-bedroomed house and shortly afterwards it exploded. Unfortunately, the inferior quality of the construction of the building provided no protection for him and he was killed as the entire building collapsed on him. Meanwhile, the rest of the assault force had gained entry to the NSO offices and were methodically clearing the buildings. Of Dumiso Dabengwa and his two colleagues, however, there was no sign, but one African was caught while trying to escape from the compound and taken prisoner.

At 07:30 hours the assault force emplaned and the helicopters flew low over the centre of Lusaka, heading south for Rhodesia. Despite warnings from the command team aboard the Dakota that Zambian MiGs (Russian-built fighter aircraft) had been scrambled to intercept it, the force succeeded in returning to Rhodesia. The haul from the raid was enormous, including several tonnes of documents which provided a mass of information on ZIPRA operations as well as full details of an NSO spy ring inside Rhodesia. Furthermore, the prisoner was identified as Alexander Brisk Vusa, the KGB-trained Deputy Head of Intelligence of NSO. Despite the death of Captain Martin Pearse and the wounding of another man, the operation was considered to be one of the most successful ever mounted by Rhodesian 1st SAS Regiment during the war.

CASEVAC Abbreviation used for the term casualty evacuation. The SAS normally have good CasEvac procedures in their operational theatre, usually including a dedicated helicopter to get the casualty directly to the field hospital. During the Oman War CasEvac helicopters would fly directly into the firefight to pick up wounded SAS soldiers.

CASHMORE, SERGEANT FRANK – AUSTRALIAN SAS REGIMENT (SASR) In South Vietnam in early 1968, aerial reconnaissance of the northern borders of Phuoc Tuy Province revealed the tracks of a tractor and trailer on a track, known as the Firestone Trail, where it crossed an area of open grassland known as LZ (landing zone) Dampier. The theft of a tractor had previously been reported by the owner of the nearby Courtenay Rubber Plantation and it was suspected that the Vietcong (VC) were using the vehicle to move weapons and stores. The Commander of 1st Australian Task Force, Brigadier Ron Hughes, gave 2 Squadron SASR the task of destroying the tractor and disrupting the VC supply route. The squadron commander, Major Brian Wade, in turn allocated the mission to Sergeant Frank Cashmore and his patrol. It was decided to carry out a demolitions ambush on the track using four 6.8kg (3lbs) 'beehive' charges and four Claymore mines initiated by a special electrical pressure switch.

On the morning of 17 March, Sergeant Cashmore and the other five members of his patrol were inserted by helicopter. Unfortunately, Private Dave Elliott injured his leg as the patrol jumped from the aircraft which was hovering about a metre from the ground. Having recalled the helicopter and evacuated Elliott, Sergeant Cashmore led his patrol to an LUP (lying-up position) some 200m (218yds) away, before heading north-west for the Firestone Trail and the ambush site. At about mid-afternoon the patrol stopped at an LUP and Sergeant Cashmore and Corporal Danny Wright moved forward to reconnoitre the Firestone Trail, which they came across some 200m (218yds) west of LZ Dampier. Cashmore selected a spot on a bend in the track for the siting of the charges, which would be buried, and for the Claymores which would be sited along the track to deal with the VC escorting the tractor. After nightfall, the patrol moved nearer to the track and at 23:20 hours observed the tractor and trailer moving west along it. At 01:45 hours, the vehicle returned eastwards and the patrol withdrew to its LUP.

At 19:20 hours the following evening, the patrol moved on to the Firestone Trail. While Privates Kim McAlear and Adrian Blacker moved off as sentries in opposite directions along the track, the demolitions team, Corporals Danny Wright and Dave Scheele, commenced digging the holes for the Beehive charges. This proved to be no easy task as the soil was heavily compacted. Meanwhile, Sergeant Cashmore sited the four Claymores to cover the entire area of the likely Vietcong advance. Once the charges and mines were in position, he recalled the two sentries.

As they returned to the ambush site, the patrol heard the sound of the tractor to the east. Rapidly connecting the Claymores and paying out the firing cable, they withdrew to a bomb crater 50m (54yds) away where they took cover and waited. Corporal Danny Wright prepared the Claymore firing unit and shortly afterwards the tractor and its escort arrived in the killing zone, although the long grass hid them from the patrol's view. Becoming concerned that the tractor's wheels had missed the pressure switch, Sergeant Cashmore stood up in the crater to check on the vehicle's location. As he did so, there was a massive explosion as the beehive charges detonated, followed by another as Corporal Danny Wright initiated the Claymores.

Complete withdrawal from the area was impossible due to the bright moonlight and thick jungle so, having left the bomb crater, the patrol crawled a further 50m (54yds) away from the ambush area to some bushes where it took cover. At dawn it moved carefully towards LZ Dampier, obeying orders to avoid contact, and surveyed the area: the only evidence of enemy activity was a single heavily bandaged Vietcong staggering across the open ground. After a while, seeing no further sign of the enemy, Sergeant Cashmore radioed the 2 Squadron base at Nui Dat and requested extraction, which took place shortly afterwards. That afternoon, the entire area was bombed with napalm by South Vietnamese Air Force Skyraiders. The mission had been a complete success as the tractor and trailer had been totally destroyed and, according to information supplied subsequently by a Vietcong defector, 21 VC had been killed.

CASTLE MARTIN TRAINING AREA   Corporal Richardson and Trooper O'Tool were two members of the SAS drowned in 1965 when their canoe capsized in heavy seas off the South Wales coast near Castle Martin. It is believed that the two men were part of an exercise practising entry techniques from a submarine.

'CAULDRON', OPERATION   In 1968 ZIPRA carried out a massive incursion into Rhodesia, primarily into the Zambesi Valley but with a few small groups succeeding in reaching some towns. These had been tasked with attacking government buildings and installations, but in the event, despite a small number of bombs being exploded, they had a negligible effect. A joint police/military operation code-named 'Cauldron' was mounted to hunt down the infiltrators, and C Squadron Rhodesian SAS played its part. During the six weeks of the operation, those terrorists landing on the southern bank of the Zambesi River encountered the security forces who, assisted by excellent intelligence, tracked the ZIPRA groups without difficulty and eliminated them.

CHALLENOR, SERGEANT 'TANKY'   Member of 2 SAS involved in Operation 'Speedwell' in Italy in 1943, during which the SAS party was divided into several small groups. Together with Lieutenant Wedderburn, Challenor destroyed two trains and a tunnel on the Bologna-Genoa line. Another train on the Pontremoli-La Spezia line was also destroyed. Of his pairing with Lieutenant Wedderburn, Challenor later wrote, 'In small raids such as the one we were engaged on, where each was dependent on the other, the formality of aloofness which existed between officers and men in a normal regiment was replaced by a mutual respect. When you eat together, sleep together and perform bodily functions in sight of each other, you can't always be returning salutes.'

As they made their way south via the high ground of the Apennines, Challenor suffered from recurring malaria, which eventually turned into jaundice, while Wedderburn was troubled by his feet. On Christmas Day 1943, to increase their chances of successfully returning to Allied lines alive, the two men split up, but were both captured. Threatened with execution for being a spy, Challenor managed to escape and fled to the cover of friendly Italians in the hills. Here he was nursed back to health from both pneumonia and malaria, before being captured for the second time in April, trying once again to reach Allied lines. Astonishingly, he managed to escape once more, finally reaching British positions seven months after the start of the operation.

Challenor saw further action in 1944–45, most notably in Operation 'Wallace' in France in 1944. Following the end of the war, he joined the London Metropolitan Police.

CHAMP A jeep-type vehicle used by the British army, including the SAS, during the late 1950s and early 1960s. It was not a particularly good vehicle and certainly no match for the Land Rover.

CHAPMAN, LANCE-CORPORAL ROGER During the Oman War Roger Chapman was one of the BATT stationed in and much involved in the defence of Mirbat in July 1972. He was awarded the Military Medal for his bravery in the action.

CHARLES, PRINCE OF WALES Prince Charles has made several visits to Hereford. His first, in 1968, was succeeded a few days later by his sister Princess Anne, who enjoyed herself tremendously at a reception in the sergeant's mess. Prince Charles also visited the new barracks where both he and Princess Diana underwent a live hostage demonstration. The couple where seated in a darkened room with targets placed in close proximity. The assaulting SAS members burst into the room throwing stun grenades and firing live ammunition. The only damage done was to Princess Diana's hair which was slightly singed.

'CHAUCER', OPERATION Conducted between 28 July and 15 August 1944 by 22 troopers of the Belgian Independent Parachute Company (5 SAS). Two patrols were dropped by parachute into the area northwest of Le Mans, France, with the task of harassing the retreating Germans. The first party was commanded by Lieutenant Ghys and landed on 28 July, the second, commanded by Captain Hazel, on 9 August. Unfortunately, however, the drop was executed too late and the operation was forced to continue on foot, managing only to meet the rear of the retreating enemy.

'CHEESE', OPERATION In September 1979 the Rhodesians decided to increase the pressure on Zambia's economy by forcing it to become more reliant on imports of maize shipped via rail through Rhodesia. To achieve this an operation, code-named 'Cheese', was mounted by Rhodesian 1st SAS Regiment (RhSAS) with the objective of destroying the Zambian rail links with Tanzania to the north. The targets were two bridges which spanned the Chambeshi River in northeastern Zambia. One major problem, however, was the fact that they were 320km (200 miles) from the Rhodesian border – the longest distance over which the RhSAS had operated so far during the entire war.

An initial attempt to launch the operation on 12 September had to be aborted due to bad weather. On 3 October the assault force of sixteen men once again travelled to a secret military airfield at Fylde, near the town of Hartley. At 22:00 hours a reconnaissance group of four free-fall parachutists, consisting of Major Dave Dodson, Lieutenant Phil Brooke, Lance-Corporal Andy Standish-White and a fourth man, emplaned a DC-7 aircraft, which took off shortly afterwards and headed for Zambia. Despite initial problems caused by cloud obscuring the dropping zone (DZ) from the air, they were despatched and landed safely. On reorganizing, however, they discovered that one container, with two canoes and an HF radio, was missing.

The loss of the canoes meant that the reconnaissance group had to walk to the target area, a distance of some 48km (30 miles). Two and a half days later, the four men reached the bridges and carried out a close reconnaissance. Returning to the DZ area, they awaited the arrival of the twelve-man main party, bringing with them replacement canoes and a radio set which had been requested earlier in a transmission.

At 01:00 hours on 8 October, the main party under Captain Bob McKenna was dropped safely and the entire force took up positions in an LUP (lying-up position) for the rest of the day. During the afternoon, however, a bush fire threatened the force and its large quantity of explosives and equipment. It was only with difficulty and a great deal of effort that the flames were stopped short of the explosives cache.

As night fell, the explosives and equipment were loaded aboard six canoes and a Zodiac inflatable powered by an outboard engine. This took longer than expected and it was not until midnight on the night of 8 October that the force was heading upriver towards the bridges. Despite having to struggle against a 15 knot current and negotiating rapids, and coping with canoes capsizing and water contaminating the outboard engine's fuel, Major Dodson and his men arrived two nights later at the bridges. After lying-up during the following day, they moved in under cover of darkness.

The twelve men in the six canoes approached the bridges first. While two pairs checked the area for guards, two others fastened a rope around the centre pier of the rail bridge to enable the Zodiac crew to hold their boat in position when attaching the explosive charges. The two other canoe pairs fastened hooks to the centre pier, on which three 100kg (45lbs) explosive charges were subsequently attached by the four men in the inflatable. The charges were attached to the hooks and then lowered below water level. An experimental explosive device, known as a demolition net, was also attached to the pier. Once all the charges were in position, the Cordtex detonating cords were attached to them and linked to a ringmain (a ring of 'det' cord connected to the initiator).

Similar treatment was accorded to the road bridge 600m (654yds) away. Meanwhile a roadblock had been set up and a 20-ton truck, carrying a load of sacks of chemical fertiliser, was commandeered. Jettisoning some of the sacks, the SAS concealed themselves, their dismantled boats and equipment aboard the vehicle. Having lit the fuses, which would give a fifteen-minute delay, Major Dave Dodson and his men left the bridges at 02:15 hours and headed south as fast as possible. Having driven through the town of Chambeshi, they halted some 12km (7.5 miles) from the target area and cut the telephone wires. As they did so, they saw the massive flash of the charges exploding in the distance to the north.

Driving on through the night and bypassing the town of Mpika, the SAS continued heading south on side roads. An unfortunate encounter with members of a power station guard force meant that they had to take to the bush and by late afternoon, with the terrain having become impassable to the truck, Major Dodson requested extraction by helicopter on the following morning. At 08:00 hours on 13 October, the helicopters arrived and Major Dodson's force flew back to the RhSAS base at Kabrit Barracks having successfully carried out its mission. As a result of the operation 18,000 tonnes of goods, including maize, were stranded at the Tanzanian port of Dar es Salaam and 10,000 tonnes of Zambian copper were left waiting for shipment to export markets. Consequently President Kaunda had no choice but to negotiate with the Rhodesians.

'CHESTNUT', OPERATION An action designed to support Operation 'Husky' (9 July 1943), the Allied invasion of Sicily. The original plan was to install two parties of 2 SAS in northern Sicily to break up enemy communications. 'Pink' party was led by Captain Pinckney, and was commanded to sever roads and telephone lines along the northeast coast of the island. In addition they were ordered to destroy the Catania-Messina railway line. By contrast, 'Brig' party, under the leadership of Captain Bridgeman-Evans, was detailed to attack hostile convoys and the enemy headquarters near Enna.

It had been the intention to land both parties, by submarine, on the north coast of Sicily. However, on 17 June, the advance of the operation was postponed by 15th Army Group, until the day before the main Allied invasion of Sicily, which was expected to take place on 11 July. On 20 June the SAS operation was cancelled, but was resurrected on 6 July, and on the night of 12 July the two parties were air-lifted.

Almost immediately, the two groups encountered serious difficulties. The majority of 'Pink' party's equipment and radios were damaged on landing, and the men were scattered over a wide area. 'Brig' party was dropped too close to urban areas, which unintentionally alerted the enemy. Bridgeman-Evans was captured but later managed to escape. On 13 July a night-time reinforcement drop was planned, but damaged radios meant that the aircraft were unable to contact either party, consequently no men were dropped. No further forces were committed to the operation.

On the ground neither party achieved anything worthwhile. The only positive result of Operation 'Chestnut' was that most of the SAS soldiers successfully returned to Allied lines.

This was 2 SAS's first parachute drop and the poor preparation became very apparent. Assembly of both parties was also made difficult because they were widely dispersed as the result of a badly executed drop. The official report on the operation stated: 'The value of damage and disorganization inflicted on the enemy was not proportionate to the number of men, amount of equipment and planes used. It provided valuable experience for future operations and pointed out the pitfalls which are inevitable in any operation which is the first of its kind.'

'CHICORY', OPERATION A follow-up to Operation 'Carpet' by the Rhodesian 1st SAS Regiment (RhSAS). As a result of lengthy interrogation of the NSO Deputy Head of Intelligence, Alexander Brisk Vusa, the Rhodesian Special Branch learned of the arrival of heavily laden convoys of trucks at a terrorist camp designated 'JZ' which was located 14km (9 miles) west of the Zambian capital, Lusaka. The Rhodesians had long been aware that Libyan aircraft had been ferrying consignments of Russian and East German-supplied weapons at night from Angola to Zambia, but had been unable to determine the location of the ZIPRA caches.

Photographic reconnaissance of the area by the Royal Rhodesian Air Force (RRAF) confirmed the presence of large caches, defensive positions and vehicle tracks over an area of some 6ha (15 acres), and it was decided to carry out a raid of the JZ camp and the cache area as soon as possible. A force of 50 men from the regiment's three Sabre Squadrons was assembled, and at 12:45 hours on Sunday 1 July 1979 it lifted off in five helicopters of 8 Squadron RRAF and headed north towards Zambia. Sixty minutes later, RRAF Hawker Hunters and Canberra bombers struck at the terrorist camp, while a Dakota, carrying a command team headed by Lieutenant-General Peter Walls, the commander of combined operations, circled overhead.

Shortly afterwards, the helicopters landed and the assault force went into action heading for the arms caches and the nearby camp. The RhSAS found 500 tents containing weapons, equipment and the possessions of the ZIPRA guerrillas which were swiftly set ablaze.

Meanwhile the demolitions teams were dealing with the arms caches, planting explosives charges which began to detonate soon afterwards, filling the air with debris and fragments. Altogether 100 tonnes of weapons, ammunition and equipment were destroyed together with a number of vehicles, boats and a large quantity of diesel fuel.

As dusk approached, the assault force withdrew to the nearby landing zone where the helicopters arrived shortly afterwards. At that moment a column of Zambian armoured vehicles appeared, but made no attempt at intervention until after the aircraft were well out of range, when a few desultory shots were fired after them. Zambian MiGs had appeared earlier but had steered clear, well aware that they were being tracked by the RRAF Hawker Hunters who were ready to shoot them down if they showed any sign of aggression.

It transpired that the caches had contained logistical reserves intended to equip ZIPRA units being trained for conventional warfare. Their destruction meant the end of Joshua Nkomo's plans for an invasion of Rhodesia until such time as he could replace them. As far as the RhSAS were concerned, the raid was a highly successful postscript to Operation 'Carpet'.

CHINESE PARLIAMENT   A form of open debate where everyone has their say. The SAS pride themselves on listening to all ranks during operational planning, and many excellent ideas have come from having a 'Chinese Parliament'. The expression is also used to convey disorder, 'a right old Chinese Parliament'.

CHINOOK   *Specification* Manufacturer: Boeing; Engines: 2×3750 shp Lycoming Turboshafts; Length: 15.54m (17yds); Height: 5.68m (6yds); Weight: 22,680kg (25 tons); Range: 370km (229 miles); Speed: 298kph (184mph) max.

The Boeing Vertol CH-47D Chinook was first delivered to the US Army in 1962 and in 1965 was deployed to Vietnam. It is a battlefield helicopter vital today for the movement of heavy logistics and assault troop transportation. It is flown by both the RAF and the Army Air Corps and is widely used by the SAS for insertion, extraction and parachuting. It will carry 44 soldiers and can lift 12 tonnes of stores. Most of the British Chinooks have recently undergone modernization, with modifications including new instrumentation which enables the helicopter to fly at night and in bad weather using precision navigation techniques. During the Gulf War, SAS patrols and fighting columns were re-supplied by the latest version of the Chinook, the MH-47, all of which operated deep behind the Iraqi lines at night.

CHIN PENG   Chin Peng was Secretary General of the Malayan Communist Party (MCP) and the leader of the Communist Terrorists (CTs) against whom British Commonwealth forces fought during the Malayan

Emergency of 1948–60. He learned the art of guerrilla warfare during World War II while heading the Malayan Peoples' Anti-Japanese Army (MPAJA), which eventually numbered 5,000 men and women. The MPAJA received training and weapons from Force 136, the arm of the Special Operations Executive (SOE) which operated throughout South and Southeast Asia. The total defeat and rout of British forces in Malaya in 1942 had enabled Chin Peng to pose as the sole effective resistance against the Japanese, and thus the British were forced to collaborate with him in achieving their objective of defeating the Japanese and regaining control of Malaya. At the end of the war, he was awarded the MBE for his performance as head of the MPAJA, which did not disband but renamed itself the Malayan Races Liberation Army (MRLA) in early 1949.

Chin Peng's aim was the establishment of a Communist state in Malaya by force of arms, ejecting the British whom he and his followers viewed as colonial oppressors. His forces comprised eight regiments of terrorists dispersed throughout the country and armed with weapons supplied by Force 136 during the period 1942–45. His plan for the Communist conquest of Malaya consisted of three phases. Phase One would consist of attacks on the country's rubber, tea and palm oil estates – whose British planters lived a lonely existence in secluded areas – as well as police stations and government officials in towns and villages. The aim of Phase One was to force the British to evacuate the rural areas and concentrate in the towns. Phase Two would be occupation of the so-called 'Liberated Areas', the establishment of terrorist bases in them and the recruitment of further forces from within the local Chinese population. Phase Three would see Communist forces moving out of the 'Liberated Areas' and attacking towns, villages and railways, eventually taking on the might of the British with the support of China.

In the event, Chin Peng's plans came to nothing. He was outmanoeuvred by the British who, among various measures, uprooted and resettled 500,000 Chinese in fortified villages and thus cut off the terrorists from the support of the Min Yuen (their civilian sympathizers). The British also took the war to the enemy, sending troops into the jungle to hunt them down. Above all, British 'hearts and minds' operations to win over the local population were successful, and contributed largely to the isolation of the terrorists. Nevertheless, Chin Peng's CTs fought a long and bitter struggle during the twelve years of the Malayan Emergency. He himself lived in the jungle of central Pahang until 1952 when, as a result of mounting CT losses, he fled with other members of his Politburo to the safety of a new base over the border in neutral Thailand.

CHIOCO I In March 1977 the Rhodesians decided to deal with a strong ZANLA garrison, numbering some 100 terrorists, based 1km (1.5

miles) south of the town of Chioco in the northern Mozambique province of Tete. A and B Troops of C Squadron Rhodesian SAS (RhSAS), numbering 22 all ranks, were given the task of carrying out a raid on the terrorist camp.

At dusk on 22 March the assault force, under Captain Dave Dodson, was inserted by helicopter in two lifts from a forward base at Mtoko. Having been dropped approximately 17km (10.5 miles) west of their objectives, Captain Dodson and his men moved off to a lying-up position (LUP) in some thick undergrowth about a kilometre's distance away, where they stayed until moonrise. Marching throughout the rest of the night, they halted just before dawn and stayed until dusk on the following evening.

At 23:00 hours on 23 March the force moved up to its objective. In the distance, coming from the direction of Chioco, they could hear music and singing, which indicated that a major celebration was being held in the town. Captain Dodson sited a three-man 60mm light mortar team, whose task was to bomb Chioco and its police station so as to prevent any attempt at reinforcement from the town during the attack on the camp. As the four assault groups moved past the mortar position, they dropped off their packs and quantities of mortar bombs before moving up to a three-strand wire fence and taking up their positions. Just before first light Captain Dave Dodson's and Sergeant Iain Bowen's groups slid under the wire and positioned ten Claymore mines along the back walls of two barrack blocks. At the same time, Corporal Nick Breytenbach was siting eight more Claymores on the northern corner of the camp.

The attack was launched at first light. Corporal Breytenbach's Claymores were initiated first, followed a split second later by those of Sergeant Bowen. At the same time, Corporal Frank Booth tossed two fragmentation grenades into a bunker holding a number of terrorists. The four assault groups then commenced their advance through the camp, firing at everything that moved. Having cleared the barrack buildings, they turned their attention to the terrorists' defensive positions, which comprised a network of trenches leading from inside the camp to outside the wire fence. The assault group threw grenades and 'bunker bombs', 1kg (.5lb) explosive charges fitted with four-second fuses, into the trenches as the terrorists attempted to escape from the camp unseen. Some of those that succeeded in doing so encountered a stop group, positioned to the north of the camp, which picked them off. Meanwhile the 60mm mortar team was bombarding Chioco from where troops of FRELIMO (Front for the Liberation of Mozambique) and ZANLA terrorists were firing at the RhSAS.

Sergeant Andy Chait's assault group approached the camp from the south. Crossing a gully via a makeshift bridge, he and his men moved through a field of maize until they came under fire from terrorists in a trench to their front. These were engaged with AK-47s, fragmentation grenades and an accurately thrown white phosphorous grenade which exploded in the trench. Those terrorists not stopped by the burning phosphorous were killed as they fled. While clearing the trench, Sergeant Chait and his men came under fire from an RPD light machine gun and shortly afterwards Chart was seriously wounded in the thigh, suffering a ruptured femoral artery. Enemy fire, including shelling by some 75mm recoilless rifles sited in bunkers nearby, prevented the RhSAS medics from carrying out emergency treatment until they had moved him to cover behind some buildings. A medevac helicopter was called and this arrived a few minutes later. Unfortunately, the medics' efforts were in vain: Sergeant Chait died during the flight to Salisbury.

Shortly afterwards, the RhSAS withdrew, leaving a scene of destruction with at least 38 ZANLA terrorists dead and a large number wounded. They made their way over a distance of a few kilometres to a landing zone from which they were extracted by helicopter under cover of four Royal Rhodesian Air Force Hunters, which were poised to carry out a strike in the event of interference by FRELIMO. The operation had been entirely successful and the enemy abandoned the camp.

CHIOCO II May 1977 saw a return to Chioco by C Squadron Rhodesian SAS (RhSAS), which had raided the nearby ZANLA camp in March of that year. Having abandoned the camp, ZANLA had subsequently moved into the town, which it proceeded to share with FRELIMO forces. The Rhodesians thus decided to attack the town and render it untenable.

Four patrols, totalling sixteen men under Captain Dave Dodson, moved into the area on foot and for the next few days mined some of the roads. Having reconnoitred Chioco, and finding the strength of the ZANLA and FRELIMO garrison larger than expected, Captain Dodson requested a further three patrols as reinforcements. These were dropped at night from a Royal Rhodesian Air Force Dakota and the entire force moved off immediately towards the town.

A 60mm mortar team set up two mortars in a field of maize while the rest of the force moved to the edge of the town where it took up positions in a ditch. Just before first light the RhSAS advanced into the town and began their attack by throwing 'bunker bombs' into buildings as they worked their way through the town. Ahead of them 60mm bombs exploded as the mortar team in the maize field brought down a creeping barrage.

Of ZANLA and FRELIMO, however, there was no sign and the RhSAS were unopposed as they swept through the town. Thirty minutes later it had been cleared and was in SAS hands. Unbeknown to Captain Dodson and his men, however, the entire ZANLA/FRELIMO force was sleeping in the bush only 20m (21yds) from the SAS mortar team's position. The latter discovered this when it suddenly came under fire. Rapidly redeploying one of the mortars, a sergeant sent several bombs into the area from where he suspected the firing had emanated. This action had the desired effect and there was no further trouble.

Special Branch personnel flew in by helicopter to collect and inspect the large quantity of documents discovered in the FRELIMO head-quarters. At the same time, a huge cache of weapons and ammunition was discovered in a stone tower nearby and this was blown up. Thereafter, Captain Dodson split his force into two: a group of eight under his command withdrew into the bush to continue harassing the enemy in the area, while the rest of the force, under Lieutenant 'Mac' McIntosh, remained on the outskirts of the town to ambush any ZANLA or FRELIMO forces which appeared. Several days later, the latter did so with Tanzanian troops in support. A patrol of three men ventured into the town but these were eliminated with a few 60mm bombs.

Shortly afterwards a force of 100 troops, supported by mortars, arrived and proceeded to bring down a heavy bombardment around the Rhodesian positions. This proved largely ineffective but Lieutenant McIntosh and Corporal Dave Arkwright were wounded by a bomb which landed near the RhSAS command position. They were evacuated shortly afterwards and Captain Bob McKenna arrived to take over command. By that stage, however, FRELIMO and the Tanzanians had lost all enthusiasm for the battle and retired to lick their wounds.

Meanwhile, Captain Dave Dodson and his group had been enjoying some success, ambushing a number of ZANLA groups and discovering information about a large camp at the nearby town of Jeque, which was immediately raided by other elements of C Squadron and the Rhodesian Light Infantry, with air support from RRAF Hawker Hunters. A few days later the entire Chioco raiding force withdrew and returned to Rhodesia and their base. They had achieved their objective because the town was never rebuilt or reoccupied by FRELIMO or ZANLA.

CHURCHILL, RANDOLPH   Son of Winston Churchill, who during World War II joined the Long Range Desert Group (LRDG) for a short while. In March 1942, he was seriously hurt in a car accident and had to be shipped back to Britain.

CIA – CENTRAL INTELLIGENCE AGENCY   During the Vietnam War, members of the Australian SAS Regiment (SASR) also served on unconventional warfare operations in which the Central Intelligence Agency (CIA) played a prominent role. In doing so, they were members of the Australian Army Training Team in Vietnam (AATTV). Prominent among these SASR personnel operating on attachment to the CIA were

Captain Ian Teague, who later commanded 1 Squadron SASR on operations in Phuoc Tuy Province, and WO2 Danny Neville who was the assistant to Captain Barry Peterson, an AATTV officer also seconded to the CIA and commander of a Montagnard force in the Central Highlands.

CIO – CENTRAL INTELLIGENCE ORGANIZATION The Rhodesian government agency handling external intelligence and internal counter-intelligence in close collaboration with the police Special Branch. Headed by its director, Ken Flower, it also liaised closely with Combined Operations Headquarters, under Lieutenant General Peter Walls, and the Rhodesian 1st SAS Regiment (RhSAS) with whom it provided intelligence. In addition, CIO clearance had to be given for all cross-border missions undertaken by the Rhodesian armed forces.

On several occasions, CIO personnel accompanied RhSAS troops on such missions. An example of this was an Operation 'Hurricane' task in early April 1974, when a CIO officer was included as a member of a force which crossed the Zambesi River to attack a ZIPRA camp known as Pondoland East 'B' which was believed to accommodate 50 terrorists.

From 1977 onwards, the CIO masterminded unconventional warfare operations against the FRELIMO government of Mozambique, which was deeply unpopular with the population of the country. It established a radio station, equipped with a 400 kilowatt transmitter and called 'The Voice of Africa', which beamed broadcasts to Mozambique, encouraging the population to support a non-existent organization called the Mozambique National Resistance (MNR). The station continued to operate until forced to close by the British in February 1980 during the Lancaster House talks, as part of the way of conceding independence to black Rhodesia.

Such was the success of the broadcasts, which resulted in hundreds of FRELIMO personnel deserting in order to join the MNR, that the CIO was rapidly forced to bring the MNR into existence. It did so by establishing a training camp for Mozambiquan anti-FRELIMO guerrillas at an abandoned farm at Odzi, near Umtali, with former RhSAS officers and men as instructors. MNR operations began in mid-1978 and in January of the following year elements of 1st SAS Regiment began operating with the guerrillas in Mozambique and continued to do so until the end of Rhodesia's unilateral independence in 1980. Thereafter the MNR operated on its own in its campaign against the FRELIMO government of Samora Machel.

CIVIL AID TEAM (CAT) Teams responsible for assisting the rebuilding of economic facilities during the Oman War. One of their tasks was to exploit the vast underground sources of fresh water. This simple act of producing water in a barren desert would make the local population dance with glee as water had previously been in short supply. The Civil Aid Teams, which were part of the 'hearts and minds' programme, also introduced new breeding stock to improve the herds of native cattle.

CLANDESTINE COMMUNIST ORGANIZATION (CCO)

Chinese terrorist group located largely in the Sarawak region of Borneo, where it had large and active cells in many towns. President Sukarno of Indonesia supplied the CCO with arms, and allowed the Communists to train in Kalimantan prior to their incursions into Borneo. However, border surveillance and patrols mounted by the SAS placed a major constraint upon CCO freedom of action.

'CLARET' OPERATIONS

In mid-1964, during the Borneo Confrontation with Indonesia, approval was given by the Malaysian and British governments to the request by the Director of Borneo Operations, Major-General Walter Walker, for permission to conduct cross-border operations into Kalimantan, the Indonesian part of the island of Borneo, in order to prevent anticipated or suspected Indonesian attacks. Initially, the maximum distance from the border was limited to 4,500m (5,000yds) but later in the same year it was increased to 18,200m (20,000yds) for a small number of specific operations. Such operations, heavily classified as Top Secret, were code-named 'Claret', and among those units which participated in them were A and D Squadrons 22 SAS Regiment, the Guards Independent Parachute Company, the Gurkha Independent Parachute Company, 1 and 2 Squadrons Australian SASR, and detachments 1st Ranger Squadron NZSAS. In addition, 1 and 2 Special Boat Sections Royal Marines also carried out small-scale raids on coastal targets on either flank.

'Claret' operations typically consisted of interdiction of tracks, rivers and other routes being used by Indonesian troops who were mainly well-trained regulars of the Indonesian National Army, the Tentera Nasional Indonesia (TNI). These included para-commandos of the Resemen Para Kommando Angaton Darat (RPKAD) and marine commandos of the Korps Kommando Operasi (KKO). Over 22,000 TNI troops were deployed in the borders areas, supported by large numbers of volunteer irregular forces.

The conduct of 'Claret' operations was governed by a set of regulations, laid down by Major-General Walker, which were known as the 'Golden Rules'. These stipulated that all operations had to be authorized by the Director of Borneo Operations personally and that every operation had to be meticulously planned, rehearsed and carried out with maximum security. Only tried and tested troops were permitted to be used and under no circumstances were troops to be captured, dead or alive, by the enemy. All operations were to be carried out with the aim of deterring and thwarting aggression by the Indonesians. Furthermore the depth of penetration from the border was to be strictly controlled, and it was emphasized that air support could not be given except in instances of extreme emergency. Artillery and mortar support was, however, available on call with 5.5in guns, 105mm pack howitzers or 81mm mortars being lifted forward singly or in pairs by helicopter to bases on the border in support of specific operations.

'Claret' operations ceased on 23 March 1966, eleven days after the overthrow of President Sukarno by General Suharto. In the main they had achieved their aim of keeping the Indonesians off balance, although early operations achieved only limited success. Within Indonesia all publicity about setbacks caused by 'Claret' raids had been suppressed, principally because President Sukarno had not wished to admit them to his people to whom he had promised that Malaysia would be crushed by 1 January 1965.

CLARK, LIEUTENANT-COLONEL LAWRIE – AUSTRALIAN SAS REGIMENT (SASR) AND AUSTRALIAN ARMY TRAINING TEAM (AATT) Vietnam
Second Lieutenant Lawrie Clark was commissioned from the Royal Military College Duntroon in 1947 and subsequently served in the Korean War with the 3rd Battalion Royal Australian Regiment (3 RAR), with whom he won the Military Cross. Thereafter he served postings as an instructor at Duntroon and adjutant of a Citizen's Military Force battalion before attending the Canadian Staff College. He was subsequently posted to the Australian Army Staff in Washington, DC, before undergoing US Special Forces training at Fort Bragg, North Carolina, and Ranger and Airborne training at Fort Benning, Georgia. In September 1960, Major Clark assumed command of 1st SAS Company RAR, a post he held until June 1963.

Six years later, in December 1969, Lieutenant-Colonel Clark assumed command of the SASR. During his time away from the regiment, he had served in Vietnam with the AATT, had been an instructor at the Jungle Warfare School at Canungra, been Chief Instructor of the Officer Training Unit and subsequently GSO1 (Land/Air Warfare) at the Directorate of Military Operations & Plans. His tenure of command saw the last twenty months of Australian operations in South Vietnam and the end of SASR operations there in October 1971. Thereafter it was a difficult period for the regiment which had to come to terms with peacetime soldiering after seven years of operations in Borneo and South Vietnam. The establishment of SASR was reduced and consequently 2 Squadron was disbanded. It was in these circumstances that Lieutenant-Colonel Lawrie Clark handed over command to Lieutenant-Colonel Ian McFarlane on 26 January 1972.

CLAYMORE ANTI-PERSONNEL MINE The American-made
Claymore mine was used by the SAS during the Borneo confrontation

and is still widely used to this day. The mine itself is a moulded plastic case measuring some 75mm (3in) high by 200mm (8in) wide. The whole case is slightly curved with 'Front Towards Enemy' embossed on the crest face. The mine is packed with a solid explosive, into which thousands of small ball bearings are set. The base of the mine has two sets of spiked legs which can be adjusted for angle, the top containing two screw-cap detonator wells. The mine is exploded by command detonation, when a hand generator is depressed. One in five mines comes with a testing device to show continuity along the command wire. The mine is perfect for perimeter defence or ambush.

COALISLAND SHOOTING, COUNTY TYRONE   On Sunday 4 December 1983 an SAS observation post (OP) which had been watching an IRA arms cache opened fire on two men who had arrived to collect the weapons with the intention of committing a murder.

The weapons were housed in a hide protected by thick hedgerow, that separated a small field from a quiet country lane, a gateway into the field providing easy access. Once the hide was discovered a full-scale operation was mounted; this involved 14 Intelligence and Security unit (14 Int) who were responsible for watching on the IRA suspect players; the SAS would act as cover for the weapons; and the RUC's intelligence group, E4A who would form a Quick Reaction Force (QRF). The SAS inserted several two-man OPs around the field, with the main OP in a ditch opposite the weapons hide, some 20m (21yds) away. Members of E4A, were positioned at Lurgan while 14 Int carried out close surveillance.

The SAS men in the OPs remained in position despite the wet and cold December weather. Around 15:15 on Sunday afternoon a car was heard slowing down and it eventually stopped opposite the gate. Two men got out and climbed the gate, leaving the driver in the car. They walked directly to the hide, knelt down and retrieved the weapons. The first terrorist, Colm McGirr, pulled out a weapon and passed it to Brian Campbell. As Campbell stood up, turning back in the direction of the car, the two SAS men challenged from the main OP. McGirr, who was still kneeling by the bush, turned with a gun in his hand and was shot dead. Campbell ran for the gate still holding the weapon. Two more shots rang out and he fell mortally wounded. The driver, on hearing the gunfire and realizing that it was a trap, drove off. An SAS soldier jumped out to stop him, firing four high velocity rounds directly into the car but failed to stop it.

A quick check indicated that McGirr was dead, but Campbell was still breathing and an SAS medic inserted an airway and administered first aid; Campbell died before the ambulance crew arrived about twenty minutes later. The area was sealed off by E4A, who were activated via radio instructions to search for the missing getaway car. It was soon located near some houses about a kilometre away, heavily stained with blood, but the injured driver was not to be found. It was later learnt that he had been whisked away by local Republican sympathizers who managed to get him across the border into the Irish Republic before major stops came into force. In the eyes of the SAS it was a clean, neat job, apart from the vehicle stop, for which the SAS soldier concerned was severely criticized by the regimental headshed (senior officer) for allowing the car to pass.

COBRA (CABINET OFFICE BRIEFING ROOM) The office where members of the government, senior police officers and military commanders meet to discuss major terrorist incidents. Director SAS is usually on hand to voice the options available from the Regiment, and to keep members of COBRA fully informed of the regiment's preparedness.

COCKERILL, HARRY A World War II SAS veteran who provided the regiment with a review on the tribes of the Radfan in Aden in 1960.

'COCKLE' CANOE Adapted from the older Folbot, the Cockle was a much improved canoe which had a wooden framework, improved buoyancy and a much better rubber outer skin. The Cockle underwent many changes from the MkI to the MkVIII, the latter being a motorized canoe that would carry up to four men plus a large amount of equipment. It had a range of 113km (70 miles) with a top speed of 6 knots.

'COCKLESHELL HEROES', OPERATION The giant man-made Lake Caborra Bassa, 248km (155 miles) long and 32km (21 miles) wide, and dominating the province of Tete in northwestern Mozambique, was the base for a six-week waterborne operation mounted by C Squadron Rhodesian SAS (RhSAS) in January 1977. A twelve-man patrol, under A Troop's commander, Captain Bob McKenna, was inserted by vehicle into the area of the Musengezi River on 17 January. At 18:00 hours that evening the patrol embarked on the river in six two-man Klepper canoes but shortly afterwards hit rapids and rough waters which capsized the canoes, some of which were damaged. After repairs had been carried out, the journey down river continued on the evening of the following day, and the intended location for the patrol's first base on the lake, a mopani forest-covered mudflat, was reached in the early hours of 19 January. Radio communications were then established with the RhSAS headquarters at Salisbury.

A week later, having received a re-supply drop, a four-man patrol under Colour Sergeant Karl Lutz was transported by canoe on to the Mozambique shore. Moving inland, it planted a mine on the Mague-

Caponda road which was a known route for ZANLA terrorists infiltrating into Rhodesia. On the evening of the following day, the group was picked up and rejoined the rest of the patrol. At 03:00 hours on the following day, the entire patrol moved to a new base on an island. At 09:15 hours, Captain McKenna and his men heard an explosion; they later learned the second-in-command of the FRELIMO garrison at Mkumbura had been killed in the explosion. A few days later, ten men of the patrol carried out an ambush on the Mague-Daque road. Nine hours after taking up their positions they ambushed a FRELIMO supply vehicle carrying ten uniformed FRELIMO troops, all of whom were killed. Having replenished their stocks of ammunition from the vehicle and laid booby traps in the area, the patrol withdrew and paddled its way back to its base.

After two weeks on the lake, Captain McKenna moved his men to the northern banks, where he established a new base. Shortly afterwards, the entire patrol carried out a raid on a small FRELIMO garrison next to a village called Nhende Aldeamento. Having planted a mine on the road that led from the lake to the village, it took up its assault positions. At 22:15 hours, the attack commenced and the patrol fired rockets, rifle grenades and small arms fire into the barracks. There was no response from the FRELIMO troops and the patrol withdrew 8km (5 miles) to its base on the banks of the lake. During the night, it relocated to a new site on an island.

At the end of the third week of the operation, the patrol carried out an ambush 14km (9 miles) east of the town of Daque, which is situated near the southern shore of the lake and which was occupied by a garrison of FRELIMO forces. Having landed at night and planted a mine on the road in the middle of the ambush killing area, the patrol was in its positions by sunrise. No vehicles appeared on that day or the next and Captain McKenna was about to lift the ambush when a tractor and trailer, carrying twelve FRELIMO troops and a load of weapons, ammunition, equipment, rations and clothing, arrived on the scene. The patrol opened fire and within a few seconds all the FRELIMO lay dead or dying with the exception of one man who, badly wounded, succeeded in making his escape. Having searched the bodies, and booby-trapped one of them, the Rhodesians withdrew to the lake and a new base.

On the following day, they heard their mine explode and subsequently learned that a company of FRELIMO troops were sweeping the area when another tractor and trailer, carrying all the dead from the previous day's ambush, detonated the mine. FRELIMO abandoned the area and bodies forthwith.

After six weeks, the operation drew to a close. The patrol had paddled a total of 536km (335 miles), caused mayhem among FRELIMO garrisons and disrupted ZANLA infiltration routes in the area. More importantly, it had proved the viability of such operations and as a result two further operations, 'Cockleshell Heroes II and III', were subsequently mounted on Lake Caborra Bassa. These in turn led to other lake operations by the RhSAS and the Selous Scouts of the Rhodesian Army.

'COLD COMFORT', OPERATION (later to be renamed 'Zombie') With the command to block the railway line leading to the Brenner Pass with a landslide, a thirteen-strong party from 3 Squadron 2 SAS was dropped by parachute on 17 February 1945, just to the north of Verona in northern Italy. A successful attack meant the Germans would be unable to send their troops south through the Alps. Unfortunately, the party was widely dispersed on landing and re-supply was an impossibility, on account of the abysmal weather. An additional complication was the hostility of the local inhabitants, who were ethnic Germans. As a result, the SAS party were forced into hiding and the group's two commander officers, Captain Littlejohn and Corporal Crowley, were captured and subsequently executed under Hitler's Commando Order. By the end of March, the mission was declared a failure and the party evacuated from Italy.

COLLINS, LIEUTENANT IAN G. The SAS liaison officer with Airborne Corps HQ, based at Moor Park outside London, who towards the end of World War II was responsible for planning, training and various other staff duties. The first role he suggested for the SAS at the close of the war in Europe was the disarmament of German troops in Norway, the hunting down of war criminals in Germany and deployment to the Far East. In particular, he was eager to prevent the Germans carrying out a demolition campaign in Norway before they left. He also advocated that the SAS operate with frontline units in Germany in order to arrest war criminals and Gestapo agents. These proposals were sensible, although a further proposal, that the whole SAS brigade be sent to the Far East, was dismissed as being too outlandish.

Collins was one of those officers who argued that the SAS was a specialist unit, a view not shared by many commanders at corps and divisional level. He was, in many ways, ahead of his time, for in late 1944 he proposed the dropping of SAS parties into Germany to conduct sabotage missions, a role which required intensive and specialist training and which was beyond the Special Air Service at that time.

COLOMBIA OPERATIONS As part of a US/British effort to combat the huge narcotics industry in Colombia, members of 22 SAS have been sent there since the 1980s to train local police anti-narcotics commandos in infiltration skills. The police commandos are taught how to work in long-range patrols in hostile areas, destroy the factories where the drugs are produced, and either to kill or capture the criminals.

The SAS would teach basic jungle tactics, plus a few counter-terrorist methods. The training continued until the early 1990s, normally with a full squadron and a section of SBS. The Americans funded a large percentage of the operational equipment supplied to Colombia, but Britain also contributed night-sights, waterproof equipment, bergens, and military-type clothing. Despite what the media say concerning the role of the SAS in Colombia, the regiment never carried out any actual operations against the drugs cartel.

COLT COMMANDO   A shorter version of the M16A2 Armalite designed to fire the SS109 standard NATO round.

COMMUNIST TERRORISTS (CTS)   Organized in so-called regiments, the Communist Terrorists (CTs) of the Malayan Races Liberation Army (MRLA) were reported as numbering some 12,000 in total at the height of the Malayan Emergency during the years 1948–60. Headed by Chin Peng, the Communist wartime guerrilla leader, they were deployed in the jungle throughout Malaya. They were well trained and armed with weapons supplied during World War II by Britain's Force 136, which had also dropped officers to train and work with Chin Peng's guerrillas, when both factions were united against the Japanese threat. After the war, Chin Peng sought to eject the British by force and establish Malaya as a Communist state.

The CT were supported by the Min Yuen, an organization numbering some 60,000 civilian sympathizers who existed at every level of life in Malaya, supplying the terrorists with food, money and information. Its members ranged from clerks in government departments and waiters in British officers' messes and clubs to schoolteachers, journalists, squatters and tappers on rubber estates.

The CT were highly skilled in their operations and particularly adept at ambushes, a skill which they had learned from their Force 136 instructors during World War II. During the early part of the campaign they were based in large camps in the jungle, some boasting facilities such as parade grounds and lecture halls as well as accommodation for 200 to 300 fighters. However, once the RAF and RAAF started carrying out aerial reconnaissance, which spotted such camps without much difficulty, and followed this up with area bombardments by Lincoln medium bombers, the CTs switched to operating in smaller groups based in smaller and heavily camouflaged camps.

For the first three years of the Emergency the CTs posed a formidable threat, carrying out attacks against the security forces and civilian population and then disappearing back to their lairs in the jungle. In 1952, however, the tide of the war turned with the arrival of General Sir Gerald Templer as High Commissioner in place of Sir Henry Gurney, who was murdered in a CT ambush on the road to Fraser's Hill on 6

October 1951. Proper use of intelligence, the reorganization and expansion of the police (in particular its Special Branch), effective use of propaganda, rewards for information on terrorists and relocation of the local population into fortified villages were just some of the measures implemented by General Templer which proved highly successful in countering the CT threat.

The CT also found that they were no longer reigning supreme in the jungle, as British, Commonwealth and Gurkha troops began to learn once again the skills of jungle warfare and put them to good use. The Malayan Scouts and subsequently 22 SAS Regiment were renowned for probing into the depths of the jungle in their hunt for the terrorists and their camps. By the end of the campaign, CT casualties during the Emergency were very heavy: 6,698 killed, 2,819 wounded and 1,286 captured. In addition a further 2,696 surrendered and in excess of 1,000 were estimated to have died, deserted or been executed by their commanders. After the end of the campaign in the early 1960s some 500 CTs operated from camps in the jungle north of the Malay-Thai border until they eventually gave up the armed struggle some years later.

COMPASS Every SAS soldier will carry a compass of one sort or another. It was traditional until the mid-1970s to use the standard issue prismatic compass which has been in service since World War II. However, most soldiers now rely on the Silva-type compass which is flat and easier to use in conjunction with an Ordnance Survey map; this type of compass also comes with a combination map romer and various distance scales. In addition to the main compass, each soldier will also have an escape compass in his survival kit.

COMPO A cardboard carton containing the food for either four or ten men, for one day. Compo is mostly tinned food with a variety of menus supplemented by basic items such as tea, sugar and coffee. The packs are designed for operational static locations, away from a British military location and where local food is not considered to be adequate. The SAS lived on Compo for most of the time spent on the mountainous Jebel during the Oman War. Compo food is made to a very high standard, but fresh rations are issued periodically to ease the boredom of eating tinned food.

'CONCRETE', OPERATION On 19 April 1970, 1st Australian Task Force with the objective of destroying a Vietcong (VC) main force unit, D445 Battalion, launched Operation 'Concrete' in the district of Xuyen Moc, in the eastern area of Phuoc Tuy Province. Three battalions plus supporting arms were involved, as were a number of patrols of 1 Squadron Australian SAS Regiment deployed in the area of the May Tao mountains to the northeast.

CONDON, TROOPER PADDY   A member of A Squadron who, due to the shortage of signallers, volunteered to join D Squadron for the tour in Borneo, in 1964. Part of Sergeant 'Smokey' Richardson's patrol, Trooper Condon became separated from the rest, after the patrol had a head-on contact with the Indonesian forces, on 14 May. Although surrounded and heavily outnumbered, Richardson and the remaining members of his patrol searched for days, finding only Condon's bergen. It was later learnt that Condon had been shot and wounded, before being taken prisoner by the Indonesians, whereupon he was tortured and killed. His body was never recovered.

CONSIDINE, SERGEANT BERNIE – AUSTRALIAN SAS REGIMENT (SASR)   In South Vietnam in mid-January 1969 Sergeant Bernie Considine's patrol of 2 Squadron SASR was inserted in the area of the Firestone Trail in Bien Hoa Province. It was one of a number of patrols deployed throughout the north of the province and tasked with locating a large Vietcong (VC) storage base in the area. Sergeant Considine's patrol had entered the area of the base and was in the process of crossing a small river when it spotted nine VC approaching from the rear. These were engaged by two members of the patrol, who killed three of them. Almost immediately afterwards the patrol came under heavy fire. The patrol then called for an air strike, which was carried out shortly afterwards, before withdrawing for extraction.

CONSIGLIO, TROOPER 'BOB' ROBERT   A former Royal Marine, Bob Consiglio joined the SAS in February 1990 and was posted to B Squadron's Mobility Troop serving, a year later, as a member of the ill-fated 'Bravo Two Zero' patrol, in the Gulf War. The patrol, operating on foot, was spotted and found themselves running for the Syrian border, hotly pursued by the Iraqis. Just a few miles short of the border, Bob Consiglio was fatally wounded, yet he continued to give covering fire while the rest continued their escape. During the whole traumatic race to freedom Bob Consiglio constantly helped those patrol members who were suffering from hypothermia by sharing his body heat. Those that survived will vouch that danger of death from the cold was greater than that of being found by the Iraqis. Trooper Consiglio was the first SAS soldier to be killed in the Gulf War.

CONTACT   The word 'contact' is reserved in the SAS to mean one thing: contact with the enemy. At the first opportunity the patrol signaller will send the simple message, 'Contact, wait out'. This will alert the base unit to stand by, organizing a relief force if necessary. The next message will be a brief contact report stating what has happened, who is dead or wounded, enemy strength and the patrol commander's intentions.

CONTACT DRILL A technique practised to prepare contingencies in the event of an SAS patrol meeting the enemy head-on at close range. Contact drills differ depending on terrain and patrol size. The basis of the contact drill is to lay down suppressive fire and extract as soon as possible, grabbing any wounded in the process. Quick reactions by the lead scout and good rehearsals beforehand make for a good contact drill.

CONTINUATION TRAINING Once a recruit has passed SAS Selection, he will go on to Continuation training. This is a series of specially designed courses covering a 14-week period in which prospective SAS troopers learn basic SAS skills, including how to operate as part of a four-man patrol. Many of the soldiers come from infantry regiments and their fieldcraft skills are excellent – however, the SAS recognize the need to incorporate soldiers from all sections of the Army. To aid non-infantry soldiers, the SAS run a special infantry tactics course. At the start of the Continuation phase members of the SBS (Special Boat Section), who have also been doing their own Selection, will arrive at Hereford. The two sets of students are then integrated into patrols of two SAS and two SBS members.

SOPs (standard operating procedures) become a priority, as does learning ambush procedures and contact drills. Weapon training for the M16 and Claymore mines are also taught prior to the jungle phase. All students will undergo a course in escape and evasion (E&E) techniques, and participate in an E&E exercise which ends with interrogation. Finally, those candidates that remain will be badged, receiving the beige beret with its famous winged dagger, before being posted to a squadron. New SAS members remain on a form of probation for the first two years.

Author's note: as any SAS man will tell you, receiving your beret is a very special moment which gives a fabulous feeling of achievement.

CONTROL RISKS A private security company started in 1973 by former SAS men with the aim of advising on kidnapping and risk assessment to insurance companies. They would provide security personnel in the case of ransom negotiations, and would deal directly with the terrorist. Control Risks have undertaken many dangerous negotiations between the terrorists and the insurance company paying the ransom.

'COONEY', OPERATION With orders to cut railway lines throughout Brittany, 54 men of 4 French Parachute Battalion (4 SAS) were dropped 'blind', on 7 June 1944, between St Malo and Vannes. Dividing the party into eighteen 3-man teams, the troopers managed to cut several railway lines before dispersing and joining the SAS base established by the 'Dingson' party.

COOPER, LIEUTENANT-COLONEL JOHNNY A most outstanding member of the SAS, contributing to a major part of its history, Cooper was an original member of L Detachment during World War II who went on to a distinguished career within the regiment. He joined the unit via a spell with the Scots Guards, in which David Stirling was a junior officer, and No. 8 Guards Commando. Arriving in North Africa in February 1941, Cooper spent time with Layforce before volunteering to serve in Stirling's new SAS command. Cooper was trained as a navigator and went on many of the SAS's desert missions, usually serving as Stirling's driver. In 1943, Cooper was sent to an Officer Cadet Training School, and at the end of that year flew back to Britain, where he was closely involved in the creation and training of the SAS Brigade in preparation for the liberation of Europe. He took command of a troop in A Squadron 1 SAS and became involved in the highly successful Operation 'Houndsworth', June 1944, tasked with severing railway lines and disrupting enemy communications in Dijon, France.

Shortly after the end of the war, Cooper accompanied most of the brigade to Norway to assist in the repatriation of German troops. He was demobilized in January 1947, though he joined the Territorial Army as a lieutenant a year later. At the beginning of 1951 he rejoined the Regular Army and was posted to Malaya to serve with 22 SAS. During his time in Malaya, Cooper held many positions within the regiment: commander of C, B and A Squadrons; officer in charge of transport; operations officer; and recruiting officer. He finally rose to the rank of major.

In January 1959, while commanding A Squadron, Cooper was badly injured 'tree-jumping' into the jungle, and was suddenly withdrawn from Malaya and transferred to Oman.

In Oman in the late 1950s, A Squadron played a diversionary role during the attempt to reach the summit of Jebel Akhdar. Unfortunately, two men died and a third was seriously injured when a stray bullet struck a grenade in one of their bergens. Mopping-up operations followed before Cooper returned to the UK in December 1959. At the beginning of the following year, Cooper left 22 SAS to take up the post of company commander of the Omani Northern Frontier Regiment, then becoming second-in-command of the Muscat Regiment. However, Cooper was soon to be once again involved with the SAS.

In 1963, he was asked to lead a covert mission into the Yemen to gather intelligence on Egypt's involvement in the conflict as well as discover their order of battle, to give assistance to loyal forces of the deposed imam, and to provide medical services to the local tribes people. His mission in the Yemen was finally completed in 1966.

COP (CLOSE OBSERVATION PLATOON) Select units from the various regiments serving in Northern Ireland. Their purpose was to watch and observe known members of the IRA and other paramilitary organizations. Most of their duties lay in manning long-term observation sites, photographing movements and amassing basic intelligence. They did much of the donkey work required in many operations, providing extremely detailed reports on local suspects. COPs were normally tasked through the regional TCG (Tactical Control Group) to avoid friendly forces contact and to allow the security organization knowledge of the COP's activities. Many COPs produced high-grade information which would require SAS or mobile surveillance assistance. The SAS used the COPs as back-up troops during many operations in which shooting could be involved.

COPEMAN, PRIVATE RUSSEL — AUSTRALIAN SAS REGIMENT (SASR)

During one of SASR's operations in South Vietnam, on 17 January 1967, Private Russel Copeman was a member of a patrol commanded by Sergeant Norm Ferguson, inserted by helicopter northwest of Binh Ba. At 10:15 hours the following day, having previously located a small Vietcong (VC) camp occupied by four men and two women, the patrol spotted VC tracks and almost immediately afterwards came under fire. Private Copeman, who was the rear member of the patrol, was hit and severely wounded as the remainder returned the enemy fire. The patrol's signaller, Private John Matten, went to his aid and, under cover of smoke from a white phosphorous grenade and covering fire from the rest of the patrol, succeeded in carrying Copeman to safety once contact had been broken with the enemy.

Private Matten then sent a signal requesting assistance and extraction, but shortly afterwards the patrol heard the sounds of VC approaching, and moved off with haste. A helicopter then arrived with an escort of two gunships. While Private Copeman was being winched up, two VC appeared nearby but these were engaged by the helicopter's door gunner and Private Matten. More enemy approached but were engaged by Sergeant Ferguson, who was by then in the process of being winched up to the aircraft. With all of the patrol aboard, the helicopter headed direct to the military hospital at Vung Tau where emergency surgery was carried out on Private Copeman. He survived the operation but some three months later, on 10 April, died as a result of complications. He was the only member of the SASR to die from enemy action during operations in South Vietnam.

COUNTER REVOLUTIONARY WARFARE (CRW)

The Counter Revolutionary Warfare unit within the regiment can trace its origins back to the Keeni-Meeni operations in Aden in the 1960s. Not long after, the regiment formed its own CRW cell, with the specific purpose of developing techniques to counter terrorism. From its inception the CRW unit was indicative of how the modern-day SAS soldier was to develop.

No longer would they always fight in military uniform; CRW tasking called for civilian clothing and a variety of new covert weaponry. Surveillance and close-quarter battle were combined with high-speed driving, and the famous 'Killing House' was built.

As the Dhofar conflict in Oman came to an end, a new enemy emerged from the Middle East – the hijacker. With the rise of international terrorism, especially after the massacre of Israeli athletes at the Munich Olympic Games in 1972, the need for CRW skills was much in demand. The Western governments became so alarmed by the lack of any measures to control such extreme acts that they looked seriously at having skilled and armed anti-terrorist units specially available to handle these incidents. The British Government tasked the SAS to take on the role, and they formed CRW.

CRW very quickly analysed the problems, and their answers provided the basis for forming the anti-terrorist team and the Northern Ireland Cell. CRW was purely an ideas and training unit, although for individual jobs men from CRW could be called upon to offer advice on a situation, such as the Moluccan train hijack in 1977. So the CRW unit became an official and an important part of the regiment.

Today the duties of the SAS CRW unit span the world. They are able to infiltrate into enemy organizations, gather intelligence, carry out ambushes, undertake demolition work, and provide bodyguards for VIPs.

COUNTY MONAGHAN It is claimed that on 10 January 1975, members of 14 Intelligence and Security unit murdered John Francis Green at an isolated farmhouse. A four-man patrol reportedly crossed the border with the Irish Republic into County Monaghan and located the building in which Green was hiding. Two of the men, said to be SAS Major Tony Ball, the detachment commander, and Captain Robert Nairac, his second-in-command, shot Green at point blank range with their pistols. No evidence ever came to light and, as both men are now dead, it will be difficult to establish the truth other than the fact that Green was assassinated. The IRA ended its Christmas truce that year after blaming Green's death on the SAS.

COURTENAY RUBBER PLANTATION – SASR The Courtenay rubber plantation was located 1,500m (1,635yds) east of Route 2 and a short distance south of the northern border of Phuoc Tuy Province in South Vietnam. The area around the plantation was the scene of much activity by the Vietcong and, in turn, of patrolling SASR squadrons during their deployment in South Vietnam from 1965 to 1971. In late March 1969 an occupied Vietcong (VC) camp, containing a headquarters, hospital and a large cache of food, was located only 300m (327yds) south of the plantation by a 3 Squadron patrol under Sergeant Ned

Kelly. V Company of the 4th Battalion Royal Australian Regiment destroyed it on 27 March.

COVENTRY, MAJOR DUDLEY Coventry commanded a volunteer squadron of the Parachute Regiment, which in 1955 joined the SAS in Malaya. He later served with the Rhodesian SAS where he commanded C Squadron.

CQB (CLOSE QUARTER BATTLE) A method of fighting that the SAS have developed since the early 1960s. It has two forms, armed and unarmed. Armed CQB covers a wide range of pistol and sub-machine gun techniques. Weapon training starts from the very basics of pistol work and encompasses all the problems of movement and weapons stoppages – which can be caused by anything from an empty magazine to a double feed into the breach. It then progresses to more advanced techniques using automatic weaponry movement and fire off the ground, and the use of both primary and secondary weapons (sub-machine gun and pistol, for example).

CQB techniques in unarmed combat are fast and deadly. They include learning about the defensive and offensive parts of the body, and how best to use them and protect against them. Something as simple as a rolled up newspaper jabbed into the solar plexus can take an opponent down, as can a fist weighted with coins. In many cases the SAS are required to carry out a hard arrest, sometimes against an enemy known to be armed, and CQB provides the techniques by which this can be safely done.

CRATER DISTRICT The town of Crater, so named because it sat at the base of an extinct volcano, was a large settlement in Aden. In December 1967 rebellious locals took to the streets, killing several Europeans. At the time the SAS was stationed in Ballycastle House, near Khormaksar airport. A small group from G Squadron was hastily assembled and lifted by helicopter on to Jebel Shamsan, a high mountain that looked down over Crater. From a good position overlooking the town, the SAS were able to observe and report the rebel activities. Many of the butchered bodies had been laid out in the street, allowing mob traffic to run over them. The patrol remained in position until Lieutenant-Colonel Mitchell ('Mad Mitch') led the Argyll and Sutherland Highlanders into Crater where they retook the town.

CREDENHILL The name of a Hereford village and home to a disused RAF barracks which had previously been used as a training establishment for catering staff. The SAS has proposed that the regiment move to Credenhill, which offers much larger accommodation and facilities. The camp is currently undergoing renovation work.

CRETE On the night of 7 June 1942 three Special Boat Section (SBS) parties landed on Crete to destroy German aircraft at Kastelli, Timbaki and Maleme airfields. Unfortunately, only the assault on Kastelli was successful, with a total of seven aircraft being destroyed. The SBS was used because, at this time, they were partially included in the SAS.

Just one week later on 13/14 June, a further operation took place. A group of SAS men including Commandant Berge, Captain the Earl Jellicoe and three Free French non-commissioned officers, transported by submarine, landed with orders to attack the German airfield at Heraklion. On the same night other airfields at Derna, Benina, Berka, Barce and Martuba were also attacked, as part of a plan to support two convoys which were endeavouring to reach beleaguered Malta.

Commandant Berge and his party successfully destroyed 21 aircraft, although only Jellicoe and one other officer managed to escape from Crete, the others being killed or captured. Incredibly, despite valiant SAS efforts, German aircraft sunk 15 of the 17 ships in the convoy. The remaining two successfully reached Malta.

CROSS-BORDER SCOUTS During the war in Borneo, 1963–66, the SAS trained and led a force of Iban trackers against Indonesian troops and Communist guerrillas. Consisting of 40 specially selected Iban Dyaks, the unit was trained for cross-border operations into Indonesian Kalimantan. The British believed the Ibans would be highly skilled at moving quietly and efficiently through the jungle and, in the event that a mission was unsuccessful, the Ibans would be the most likely to escape alive. Under the supervision of Major John Edwardes of A Squadron, 22 SAS, training began in the summer of 1964. The Scouts' first mission was in August, following which they were employed along the border, especially in western Sarawak and around Bemban.

CROSSMAGLEN A British Army outpost in South Armagh near the border with the Irish Republic. On the evening of 15 April 1976, the IRA fired on a helicopter which was landing at the base. The SAS who had been operating in the surrounding countryside arrested an IRA suspect, Peter Cleary, at the home of his fiancée's sister, who lived at Tievecrum just north of the border. The house had been under observation for some time and, knowing that Cleary was soon to be married, it was just a matter of waiting. Once Cleary had been taken into captivity, the SAS patrol moved to a pick-up point in a nearby field and waited for their helicopter. During this time Cleary made to escape, and he was shot dead. Despite the claim by the SAS that Cleary grabbed at the rifle barrel of the soldier who was guarding him, and was shot while trying to escape, the media had a field-day alleging the SAS had arrived in the province with a 'shoot to kill' policy.

CROSS TRAINING Every SAS soldier is given the opportunity to train in several different personal or troop skills. He will already be skilled in at least one, such as medic, linguist, signaller or demolitions, as well as having troop skills like skiing, mountaineering, free-fall etc. It is not always easy to fit the right men with the right skills into a four-man patrol, and cross training ensures that an average patrol will possess a variety of abilities and experience that will help to ensure its survival in hostile conditions.

'CRUSADER', OPERATION A British operation in North Africa beginning on 17 November 1941. The operation was devised by General Sir Claude Auchinleck, Commander-in-Chief Middle East, to evict General Erwin Rommel, commander of the Afrika Korps, from Cyrenaica. 'Crusader' was the largest armoured operation undertaken by British forces at the time. The raids were also the first to be executed by the newly formed L Detachment, SAS, which attacked airfields at Tmimi and Gazala.

L Detachment was divided among five aircraft, provided by 216 Squadron, and were commanded by David Stirling, Paddy Mayne, Eoin McGonigal, Jock Lewes and Lieutenant Bonnington respectively. It was intended to drop the group by parachute on the night of 16/17 November. The men were then to wait for nightfall before packing their bombs into the aircraft stationed on the airfields, in a move to coincide with the start of the offensive.

L Detachment took off from Bagoush airfield on schedule, but navigation was hampered by strong winds and the aircraft encountered heavy flak. The drop was disastrous, with the men being scattered over a wide area on landing and several injuries being sustained – Stirling himself was knocked unconscious. The operation was abandoned as a result, individual soldiers having to make their own way to the rendezvous with the Long Range Desert Group (LRDG). Only 22 of the 64 men dropped made it successfully.

CS GRENADE *Specification* Delay: 1.5–3 seconds; Burn time: 10–40 seconds; Weight: 450g (1lb); CS content: 53g (2oz).

The CS grenade is a hand-thrown weapon used in circumstances where a rapid development of CS irritant is required. The metal canister has a ring-pull safety pin which holds a spring release lever. When this pin is pulled and the grenade thrown the lever flies off, allowing the percussion mechanism to operate the delay. Once fired the gas build-up is instantaneous.

CTR (CLOSE TARGET RECCE) This takes place once the patrol is near the target.

CULLINAN, MAJOR PAT – AUSTRALIAN SAS REGIMENT

(SASR) On 25 May 1988, together with a civilian named Paul Baynes, Major Pat Cullinan reached the summit of Mount Everest as a member of the Australian Bicentenary Everest Expedition, which had been mounted by the Australian Army Alpine Association and the Australian Alpine Climbing Club. Among the other members of the expedition were two former members of SASR, Majors Jim Truscott and Rick Moor, and a serving member of the regiment, Sergeant Norm Crookston. A keen mountaineer, Major Cullinan had earlier commanded a climbing troop in SASR. In 1980 he had led the first Australian expedition to climb in the Himalayas and a number of others, including one to Pakistan, where they made an ascent of Broad Peak, 7,950m (26,153ft). It was during the subsequent return descent of Broad Peak that Cullinan encountered an exhausted German climber in difficulties and kept him alive for 24 hours, at which point a rescue expedition arrived. Cullinan was subsequently awarded the Australian Star of Courage.

CUMPER, CAPTAIN WILLIAM, 'BILL'

A Royal Engineers Officer, and an expert in explosives. He trained the Free French in demolitions and was instrumental in acquiring small boats for the raids on German shipping. He accompanied David Stirling on the raid on Benghazi (see Raid on), on the North African coast, in September 1942 and took part in the attack on the Greek island of Simi in July 1944.

'CUNG CHUNG' II AND III, OPERATIONS, AUSTRALIAN SAS REGIMENT (SASR)

During the period August to September 1970, 1 Squadron SASR provided support for Operations 'Cung Chung' I and II in South Vietnam. These were carried out by the 7th Battalion Royal Australian Regiment (7 RAR), to deny the areas of the villages of Xuyen Moc, Dat Do and Lang Phuoc Hai to the Vietcong (VC). During the first week of September a patrol, under Sergeant John Ward, was deployed in the infantry role in support of a section of armoured personnel carriers (APCs) in the coastal area, on the border between the provinces of Phuoc Tuy and Binh Tuy. On 6 September it discovered a VC camp and on the following day located a bunker complex, both of which were subsequently destroyed. Two days later, the APCs having departed, the patrol took up an ambush position and on the following day ambushed three VC, killing two of them.

Thereafter, 7 RAR assumed responsibility for this task and one of its platoons was trained by 1 Squadron in a reconnaissance-ambush role. These operations proved very successful in denying the VC access to the villages and their populations. Captured documents subsequently showed that the enemy was suffering from a shortage of food and that constant interdiction of their courier routes was having an adverse effect on VC operations.

CURTIS, BRIGADIER ROD – AUSTRALIAN SAS REGIMENT

(SASR) Lieutenant-Colonel Rod Curtis assumed command of the SASR on 22 December 1979, succeeding Lieutenant-Colonel Reg Beesley. Commissioned into the Royal Australian Regiment from the Royal Military Academy Duntroon in December 1963, he served with the 4th Battalion (4 RAR) in Borneo, where he won the Military Cross. Thereafter he served with 9 RAR in South Vietnam as intelligence officer and company second-in-command. In 1972 he joined the SASR as a squadron commander before going to the United Kingdom in 1974 as an instructor. In 1976 he attended the Australian Army Staff College and subsequently was posted as Chief Instructor at the Royal Military College Duntroon.

On 22 December 1982, Lieutenant-Colonel Rod Curtis relinquished command of the SASR, handing over to Lieutenant-Colonel Chris Roberts.

CYPRUS In 1988 the SAS anti-terrorist team were sent to Cyprus where they prepared for an assault on a Boeing 737 airliner. The aircraft would be flying out of Lebanon into Libya, and in the course of its flight would be forced to land by Lightning fighters which were stationed at a British RAF base, where men of the SAS would attack it. The aircraft was carrying two British Lecturers who had previously been kidnapped. The 737 never flew, and after three weeks the plan was called off and the SAS returned to Hereford.

D

DAKOTA (DC-3) *Specification* Engines: 2 × Pratt & Whitney radial piston engines of 1,200hp; Wingspan: 28.96m (31.5yds); Height: 5.61m (6yds); Length: 19.66m (21yds); Weight: 7,650kg (7.5 tons); Speed: 371km/h (230 mph); Range: 3,862km (2,414 miles).

The British used a Douglas Dakota, which was the twin of its famous American counterpart, the DC-3. The DC-3 came into service in 1941 and is acclaimed as the first modern military transport, with over 10,000 being produced during World War II. It has a crew of three, but can be flown by a single pilot. Under the Lease-Lend programme, Britain received around 2,000, many which lasted until the early 1970s. The Dakota saw service with the SAS in 1943 when it parachuted men into Europe, and again in 1950 when it was used in Malaya. In the latter case the Dakotas were borrowed from the RAF Far East parachute school at Changi airfield, Singapore.

DAVIES, STAFF SERGEANT Joined the SAS from the Welsh Guards, passing Selection in 1966. He served most of his time with Mountain Troop, G Squadron. Together with Major Alastair Morrison he was sent to assist the German GSG9 during the 1977 Mogadishu hijack. He is also the author of this book.

DEANE-DRUMMOND, MAJOR-GENERAL TONY Served extensively in Italy and northern Europe during World War II and played a major part in the Arnhem operation in 1944, during which he was forced to hide in enemy territory for three days in a cupboard in a house to avoid capture.

In 1958 he took command of 22 SAS, and in that role he was instrumental in planning the capture of the Jebel Akhdar in Oman the following year. A patrol stormed the mountain in a night-time assault which secured victory over the rebels. Deane-Drummond was awarded the Distinguished Service Order for his part in the action.

'DEFOE', OPERATION An unsuccessful mission undertaken between 19 July and 23 August 1944 by Captain McGibbon-Lewis and 21 men of 2 SAS. The aim was a reconnaissance of the Argentan area of Normandy. On 15 August a Lieutenant Silly commanded a patrol of armoured cars, whilst McGibbon-Lewis and his group, using jeeps and a truck, patrolled the areas of Flers, Argentan and Falaise. Unfortunately, they were caught up in the battles around the Falaise Pocket, but managed to avoid injury and successfully returned to British lines by 18 August.

DE LA BILLIÈRE, GENERAL SIR PETER, MM   The man who, for most, epitomizes the perfect SAS soldier, was born in 1934 and educated at Harrow School. He originally joined the KSLI (King's Shropshire Light Infantry) in 1952 and served with the Durham Light Infantry before joining the SAS in 1955, as a captain in Malaya. A troop commander with D Squadron, he parachuted into the Telok Anson swamp and spent 20 days there in February 1958, making a significant contribution to the capture of the notorious terrorist Ah Hoi. Between December 1958 and January 1959, de la Billière also took part in the victorious assault on the Jebel Akhdar in Oman and was awarded the Military Medal for his actions. Staying in the Middle East, he spent the winter of 1963–64 on attachment with the Federal Regular Army in Aden, later in 1964 being promoted to major and being given the command of A Squadron in the Radfan. He devised and established a CQB (close quarter battle) course for the soldiers engaged in the Keeni-Meeni operations in the colony, as part of his continuing efforts on anti-terrorism.

In 1965 he, and A Squadron, were despatched to Borneo. Here he undertook a thorough re-organization of the SAS in an attempt to make the unit more efficient, most notably improving transportation to ensure that supplies were successfully delivered to the jungle patrols. Together with A Squadron, de la Billière undertook a three-week sweep of the area between the Bemban and Sempayang Rivers, working in conjunction with the Gurkhas on the cross-border 'Claret' raids. In addition, as we have come to expect from the SAS, he engaged on a series of lone reconnaissance expeditions into the jungle. In 1966 for his services he was awarded a bar to his Military Medal.

From 1972 to 1974 de la Billière held the position of commander of 22 SAS, before becoming Director of the SAS and Commander of the SAS Group in 1978, by which time he had a Distinguished Service Order to add to his Military Medal. He was the major force behind the transformation of the regiment into a crack counter-terrorist unit, and played a critical command role in the Iranian Embassy Siege in 1980.

By the time the Falklands War began in 1982, he had been promoted to brigadier and was instrumental in the decision to include the SAS in the Task Force, convinced, rightly so, that they were ideally suited to the campaign.

In October 1990 de la Billière commanded 45,000 men and women of the British Forces during the Gulf War, as part of the United Nations contingent against Iraq. By now fluent in Arabic, and with 15 years experience of the Arabian Gulf, he earned himself enormous respect, both for his diplomacy and his ability to work closely and effectively with both his Arab allies and General Norman Schwarzkopf, Commander of the Allied Ground Forces. It was de la Billière who convinced Schwarzkopf to employ the SAS to operate behind enemy lines, and the outstanding success of the ground offensive in February 1991 was largely due to this partnership. When he returned to the UK, de la Billière was awarded a knighthood, CBE and promoted to full general. He retired from active service in June 1992.

DELGADO, SERGEANT VERN – AUSTRALIAN SAS REGIMENT (SASR) In mid-October 1968 a patrol of 2 Squadron SASR was operating in the north-east of Phuoc Tuy Province in South Vietnam. On the evening of 16 October, while eating their evening meal, its members spotted five Vietcong (VC) moving towards their position, following the patrol's tracks. These were engaged and three VC were killed, Corporal Ron Harris noting at the time that one of the enemy was of European appearance. As dusk fell, the patrol withdrew and, having failed to establish communications with the squadron base to request extraction, moved to an LUP (lying-up position) on an island in a lake. A Claymore mine was set up to cover the most likely avenue of approach by the enemy while repeated efforts were made to make contact with 2 Squadron. These were eventually successful just before dawn on the following day, and the patrol was extracted shortly afterwards.

DELTA FORCE The US counter-terrorist unit raised by Colonel Charles Beckwith in 1977. This elite and secretive force is modelled on the SAS, with similar Selection procedures, training, and also a close quarter battle wing called the 'house of horrors'. They are stationed in the old stockade (jail) in the Special Forces base at Fort Bragg, North Carolina. Delta also undertake exchange training with the SAS, the French GIGN and the German GSG9. It is made up of two operational squadrons and tends to involve itself with incidents outside the US but which affect US interests. In 1980 it took part in Operation 'Eagle Claw', the failed attempt to rescue American hostages held in Iran. They have also been involved in action in Panama (1983), Grenada (1989) and the Gulf War (1991).

DELTA PROJECT A training programme under which Detachment B-52 of the US 5th Special Forces Group (Airborne) trained South Vietnamese Special Forces (LLDB) and irregular troops in strategic Long Range Reconnaissance Patrol (LRRP) operations. Delta missions included the gathering of strategic intelligence in enemy-controlled areas, hunter-killer missions, direction of air strikes on to Vietcong (VC) or North Vietnamese Army (NVA) bases, rescue and recovery of downed Allied aircrew or PoWs, wiretapping of VC or NVA communications, deception and disinformation missions, and psychological warfare operations.

Delta comprised 450 men organized in twelve reconnaissance/hunter-killer teams, each comprising six Vietnamese LLDB and two US Green Berets, six 'Roadrunner' teams of Vietnamese dressed and equipped as VC or NVA, a security company and a Ranger battalion which acted as a rapid-reaction force. In addition, it possessed its own dedicated aviation support in the form of the 281st Helicopter Assault Company and forward air controllers from the US Air Force and US Marine Corps. The headquarters element was provided by Detachment B-52.

Headquarters Military Assistance Command Vietnam (MACV) was keen that the Special Forces should benefit from Australian SAS (SASR) experience and expertise. In July the Deputy Commander of the 5th Special Forces Group visited 3 Squadron SASR, commanded by Major John Murphy, with a view to obtaining some SAS instructors for the Delta training camp at Nha Trang. Major Murphy was unable to grant the Americans' request but agreed to an exchange programme, which was subsequently approved officially. On 15 August 1966 six members of 3 Squadron SASR joined the Delta team as instructors for six weeks, while six Green Berets were attached to the squadron during the same period.

DELVES, MAJOR CEDRIC Commanded D Squadron in the Falklands War in 1982. He was responsible for accepting the Argentinian surrender on South Georgia, and other SAS missions such as leading the raid on Pebble Island airstrip. He was awarded the Distinguished Service Order for his actions.

DEMOLITIONS WING The SAS Demolition Course is perhaps the most interesting one of all, with several different courses teaching all aspects from the basics to planning for a full target attack. The basic four-week course combines theory with practical demonstrations, and covers a wide range of skills. The practical work progresses slowly from the fundamental rules of handling explosives, to actually making the home-made explosives. This course also includes many excursions to such strategic targets as oil refineries, railway stations, and telephone exchanges.

In any major conflict, demolitions will play a large part. Industrialized nations rely on centres producing war materials to sustain their front line troops, and destroying these installations will help defeat the enemy. But every target offers a different problem for the demolitions team, as do the circumstances governing the attack; for example, in most cases the target will be heavily guarded. The aim of the SAS demolition course is to teach the men how to overcome obstacles and achieve their objective using the minimum amount of effort, and to place the explosive where it will do the most damage.

DEMPSEY, GENERAL SIR MILES Very successful World War II British general who commanded XII Corps. Dempsey worked with the SAS in Sicily and Italy and expressed great admiration for their abilities. In his farewell speech he listed six reasons for the success of the unit: good training, fair discipline, physical fitness, the men's confidence in their abilities, careful planning, and the right spirit. In praise of the SAS he said, 'In all my military career, and in my time I have commanded many units, I have never yet met a unit in which I had such confidence as I have in yours. And I mean that!'

DENBURY, LANCE-CORPORAL DAVID 'SHUG', MM Joined the SAS in February 1989 from 9 Parachute Squadron of the Royal Engineers. During the Gulf War he was a motorbike outrider with one of A Squadron's fighting columns. On 21 February 1991 the column were carrying out a demolition task at the side of a MSR (main supply route). As they were busy placing their explosives, two Iraqi trucks carrying missiles drove straight past them. The SAS chased the fleeing Iraqis, with the bikes racing ahead trying to cut them off. Once the Iraqi vehicles had been stopped, 'Shug' Denbury dumped his bike and ran forward to engage the soldiers. At this time he was fatally hit and died from his wounds. He was awarded a posthumous Military Medal. Prior to the Gulf War, Denbury had also served in Northern Ireland where he was awarded the Queen's Gallantry medal.

DENEHEY, LANCE-CORPORAL PAUL – AUSTRALIAN SAS REGIMENT (SASR) A member of a 1 Squadron SASR patrol, commanded by Sergeant Roy Weir, which was inserted on 24 May 1965 by helicopter into a landing-zone (LZ) on the border between the Malaysian state of Sabah and Indonesian Kalimantan, some 35km (21 miles) southeast of Pensiangan. Its cross-border reconnaissance task, carried out under the auspices of Operation 'Claret', was to discover whether Indonesian forces were moving between Labuk, located in Indonesia on the Sembatung River, and Sabah to the north.

On the afternoon of 2 June the patrol was attacked by a large rogue elephant which, despite being hit repeatedly by fire from Lance-Corporal Stephen Bloomfield, the patrols medic, and Sergeant Weir, caught Lance-Corporal Denehey and gored him very severely in the left side before disappearing from sight. Lance-Corporal Bloomfield applied emergency medical treatment and the patrol attempted unsuccessfully to contact the 1 Squadron base in Brunei by radio to request extraction.

Sergeant Weir, assuming that the messages had not been received, set off for the border with Corporal Bryan Littler to summon assistance, leaving Lance-Corporal Bloomfield to look after Lance-Corporal Denehey. Two days later they reached the LZ and shortly afterwards made contact with a helicopter with their **SARBE** beacon/radio. At 15:00 hours another aircraft extracted them and flew them to an LZ nearer to where they had left Bloomfield and Denehey. There they met another 1 Squadron patrol, under Sergeant Chris Pope, and ten **Gurkhas** from the 2nd Battalion, 7th Duke of Edinburgh's Own (DEO) Gurkha Rifles. It took two days to reach the location of Lance-Corporal Denehey who was found dead, having succumbed to his wounds. He was also alone as, after two days of waiting for Sergeant Weir to return with help and having given Denehey the last of his morphia, Lance-Corporal Bloomfield had also gone for assistance.

DEPONT TRAIN INCIDENT A train travelling between Assen and Groningen in Holland was hijacked by nine Moluccan terrorists on 23 May 1977, and 51 hostages were taken. At the same time 110 hostages, mostly children, were seized at an elementary school at Bovensmilde – although 106 were released a few days later with a stomach virus. The stand-off lasted for three weeks until the psychiatrist who was conducting negotiations on behalf of the Dutch Government disclosed his concern that the terrorists were about to start killing the hostages.

The Royal Dutch Marines Close Combat Unit, working in five-man teams, prepared to storm the train at 04:53. SAS advisors were in close contact throughout the hijack and recommended the use of stun grenades, but the Dutch decided against this form of action, preferring instead to instigate the assault under the distraction of six F104 Starfighters flying low over the train. Six of the terrorists were killed and three surrendered in the attack. Two hostages, who panicked when the firing began, were killed. One other hostage was also shot, though not fatally.

In a simultaneous assault on the school the results were much better. Three of the four terrorists were caught unawares, asleep in their underwear, when the Marines broke through the school wall with an armoured vehicle. All four terrorists were captured and the hostages safely released.

DERNA The location of an Axis airfield complex in North Africa – one of a number that were raided by the SAS on the night of 13 June 1942. The party for Derna consisted of Captain Buck, Lieutenant Jordan, Free French volunteers and a number of Special Interrogation Group personnel (Jewish immigrants to Palestine who spoke fluent German and dressed in German uniforms), as well as one ex-Afrika Korps soldier called Brueckner who had been recruited by Buck. Transportation consisted of four German trucks driven by the Jewish volunteers. For the attack on the airfield, Jordan and Corporal Bourmont set off with four men each, travelling in a single truck driven by Brueckner. However, the latter betrayed the SAS men and the truck was duly surrounded by German soldiers. Following a brief battle only Buck, Jordan and two others made it back to the rendezvous with the Long Range Desert Group (LRDG).

'DERRI' HUNT   The word 'derri' is short for derelict. Some of the SAS patrols in South Armagh would be tasked to check out, or use for observation posts (OPs), some of the disused houses scattered around the border area. In some cases these houses had been left abandoned, but partly furnished. For a short while members would liberate derelict items such as old brass fittings and small pieces of furniture. Restoring these to good order served to fill the boredom when confined to Bessbrook Mill between operations.

'DERRY', OPERATION   A very successful mission conducted between 5 and 18 August 1944, by 89 men of 3 French Parachute Battalion (3 SAS). Led by Commandant Conan, the group was dropped by parachute into the Finistère area of Brittany. The plan was to suppress the German advance on Brest, and prevent the destruction of the viaducts at Morlaix and Plougastel. The mission was successful and enormous damage and injury was inflicted on the enemy.

DESERT FIGHTING COLUMNS   The desert columns were formed by the SAS during the 1990–91 Gulf War and were designed to infiltrate deep into Iraqi territory to carry out search and destroy missions. The firepower carried was enough to ensure that they could destroy just about anything they could find. This strategy was employed to force the Iraqis to deploy large forces in order to locate them. Each squadron was divided up into two mobile fighting columns, training for which had been carried out in the United Arab Emirates. In each column a Unimog, a Mercedes-made short-wheel based open truck ideal for cross-country work, was used as the mother vehicle. This would carry the bulk of the extra stores, rations, fuel, ammunition for several types of gun, NBC (Nuclear, Biological and Chemical) equipment and spares. The fighting vehicles in each column consisted of between eight and twelve type 110 Land Rovers, each of which was armed with a Browning .50 heavy machine gun. Additional weapons included GPMGs, American Mark 19 40mm grenade launchers and Milan anti-tank missiles. The latter, excellent for night operations, was fitted with thermal imaging sights and could be used at ranges of up to 8km (5 miles).

The desert columns had great success, none more so than when they operated totally at night, preferring to lay-up during the day to avoid detection. All the SAS columns stayed inside Iraq for the full duration of the war. At one point a maintenance column of several 4-ton trucks rendezvoused with the columns in order to carry out running repairs and re-supply ammunition etc.

DETACHMENT The 'detachment' or 'Det' was another name for 14 Intelligence and Security Unit.

DETONATING CORD A plastic coated cord filled with PETN or RDX explosive, which is used to transfer detonations from an initiation point to a single or multiple set of explosive charges. Type two (military specification), which contains 40 to 42 grams of PETN per metre, has a detonation velocity of 6,500m (7,085yds) per second.

DEVLIN, BERNADETTE In 1981 the SAS mounted an operation against the Ulster Defence Association (UDA) when it was discovered that they intended to kill the Republican activist and former MP, Bernadette McAliskey (née Devlin). Intelligence indicated that the UDA planned to kill McAliskey, together with her husband Michael, at their isolated farmhouse near Coalisland on 6 January. The SAS put the house under observation, but the nearest they could conceal themselves was some 200m (218yds) from the building. When the three gunmen arrived by car, they did so at speed, driving directly to the house. The SAS team responded immediately, but by the time they reached the house, the UDA had smashed the door in and shots were heard. The gunmen were arrested as they made their escape, and on checking inside the house the soldiers found Michael McAliskey bleeding from a severed artery and in a grave condition. Bernadette, although shot several times, was not so critical. The SAS medic kept them both alive until an ambulance arrived. The McAliskeys survived and the three UDA gunmen were sentenced to between fifteen years and life imprisonment.

'DEVON', OPERATION Following its operation at Bagnara, in southern Italy in September 1943 the Special Raiding Squadron (SRS), commanded by Paddy Mayne, was tasked with the capture of Termoli to aid the Eighth Army's breaking of the German Termoli Line north of Bari. The SRS was part of a combined force comprising two commandos and various support units. The 207-strong SRS sailed from Monfredonia in a large landing craft on 2 October, and arrived off Termoli the following morning. After No. 3 Commando had seized the beach, the SRS went in smaller landing craft.

The Germans were occupying the surrounding countryside, and very soon a series of small battles developed. Paddy Mayne pulled his men back into the town that evening, by which time Roy Farran and twenty soldiers from 2 SAS had also arrived at Termoli.

The next day was quiet, with troops from the 78th Division arriving and the two commandos taking their leave. It was the lull before the storm, for on 5 October the Germans launched a strong counter-attack. Mayne and his men plugged the gaps in the line as the enemy tried to retake Termoli. During the savage battle that ensued, a shell hit an SAS lorry, killing eighteen men. The fighting, which went on through the night and into the following day, was particularly heavy around the cemetery and beside the railway line.

The landing of the Irish Brigade in the harbour tipped the scales in favour of the British, and the town was eventually secured. It was a sobering experience for the SRS, and turned out to be the unit's last action in Italy.

DHOFAR A region in the west of Oman. The Dhofaris, most of whom live on the high ground of the Jebel Dhofar, are a proud and independent people, with a culture different from the surrounding Arabs and Baluchis. Their repression by the Sultan of Oman, Said bin Taimur, caused much resentment which turned into open rebellion in 1962, and resulted in the formation of the Dhofar Liberation Front (DLF). When the SAS became involved in the conflict in 1970, after Said had been deposed by his son Qaboos, they embarked upon a 'hearts and minds' campaign to win back the Dhofaris to the cause of the new ruler.

DHOFAR DEFENSIVE LINES During the Dhofar campaign of 1970–76 in the Sultanate of Oman, a series of five fortified defensive lines or barriers were established to provide protection for the areas under government control as they expanded. They comprised barbed wire fences and minefields with defended bases from which units of the Sultan's Armed Forces (SAF) units could operate, patrolling the areas around them.

The most prominent and effective of these was the Hornbeam Line which stretched from Mugsayl on the coast 64km (40 miles) inland to Oven which was its northernmost end. A defensive position was sited every 1,800m (2,000yds) on high ground, being linked to others by a barbed wire fence and minefields. Others included the Demavend Line which was completed in April 1975, and was manned by Iranian Special Forces units, the first battalion of which had arrived in early 1973, with the remainder following in December of that year. The Leopard Line stretched from above the Jebel Khaftawt down to Windy Ridge with three defensive positions positioned throughout its length; it was withdrawn in mid-1972 because of SAF inability to keep it supplied during the monsoon. The Hammer Line was established during 1974 on the Jebel Khaftawt as a 'long stop' in support of the Hornbeam Line, occupying similar positions to the Leopard Line. The Simba Line, manned by a regular battalion and a Firqat, was located at Sarfait on the border with the People's Democratic Republic of Yemen; it had been established with the aim of cutting off enemy supply routes but achieved only limited success as it was overlooked by hills of which the guerrilla supply convoys took good advantage.

DHOFAR LIBERATION FRONT The Dhofar Liberation Front (DLF) was formed in response to the repressive and traditionalist measures imposed on the Dhofari people by the Sultan of Oman, Said bin Taimur. They wanted the province to be modernized with a greater independence and so organized themselves into a fighting force. However, although some of the soldiers had fought with other Arab armies, they were, in the main, poorly armed and equipped. In neighbouring Yemen, another rebel group, the People's Front for the Liberation of the Occupied Arabian Gulf (PFLOAG) were faring a little better. As Communists, they were supplied by the Chinese and Soviet Union and were considerably better equipped. PFLOAG made an offer to the DLF to amalgamate and share their fight.

After much discussion, the DLF agreed to PFLOAG's offer, but this decision ultimately worked against them. PFLOAG was a dominant and ruthless organization and had soon spread its influence very widely throughout the Jebel Dhofar, controlling the tribes-people with threats. The proud Dhofaris resented the arrogance and dominance of PFLOAG and soon began to fight back. PFLOAG ordered their disarmament which in turn led to many battles between the two organizations.

The SAS exploited the split even more with its 'hearts and minds' policy, persuading many of the erstwhile Dhofari guerrillas to surrender to the government, now under the rule of Sultan Qaboos, the son of Said bin Taimur. Many of these Dhofaris then joined the Firqat troops, trained and commanded by the SAS under the cover name of the British Army Training Team (BATT).

'DIANAS' Name given to a series of SAS defensive positions situated along the southern edge of the Jebel Massive in Oman, 1973–75. Five 'Dianas' were formed and designed to keep the rebels from bringing long-range weapons to the lip of the Jebel, from where they could observe and fire down on the RAF base and nearby town of Salala. The 'Dianas' came under constant attack and were heavily defended by mainly SAS personnel.

'DICE', OPERATION During November 1979 an operation was mounted to counter the threat of a major invasion of Rhodesia by Russian and Cuban-trained ZIPRA conventional forces, numbering up to 25,000 men. These had already been preceded by 3,000 guerrillas who had crossed the border from Zambia and were waiting to link up with motorized infantry units which would cross the Zambesi River with air support from Russian-supplied MiG fighters. Rhodesian 1st SAS Regiment (RhSAS) was given the task of blowing a number of bridges along routes to be used by the ZIPRA main force units, which would travel south to concentrate at an assembly point some 50km (31 miles) to the northeast of the Zambian capital Lusaka. In the meantime, other units would be deployed to stop any further crossings of the border by ZIPRA guerrillas.

On 16 November B Squadron, commanded by Captain Colin Willis, was inserted by helicopter into Zambian territory where it attacked three road bridges 30km (18 miles) to the west of the town of Chirundu. While the three demolitions teams, under Captain Willis and Lieutenants Mike Rich and Pete Cole, went about their tasks, a protection party under Colour Sergeant Nick Breytenbach, sited on mountains overlooking the road from Chirundu and equipped with two 20mm cannon and a 60mm mortar, engaged Zambian army units. These were kept at bay until after the bridges were blown and the demolition teams had withdrawn south for extraction, after which Colour Sergeant Breytenbach and his men were also extracted by helicopter.

On 18 November B Squadron was deployed again, this time for an attack on a bridge on the Great North Road, 70km (43 miles) south of Lusaka. However, on arrival the target was found to be heavily guarded by Zambian troops and so a larger bridge over the Kaleya River, 20km (12 miles) further north and unguarded, was selected by Captain Willis instead. Having completed the laying of charges within twenty minutes, the squadron withdrew and shortly afterwards the bridge was blown and completely demolished. Commandeering a truck, Captain Willis and his men made good their escape, and having reached a location some 60km (37 miles) south of the bridge, were extracted by helicopter.

On 19 November 1979, C Squadron, commanded by Captain Bob McKenna, attacked a pair of road and rail bridges 150km (93 miles) east of Lusaka. A force of twenty was inserted and shortly afterwards came under fire from Zambian police units which were dealt with by two Royal Rhodesian Air Force (RRAF) Cessna 337 Lynx ground attack aircraft circling above the area. In front of a large crowd of onlookers, the demolitions team placed its charges and shortly afterwards both bridges were blown, the destruction of the rail bridge severing the link with Tanzania. Three hours after being inserted, the squadron was extracted and was heading back to its base.

Meanwhile, B Squadron was attacking a road bridge over the Chongwe River, some 35km (21 miles) from Lusaka. While the demolitions team placed their charges, a 20mm cannon crew under Colour Sergeant Nick Breytenbach opened fire on a nearby Zambian army camp while the rest of the squadron established a roadblock and engaged a platoon of troops in the vicinity of the bridge. Thirty minutes later, when the squadron had landed at its target, the bridge was blown.

The following day, 20 November, an A Squadron patrol under Lieutenant Dale Scott carried out an attack on two bridges with the help of a patrol from the Rhodesian Light Infantry (RLI). Both were successfully blown and shortly afterwards the RhSAS patrol ambushed a vehicle carrying eighteen armed men, ten of whom were killed. A road bridge over the Lufua River was also blown on the same day by the SAS, bringing the total to ten.

Operation 'Dice' was entirely successful. It not only prevented ZIPRA concentrating its forces at the assembly area, which was bombed by the RRAF, but also put further pressure on Zambia by cutting its road and rail links with Tanzania and Malawi, whilst also preventing shipment of its exports to the Mozambique port of Beira. This had the desired effect of prompting President Kenneth Kaunda to pressure the ZIPRA leader Joshua Nkomo into continuing to participate in the Lancaster House talks in London rather than attempting to invade Rhodesia.

'DINGO', OPERATION A two-phase attack on two huge ZANLA bases at Chimoio and Tembue, 90 and 225km (55 and 139 miles) respectively inside Mozambique. The base at Chimoio was enormous, comprising thirteen camps holding 9,000 guerrillas, and was ZANLA's headquarters and main base in Mozambique. It was thus well equipped with strong defences organized around trench systems and bunkers, and including well-sited 12.7mm and 13.7mm anti-aircraft machine guns. The base at Tembue, located northeast of Lake Caborra Bassa, was smaller and consisted of two camps accommodating 4,000 guerrillas.

Operation 'Dingo' was launched on 23 November 1977. At 05:00 hours ten troop carrier helicopters, carrying 40 men of the Rhodesian Light Infantry (RLI), took off from the Royal Rhodesian Air Force (RRAF) air base at New Sarum. K-Car Alouette gunships and a command helicopter flown by Group Captain Walsh with the commander of C Squadron Rhodesian SAS (RhSAS), Major Brian Robinson, accompanied them. They were subsequently followed by six Dakotas carrying 97 members of C Squadron and 48 paratroopers of the RLI. After these came eight Hawker Hunters, six Vampires, three Canberra bombers and twelve Cessna 337 Lynx ground attack aircraft.

Having landed briefly at a forward refuelling point at Lake Alexander, just inside the Rhodesian border, the helicopters flew on into Mozambique. By the time they arrived at Chimoio, the Canberras had dropped their bombs and shortly afterwards the Hunters and K-Car gunships commenced their air strikes. At the same time, the six Dakotas dropped their RhSAS and RLI parachutists who went into action immediately after landing. Heavy fire was coming from the ZANLA defensive positions and all aircraft were hit, including Major Robinson's command helicopter.

The battle continued throughout the day with the RhSAS and RLI having to fight their way through the five main camps within the complex. That night fighting died down and on the following morning the assault force carried out another sweep, clearing the camps of terrorists, collecting a large amount of documents and destroying weapons and equipment. During the afternoon the entire force was extracted by helicopter, firstly to the forward support base and then subsequently, via the refuelling point at Lake Alexander, back into Rhodesia. That night was spent in preparations for the second phase of the operation: the attack on Tembue.

Before dawn on the following day, the force was in the air once more. The helicopter-borne element flew to a forward support base, located on a mountain south of Lake Caborra Bassa, to refuel before heading for Tembue. The parachutists once again took off from Salisbury in their Dakotas and flew direct to the objective, accompanied once again by the Canberras, Hunters and Lynx. As the air strikes commenced, C Squadron and the RLI paratroopers dropped to join the helicopter-borne troops who were already on the ground and in action. Having established a cordon, the force swept through both camps, flushing out the terrorists who attempted to flee. During the battle, three members of C Squadron killed 86 enemy in a particularly fierce engagement lasting only three minutes.

The fighting had died down by dusk and the helicopters started to extract the force back to Rhodesia, with the exception of Captain Bob McKenna and some of C Squadron who were extracted early on the following morning. Operation 'Dingo' had been a brilliant success. Over 2,000 enemy had been killed, both bases and large amounts of weapons destroyed, and a considerable amount of documentation on ZANLA's operations captured.

'DINGSON', OPERATION One hundred and sixty men of 4 French Parachute Battalion (4 SAS), and with four jeeps, landed by parachute in the Vannes area of Brittany on 6 June 1944, where they established the 'Dingson' base. Once established, they took over the organization of the local Resistance Maquis and began to investigate how to interrupt the movements of enemy forces. By 18 June, the leader of the SAS party, Commandant Bourgoin, had a company of gendarmes and three fully equipped battalions of Resistance fighters. Unfortunately, however, these men had little or no military training and were quickly dispersed when the base was attacked by the Germans later that day. Around 40 SAS men managed to escape with no loss of life and a new base was quickly established near Pontivy, code-named 'Grog'.

'DINKY', OPERATION In April 1979 an operation was mounted by the Rhodesians to destroy the Kazangula Ferry which, apart from the railway, was Zambia's only link with countries to the south. Operating between Kazangula in Zambia and Botswana, it carried passengers and freight. The Rhodesians were aware that ZIPRA, despite having been refused permission previously by Zambia, had been using the ferry for transportation of terrorists from Zambia to Botswana, from where they travelled by road to Matabeleland. Rhodesian Special Branch had learned that ZIPRA was using the ferry to move weapons and mines concealed in 200-litre (44 gallon) fuel drums, which were unloaded and cached in Botswana. The caches were found and emptied by the Rhodesians so ZIPRA, believing they had been discovered by the Botswana security forces, switched to using trucks which travelled regularly on the ferry and were fitted with secret compartments beneath their floors. Further evidence had also been collected by patrols of Rhodesian 1st SAS Regiment (RhSAS), the Selous Scouts and other Rhodesian units, which had kept the ferry under surveillance from covert observation posts (OPs).

After lengthy deliberation, Combined Operations Headquarters decided to destroy the ferry, and the task was allocated to B Squadron 1st RhSAS, commanded by Captain Colin Willis, who had already drawn up plans for such an operation. At 20:00 hours on 12 April, twelve men led by Captain Pete Fritz moved from a forward base near Victoria Falls to the border with Botswana. Leaving four men with the vehicles, the remainder set off along the border and crossed over from Rhodesia into Botswana where Lieutenant Laurie Walters and two NCOs established a command post. Captain Fritz and four men moved to the ferry slipway, which was some 130m (141yds) away, and planted a 110kg (53lbs) charge of Pentolite explosive below the surface of the water. This was positioned so as to blast up through the bottom of the ferry when initiated, after the vessel was in position on the slipway. Connected to its detonators by cable was a command-activated radio receiver, which was concealed nearby.

Captain Fritz and his men returned to the command post and prepared the radio transmitter for initiation of the explosive charge once the ferry had berthed on the slipway. At 10:00 hours they heard the sound of the ferry, which was on the Zambian side, as it crossed towards Botswana. Minutes later it came into view and shortly afterwards slid into position on the slipway. Waiting until its passengers and vehicles had disembarked, Captain Fritz gave the command to fire. Lieutenant Laurie Walters pressed the transmit button and seconds later the charge exploded, blowing the ferry in half. This was followed by another small explosion, as the radio receiver exploded on command from another signal transmitted by Lieutenant Walters, destroying all evidence of its existence.

DONNE HOLDINGS Headed by Major (retired) Freddie Mace, a former officer in the British Army's Intelligence Corps, Donne Holdings was a London-based security consultancy. In 1977 the company was contracted by the Libyan Government to provide training for bodyguard teams for Colonel Muammar Ghaddafi. Instructors were initially recruited from former members of 21 SAS and thereafter from former 22 SAS personnel. The contract was carried out with the knowledge of the British Government, with Mace liaising regularly with the relevant desk of the Secret Intelligence Service, and Headquarters SAS Group, which was kept informed by the former SAS personnel employed by the company.

'DOOMSDAY', OPERATION   A large group of SAS soldiers undertook this mission to disarm German troops stationed in Norway at the end of World War II.

'DOUBLE TAP'   A technique by which two shots are fired, from a handgun, in quick succession. This used to be considered, particularly for counter-terrorist or hostage rescue scenarios, the most effective way to kill a hostile. It has since been recognized, however, that two shots are not always enough to stop an attacker, particularly if he has access to a remote detonation device. Current teachings advocate the use of sustained and accurate firepower from a high-power handgun, which can discharge 13 rounds in less than three seconds – more than enough to stop a terrorist getting close to a weapon or detonating device.

'DRIFTWOOD', OPERATION   Part of Operation 'Maple' in January 1944, involving a series of unsuccessful attacks on the Urbino-Fabriano and Ancona-Rimini railway lines in northern and central Italy. Two four-man teams from 2 SAS, led by Captain Gunston, were commanded to undertake the operation, and yet not one of the parties reached the sea evacuation point; the soldiers were last seen attempting to make their escape by rowing boat on 7 March. Since they never returned to base it can only be assumed that either they sank or were captured and shot.

DRUCE, CAPTAIN HENRY   Also nicknamed the 'Drake' and 'Docker', Druce joined 2 SAS late in World War II and led a reconnaissance party into eastern France in August 1944 to prepare the way for Operation 'Loyton'. In the early part of the war, he had been in Belgium and Holland (he was fluent in Flemish), undertaking secret missions on behalf of MI6. Following the arrival of the main force on 1 September, he took part in numerous raids before breaking through enemy lines with valuable captured documents. Druce later took part in Operation 'Keystone', tasked with disrupting enemy movements south of the Ijsselmeer in Holland, leading a force of ten armoured jeeps.

DRUMMAKAVAL   Seamus Harvey, a twenty-year-old farm labourer from Drummakaval in Northern Ireland was an IRA operative killed by the

SAS on 16 January 1977. Intelligence had been received which indicated that a car parked at Culderry near Armagh was to be used by the IRA on an operation. Acting on this, an SAS patrol hid itself in nearby undergrowth in order to observe any activity. In the afternoon a man appeared dressed in military-style clothing and carrying a sawn-off shotgun. Two of the SAS stood up and made the move to arrest him, but were met with a hail of bullets from other IRA men who had been covering Harvey's approach. In the ensuing firefight Harvey was killed, hit by 11 SAS bullets and two from his own men.

DRUMNAKILLY   The location of an SAS ambush in Northern Ireland on 30 August 1988, which resulted in the death of three members of the IRA's Mid-Tyrone Brigade. Martin and Gerard Harte and Brian Mullan were suspected of committing over 32 murders, but none had ever been proved and the three men remained at large. Intelligence showed their next target to be a retired officer of the Ulster Defence Regiment (UDR), working in the bandit country around Omagh. Troops had also uncovered a dump nearby which, it was believed, was the cache of personal weapons belonging to Mullan and the Hartes.

An observation post (OP) was set up to watch the weapons cache for any activity and the UDR officer was given a Leyland truck with an armoured cab, and advised to establish a predictable daily route on his way to and from work, along a quiet country road. The plan was to spur the terrorists into recovering their weapons, thereby indicating to the SAS when they intended to strike. The UDR man was to be substituted by an SAS man and the truck designed to 'break down' in a designated place, thus setting the ambush.

However, before any of this could take place, the Mid-Tyrone Brigade attacked another target. On the afternoon of 20 August 1988, a bomb was exploded in a small trailer parked by the side of the road just as a bus carrying soldiers of the 1st Battalion Light Infantry was returning to the Omagh Barracks. Twenty-two kilos (48lbs) of Semtex threw the bus into the air, killing eight soldiers, injuring twenty-seven others and creating a 2m (6ft) deep crater in the road. This victory for the IRA, however, was to be short-lived.

Nine days later the OP at the weapons cache saw the terrorists approach to collect their weapons. This message was relayed immediately, assuming that the Mid-Tyrone Brigade was planning the murder of the UDR man the next morning. Shortly before dawn, three SAS soldiers set out on foot to the location of the planned ambush, a deserted farm just outside the village of Drumnakilly, where they hid and waited. Another SAS soldier, dressed in the UDR man's overalls, began the drive along the route until the truck 'broke down' near to the farmhouse, when the soldier got out to try and 'mend' it. Unbelievably, it took six hours for the news to reach the terrorists, who eventually turned up in a stolen car, but not the one that had been expected. The SAS driver masquerading as the UDR man was caught unprotected as the terrorists, dressed in the standard uniform of blue boiler suits and black balaclavas, began to fire at him. He managed to use a brick gatepost as cover, which allowed the other SAS soldiers a clear view of the terrorists. Seeing their target hide behind the gatepost, the terrorists got out of their vehicle to complete their task but were killed outright by unrelenting firepower from the SAS soldiers in their hide-outs. The successful operation was completed when a Lynx helicopter arrived to return the soldiers to their base, within minutes of the shooting, even before the press arrived. The whole exercise was deemed a great success for both the SAS and the Security Services in Northern Ireland.

'DUCK', OPERATION AUSTRALIAN SAS REGIMENT (SASR)

On 14 December 1966, five patrols of 3 Squadron SASR were inserted into the area north of Nui Thi Vai and Nui Dinh, in the western part of South Vietnam's Phuoc Tuy Province. They were deployed in support of Operation 'Duck' which was being carried out by the 6th Battalion Royal Australian Regiment (6 RAR) to clear Highway 15, the coastal road heading north west from the provincial capital of Baria to Bien Hoa Province. A considerable number of Vietcong (VC) were sighted and several contacts took place during this operation.

On 18 December Sergeant Jock Thorburn's patrol located an enemy base camp in a cave near Nui Toc Tien and killed four VC in the ensuing firefight, withdrawing on the approach of a further force of VC. On 20 December a patrol under Lance-Corporal Reg Causton spotted nine heavily armed VC, while Sergeant Des Kennedy and his patrol saw some 50 VC in the area northeast of Nui Dinh during the three days of their patrol. On 22 December, Lance-Corporal Ronald Gammie and his patrol were in an observation post when some VC spotted them. Having killed two enemy and wounded a third, the patrol withdrew under fire from another group of enemy.

'DUNHILL', OPERATION

On 3 August 1944, 59 men of 2 SAS, divided into five parties and accompanied by Lieutenant Johnston and a 'Phantom' communications troop, were dropped into eastern Brittany to observe enemy movements in the Rennes-Laval area. However, the area of operation assigned to 'Dunhill' was overtaken by events, as the Americans managed to move inland from the Normandy beaches, and four of the parties were overrun within 24 hours of landing. The SAS switched their attention to helping to rescue pilots who were shot down over the forward edge of the battle area. The main result of the operation, which was completed by 24 August, was the rescue of 200 downed Allied airmen.

DUNLOY SHOOTING, COUNTY ANTRIM A tragic incident which took place in the village of Dunloy, Northern Ireland, in 1978. On 10 June in the graveyard of the village, John Boyle, a sixteen-year-old Catholic boy, came across a cache of weapons belonging to the IRA. His family informed the Royal Ulster Constabulary (RUC) who, in turn, informed the British Army. The SAS were called in and mounted a covert observation on the hide in the hope of making an arrest. Unfortunately, due to a breakdown in communications, the SAS were mistakenly told that John Boyle was a child, not a young man. They were also unaware that the Boyle family had not been warned to stay away from the graveyard. One evening, after several days lying in a waterfilled ditch, the patrol saw a young man approach the hide. After removing a stone, he lifted out an AK-47 assault rifle and pointed it in the direction of the SAS observation post. Thinking he was an IRA operative about to shoot, a patrol member shot the young man dead, not realizing that he was in fact John Boyle, who had returned to the graveyard out of curiosity.

The two SAS soldiers were charged with his murder and two pathologists' reports revealed that one bullet had entered the young man's head from the front whilst two more had entered from the back. The two SAS soldiers stuck to their story, insisting that the suspect had been facing them when they opened fire, and that the other rounds had entered the body due to a twisting action as he fell. The soldiers were acquitted. The IRA, however, turned the whole incident into a huge propaganda campaign, claiming the killing was proof of the SAS's shoot to kill policy, an accusation which threatened to damage the regiment's reputation.

E

'E' SQUADRON   The Gulf War presented many problems for the SAS, one of which was how to re-supply and repair the vehicles of the fighting columns. Although helicopters could have been used to ferry the vast amount of replenishment stores and the engineering equipment required to set up a field repair centre, it would have required a dozen helicopters all under threat from Iraqi anti-aircraft guns.

In the end the SAS decided to run their own re-supply convoy, sending ten trucks and a heavily armed Land Rover escort to a rendezvous (RV) some 139km (87 miles) inside Iraq, where they would meet up with the fighting columns. The re-supply convoy, temporarily called 'E' Squadron, left on the morning of the 10 February; crossing the Iraqi border two days later at 04:00 on 12 February, by 15:00 hours they had reached the RV.

The RV became a hive of activity as the columns converged, all waiting their turn to have their vehicles serviced or repaired. One of the columns had brought in two Iraqi prisoners who were to return with the convoy. As there were so many of the regiment in one place, the RSM decided to hold a Warrant Officers and Sergeants Mess meeting, which was held on the 16 February and consisted of over 30 senior NCOs. One of the items voted on was the purchase of new leather furniture for the mess. The re-supply convoy returned safely back to Saudi Arabia on the 17 February and 'E' Squadron ceased to exist.

'EAGLE CLAW', OPERATION (USA)   An American operation initiated in 1980 from an old air base on Masirah island, off southeastern Oman, and the aircraft carrier USS *Nimitz*, which was sailing in the Gulf of Oman. The aim was to covertly position Delta Force, the American anti-terrorist team, in Iran from where they would effect the rescue of American hostages held in the American Embassy in Tehran.

The bold plan was initially to establish a secure base about 320km (200 miles) south of Tehran, to be known as Desert One. Delta was to fly to Desert One from Masirah by a series of C-130 transport aircraft, three carrying fuel and three carrying Delta, together with a company of Rangers, whose job it was to give extra protection.

Dead **Adoo**. This is the Arabic word for 'enemy' and a term used by the SAS in Oman for the guerilla forces of the **Peoples Front for the Liberation of the Occupied Arabian Gulf (PFLOAG)** and the **Dhofar Liberation Front (DLF).**

Below: A typical **BATT** (SAS) unit during the Oman war.

Bodyguard training plays a large part in SAS life. Many former members of the regiment continue to protect some of the world's most senior VIPs.

Left: **Brigadier Mike Calvert**, the man much responsible for resurrecting the SAS in the 1950s. (IWM)

Above: SAS soldiers at the start of an **escape and evasion** exercise.

Below: Two men about to enter a high security compound during an exercise at the **ILRRP School**.

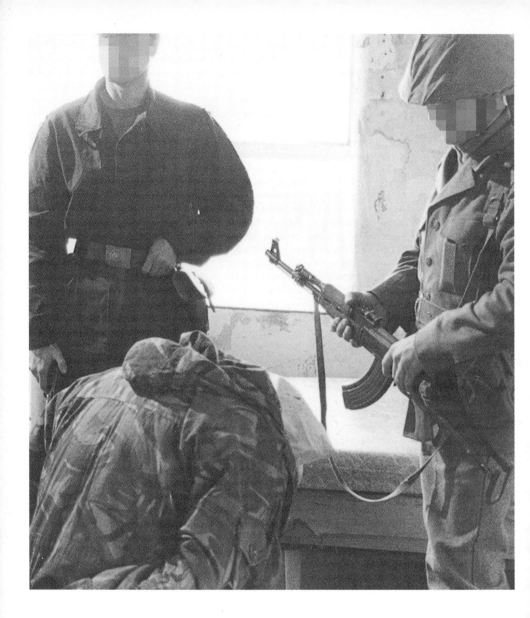

Above: The **JSIU** makes interrogation training as realistic as possible.

Right: **Lieutenant-Colonel 'Paddy' Mayne**, distinguished sportsman and soldier. (IWM)

Left: The **Milan** wire-guided anti-armour missile's **MIRA** sight proved to be most beneficial during the **Gulf War**.

Above: **Pea Green House** in Kuching, Sarawak, Borneo, the SAS regimental HQ from 1965.

Below: Pigeon lofts in St James's Park, London. Pigeons supplemented GHQ (**Phantoms**) radio system from 1940 to 1945.

Left: Protection of the **Royal Family** has fallen on the shoulders of the SAS; here Princess Anne is experiencing a hostage rescue scenario.

Below: In an effort to stop Scud missiles falling on Israel during the Gulf War, **General Schwarzkopf** (fifth from left) personally committed the SAS into Iraq.

David Sillito. (IWM)

Colonel David Stirling, founder of the SAS.

St Martin's Church, Hereford,
the final resting place for many outstanding SAS men.

Once the aircraft had safely landed at Desert One, eight RH-53D helicopters would be despatched from the aircraft carrier to join them. Re-fuelling at the base, they would transport Delta Force to a secret position just outside Tehran, where they would stay, ready to attack by night. They planned to assault the Embassy covertly and rescue the hostages that night, with the assistance of the DOD (Department of Defense) agents. The helicopters would remain on stand-by, ready to airlift everyone to an airfield called Manzariyeh, about 48km (30 miles) south of Tehran, which would have been secured by a force of US Rangers. From here the rescue would be continued using a giant C-141 Starlifter. Resistance by the Iranian Revolutionary Guard and any support from other Iranian troops was to be suppressed. Helicopter gunships were ready to offer aid if required.

On the evening of 24 April the raid began, but was beset with problems almost from the start. The landing strip at Desert One was supposed to be a deserted road, but in the event it turned out to be well used. As soon as the C-130s carrying Delta touched down, a Mercedes bus with about 30 passengers on board showed up. Delta were forced to stop the bus; the passengers were held hostage and later released. Then unbelievably a petrol tanker going about its normal business appeared from the opposite direction. As it tried to escape, one of the Rangers accompanying Delta fired an LAW anti-tank rocket at the tanker, which instantly burst into flames. At the same time a smaller truck drove up behind the tanker witnessing everything, but before the rescue force could take any further action, the driver of the tanker escaped from his burning vehicle and made off at speed, with the other driver, in the smaller truck.

In spite of this set-back, Delta attempted to continue with the raid, but encountered further problems. Eventually, over an hour and a half later than planned, only six of the eight helicopters arrived, and straightaway one of them developed technical problems. In order for the mission to continue Delta needed a minimum of six serviceable helicopters. To further add to the mayhem at Desert One, a C-130 aircraft and one of the choppers collided, creating an instant fireball as a mixture of ammunition and fuel ignited. Five aircrew in the C-130 and three marines in the RH-53 were killed.

Unable to pursue the mission, the operation was called off, Delta and the remaining aircraft returning to Masirah and the carrier *Nimitz*. The helicopters that had to be abandoned were later destroyed by a jet strike. The American hostages were eventually released safely following demanding negotiations on both sides.

EDWARDS, CAPTAIN ROBIN   On the evening of 29 April 1964, Captain Robin Edwards of 22 SAS led a patrol of ten men from 3 Troop

A Squadron into the Radfan mountains of Aden. The aim of the patrol was to secure a drop-zone (DZ) onto which soldiers of 3rd Battalion The Parachute Regiment would land. The SAS patrol were ferried by armoured cars which drove them down the Dhala road and into the Wadi Rabwa. As darkness fell the patrol parted with their escort and, shouldering their heavy bergens, made their way towards the DZ on foot. They had about 12km (8 miles) to cover and while Edwards' men were tough, most having experience in Borneo and Malaya, movement through the wadi was hard going. Their objective was the high plateau of Jebel Ashquab, which Edwards hoped to reach undetected before dawn the next morning. Progress was slow, mainly due to the rough terrain and partly due to the signaller, Trooper Warburton, who was suffering from severe stomach cramps. The patrol was forced to pause for several intervals and allow him to catch up, and after a while it became apparent that he was getting weaker, slower and was finding it a struggle to keep going.

By 01:00 in the morning the patrol had become fragmented, as they were forced to stop and wait for the ailing signaller. By now Edwards realized that they would not reach their objective by daylight, and decided to find some form of cover where they could shelter throughout the day. Edwards sent out a recce group who reported that they were still some way off from their objective at Jebel Ashquab, but that they had found two old rock-built sangars in which the patrol could shelter throughout the day. Edwards decided to use these and lay-up for the day, giving Warburton time to recover, then later that evening the patrol would proceed to the DZ and mark it with torches. They radioed their position back to the SAS squadron commander and lay-up successfully for the rest of the night, but some time during the following morning their presence was detected.

The SAS position was quickly surrounded by rebel tribesmen who, as the alarm was raised, came pouring out from nearby villages. A gun battle ensued, from long range at first, but later as the tribesmen became bolder they climbed the rocky slopes that overlooked the two SAS sangars. Edwards reported the situation back to SAS headquarters in Thumier which in turn requested air-support from the RAF in Aden. Hunter ground-attack fighters were despatched and during the daylight hours managed to force the tribesmen back. However, by this time the rebels had completely surrounded the sangars leaving the SAS with no way out. By dusk, the fighters were unable to assist and the rebels moved to within 50m (54yds), and were preparing to rush the SAS position. As the drop-zone could not be marked, the parachute drop was abandoned, and headquarters advised them to try and break out just after dark and make their way back to the Dhala road. An artillery barrage around their position would start at 19:00 hours, which would help keep the rebels heads down while the patrol made good their escape.

The rebels, sensing victory, increased their fire on the two sangars and two men were hit in the legs. Knowing they must move Edwards decided to send one last message, but when he went to speak to the signaller, he found Trooper Warburton dead. With the situation worsening Edwards gave the order to break out, but just as they did so a barrage of fire swept the sangars and Edwards was hit several times and fell to the ground dead.

The rest of the patrol kept going, and once they had cleared the immediate area they slowed, but continued climbing to avoid the rebels. Progress was difficult especially for the wounded men, but eventually they found their way off the hill and onto a small track which was heading in the right direction and would eventually lead them to the Dhala road. Meanwhile the rebel tribesmen, having recovered the dead bodies of Edwards and Warburton, continued to follow the patrol. Two of the slower SAS men, one of whom was wounded, lay in wait and as four rebels appeared out of the darkness, sacrificing speed for caution, the two SAS men shot all four dead. The fleeing SAS men applied this same tactic several times, killing several more, until at last the rebels started to wise up and broke off the chase. Having beaten off their immediate pursuers, what remained of Captain Edwards' patrol made its way back towards the Dhala road. All efforts were made to help the beleaguered patrol and by dawn the first pair were spotted and were picked up by armoured cars and brought safely back to their base.

A few days later it was reported that the heads of two British servicemen had been displayed impaled on stakes in the main square of Taiz, across the North Yemen border. This grotesque incident was confirmed a week later when a patrol found the decapitated bodies of Edwards and Warburton buried in a shallow grave near the two sangars. Their bodies were removed and buried with full military honours.

E4A A unit of the Royal Ulster Constabulary (RUC) in Northern Ireland that specializes in surveillance and the gathering of intelligence. Their initial training was undertaken by the SAS at Hereford and continued until the unit became fully operational in 1978. As E4A proved their worth, they took over much of the work previously undertaken by the British Army's 14 Intelligence and Security Unit.

ELAS/EAM ELAS (Hellenic People's Army of Liberation) were the military arm of EAM (Greek National Liberation Front), a Greek force with strong communist political views who opposed the Germans, and which in October 1942 the SOE (Special Operations Executive) and SAS tried to cultivate as allies. Unfortunately, the Greeks were more interested in their own internal civil wars and open rivalry between other factions. On 3 December the SAS under Captain Lassen were sent to raid Heraklion in Crete only to find that the various Greek factions, mainly those of ELAS, were not too keen on fighting, with the result that the attack ended up in shambles. The SAS would have no more to do with ELAS.

'ELBOW', OPERATION   During the first half of 1978, repeated raids by Rhodesian 1st SAS Regiment had forced ZIPRA guerrillas to withdraw their forward bases from near the banks of the Zambesi River to locations deeper inside Zambia. Reconnaissance had revealed that ZIPRA terrorists were travelling south in Russian-supplied trucks at night from the area of Kabanga to a staging post at Simani before heading over the border into Rhodesia. On the evening of 13 June twelve men of B Squadron under Captain Peter Fritz were inserted into a landing zone inside Zambia with the task of ambushing the stretch of road between Kabanga and Simani. Moving through the night, they halted at 04:00 hours and lay up until the afternoon when they set off once more, reaching the ambush area in the early hours of 15 June. Having carried out a reconnaissance of the area, Captain Fritz positioned his men in their ambush positions. Squadron Sergeant-Major Pete Cole and an NCO then mined the road with a single command-detonated mine augmented with a further 13kg (5.8lbs) of plastic explosive.

It was not until 24 June that an enemy convoy appeared. At 11:15 hours three trucks containing fully armed and equipped ZIPRA guerrillas drove slowly down the road, preceded by a small party checking the road for mines. Fortunately they abandoned this process about 10m (11yds) short of the ambush area, and as the leading vehicle drove over the mine, Sergeant-Major Cole detonated it. A split second later the other two vehicles came under heavy automatic fire, which set the guerrillas ablaze and cut them down as they tried to flee. When a body count was carried out, the figure reached 69.

Shortly afterwards, the entire force was lifted out by three helicopters. While two headed back to Rhodesia, the third carrying Sergeant Phil Cripps flew to the area of the Simani Mine where a mine was laid in the road towards Kabanga. Three days later a senior ZIPRA commander, Alfred Mangena, visited the area to inspect the damage caused by the ambush. While returning to Kabanga his Land Rover activated Sergeant Cripps' mine and he was killed. His death was a major blow to ZIPRA.

EL DABA   German airfield in North Africa raided on 7 and 11 July 1942 by the SAS. The first attack, which was a hit and run affair using jeeps and led by Captain the Earl Jellicoe, blasted through the wire but failed to penetrate the perimeter. The second raid four days later proved equally difficult as the Germans had improved their defences, and the attack had to be called off.

EL FASCIA An SAS forward base used in the North Africa campaign in December 1942. Shortly after it was formed, David Stirling sent B Squadron to establish the base, which was, at the time, behind the German lines. From El Fascia they could patrol and harass the Germans, who were in retreat after the Battle of El Alamein. B Squadron did exceptionally well raiding, but the price of their success was to attract a large force of Germans who discovered their base. On the night of 23 December the base was surrounded and a fierce fight ensued. A few SAS men managed to escape and link up with A Squadron, but the majority, heavily outnumbered, surrendered.

EMERGENCY SLEEPING BAG Carried by most members of SAS as part of their survival kit. It is normally a lightweight clear polythene bag that when folded will fit into a sealed bag, 13cm × 8cm × 2cm (5in × 3in × .8in), and weighs 33gm (1oz). This simple sack will protect the body from both wind and rain, and will help prevent hypothermia. A new Kevalite foil bag which maximizes body heat has recently been trialed by the SAS Ops research team.

EMPTY QUARTER A large desert area in Oman which lies in the centre of the country. In 1969 the SAS reclaimed several old 'Pink Panther' Land Rovers which had been left in storage at the British garrison in Sharjah and drove them south through the Empty Quarter into the town of Salalah.

ENTEBBE On 27 June 1976 a joint group of German Baader-Meinhof and Palestinian PFLP hijacked an Air France airliner with 254 passengers on board, and forced the crew to fly to Entebbe Airport in Uganda, where Idi Amin was the ruling power. Israel immediately reacted by deploying their newly formed anti-terrorist units, in what was to become the first in a series of intrepid raids. They called in their most elite soldiers for the task, in particular Colonel Netanyahu, known to all Israelis as 'Yoni', a 30-year-old American-born Jew who, like so many of his predecessors, had returned to his homeland, Israel.

One of the biggest hurdles to overcome was the enormous flying distance between Israel and Entebbe. The only way to avoid the enemy radar was for the three C-130s to fly very low in close formation for the 3,200km (2,000 mile) journey, down over the Red Sea, across Ethiopia then directly into Uganda.

After numerous practice runs of unloading the armoured jeeps from the C-130s, tearing across the 500m (545yds) of tarmac and assaulting the buildings, the Israelis were finally ready to embark on this most important of missions. The assault team boarded the C-130s, their equipment was loaded, and the aircraft took off. In a relatively short time the planes reached their maximum speed of just a little over

614km/h (384mph), whilst flying just a few metres above the waves, which made most of the 150 men on board violently sick for the entire journey.

Meanwhile, the Israeli intelligence service, Mossad, had instructed its agents in Kenya and Uganda to start cutting telephone wires, creating distractions and relaying vital information to the command aircraft flying in the shadow of a commercial airliner.

Two hours after take-off, the three C-130s, with the assault teams aboard, flew low into Entebbe and were able to land totally undetected by the radar operators. A large black Mercedes, with an escort of two British Land Rovers, discreetly emerged from the rear door of the C-130 and, looking exactly like Idi Amin's entourage, drove swiftly across the tarmac towards the main doors of a disused terminal building, where the hostages were being held. This small convoy was immediately followed by Colonel Netanyahu and his men, to the surprise of both the German terrorists, Gabrielle Tiedemann and Wilfred Boese, who were standing with some Ugandan officers outside the doors of the terminal block.

Suddenly it dawned on Boese that something had gone horribly wrong, and he immediately rushed inside to get his machine gun. As he returned from the terminal the approaching Israeli convoy opened fire and he was killed instantly. Colonel Netanyahu and his team went on to storm the terminal building and attack the PFLP terrorists, but the Ugandan soldiers began to regroup and retaliate, fatally wounding Colonel Netanyahu, who died almost immediately.

The Israeli soldiers successfully rescued the hostages and quickly transferred them to the waiting aircraft, whilst the medics and doctors rushed to treat those who had been injured in the action. Once all were safely aboard, the three aircraft took off, returning across the Red Sea towards Israel, under cover of squadrons of Phantoms and Mirage fighters which had been scrambled to give protection.

ENTRY TECHNIQUES   For the SAS, entry techniques fall into two different categories: entry into an operational area, and entry into a location such as a building, aircraft or train. Both methods of entry can also be covert or overt. Entry into an operational area can be by land, sea and air, by parachute, vehicle or on foot. Entry into a building or aircraft can be made using cutting devices, shotguns, thermal lances or 'Harvey Wallbanger' wall-busting cannon.

ESCAPE AND EVASION   The final exercise in the Combat and Survival phase of SAS Continuation training. The candidate is dressed in an old overcoat and his boots tied up with string, before being dropped off in an unknown location with directions to a rendezvous point. He is not allowed to carry any rations or survival kit and is, in fact, searched for banned items beforehand. In addition, an 'enemy' force – usually an infantry battalion – pursues him. The aim is to avoid capture and stay on the run until either he is taken prisoner, or the allotted time is up, in which case he must surrender. During the evasion phase the student must make use of all he has learnt to stay free: camouflage; selecting the least obvious routes; concealment; laying false trails; the best time of day to move and so on. The best students will also be able to formulate alternative plans of action in case the first one goes wrong, or the unexpected crops up. He will also be expected to think clearly even when tired, cold, hungry, wet and under stress.

At the end of the evasion phase of the exercise, whether he is captured or he surrenders, the student has to undergo 24 hours of a **Resistance to Interrogation** exercise. This is to test how he will react under intense psychological pressure: threats, bribes, friendly overtures and sensory deprivation are all used, as they would be if the soldier was interrogated by an enemy force. The only information the student is allowed to offer during this time is name, rank, service number and date of birth. Various psychological tricks are used to disorientate the prisoners; these include the use of white sound, cold environment, food deprivation and disorientation. Finally, each student is debriefed to assess his resistance to interrogation training.

ESCAPE KIT The essentials of an SAS escape which, for most SAS soldiers, is housed in a tobacco tin, the contents of which will depend on the theatre of operation. Items can include a button compass that can be swallowed, a wire saw that will cut through the hardest metal, a condom for collecting water, and a Tampax for use in fire-lighting. In addition to the basic survival items, specialist equipment is also issued such as a silk escape map, or lock-picking tools.

A typical SAS survival kit will contain the following: button compass; wire saw; wind and waterproof matches; flint and steel; safety pins; candle; signal mirror; fishing kit; puritabs; razor blade; condoms; snare wire; Tampax; polythene survival bag.

EVEREST In 1976 the Army Mountaineering Association invited interested and able members to participate in an ascent of Mount Everest. Included in the group were three members of the SAS, two of whom emerged during practice as the most likely to reach the summit. The men, Corporal Michael 'Bronco' Lane and Sergeant John 'Brummie' Stokes, had climbed together for years and were extremely fit.

Supported by a team of four, the summit pair pushed forward to Camp 6 at 8,880m (27,000ft), where they were left alone to make their attempt next day. However, the weather worsened and they remained in Camp 6 for 36 hours before making their attempt on the summit at 06:30. Despite being just 425m (1,400ft) from the summit the weather delayed them and it was not until 15:00 that the two men found themselves standing on the roof of the world.

The two men quickly took photographs, preferring not to dally as time and the weather were against them – they had to make it back to Camp 6 before dark. The descent was not easy and worsening visibility served only to slow them even more. Then by luck, they came across some oxygen bottles that they had cached on the way up. Although this gave them an indication of their whereabouts, it also told them that Camp 6 was still over 300m (1,000ft) below them. To stumble on in the dark meant certain death so there was only one thing to do – dig in. Scooping a hole in the snow, the two men huddled together to wait out the long night, the reclaimed oxygen being their only saviour.

They made it through the night, but by dawn neither was in any physical state to move or even contemplate walking down to Camp 6; their only hope of assistance lay with the support party in Camp 5 760m (2,500ft) below them. Stokes was totally snow blind by now, but the sun began to shine and once more luck was with them. At 09:00 the alternative summit team reached them and they were safe. They were flown from Base Camp to the hospital in Kathmandu where they received medical treatment for advanced frostbite; Stokes lost several of his toes while Lane had to have fingers amputated from his right hand.

In 1984 both 'Brummie' Stokes and 'Bronco' Lane were back on Everest, this time leading an all-SAS team consisting of soldiers from the regiment's various **Mountain Troops**. The expedition was well planned, and by 2 April the front runners were already at 6,930m (22,800ft). Then disaster struck. A little after dawn on the morning of 3 April a huge avalanche, initiated by falling ice, swept down the mountain heading directly for Advanced Base Camp. It completely ravaged the camp, propelling it and the men down the mountainside. As a result of the avalanche Corporal Tony Swierzy was killed and several others lay badly injured, with Sergeant Andy **Baxter** suffering the worst injuries.

EXOCET   A French-built surface-skimming missile which caused tremendous damage to British shipping during the **Falklands War**. A raid was planned by the SAS in which they would fly directly to the Argentinian airfield and destroy both the delivery aircraft and the missiles. This raid was deemed highly politically sensitive and was consequently called off in mid-flight.

EYEBALL   The word means to keep an eye on, or watch someone or something. The word is used a lot during surveillance when the operators will 'eyeball' a suspect.

EYLES, LIEUTENANT-COLONEL LEN – AUSTRALIAN SAS REGIMENT (SASR)   Major Len Eyles assumed command of 1st SAS

Company (Royal Australian Infantry) on 1 February 1958, six months after its formation on 25 July 1957. During the period of his command, 1st SAS Company grew to full strength and developed specialist skills such as small boat handling, diving, roping, and amphibious raiding. In the earlier stages it devoted considerable time to vehicle-borne reconnaissance patrol skills which included driving, vehicle maintenance, navigation and long-range radio communications. In June–July 1958, Major Eyles led a month-long expedition from Perth to Darwin and back. On 11 September 1960, he handed over command to Major Lawrie Clark.

Six and a half years later, on 29 March 1967, Lieutenant-Colonel Eyles returned to Swanbourne to assume command of the SAS Regiment, taking over from Lieutenant-Colonel Bill Brathwaite. Since commanding 1st SAS Company he had attended the Australian Army Staff College, thereafter serving on the staff of Headquarters 28 Commonwealth Brigade in Malaysia before taking up the post of deployed Assistant Adjutant General at Headquarters Eastern Command in Australia.

Eyles' tenure of command saw all three of the regiment's Sabre Squadrons on twelve-month tours of operations in Vietnam, and his main concern during that period was to ensure that they were fully prepared. Another matter of high priority was the maintaining of a constant flow of new manpower into the SASR in order to ensure that squadrons on operations were maintained at full strength.

F

F SQUADRON A squadron from the GHQ Liaison Regiment known as 'Phantom' which is attached to the SAS.

'FABIAN', OPERATION Originally code-named 'Regan', Operation Fabian was a six-month mission carried out by five men of the Belgian Independent Parachute Company (5 SAS). They operated around Arnhem, Holland, between 16 September 1944 and 14 March 1945, collecting intelligence concerning enemy concentrations in northwest Holland, as well as the launch sites of V2 rockets. This was one of those SAS operations which was sidelined, for Belgian soldiers became involved with the Dutch Resistance in helping Allied paratroopers escape in the aftermath of the landings around Arnhem in September 1944. As a result, their intelligence-gathering work took second place, and the mission's results were mediocre at best.

FALKLANDS WAR The Falklands are a group of islands in the South Atlantic which have been under British sovereignty since 1833. When the Argentinians invaded the Falklands on 2 April 1982 the British prime minister, Margaret Thatcher, announced that Britain would win the islands back, taking them by force if necessary. Under Operation 'Corporate', a task force was immediately assembled and sent on its way south. Both Brigadier Peter de la Billière and Lieutenant-Colonel Mike Rose, the Commander of 22 SAS, fought hard to have the regiment included in the task force. By early April, members of D and G Squadrons were on their way.

The SAS saw their first action on the little island of South Georgia, 500km (310 miles) south of the Falklands. With its small Argentine garrison, retaking the island was seen as a low-risk, high propaganda measure; men from the SAS, SBS and M Company of 42 Commando achieved the task on 26 April.

The SAS mounted a diversionary raid the night before the main task force landing at San Carlos on East Falkland. This involved 60 men of D Squadron hitting the garrison at Goose Green with the aim of simulating a battalion-sized attack. Using a vast amount of 66mm rockets, and automatic gunfire, the SAS laid down a ferocious barrage. Early next morning, with the main landing completed, the SAS withdrew from Goose Green.

The night of 14/15 May saw one of the most daring raids carried out by the SAS during the conflict. A reconnaissance group from D Squadron had already reported the presence of eleven aircraft at the Pebble Island airstrip on West Falkland.

Twenty members of Mountain Troop, D Squadron, led by Captain John Hamilton, assaulted the airstrip with orders to destroy all aircraft. Despite a few last-minute hitches, by the time they finished, all the aircraft had been destroyed or rendered irreparable, and one Argentinian lay dead. Two of the squadron were wounded by shrapnel when a mine exploded, though they were not seriously hurt. The success of the mission was a serious blow to Argentine morale.

On 19 May the regiment suffered a tragic blow when a Sea King helicopter, carrying a large group of SAS troops cross-decking from HMS *Hermes* to HMS *Intrepid*, accidentally crashed killing 22 men.

For the next few weeks the SAS continued their aggressive actions, and at the end of May, D Squadron seized Mount Kent, some 64km (40 miles) behind enemy lines and held it until relieved by 42 Marine Commando.

The last major SAS raid was mounted in East Falkland on the night of 14 June. This involved attacking the Argentinian rear while 2 Para assaulted Wireless Ridge, just a few kilometres west of Port Stanley. A total of 60 men from D and G Squadrons and six men from the SBS used Rigid Raiders to assault Port Stanley harbour, setting fire to the oil-storage tanks while laying down suppressive fire. The Argentinians retaliated in overwhelming numbers and the raiders were forced to retreat. Shortly afterwards the Argentine surrender was effectively instigated by 22 SAS's commanding officer, Mike Rose. See also Argentina; Fortuna Glacier; Goose Green; Grytviken Story; Capt. John Hamilton; Pebble Island.

'FAN DANCE' The Fan Dance is a march over the Brecon Beacons during SAS Selection. Candidates are placed in a group and given a colour; each group has its own Directing Staff (DS). Students carry a bergen weighing 88kg (40lbs), belt kit and rifle. At this stage of Selection there are still high numbers on the course and DS will normally race off in an effort to burn out the men who are trying to catch them. Depending on the weather, Fan Dance must be completed inside four hours in order for a candidate to pass.

FARRAN, MAJOR ROY Led Operation 'Narcissus' not long after joining 2 SAS in the later stages of the war in North Africa. Commanding the operation, he led a daring attack on Axis positions in Sicily before the main Allied landings of Operation 'Husky'. In 1943 he was involved in the activities at Termoli with B Squadron before withdrawing his men and returning to Britain to start preparations for coming missions in France. Farran led the highly successful Operation 'Wallace' following D-Day, and in December 1944 he was made commander of 3 Squadron and sent to Italy to undertake Operation 'Tombola'. Since he had previously escaped from the Germans, he was forced to work under the false name of Major Patrick McGinty, which he took from the song about an Irish goat which swallowed a stick of dynamite.

FAV/LSV (FAST ATTACK VEHICLE/LIGHT STRIKE VE-HICLE) *Specification* Length: 3.9m (4.2yds); Width: 1.86m (2yds); Height: 1.73m (1.8yds); Weight: 1,100kg (2,420lbs).

Light Strike Vehicles (LSVs) were used by the SAS during the Gulf War. Two British variants were considered but neither proved as reliable as the Land Rover 110. The Longline LSV has a VW 1.91 flat-four water-cooled petrol engine, while the Wessex Saker has a Perkins Prima 80T 1.993, 4-cylinder, water-cooled, turbo-charged diesel engine. Although there are four-man LSVs, most are designed to carry two or three soldiers, with stowage for the crew's kit in panniers and racks along the sides of the vehicle. Despite their 'beach buggy' appearance, the vehicles are not cheap to produce, and additional items such as Kevlar armour, and ignition retardant fuel tanks come as extra. After initial trials during their warm-up training in the Gulf, the SAS decided to drop the LSVs from the mobile fighting columns.

'FEATHER MEN' *The Feather Men* was the title of a book written by Sir Ranulph Fiennes about four men, two of whom were SAS, who were murdered by a contract organization called the Clinic. The contract had allegedly been arranged by an Arab sheikh, whose sons had died in the Dhofar conflict. Although Fiennes attempted SAS Selection and also served in Oman on secondment, he was never in the regiment. Allegations that an organization exists known as the 'Feather Men', whose purpose is to protect ex-members of the SAS, are totally unfounded.

It is true that many ex-members of the SAS, especially some Malayan veterans, previously unknown to one other may introduce themselves by asking 'Are you a Pilgrim, brother?', taking the phrase from the inscription on the SAS Clock Tower.

FENWICK, MAJOR IAN Commander of D Squadron, 1 SAS, who took part in Operation 'Gain' in France during June and August 1944. D Squadron had been particularly active under Fenwick, but his daring had a price: he was killed in action in the village of Chambon on 6 August.

'FERRET FORCE'   Established during the Malayan Emergency (1948–60) by the British, its task was to reach Communists in their jungle bases, and as such it was a highly offensive unit. It was formed in July 1948 by an ex-Chindit officer, R.G.K. Thompson of the Government Planning Staff, and three former officers of Force 136. It was made up of volunteers from British, Gurkha and Malay battalions, the Malayan Police, as well as Iban trackers brought in from Borneo. 'Ferret' scouts led fighting patrols of regular Commonwealth infantry units into the jungle to look for Communist bases. The results were quite promising: in their first operation British infantry and Gurkhas discovered twelve guerrilla camps thanks to 'Ferret Force'.

However, the unit could only last for a few months, as most of its leaders had to return to other military duties or civilian life. But, importantly, a precedent had been set for creating a unit for offensive jungle operations, which would lead to the reforming of 22 SAS for just such a role.

FIELD POLICE FORCE   The Field Police Force was part of the Federation of Malaya Police Force during the Malayan Emergency (1948–60). This unit deployed 22 Jungle Companies, each having a strength of 180 men, to fight the Communists. The SAS worked with the Field Police Force during the implementation of the 'Briggs Plan', when large numbers of villagers were moved into fortified settlements to protect them from Communist infiltration.

FIELD SURGICAL TEAMS (FST)   Consist of four medical specialists, including two surgeons. These teams of highly trained doctors and medical staff are present wherever the SAS operate in a theatre of war. During the Oman conflict, field surgical teams were stationed at the RAF air base in Salalah, making the delivery, by helicopter, of SAS casualties into the FST in under twenty minutes. During the Gulf War the British had more than 40 such mobile operating theatres in readiness.

FIJIANS   In September 1952 D Company of the 1st Fijian Infantry took part in Operation 'Hive', together with two squadrons of SAS. By the early 1960s a number of Fijians joined the British Army, many making their way into the SAS, where they achieved great standing with their peers. In particular, the two Fijians, Corporal Labalaba and Trooper Takevesi, are remembered for their outstanding courage during the Battle of Mirbat in 1972.

FINES   Whereas most regiments in the British Army have procedures for discipline that include fines, loss of privileges and custodial sentencing, the SAS relies mainly on its own fine system. Fines can be imposed by senior ranks, both commissioned and non-commissioned, with the money being paid into regimental or squadron funds. Such funds are normally spent on PRI (President of the Regimental Institute) equipment or squadron entertainment. Most SAS soldiers accept the fine system, as it involves little time or paperwork and is not normally entered on their record card. In many instances, where SAS soldiers have committed a minor misdemeanour or not complied with SOPs (standard operating procedures) they have seen fit to fine themselves. These fines are normally accepted without question or query. Serious breaches of SOPs or discipline will result in the harshest treatment – instant RTU (return to unit) and an end to the soldier's career in the regiment.

'FIRKINS'   SAS slang for Firqat troops.

FIRQAT   The name Firqat is a rough Arabic translation for a military company, and was used to describe the irregular Dhofari troops during the Oman War. Many were from the southern coastal villages, whilst others had previously served as anti-government guerrillas and had been granted amnesty by the sultan. These men were raised and trained by the SAS and formed into Firqat companies.

The idea of Firqat troops was first put forward in 1971, after a meeting between Major Tony Jeapes of 22 SAS and Salim Mubarak, a former leading figure within the Dhofar Liberation Front. Mubarak suggested that an anti-guerrilla fighting force could be formed using disgruntled Dhofari tribesmen; he also suggested a name – Firqat Salahadin (Company of Salahadin). Jeapes agreed and soon, with the co-operation of local tribal elders, the SAS were training Firqats at Mirbat. Although they took part in battles, the Firqat were considered to be reconnaissance troops rather than infantry troops. Their task was to gather intelligence, usually through village gossip, and to pass it on to the British.

The first successful action of the Firqat Salahadin was the taking of Sudh, 30km (18 miles) east of Mirbat. Other successes followed, which encouraged more men to join. Initially, each company numbered 30–40 men, but the numbers grew until by the end of the war the combined strengths of Firqats was 2,000 men. Although Firqat Salahadin was the first company, others followed – Firqat A'asifat, Firqat Al Nasr, Firqat Tariq Bin Zeead amongst others.

The Firqat forces proved a great bonus to the British effort in Oman. However, after the end of the war, the men went back to their individual tribes and families and the Firqats were all but disbanded.

FIRQAT FUNDS   In August 1974 it was discovered that certain members of the SAS had been illegally taking money from a variety of sources during the Oman War. SAS troops working in outposts were tasked with raising local tribesmen into Firqats. For each weapon they issued to a Firqat member there would be a corresponding monthly pay packet. It materialized, however, that some Firqat members were fictitious and the money remained with the controlling SAS unit. In addition to this, the Firqat were encouraged to locate enemy weapons, for which they received a bounty, many a time sharing this money with their SAS counterparts who had not been granted the same privilege.

At the end of each tour the money would be evenly divided among the SAS soldiers in that particular location. When the fraud came to light, much of the money was returned and those soldiers involved were punished. In fairness, the monetary system itself was partly to blame; SAS soldiers in the field are not paymasters and such activities are commonly seen as fringe benefits in the Arab world.

FIRST LIGHT First light is important for any soldier on operations, as it is a time of heightened enemy activity, and it is not unusual for a position to be attacked at first light. Following a procedure shared by soldiers for generations, SAS soldiers will always stand-to at first light. However, over the past few years, battle techniques have changed dramatically, with most of the fighting happening during the hours of darkness. This change has come about mainly due to the rapid advancement in night-fighting technology that allows the SAS to operate equally effectively in the dark.

FIR TREE SNOW SHELTER A simple shelter formed under a large fir tree, using a natural hollow in the snow around the base of the trunk. This type of shelter is regularly used by the SAS during winter exercises in Norway and is one of the basic lessons learnt during survival training.

FIVE FRONTS CAMPAIGN During the Oman War, this campaign was undertaken on the recommendations of Lieutenant-Colonel Johnny Watts, who was commanding officer of 22 SAS prior to their main assault on the Jebel Massive, and who was tasked to make an assessment of what an SAS presence could offer Oman. His basic strategy was to get the SAS and SAF (Sultan's Armed Forces) back on to the dominating high ground of the Jebel and remain there. Watts realized that defeating the enemy would require not just fighting the Adoo but also the winning of support of the Jebel tribesmen, and that of the coastal Omani people. His plan had five main points, although this was later revised.

1. To establish an intelligence operation.
2. To set up an information network (Psy Ops).
3. To provide medical aid.
4. To provide economic aid.
5. To raise an army from the local people who would fight for the new sultan.

The Five Fronts campaign is a classic example of how, with careful planning and a few select Special Forces, a military operation can change the fate of a government and its people. The medical and economic aid helped build a bond that even the simplest of Jebel tribesmen could understand. Well-versed psychological operations and radio broadcasts helped inform the people and the Adoo as to the new order. But the brilliance of Watts' plan lay in raising the locals into Firqats and training them to fight for their own country.

FLAG-MARCHES A type of 'hearts and minds' campaign used in the Middle East. It normally meant visiting the inhabitants of isolated villages and spreading news or giving assistance. Used during the Jebel Akhdar campaign and the Oman War.

FLASH-BANG See Stun Grenade.

'FLAVIUS', OPERATION Late in 1987 Sean Savage, an infamous IRA bomb-maker, was discovered living in Spain with another IRA suspect, Daniel McCann. For six months MI5 kept the two under surveillance, convinced that they were planning further bombings.

Their suspicions were further increased when Maraid Farrell arrived at Malaga Airport on 4 March 1988, where she was met by Savage and McCann. The trio – later acknowledged by the IRA to be an active unit cell – were kept under close observation by M15 and several of their conversations were recorded. Before long M15 discovered that they were planning to attack the British garrison in Gibraltar, with a car bomb at a military ceremony where several regimental bands would be parading.

The Gibraltar police were informed and the SAS were requested to send in an anti-terrorist team, under the operational name of 'Flavius', with instructions that the IRA active service unit was to be seized. Although contact with the IRA cell was lost for a short while, the SAS believed they understood the IRA's plan. They suspected that a car, designed as a decoy, would be delivered to Gibraltar and parked in a prominent position along the planned route for the military parade, thus guaranteeing a parking space for the actual car bomb. Most of the troops and public would assemble in the plaza, which the SAS correctly assumed to be the IRA's target area since it was obvious that a bomb here would cause the greatest destruction. At 14:00 on 5 March Savage was seen parking a white Renault 5 and was thought to be setting up the bomb triggering device. At about the same time Farrell and McCann were observed crossing the Spanish border, making their way into town.

As soon as Savage left the scene the SAS men were called into action, using an explosives expert to undertake a walk-past of the Renault. Although there were no obvious signs of a bomb, such as the rear suspension being depressed, it was agreed that the car probably did contain an explosive device, possibly Semtex, which is relatively easy to conceal. Joseph Canepa, the local police chief, immediately passed control to the SAS, whose orders were to capture the three IRA members alive, if at all possible. However, as in all such situations where lives may be at risk, the SAS have the right to shoot to kill.

Each SAS soldier was dressed in casual clothes and was armed with a **Browning 9mm Hi-Power**. Each was able to maintain contact with the rest of the team via small hidden radios. Savage having rejoined McCann and Farrell, all three IRA suspects made their way back towards the Spanish border, closely followed by four of the SAS team. The team was forced to split into two, however, when Savage, for no apparent reason, turned round and began to make his way back into the town.

A few moments later a local policeman was recalled to his police station, just as he happened to drive past McCann and Farrell, causing them to turn nervously. McCann instantly made eye contact with one of the SAS soldiers, who started to issue a challenge, being no more than 10m (11yds) away from the suspects. McCann immediately moved his arm across his body and, fearing he was about to remotely detonate the bomb, the soldier shot him in the back. Farrell, it is said, distinctly went for her bag and was shot with a single round. By this time the second soldier had also opened fire, hitting both terrorists. Savage heard the shots and turned back, only to be confronted by the remaining two SAS men, who shouted a warning to him. Savage ignored the warning and tried to reach what the soldiers took to be a weapon. Both SAS men fired and Savage was killed outright.

At first the mission was hailed as an outstanding success, but the euphoria was short-lived. All three terrorists were found to have been unarmed, and whilst a bomb was later discovered in Malaga, one was never found in the suspects' car. Allegations were made, and accusations flew from 'witnesses' who claimed to have seen the whole episode. They claimed that the three had surrendered with their arms in the air, but had been shot at point-blank range while they lay on the ground by the 'unscrupulous' SAS, operating their shoot to kill policy.

A two-week inquest followed in September 1988, at the end of which the jury returned a majority verdict of lawful killing. Outraged by the outcome, relatives of the three IRA members took the SAS soldiers responsible for the killing to court, but the European Commission of Human Rights in Strasbourg decided, eleven to six, that the SAS did not use unnecessary force. It was decreed that the soldiers were justified in opening fire given the circumstances. However, because the case was referred to the European Court of Human Rights the British Government was forced to pay compensation.

FLIP-FLOP CLUB Name of a private club in the old 'spider' accommodation of **Bradbury Lines**. It was created in 1970 by members of G Squadron, on their return from **Oman** and their first tour of duty on Operation 'Storm'. The club had a committee and the commanding officer's somewhat tacit agreement. Opening hours were from 22:00 till early morning. Only SAS members were allowed in with the exception of the female population of Hereford. It derived its name from a flip-flop sandal someone had nailed to the door. B Squadron ran a similar club named the 'Valhalla'. These clubs were the forerunner of the all-ranks 'Paludrine Club', which exists to this day.

FLYING FINGER The name given to an operation widely used in Oman, whereby an enemy captive would be taken by helicopter and flown over the rebel-held area. He would be asked to indicate enemy strongholds and his old hiding places by pointing. These flights were known as 'flying fingers', as the helicopter was normally followed by several jet fighters who, once the helicopter had departed the area, would then proceed to drop 500kg (1,100lbs) bombs on the indicated area.

FOLBOT An early version of the two-man canoe, the Folbot had a wooden frame inside a rubberized canvas cover, was 1.52m (5ft) long and equipped with a rudder.

It had been developed by the Folbot Company who, due to lack of orders, went out of business in 1940. During World War II, however, the boat was used by the SAS, commandos and Special Boat Section, despite its metal tubular frame, which had a history of coming apart while at sea. Such a craft accompanied David Stirling during his raid on Benghazi (see Raid on) in March 1942, though in the event it was damaged and could not be used. The Folbot was replaced with a much modified model which was renamed the 'Cockle'.

FORCE 136 A secret resistance force set up by the British Special Operations Executive (SOE) during World War II to attack enemy targets in Japanese-occupied Malaya. The unit, led by British military personnel, trained and armed members of the local Chinese community, mostly members of the Communist Party of Malaya, to conduct a sabotage campaign against the Japanese, using the jungle to hide their bases.

There was little thought given to what would happen after the war, when an organization which was full of heavily armed Malayan nationalists would turn their attention to the colonial rulers. Unsurprisingly, Force 136 turned its guns on the British administration in Malaya. Ironically, its leader, Chin Peng, was an ex-member of Force 136 and had been awarded an OBE for his efforts against the Japanese. Those non-Chinese members of Force 136 joined 'Ferret Force' and, later, the Malayan Scouts, and thus fought against their former comrades.

FORKHILL A border town in South Armagh, Northern Ireland, where the British Army and RUC manned a fortified police post. The town has seen much violence over the years, and several British soldiers have been killed in or around the town. In the early days of their involvement in Northern Ireland, the SAS used the Forkhill base as a launch pad for many of their border operations.

FORT BROOKE One of the jungle bases built by the SAS during its Malayan campaign, Fort Brooke was constructed at the end of 1953 in the Cameron Highlands. The forts were invariably situated deep in the jungle on cleared sites, and were usually reached by helicopter or aircraft. From these outposts long-range patrols were launched against the Communist Terrorists (CTs).

D Squadron sent in a patrol to recce a location for Fort Brooke, and after a long hard trek through thick jungle, they finally arrived at the site. The SAS spent months at the location building huts and a helicopter pad, plus making friends with the local people. As the SAS became established, their patrols cleared the area of any CT camps, losing two men as a result of an enemy ambush. The fort was finally handed over to the local police, but not before half the squadron had contracted a tropical disease and had to be evacuated.

FORTH BRIDGE INCIDENT In 1968 three territorial members of 23 SAS were on a train between Edinburgh and Aberdeen when they decided, for a bet, to leave the carriage. They crawled out of the window and up on to the roof of the train. Although a British Rail employee spotted them as the train crossed the Forth Bridge and subsequently had the train stopped, one of the three fell off and was killed.

FORTUNA GLACIER The location of an incident which occurred on the island of South Georgia, and which could have ended tragically for the SAS. It was decided during the Falklands War in 1982 to land Mountain Troop of D Squadron on Fortuna Glacier, where they would be able to establish observation posts around the town of Leith in anticipation of British forces retaking the island.

Wessex helicopters from HMS *Antrim* and HMS *Tidespring* dropped the troop, commanded by Captain John Hamilton, with their equipment and some pulks (ice sleds), on the glacier. Icy conditions on the glacier hindered their progress and the situation was to deteriorate as night fell. One of the two tents was destroyed in a blizzard, increasing the risk of hypothermia and frostbite, and Hamilton, knowing they would not survive another night, requested an evacuation.

The next morning, although still hampered by the blizzard, three helicopters, led by a radar-equipped Wessex, flew over the glacier in an attempt to retrieve the soldiers. They succeeded in rescuing all of the team, but as they took off again, one of the helicopters crashed into the glacier. Amazingly, only one man was superficially injured. The other two helicopters returned to help, dumping fuel and equipment in an effort to create room for the crew of the downed helicopter. Suddenly the weather deteriorated even more and a second helicopter crashed into an ice ridge, leaving the one remaining helicopter, known as 'Humphrey', no choice but to fly back to the *Antrim*. Flown by Lieutenant-Commander Ian Stanley, RN, 'Humphrey' returned, later in the day, to the blizzard-bound glacier, where the remaining survivors were located and rescued. However, the helicopter was now dangerously overloaded and struggled precariously back to the ship, eventually crash-landing on the deck. Stanley was awarded the DSO for his bravery and professionalism.

FOUR-MAN PATROL David Stirling's original concept of a five-man patrol was later refined to a four-man unit operating on intelligence-gathering missions in the jungles of Malaya.

Small enough to have good mobility and the advantage of surprise, and yet large enough to have sufficient firepower if necessary, a four-man patrol became and remains the SAS norm to this day.

Men operating in a four-man patrol are normally cross-trained in specific skills, such as medicine, languages, communications and demolition, which makes them a formidable force on covert operations behind enemy lines where self-sufficiency is vital.

'FOUR SQUARE LAUNDRY' An operation set up by a force known as the Military Reconnaissance Force (MRF), an undercover unit that functioned in Northern Ireland in the early 1970s. One of their tasks was to operate a mobile laundry service collecting from house to house. They were assured of good custom, as their prices were far lower than their nearest rivals. Prior to washing, all the clothes would pass through a forensic test for explosives, any traces found indicating where bombs were being assembled. Unfortunately, several members of the MRF who had been former members of the IRA converted to work for the British switched their allegiance again. This led to a Four Square Laundry van being shot up, killing the male driver, though his female companion managed to escape; both were British soldiers.

14 INTELLIGENCE AND SECURITY UNIT An intelligence-gathering unit used in Northern Ireland between 1974 and 1994. Personnel for the unit were selected and trained by the SAS. The role of 14 Intelligence and Security was to monitor the movements of IRA suspects. This information was then passed to the resident SAS detachment for action. Members of '14 Int', as they became known, were on secondment from a variety of army units and consisted of both sexes. They were trained in clandestine surveillance, communications and agent running; they wore civilian clothes and drove specially equipped cars and vans.

FOXLEY, SERGEANT ARCH – AUSTRALIAN SAS REGIMENT (SASR) The longest patrol in the history of the SASR was carried out by a 1 Squadron patrol commanded by Sergeant Arch Foxley during the Borneo Confrontation campaign against Indonesia. Inserted by helicopter on 29 March 1965 in the area of the upper Batam Baram River, in the southeast of the Fourth Division of Sarawak, the patrol was tasked with providing medical aid and other assistance to the groups of Punan tribesmen in the area. This role had previously been carried out by C (Independent) Company of the 2nd Battalion The Parachute Regiment before being relieved by 1 Squadron. The patrol was extracted on 26 June, having been in the jungle for a period of 89 days.

FRAME CHARGE/FLEXIBLE CUTTING CHARGE Originally a wooden frame to which a metal-cased explosive was attached with the aim of blowing a hole through a wall. The size of the frame depended on the area which was to be blown, and the amount of explosive depended on the thickness of the wall. The early frame charge has since been developed by Royal Ordnance into a cutting explosive known as 'Blade'. This is a linear shaped charge made from DEMIEX 200, an EDX based plastic explosive, which detonates in excess of 7,600m (25,000ft) per second. Internally, copper produces a shaped charge jet which, on initiation by an L2A1/L1A1 detonator, cuts with fine precision. Blade is fitted with a self-adhesive strip for attaching it to the target. The charge is then covered by a sheath of close-cell foam. Blade comes in five different weights and thicknesses, each of which can be cut with a knife and tailored into a design of cutting charge. Blade can be incorporated into a conventional explosive ring-main with charges linked together with detonating cord for simultaneous detonation.

Developing the frame charge was an interesting experiment, as the SAS have a tendency to add more explosive than is necessary. During several early experiments the frame charges have been known to knock down a whole house, instead of just making a hole in the wall. The value of frame charges was clearly illustrated during the Iranian Embassy Siege in London, when the front assault team attached one to the French window. Although still available, frame charges have been superseded by the less lethal 'Harvey Wallbanger' wall-breaching cannon.

'FRANKLIN', OPERATION This operation was conducted by 186 men of 4 French Parachute Battalion (4 SAS) between 24 December 1944 and 25 January 1945. They operated around St Hubert and Houffalize, in the Belgian Ardennes, in support of the left flank of the US VIII Corps during the German Ardennes Offensive. In an operation typical of the SAS, the party, commanded by Captain Puech-Samson, was mounted on 31 jeeps and undertook reconnaissance. However, in order to stem the German attack the Allied High Command used all available troops, and so the SAS men also fought alongside regular troops.

FRANKS, LIEUTENANT-COLONEL BRIAN   A key figure in the early days of the SAS, Franks joined the unit after spells with 'Phantom' and the commandos. He saw service in Italy with the Special Raiding Squadron (SRS) as the unit's second-in-command, and then became commander of 2 SAS during the liberation of Europe following D-Day, after its original commander, Lieutenant-Colonel William Stirling, had resigned. He played a major role in Operations 'Loyton' and 'Archway' before the defeat of Germany. During the campaign in northwest Europe he was particularly critical of SOE with regard to SAS drops in France: 'There is a prevalent view amongst some members of staff at SOE that uniformed troops are not welcomed by the Maquis, and further, that in known Maquis areas, it is better to supply them with arms and explosives and let them do the tasks rather than send the SAS to the area. This is in strict contradiction to the views of both French and British Maquis leaders who have returned recently to this country.'

At the end of the war he took part in the re-establishment of the SAS as a territorial unit, and became the first commander of 21 SAS in 1947. Franks was also tasked with hunting down German war criminals responsible for the murder of captured SAS personnel, a task which he pursued with vigour.

FRASER, MAJOR BILL   One of the original members of L Detachment who took part in many of the raids in North Africa, winning a Military Cross for his part in the raid against Agedabia airfield in December 1941. His most famous exploit, however, was an epic 320km (200-mile) slog through the desert after a raid against Marble Arch airfield. From April 1943 he commanded One Troop of the Special Raiding Squadron (SRS), which later became A Squadron when the SRS reverted to being called 1 SAS. In Europe he played an active role in Operations 'Houndsworth' and 'Archway', and was wounded during the latter.

FRASER, SERGEANT LAWRIE — AUSTRALIAN SAS REGIMENT (SASR)   A patrol commander in C Troop 1 Squadron SASR during its tour of operations in South Vietnam from March 1967 to February 1968. On the evening of 3 May 1967 his patrol was inserted by helicopter into a landing zone 5km (3 miles) northeast of Nui Thi Vai, in the western part of Phuoc Tuy Province. As they disembarked from the aircraft, Sergeant Fraser spotted tracks and the patrol came under fire almost immediately. The helicopter light-fire team covering the insertion laid down suppressive fire while the patrol recalled their aircraft which returned and extracted them.

On the afternoon of 18 May the patrol was inserted 10km (6 miles) northwest of Binh Ba to carry out an ambush operation. While crossing a track shortly after leaving the LZ, a Vietcong (VC) appeared and was killed by a 40mm grenade fired by Private Jim Harvey. The patrol immediately came under fire from a group of VC with a heavy machine gun and Harvey was wounded. Withdrawing under cover of smoke, the patrol requested extraction as the VC attempted a flanking move to cut it off from the LZ. Suppressive fire was laid down by a helicopter light-fire team while the patrol was extracted under heavy enemy actions.

On 7 June, Sergeant Fraser and his patrol were inserted into an area of primary jungle 7km (4 miles) northeast of Nui Dat Two which lay some 5km (3 miles) east of 1 Squadron's base at Nui Dat. Two days later, on the morning of 9 June, they established a Claymore ambush on a track and at 14:45 hours six VC entered the killing area. The ambush was initiated, killing one VC who was found to be a tax collector in possession of a large sum of money. The patrol was winched out by helicopter shortly afterwards and returned to Nui Dat.

'FREE BEER' An SAS code word from the early 1970s which required soldiers to report immediately to camp with their kit. In the event of a pending operation, personnel would be sent around the married quarters, knocking on doors and quoting the code word.

FREE FRENCH SAS Free French SAS volunteers were attached to the SAS from December 1941, when Commandant Georges Berge and a group of parachute-trained volunteers joined the unit in North Africa. The Free French contingent soon grew in number and became operational in March 1942. Though they were part of the SAS and wore the same uniforms and insignia, they were in reality a separate unit because of language difficulties. By the end of the campaign in North Africa they made up a full squadron of 1 SAS.

In mid-March 1943, the squadron was handed over to the Free French Army, but the men were later to form the nucleus of the two Free French parachute battalions that joined the SAS Brigade prior to D-Day and became 3 and 4 SAS respectively. These two units fought with distinction in northwest Europe in 1944–45, though during the early part of the campaign they caused a few difficulties. When a French party landed behind enemy lines, the local population were ecstatic, believing liberation from the Germans was at hand. Suddenly the area was filled with celebrating civilians, which naturally alerted the Germans. During Operation 'Samwest', for example, the French SAS commander soon found himself in command of 2,500 Maquis. This sounds impressive, but they were for the most part ill-equipped and devoid of military training. When the SAS base was subsequently attacked the Maquis were scattered.

FRELIMO   Headed by Samora Machel, the Front for The Liberation of Mozambique (FRELIMO) formally came to power in June 1975 as a direct result of the left-wing military coup d'état in Portugal on 25 April 1974. Since the early 1960s, the movement had been waging a guerrilla war against its colonial masters, and the sudden capitulation and departure of the Portuguese took it by surprise as it had envisaged a long struggle to win black majority rule.

Despite the very high cost of the war, and suffering 7,600 casualties, the Portuguese army had been largely successful in containing its problems with FRELIMO, and this was partly due to covert assistance from Rhodesia. During 1968 FRELIMO had commenced operations in the Tete province in Northern Mozambique which shared a border with the eastern part of Rhodesia. In March of the following year the Portuguese requested assistance from the Rhodesians in dealing with FRELIMO guerrillas in Tete. The Rhodesians had agreed to help and elements of C Squadron Rhodesian SAS (RhSAS) were secretly despatched, subsequently taking part in covert operations north of the Zambezi River in the far north of Mozambique.

Initially, FRELIMO supported the ZIPRA movement of Joshua Nkomo but during the early 1970s an agreement was reached with Robert Mugabe's ZANLA group and thereafter FRELIMO supported the latter, allowing it to establish bases in the areas controlled by it in the north of Mozambique. After the departure of the Portuguese, FRELIMO support for ZANLA increased with the latter's presence expanding in northern Mozambique. This resulted in a large number of cross-border operations being carried out in the country by Rhodesian forces, notably the RhSAS.

FRONT FOR THE LIBERATION OF OCCUPIED SOUTH YEMEN (FLOSY)   An Arab nationalist group backed by the Nasser regime in Egypt in the 1960s. Similar support earlier within Yemen had resulted in the formation of the Yemen Arab Republic. Now British-held Aden was the target. The Front for the Liberation of Occupied South Yemen (FLOSY) was provided with training, weapons and camps by Egypt. However, not only did FLOSY find itself battling with the British forces in Yemen, but also another Arab nationalist group, the National Liberation Front, in order to determine who would control the country after the end of British involvement.

F TROOP   Name given to the SAS unit stationed in Belize when the country was used for jungle training during the 1980s.

FUKA   Two Axis airfields were located here in North Africa in World War II: Fuka Main and its satellite. As such, they were the target for SAS jeep raids on the night of 7 July 1942. The airfields were heavily guarded, however, with the result that only eight aircraft were destroyed at Fuka Main and six at the satellite field. Fuka Main was raided again on the night of 12 July, the SAS managing to destroy 22 aircraft.

G

G-DAY Start of the ground war during the Gulf War. It began at 04:00 hours on Sunday 24 February 1991, when two major invasion forces crossed the borders of Iraq and Kuwait simultaneously.

G7 In the 1973 G7 talks, which took place shortly after the Munich Olympics Massacre, special anti-terrorist units were ordered to be set up around the world immediately. The heads of each government also agreed that all steps should be taken, if necessary in co-operation, to put a stop to the hijackings of airliners by terrorists.

GABES GAP At the beginning of 1943 General Montgomery was pushing Rommel back towards Tunisia, and David Stirling was determined that the SAS should play its part in the destruction of the Afrika Korps. To this end he proposed using his men to cause havoc to the rear of enemy-held positions to the west of Tripoli.

His plan had four main points. First, Lieutenant Poat was to take a jeep force and raid to the west of Tripoli. Second, Lieutenant Jordan with more jeeps was to raid the Gabes Gap, the area between the Great Sea Erg and Gabes on the coast, which had become a bottle-neck for enemy communications. If the timing was right, the SAS could cause Rommel major problems. Third, the SAS was to undertake to cross the line of bunkers and anti-tank ditches known as the Mareth Line. Last, David Stirling was to take a small force and drive through the enemy lines to link up with the British First Army that had landed in Algeria.

The SAS units assembled at Eighth Army headquarters at Bouerat, and then advanced to Bir Guedaffia to determine final plans. First to depart was Poat and his party, who would link up with the main party again at Bir Soltane. The main party then set off.

At first the going was good, but progress slowed considerably when the Great Sea Erg was encountered, an area of soft sand and high dunes. On reaching Bir Soltane, Stirling heard by radio that Tripoli had fallen to the British on 23 January, and so it was imperative for Jordan to strike for the Gabes Gap and hit Axis communications; he was duly despatched.

Stirling decided to follow Jordan through the Gap, and set off with five jeeps. On 24 January the SAS soldiers encountered a German armoured unit parked up by the side of the road, and in typical SAS fashion drove right past them. The jeeps left the road and laid up in some low hills. Unusually, no sentries were posted – a bad mistake. The camp was consequently surrounded by the Germans and the SAS party was forced to disperse. It was every man for himself, and at first Stirling made good his escape. However, he was cornered in a cave and captured. Despite escaping two nights later, he was recaptured after being betrayed by an Arab.

What of Jordan's group? At first it managed to inflict some damage, but eventually all but one – Lieutenant Martin – were captured. Once they had got through the Gabes Gap they discovered that the area was densely populated and unsuitable for SAS operations. The loss of Stirling was a grievous blow, but it was not to be fatal for the SAS.

'GAFF', OPERATION   This was an attempt to kill Field Marshal Rommel at his headquarters at La Roche Guyon, a château on the River Seine. Captain William Lee and six men were dropped into the area on 25 July 1944 from an Albemarle aircraft. Accompanying the SAS soldiers were two Frenchmen, an Englishman, three ex-French Foreign Legionnaires, a German and a Russian. The mission got off to a poor start, with Lee falling ill with malaria after landing, and being forced to lie up in a farmhouse for two days. While there, he heard that Rommel had been hurt, perhaps even killed, in his staff car after being strafed by Allied aircraft. Technically their mission was over, but Lee decided to make himself useful by hitting German targets. The SAS soldiers discovered that there was an enemy headquarters in the town of Mantes, which Lee decided to attack at night. In a daring raid the SAS soldiers stormed the building and raked it with gunfire. The fracas inevitably led to German reinforcements arriving, though the SAS men managed to make good their escape to nearby woods. Though they had killed twelve enemy soldiers, they were running very low on ammunition. What followed next day was typical of SAS officers during the war: Lee dressed up as a gendarme and decided to contact the Americans and bring back reinforcements. He rode a bicycle through enemy lines and reached General Patton's headquarters at Le Mans. He debriefed them as to German locations and strengths, but was denied reinforcements and was placed on an aircraft back to Britain. The men he left behind were encountered by advancing American forces a few days later.

'GAIN', OPERATION   An operation in France carried out by Major Ian Fenwick's D Squadron, 1 SAS. The advance party, commanded by Captain Jock Riding, dropped on the night of 13 June 1944 into the area of the Forest of Fontainebleau to the south of Paris. Its job was to find a suitable base for Fenwick and the main party, due to land three nights later. Another party, led by Lieutenant Watson, landed at the same time to attack railway lines before linking up with the main party.

Fenwick and his men arrived on the night of 18 June and made their camp in woods to the west of Pithiviers. Their task was to co-ordinate the local French into fighting the Germans, causing as much disruption as possible prior to the D-Day landings. Though they soon discovered that Maquis security was poor, the SAS soldiers nevertheless undertook foot patrols to blow up nearby railway lines. The dropping of a number of jeeps and their drivers meant Fenwick could extend their operations. The base was moved south to the Forest of Orleans, though Riding and his troop remained at the old base.

A reinforcement drop of twelve men under Captain Garston landed on 4 July, but the Germans were waiting for them. The result was that nine men were captured and three escaped. The nine captives were taken to Paris, with Lieutenant Weihe and Corporal Lutton being taken to hospital (Lutton died of his wounds the next day). The other seven were taken to woods near Beauvais on 8 August and shot. Amazingly, two – Jones and Vaculik – managed to escape and made their way back to Allied lines. Despite this tragedy Operation 'Gain' continued, Watson knocking out a train at Beaune, and then raiding the Malesherbes-Corbeil line. Fenwick was deceived by the Maquis into believing that there were locomotives in a shed at Beligarde. However, they had been betrayed and were surrounded by Germans. A brisk firefight ensued and the SAS soldiers managed to reach their jeeps safely.

At the beginning of August Fenwick was ordered to stop offensive action and concentrate on intelligence gathering. An airborne drop was planned for the Orleans Gap and so the High Command wished to lull the Germans into a false sense of security. Just as well, for Fenwick had his hands full defeating Maquis treachery, being forced to change bases regularly. It was not enough, for on the afternoon of 6 August the camp in the Forest of Orleans was attacked by the Germans. Fenwick, after being told what had happened, determined to find out why. He and four others in a jeep approached the village of Chambon, but before they arrived they were flagged down by a woman, who told the SAS soldiers that the Germans were waiting for them in the village. By this time Fenwick was in a foul temper, and decided to drive ahead at high speed. Racing into the village, the jeep hit a wall of gunfire which killed three of the SAS soldiers, including Fenwick. Sergeant Dunkley was captured, later to be murdered. Corporal Duffy was wounded and taken to hospital, from where he managed to escape and reach American lines. He was subsequently awarded the Purple Heart.

What was left of D Squadron was ordered by Paddy Mayne (who had driven all the way from the 'Houndsworth' base) to disperse and continue intelligence gathering prior to the airborne drop. Maquis treachery continued, with the raid on another base on 10 August. In addition, two more SAS soldiers were captured and executed. The Americans overran the SAS party in mid-August, bringing Operation 'Gain' to an end.

'GALIA', OPERATION This was an operation conducted in 1944 by 34 men of 3 Squadron, 2 SAS, commanded by Captain Walker-Brown, on the Italian Riviera between Genoa and La Spezia. The objective was to support a proposed American offensive in the area, and deceive the Germans into believing an airborne battalion was operating in Italy. The drop took place on 27 December 1944, with five officers and 29 men dropping in daylight north of La Spezia. On the ground the SAS party was divided into a headquarters and five sections. The conditions were appalling, with freezing weather and difficult mountainous terrain. Nevertheless, losses were inflicted on enemy transport and personnel, and at one time the Germans deployed around 6,000 troops to hunt down Walker-Brown's party. Despite cases of frostbite and exposure, the SAS party kept up the pressure, ambushing the enemy and mining roads. The operation was over by 10 February, and Walker-Brown was awarded the DSO for what was a very successful and daring operation.

GALLAGHER, SQUADRON SERGEANT-MAJOR LAWRENCE 'LOFTY' A much respected member of the SAS, who arrived in Hereford in January 1968, from 9 Field Squadron Royal Engineers. He was nicknamed 'Lofty' due to his height and physical strength, something he often took advantage of on the sports field. Originally serving as a member of D Squadron's Boat Troop, 'Lofty' reached the rank of WO11, and was awarded the British Empire Medal. Among his many achievements, he was responsible for raising the British flag on South Georgia after participating in its re-capture. He was tragically killed in a helicopter accident during a cross-decking operation towards the end of the Falklands War.

GAMBIA, THE A potentially embarrassing situation was saved when a small SAS contingent thwarted a coup in The Gambia, West Africa. At the time The Gambia's leader, President Jawara, was in London attending the wedding of Prince Charles to Lady Diana Spencer. In late July 1981, 500 Cuban and Libyan-backed rebels of the Gambian Socialist Revolutionary Party, which was headed by a young Marxist named Kukoi Samba Sanyang, attempted to overthrow Jawara and seize control of The Gambia, securing the capital, Banjul, and the airport in the process.

The coup erupted at 05:00 on Thursday 30 July. Usman Bojang, former deputy commander of Gambia's 300-man Police Field Force – a paramilitary organization charged with preserving order in the tiny country – added muscle to the insurgents, and managed to persuade or force the contingent based in the town of Bakau to join the coup. This group, which amounted to about one-third of the organization, disarmed most of the loyal police, then quickly took over the nearby transmitter for Radio Gambia and moved into Banjul. On the way, they opened the country's largest prison and distributed weapons from the police armoury, not only to the inmates but to virtually anyone who happened to come along.

Not long after daybreak, citizens and former prisoners alike began rampaging through the streets and looting shops. Soon, a free-for-all erupted. Within the first few hours of the coup, scores of bodies – those of policemen, criminals and civilians – littered the streets of Banjul. Arriving at Radio Gambia shortly after rebel policemen seized the station, Sanyang closed the country's borders and its airport at Yundum, some 24km (15miles) east of Banjul. Then he proclaimed a 'dictatorship of the proletariat' and charged the 'bourgeois' Jawara government with corruption, injustice and nepotism and took one of Jawara's wives, Lady Chilel, and four children hostage.

Most Europeans and Americans working in business or holding government posts stayed off the streets, while other foreigners and tourists stayed in the capital, or kept to their hotels in the nearby communities at Bakau and Fajara. Many rebel Gambian policemen, who saw no profit in harming Western individuals, guided anxious foreigners to the residence of the United States ambassador, Larry G. Piper. The house was soon haven to 123 nervous guests, 80 of them American citizens.

On hearing the news, Britain decided to quietly send an SAS team to see what it could do to help. The two-man team, headed by Major Ian Crooke, the second-in command of 22 SAS, left for Banjul immediately. They were dressed in civilian clothes, but their luggage contained anything but holiday clothes: grenades, weapons and a satellite communication system were all concealed within the suitcases. With that sort of gear, security checks could have proved a problem, but diplomatic strings were pulled to make their way clear. Meanwhile, some French-trained paratroopers had been sent in from Senegal in response to the emergency. They had managed to secure the airport, but had been unsuccessful in routing the rebels from the capital.

The two SAS men managed to get seats on a plane bound for Yundum airport. Upon arrival they met up with the Senegalese paratroop commander, Lieutenant-Colonel Abdourah-man N'Gom, who had established his headquarters in the airport confines.

No sooner had they arrived in The Gambia, than Crooke met up with Clive Lee, a hulking six-foot-six retired SAS major who was employed as a civilian adviser to the Gambian Pioneer Corps. Lee had rounded up 23 Pioneer Corps members, armed them, and set off for Banjul. For the

Senegalese troops, capturing Yundum airport had not been easy. During a fierce battle almost half the 120 paratroops making the assault had been wounded or killed. Once this task was completed, Senegalese soldiers entered Banjul, and within a few hours they had cleared it of rebels. They had also gained control of Denton bridge across Oyster Creek, which would prevent insurgents from re-entering the capital from their concentrations in Bakau and Fajara. A combination of these actions secured the route from Banjul to the airport.

Arriving at the British high commissioner's offices, Crooke learned that armed rebel guards had escorted President Jawara's wife and her four ailing children – one of them an infant of only five weeks – to a British clinic. Crooke decided to rescue the president's wife and children, but on approaching the clinic he noticed two armed guards posted at the entrance. Handing his sub-machine gun to his companions, the major then had them circle behind the guards, before he walked up to the pair and distracted them in conversation as the other two SAS men crept up from the rear. Crooke's ruse worked, and the two guards froze when they felt gun muzzles at the back of their heads.

Leaving the captives in the hands of his able comrades, Crooke slipped inside the clinic. He surprised Lady Chilel's weaponless escorts as they watched the children being treated and promptly took them prisoner. After conducting the president's wife and children to the high commissioner's office, Crooke and his party retreated to N'Gom's headquarters at the airport.

N'Gom paced his advance slowly. Panic among the rebels might cause them to begin killing their prisoners. The Senegalese paratroops edged up to one side of the police barracks, leaving several exits unguarded for the rebels to flee. After a tense hour or so, the hostages walked free, and the insurgents dispersed, to be captured later.

Eight days later the rebellion was all over, but it had caused over 1,000 deaths. President Jawara was once again the unchallenged and elected head of the Gambian government. Kukoi Sanyang was eventually arrested in the neighbouring country of Guinea-Bissau, but the socialist government there later released him, despite Gambian requests for his extradition. Senegalese troops captured more than a hundred of the rebels and convicts, seven of whom were ultimately condemned to death. Crooke remained in Gambia for a couple of days before slipping back into the UK, the only confirmation of the SAS presence coming from a Senegalese officer, who told reporters that SAS personnel had indeed participated in restoring order. As always the British Government said nothing.

GAP The Gap was an uncharted area in southern Sabah, near the border with Kalimantan. During the 1963–66 Borneo campaign, the SAS sent a patrol to investigate this uninhabited jungle region. The patrol commander was Captain Dennison, but in the event it was Sergeant Eddie Lillico who actually took responsibility for the mission. The maps issued were nothing more than blank pieces of paper displaying the odd river-line or feature. In addition to making sure there were no enemy present, Lillico's task was to plot and chart the area including types of fauna and flora.

GARDAI In the Irish Republic on the evening of 5 May 1976 the Irish police, the Gardai, stopped two men in a car at a check-point. Just before their apprehension, the men had radioed for back-up support and two vehicles arrived. As a result, eight members of the SAS, together with their vehicles and a large number of weapons, were taken into custody. The republican newspapers had a ball, exploiting the obvious evidence that the SAS operated on both sides of the border. Taken first to Dundalk and then to Dublin, all the men were charged, which proved as embarrassing for the Irish Republic as it was for the SAS, especially since they had only been doing their job and searching for terrorists. The SAS men were finally released, although most of them were fined £100 for carrying unlicensed weapons.

GARLAND, MAJOR ALF – AUSTRALIAN SAS REGIMENT (SASR) Assumed command of 1st SAS Company Royal Australian Regiment (RAR) on 15 March 1963. Commissioned into the RAR from the Royal Military College Duntroon in 1953, he had served with the 1st and 3rd Battalions in Korea after the end of the war. In 1962 he underwent US Army Special Forces training at Fort Bragg, North Carolina, and attended a Ranger course at Fort Benning, Georgia. Thereafter he was attached to a unit of the 101st Airborne Division and subsequently to the US Marine Corps Force Reconnaissance Unit.

During 1963 and 1964, after requests from Britain and much deliberation by the Australian Government, there was an increasing likelihood that 1st SAS Company would be deployed to Borneo as a reinforcement squadron for 22 SAS Regiment, which was already on operations there. Garland thus concentrated on training the squadron for such a role, reorganizing it from a headquarters element and four platoons, by reducing the latter into troops of twenty-one men divided into a headquarters and three patrols of six men. This produced sufficient troops to enable the company, which numbered some 230 all ranks in total, to be reorganized into two squadrons, each comprising a headquarters and three troops.

On formation of the SAS Regiment on 4 September 1964, Major Garland assumed command of 1 Squadron SASR. During February 1965 the squadron deployed to Brunei, in the northeast of Borneo, where it joined 22 SAS Regiment.

GARTHWAITE, CAPTAIN SIMON A charismatic officer of the SAS, who served in Oman. Respected by both his men and the Firqat, he was killed in 1974 while going to assist a Firqat soldier pinned down by heavy enemy fire, proving to the locals that the SAS did not abandon its allies.

'GATLING', OPERATION In October 1978, Rhodesian forces launched a major operation code-named 'Gatling' against three large targets in Zambia. The first was a ZIPRA base known as 'Freedom Camp' situated at Westlands Farm, about 15km (9 miles) north of the Zambian capital, Lusaka. It was the headquarters of ZIPRA's military command and was the nerve centre of its operations inside Rhodesia. Moreover, it housed 4,000 terrorists undergoing training. The second target was a smaller base at Mkushi, 125km (77 miles) northeast of Lusaka, which accommodated some 1,000 terrorists. The third was another large base called CGT-2, which was situated 100km (62 miles) east of Lusaka and accommodated over 4,000 terrorists. Air strikes would be carried out on all three bases followed immediately afterwards by airborne assaults on two of them: Rhodesian 1st SAS Regiment (RhSAS) was allocated the camp at Mkushi while the Rhodesian Light Infantry (RLI) was tasked with attacking CGT-2.

At 08:30 hours on 19 October two Royal Rhodesian Air Force (RRAF) Hawker Hunters, four Canberra bombers and four K-Car Alouette helicopter gunships attacked Freedom Camp, while other Hunters stationed themselves over Lusaka's airport and the Zambian Air Force's base at Mumbwa, ready to counter any threat. Having pulverized their target, the aircraft flew back to Rhodesia to refuel and rearm.

Meanwhile the force of 120 men of 1st SAS Regiment was airborne in six Dakotas and heading for Mkushi. Forty-five more took off in helicopters from a forward base at Mana Pools just inside Rhodesia's border with Zambia. The air strikes on Mkushi went in on time, followed at just after 11:45 hours by the Dakotas carrying the SAS parachutists who went into action immediately on landing. They were joined by their helicopter-borne element, under Captain Bob McKenna, which included an 81mm mortar team. The K-Car gunships laid down a carpet of suppressive fire in front of the SAS as they advanced on the camp.

By 16:00 hours the fighting was over and the base cleared of enemy. Meanwhile the RRAF had attacked the CGT-2 base, followed immediately afterwards by the RLI airborne assault, by which time most of the enemy had fled. The following morning, just prior to withdrawing, the RhSAS ambushed a combined force of ZIPRA and Zambian security forces which approached the base, killing 47 and capturing two prisoners. The operation had been a resounding success and a major setback for ZIPRA. Between 800 and 1,000 terrorists had been killed and some 600 wounded by the air strikes on Freedom Camp. A further 600 had been killed at Mkushi and fifty at CGT-2.

GAZA PROVINCE   In October 1977, Rhodesian 1st SAS Regiment (RhSAS) was withdrawn from operations in Tete Province in northern Mozambique and given the task of carrying out harassing operations in the southeast of the country, in Gaza Province. On its first operation, it was to target the roads between the towns of Mapai and Barragem to the south. On the night of 11 October, a stick of 24 HALO free-fall parachutists, commanded by Captain Dave Dodson, emplaned on a Rhodesian civilian-owned DC-7 aircraft, and in the early hours of the following day, minus one man who collapsed from lack of oxygen, dropped from 3,640m (12,000ft) into an area some 20km (12 miles) east of Mapai. The stick was scattered on landing, and by the time it rallied it was discovered that four men were injured and one was missing. The latter was the medic, Sergeant Jan Greyling, who turned up fifteen hours later.

Leaving the injured in a lying-up position (LUP), Captain Dodson led his men 8km (5 miles) to an ambush site located by the main road and railway line 3km (1.8 miles) from Mapai. Shortly after they took up their positions, a ZANLA convoy of three trucks heavily loaded with ammunition and guerrillas drove into the killing area and the ambush was initiated. Heavy automatic fire was brought to bear on the leading vehicle and all but two of the 22 terrorists aboard it were killed. One succeeded in returning the Rhodesian fire, hitting Trooper Dave Collins in the head and wounding two other members of the ambush group, before being cut down.

The three wounded were evacuated shortly afterwards by helicopter and the ambush force was reinforced by a further eighteen RhSAS dropped from a Dakota, the entire force then splitting into three groups for the rest of the operation. During subsequent operations, the RhSAS found that Gaza Province proved to be a difficult area in which to operate: in addition to suffering from a lack of water and a local population hostile to the Rhodesians, it was heavily garrisoned with FRELIMO troops equipped with armour. Furthermore, it was too far for it to be practicable for the RRAF to provide close air support with helicopters.

GEBHARDT, SERGEANT JACK – AUSTRALIAN SAS REGIMENT (SASR)   In South Vietnam on 30 April 1970, a patrol led by Sergeant Jack Gebhardt was one of a number deployed by 1 Squadron SASR, in support of a 1st Australian Task Force operation to destroy a Vietcong (VC) main force unit, D445 Battalion, and its base in the area of Xuyen Moc, in the eastern part of Phuoc Tuy Province. The patrol located a suspected VC camp some 11km (6 miles) south of Nui May Tao, but shortly afterwards discovered that it was being trailed by a VC force. Efforts to shake it off were unsuccessful and a contact ensued in which two VC were killed. At 19:15 hours Sergeant Gebhardt requested an extraction and 30 minutes later two helicopter gunships arrived, followed by two troop-carrying aircraft. While heavy suppressive fire was brought down on the area occupied by the VC, one helicopter illuminated the patrol's position so that the other could winch the members of the patrol up through the jungle canopy. Fortunately none of the aircraft was hit by enemy fire and the patrol was safely extracted.

GEMINI LANDING CRAFT   A black rubber, inflatable boat, with hinged plywood decking, that will carry up to eight men. It is powered by either 18 or 40 hp outboard motors. There are also 10- and 12-man versions. The Gemini is in current use by both the SAS and SBS for waterborne insertion.

GIBRALTAR   See Operation 'Flavius'.

GIGN   Acronym for Groupement d'Intervention de la Gendarmerie Nationale, France's elite counter-terrorist unit. It was formed in November 1973 shortly after the takeover of the Saudi Arabian Embassy in Paris, in September of that year. The GIGN was initially split into four separate units with GIGN 1 (Paris) under the command of Lieutenant Prouteau. This changed in 1976, and the units merged into one, under Prouteau, who was promoted to captain.

Training for the GIGN is not dissimilar to that of the SAS, although the French place great emphasis on unit fitness, especially swimming. Although under control of the French Ministry of Defence, they are basically policemen and certain military skills have to be taught, which include parachute training at the school in Pau in the southwest of France.

As with other counter-terrorist units, GIGN often undertakes exchange training with similar units including the SAS, in order to practise hostage rescue and counter-terrorist tactics. They also send out training teams to such countries as Saudi Arabia, where they trained the National Guard.

The GIGN had their day in 1994 when four Islamic fundamentalists hijacked an Air France Airbus in Algiers with 220 passengers and 12 crew onboard. Shortly after, they increased their profile by releasing nineteen people, mainly woman and children. However, this act of mercy was soon overshadowed when the terrorists shot and killed two hostages, an Algerian policeman and a Vietnamese diplomat. Hours later, early on Christmas morning they released more women and children, bringing the total to 63. A few hours later, a third hostage was shot, a 27-year-old Frenchman who was a cook with the French Embassy in Algiers. Soon after the aircraft took off, landing early next morning in Marseilles.

While at Marseilles the aircraft was immediately surrounded by snipers and assault personnel of the GIGN. In the late afternoon the aircraft moved towards the control tower without permission, despite demands from the authorities for it to stop. By this time the GIGN commander ordered immediate action (IA), and his men raced towards the aircraft under cover of sniper fire. The team commander, Denis Favier, together with his second-in-command, Oliver Kim, stormed the front right door. They used normal airport landing steps to gain entry, and despite trouble with the door, in the conditions the entry was very slick. At the same time Captain Tardy led another unit in via the right rear door, using the same entry method. Once on board, both groups made their way towards the cockpit where most of the terrorists had gathered. A third group of the GIGN moved into position under the belly of the aircraft, ready to receive the hostages.

By 17:39 hours the four terrorists lay dead. Although the hostages got away with a few minor cuts and bruises, the cost to the GIGN and the crew was heavy. Nine GIGN were wounded, two quite severely, one lost two fingers of his hand and one was shot in the foot. The three members of the crew that were hurt had unfortunately been trapped with the terrorists in the cockpit area; during the assault by the GIGN the co-pilot managed to climb out of a small window and throw himself to the ground, and despite a broken leg managed to escape.

Later reports indicated that the terrorist plan was to fill the aircraft full of fuel and blow it up over Paris; this theory was enforced when twenty sticks of dynamite were found under the front and mid-section seats.

GILLIE SUIT A camouflage suit used by snipers for concealment. The word 'gillie' originates from the name given to a guide of hunting and fishing. Modern day gillie suits offer a wide range of camouflage designs for concealment in all terrain. A new 'stealth' type suit has been developed, which literally makes the sniper totally invisible to infra-red and low-light thermal imagery.

'GIMPY' A nickname used by the SAS for the L7A2 General Purpose Machine Gun (GPMG).

GLOCK MODEL 17 SEMI-AUTOMATIC PISTOL *Specifications* Calibre: 9mm Parabellum; Length: 188mm (7.5in); Weight: 650g (23oz); Magazine: 17-round, box; Muzzle velocity: 350m (381yds) per second.

The Glock Model 17 was trialed by the SAS as one of the weapons to replace the ageing Browning 9mm Hi-Power. Developed in 1980 by an

Austrian firm of the same name, which had previously manufactured bayonets and knives, the Model 17 was their first venture into pistols. The weapon is a short recoil, semi-automatic which has many innovative features including no hammer or safety catch, both of which are controlled by the trigger mechanism. The Glock achieved media notoriety when it was claimed that its plastic body would pass undetected through airport security. This is untrue: 60 per cent of the moulded parts of the weapon are steel impregnated, and this makes it visible under standard airport X-ray.

GLOVER, SERGEANT BARRY 'TEX' – AUSTRALIAN SAS REGIMENT (SASR) Was the commander of a 1 Squadron SASR patrol inserted at 18:05 hours on 21 June 1967 into an area 5km (3 miles) northeast of Thua Tich in the northeastern part of Phuoc Tuy Province. After leaving the landing zone (LZ), the patrol suddenly came upon a Vietcong (VC) camp, but managed to withdraw unseen to the north and subsequently moved into a lying-up position (LUP). However, three VC then appeared within a few metres of a member of the patrol who opened fire, killing two of them. The patrol moved out swiftly, but the rear man, Corporal Steve Bloomfield, reported that the enemy were moving up behind.

Sergeant Glover deployed his men into a temporary defensive position and shortly afterwards the VC, numbering about twenty, advanced on the patrol's position. A fierce battle ensued and some VC were killed. Eventually, however, the patrol succeeding in breaking contact and moving off unseen to an LUP. The VC, however, proceeded to mortar the area throughout the night and it was not until midday on 22 June that Sergeant Glover was able to make radio contact with an American aircraft overhead and request extraction.

As the helicopters arrived, the enemy brought heavy fire to bear despite the suppressive firepower laid down by gunships. Nevertheless, the patrol was winched up safely through the jungle canopy, which was about 36m (120ft) from the ground. Those members of the patrol still on the ground also provided covering fire as the extraction was carried out; on reaching the helicopter they added to the considerable firepower being directed at the VC, which were later estimated at being of company strength. Despite the heavy fire from the enemy, the patrol was extracted safely and returned to the 1 Squadron base at Nui Dat.

GLOVES Northern Ireland saw the first specialist gloves (NI Gloves) issued to British forces outside of Arctic warfare training. The gloves are made of black leather with a light cotton inner and a padded back-fist.

Assault gloves are used by the anti-terrorist teams and are designed to provide protection for the wearer's hands while still permitting full and free movement of the fingers. Manufactured in black Kevlar/Cordura flame-resistant and waterproof fabric, each glove is fitted with a soft leather trigger finger and soft reversed-calf leather on the palm, for protection against friction burns during abseiling and fast roping. Each glove is also fitted with an adjustable strap on the back of the wrist.

'GOBBO', OPERATION   During World War II, this mission (originally code-named 'Portia') was to determine whether an SAS base could be established in the Drente area of northern Holland, to disrupt the German retreat through Friesland toward the German border. Lieutenant Debevfe and five others, including two signallers, dropped on the night of 26 September 1944. Very soon the SAS soldiers were transmitting intelligence back to headquarters, including the information that the area was too densely populated to support a larger SAS party. Notwithstanding this, the 'Gobbo' men remained in Holland until March 1945, and continued to provide the Allies with timely intelligence.

GOLD WINGED DAGGER   A solid gold winged dagger that has its origins in the Gulf War. The dagger really exists although its whereabouts is unknown. The emblem is said to have been cast by an Arab jeweller from thirteen half sovereigns of the issued 'blood money'.

GOLOK   A type of jungle knife so named because it resembles a fighting machete of the same name used by the Indonesians. The British Army issue such a blade for jungle operation. The blade is 35cm (14in) long with a riveted wooded handle and is housed in a Model 58 webbing pattern canvas sheath. The blade is very thick but is difficult to keep sharp. Every SAS soldier is issued one as standard.

GOOSE GREEN   On the eve of the main Task Force landing at San Carlos in the Falkland Islands, the SAS, in one of several diversionary raids, dropped 60 men from D Squadron to attack the Argentinian garrison at Goose Green. The soldiers had to march for 20 hours to reach the hills north of Darwin before attacking the Argentinians with LAWs, Milan missiles, GMPG rounds and tracer. The plan was to simulate a battalion-sized attack, which would normally consist of 600 men, and they conducted the attack with such ferocity that the enemy were taken completely by surprise, unable to pinpoint the SAS positions, and only able to retaliate with sporadic fire. By the following morning the main landing had been completed, and the SAS left Goose Green and began the march northwards to join 2 Para, who were moving inland. However, on the way the SAS soldiers were cut off by a Pucara ground-attack aircraft. It seemed that disaster was inevitable, but just in the nick of time an SAS trooper saved the day when he launched an American Stinger missile at the aircraft, hitting it and blowing it up.

GPMG L7A2 GENERAL PURPOSE MACHINE GUN *Specification* Calibre: 7.62mm × 51 NATO standard; Weight: 5kg (10.9lbs) as light machine gun with bipod, 14kg (32lbs) in sustained fire role with tripod and sighting unit; Muzzle velocity: 838m (913yds) per second; Magazine capacity: belt fed.

The British-built GPMG (or 'Gimpy' as it is more familiarly known) is based on the Belgian FN MAG. There are many variations of the GPMG, but all possess the same reliability, stopping power and accuracy. Once the general purpose machine gun of the British Army, its light machine gun role has now supposedly been replaced by the 5.56mm Light Support Weapon, leaving the GPMG for sustained firing duties only.

The Gimpy has been in service with the British Army since the early 1960s, where it has been used as the standard section support weapon. The SAS rarely carry it in a four-man patrol, but prefer instead to use it from a fixed position in a sustained fire role. During the Oman War, mobile three-man gun teams were set up to support forward units pinned down under heavy fire. All established base units on the Jebel would also deploy several Gimpys for defence. During the days of the 'Pink Panther' Land Rover, Mobility Troops would use the Gimpy fixed both front and rear as a main weapon. It is still in use.

GPS (Global Positioning System) A modern navigational aid which, despite being a similar size to a mobile phone, is a powerful piece of equipment. Over the past few years, this type of navigation has advanced rapidly, allowing for accurate fixes on the Earth's surface to be calculated instantly. The SAS have taken advantage of this, none more so than when travelling and fighting at night during the Gulf War.

GPS was developed by the American Department of Defense, and is based around a network of about 24 satellites in the Earth's orbit. These satellites send out continuous information about their position in relation to the Earth. By using a receiver to acquire information from several of the satellites it is possible to fix a position and orientation at any given point on the Earth's surface.

The accuracy of the information depends on the efficiency of the receiving device. In fact, as the GPS satellites can be accessed by anyone including the Chinese, Russians and Iraqis, the system has a deliberate error built into it, designed to make their receiving equipment inaccurate; this is known as 'selective availability' (SA). This dithers the signal so that only a 'coarse acquisition' (CA) is available. Accuracy under CA reception is about 40m (42yds). In military use this problem is overcome for friendly forces by using the so-called P Code, a very expensive piece of equipment which overrides SA to give accuracy to 10m (11yds) or even less. Almost all aircraft, shipping, tanks and even infantry soldiers now rely on GPS for guidance during wartime.

The GPS works by searching the sky for satellite signals, which it locks on to immediately. A minimum of four such signals will prove satisfactory for the GPS's purposes, although a greater number will improve its accuracy. The information from the satellites is then computed into the form required by the user – to provide, for example, a grid reference, a longitude and latitude, or a height above sea level. Most modern receivers can be programmed to meet individual requirements, either at sea or on land. The receiver can calculate an individual's position by a technique called satellite ranging, simply measuring his position in relation to a set of known objects. It will continually update his position, providing track and speed information, while he is moving. It will also record – without the need for a landmark – waypoints for future use.

'GRANBY', OPERATION The operational name, given by the Ministry of Defence (MoD), for the initial deployment of troops into the Gulf War. The name Granby was chosen by the MoD computer and taken from the distinguished eighteenth-century commander who fought in the Battle of Minden during the Seven Years War. Most people, however, refer to the Gulf War by the American operational name 'Desert Storm'.

GRAPNEL LAUNCHER Shoulder-fired, compressed and air powered, the Grapnel Launcher was created for the purpose of sending a grapnel with a 9mm climbing rope into the target area at ranges of up to 45m (49yds), at 45 degrees elevation, and 55m (59yds) at the horizontal. As an alternative, instead of a rope, a lightweight wire ladder may be attached. In assaults on buildings the launcher allows members of the assault team to utilize upper level entry points from either ground level, roofs or even the upper storeys of adjoining premises. When used in marine operations, the launcher is often employed as a means of covertly boarding vessels, when it is fired from a smaller craft alongside the target.

The launcher is of 50mm (2in) calibre and weighs 9.5kg (22lbs). It is manufactured from high quality anodised aluminium and steel, and is powered by a rechargeable, replaceable 0.5 litre cylinder of compressed air positioned under the barrel, which allows three firings at an operating pressure of 160 bar. Additionally, a rope storage canister can also be positioned under the barrel, in front of the air cylinder, into which the rope has been carefully coiled beforehand, ensuring that, when the launcher is fired, the rope is paid out from the canister smoothly and tangle-free.

The grapnel is made in high strength aluminium and fitted with three spring-loaded folding titanium tines. A flexible stainless steel cable shaft with a rope-ladder attachment is protected by a durable sleeve, which is also part of the standard equipment. Both the head of the grapnel and the end of the shaft have neoprene O-ring seals which guarantee an airtight seal in the barrel and ensure that full pressure is retained for maximum propulsion. The overall length of the grapnel is 720mm (28in) and the weight is 1.5kg (3.5lbs)

The launcher is supplied with a case which also converts into a valise for carrying the launcher, two spare grapnels, air cylinders, ropes and canisters, rope flaking frames, spare neoprene O-ring seals, seal grease and seal replacement tools. The size of the case is 1,280mm × 410mm × 450mm (49in × 15in × 17in) and the total weight, fully packed with launcher and accessories, is 21kg (47lbs).

GREEN MACHINE A general name used when talking about the British Army.

GREEN MAGGOT A popular name for a sleeping bag. The nickname evolved from the appearance of a man snuggled up in his military green coloured sleeping bag, the lateral, ribbed stitching making him look like a giant green maggot.

'GREEN SLIME' Discourteous slang used by the SAS to describe members of the Intelligence Corps, so named because of their green berets.

GRENADE – L2A2 FRAGMENTATION *Specification* Weight: 450g (1lb); Length: 99mm (4in); Diameter: 57mm (2in); Delay: 4 seconds; Explosive: 170g (6oz).

The L2A2 Fragmentation Grenade is designed around the American-made M61 equivalent. The grenade body is drab olive green with a yellow band and lettering. It consists of an explosive core with a threaded fuse-well into which a conventional detonator with a safety split-pin and fly-off handle is screwed. Between the metal outer casing and the explosive charge is a coil of pre-slit wire that fragments and is capable of injuring troops within a radius of up to 20m (22yds).

Gripping the fly-off handle, removing the safety split-pin and throwing the grenade activates it. Release of the handle activates a spring-loaded hammer that, in turn, strikes a percussion cap. After a delay of 4 to 5 seconds the detonator explodes. The SAS also rig the grenade as a trip-wire booby-trap or attach it to an A-type ambush that can be detonated by command wire.

GREVILLE-BELL, LIEUTENANT ANTHONY Served with 2 SAS in Italy during World War II. He took part in Operation 'Speedwell' in northern Italy in September 1944, during which he suffered a bad injury to his back, as well as suffering two broken ribs. Notwithstanding these injuries, plus snow blindness during the 73 days he and his men remained in enemy territory, he displayed that fortitude which is the hallmark of SAS officers.

Greville-Bell went on to serve in northwest Europe before the war ended, but his service with the SAS was far from over. In 1950, when North Korean troops stormed over the 38th Parallel, a squadron of volunteers – M Squadron – was raised by him to fight in the war. However, he did have reservations about Caucasian soldiers being able to operate clandestinely behind enemy lines amid an Oriental population. His list of enemy targets included communications centres, railways, bridges and supply dumps. In the event M Squadron never served in the Korean War, but was instead diverted to Singapore to become B Squadron of the Malayan Scouts. Major Greville-Bell's soldiers were mostly veterans of World War II, and as such they were a welcome addition to Mike Calvert's force.

GRIK The site of an SAS training camp situated on the Thai border with Malaysia. The camp was used to accommodate the troops before and after jungle operations. During the mid-1960s candidates from SAS Selection were also sent to the camp, which was used for jungle training after the end of the Malayan Emergency.

GRYTVIKEN STORY During the Falklands War of 1982, British Task Force commanders needed more information about Argentinian activity on South Georgia, and particularly in the port of Grytviken, yet events on the Fortuna Glacier meant their helicopter capability had been severely curtailed. As a result, a second attempt to get men ashore resulted in D Squadron's Boat Troop being launched on 22 April. Despite two of the five Gemini inflatable boats suffering engine problems, three crews managed to land on the island and set up a watch on the settlements of Leith and Stromnes. An SBS patrol was positioned, by helicopter, just a few kilometres from Grytviken. On his return to HMS *Antrim* the pilot saw the Argentinian submarine *Santa Fe* just surfacing in the ocean below him. The submarine was immediately attacked by helicopters from HMS *Endurance* and the frigate HMS *Brilliant* using depth charges. Badly damaged and listing terribly, the *Santa Fe* struggled back to Grytviken, causing panic in the 130-strong enemy garrison when it was realized that the British were close behind. In an effort to exploit the weakness of the Argentinian position, a joint force of SAS and SBS under the command of Major Cedric Delves mustered 75 men and moved in. Under the instruction of a Royal Artillery commando officer, an SAS troop landed about 3km (2 miles) from the port with two composite Royal Marine/SBS Troops close behind them.

The SAS began to close in on Grytviken, hidden from enemy view by a small mountain. The pressure was beginning to tell; at one point the soldiers shot a group of elephant seals, mistaking them for Argentinian troops, and then destroyed an ancient piece of scrap iron with a Milan missile, thinking it a prominent enemy stronghold. Nevertheless, the men continued their ascent to the top of Brown Mountain where they were surprised to see the buildings of the port below them displaying white flags. The Argentinian troops had surrendered without a shot being fired and Sergeant-Major Gallagher of D Squadron raised the Union Jack immediately. Unbelievably it was later discovered, from conversations with an English-speaking enemy soldier, that the SAS assault party, totally unaware, had walked through a minefield, which surrounded the Argentinian weapons pits. The following morning the Leith garrison surrendered without a fight to two troops from D Squadron and an SBS team, leaving South Georgia in British hands once more.

GSG9 Acronym for Grenzschutzgruppe 9, an elite German counter-terrorist unit formed from the Federal Border Police. Like many of the counter-terrorist units, it was formed in response to the Munich Olympics Massacre in 1972. It consists of approximately 220 men who are stationed at St Augustin, on the outskirts of Bonn. It has close links with the SAS, not only through training but also through operations. GSG9's first leader, Ulrich Wegener, led the German unit's assault on the hijacked aircraft at Mogadishu airport in 1977. Two members of the SAS were also present during the rescue attempt.

GUARDS INDEPENDENT PARACHUTE COMPANY The Guards Independent Parachute Company first became involved with the SAS during the Borneo campaign. The SAS were suffering from a manpower crisis and Major-General Walter Walker pushed for the inclusion of a third squadron of SAS in the battle against the Indonesians. It was decided that the Guards Independent Parachute company would be trained in SAS jungle tactics. Initially used for border surveillance, in September 1965 the Company, under Major L. G. S. Head were allowed to carry out cross-border operations. They achieved excellent results, in one instance ambushing 40 Indonesian soldiers, killing nine and wounding many others. In 1965, several members who had served with the SAS in Borneo were chosen to form the backbone of 'G' Squadron.

GULF WAR In August 1990 Iraq invaded the small, defenceless, oil-rich state of Kuwait, creating a situation which resulted in conflict with the combined forces of the United Nations. Despite attempting to negotiate with Iraq, it became apparent that military action was inevitable, and a huge coalition force began to make its way out to the Persian Gulf. The overall UN Commander was the US General Norman Schwarzkopf, who was a veteran of Vietnam and who had also been involved in operations in Grenada. Both theatres had left him with little regard for unconventional warfare. As a result, it seemed unlikely that US Special Forces and the British SAS, a unit originally created for desert warfare, were going to be used. Fortunately, the commander of the British forces, Lieutenant-General Peter de la Billière, himself an SAS veteran and former commander of 22 SAS, managed to convince Schwarzkopf that the very special skills of the SAS would be invaluable.

Shortly after Christmas 1990, the SAS, having been on standby for action for months, left for the Gulf, activating the largest deployment of the regiment since 1945, with men from A, B and D Squadrons. However, there appeared to be no immediate requirement for them since the US Special Forces and SEALs (Sea, Air and Land) teams had already taken all the border reconnaissance roles. It was proposed to use the SAS and Delta Force to rescue the hundreds of foreign nationals being held as hostages in Saddam Hussein's 'human shield' policy. But this was a logistical impossibility as the hostages were held in various locations all over the country, and too many lives, both soldiers' and hostages', would be lost.

By mid-January 1991, Lieutenent-General de la Billière decided the SAS could be effective in creating diversions ahead of the main attack, destroying Iraqi communications facilities and tracking down the mobile Scud missile launchers which, so far, had eluded both satellite reconnaissance and the air strikes. The SAS were to undertake these operations on the night of the 22/23 January, six days prior to the anticipated start of the main hostilities. In the event, the speed of events took most people by surprise. Just before dawn on 17 January, eight Apache helicopters from the US Army's 101st Airborne Division destroyed Iraqi air defence radars, creating safe corridors along which Allied aircraft could fly. The air war had begun.

Iraq, completely unprepared for such an attack, suffered substantial damage to its infrastructure and a devastating blow to its morale. In a desperate move to retaliate, Saddam Hussein turned his Scuds on Israel and launched twelve missiles on the suburbs of Tel Aviv. Miraculously most inhabitants avoided injury, but the consequences could have been devastating. Scuds are not particularly accurate, but they do have the facility to carry warheads with a chemical or biological weapon capability. Saddam had both of these weapons of mass destruction and, as he had proved with his actions against the Iranians and the Kurds, he was prepared to use them.

The missiles that targeted Tel Aviv that night were carrying conventional warheads, but the realization of what could have happened caused mass panic. Israel threatened to invade Iraq and destroy the Scud sites and launchers. It also declared that it would respond with a nuclear strike on Baghdad if Iraq used a chemical or biological weapon against its people. For United Nations commanders this posed a nightmare situation. If Israel became involved in the war, it would cause massive disagreements amongst the Coalition's Arab allies and the whole war plan would be destroyed – something which Saddam Hussein was acutely aware of, and which was the very reason for his Scud attack.

The SAS were immediately ordered to find and destroy the mobile Scud launchers, and set about their task with road watch patrols and mobile fighting columns. As a result, Israel backed down – at least for the time being. The road watch patrols, positioned far behind enemy lines by helicopter, consisted of eight-man teams who set up static observation posts to survey the main supply routes (MSRs) for the movement of Scud launchers. They would then call by radio for air strikes to destroy the vehicles.

The first patrol wanted to survey their surroundings and requested that the helicopter wait on landing. They decided that the flat terrain offered too little cover, making it dangerous to continue their mission and they returned via the waiting helicopter. The second patrol did not ask their helicopter to wait, but again, after surveying the surroundings, decided it was too risky to continue and decided to drive back to the Saudi border in the only vehicle they had with them. Just before they departed they requested an air strike on a nearby mobile radar station. The US A10 aircraft mistook them for the target; however, realizing his mistake, the pilot managed to pull away just in time to destroy the intended target.

The area the SAS were working in was suffering its most severe weather ever, with freezing temperatures, snow, sleet and rain. The men had been supplied with only desert attire and consequently suffered badly from frostbite and hypothermia. The bitter cold also affected the mobile fighting columns – the other SAS line of attack against the Scuds. Each column consisted of approximately 30 men, twelve heavily armed four-wheel drive vehicles, and motorcycle outriders. There were four of these columns in total – two drawn from A Squadron and two drawn from D Squadron.

By the end of the war, both the SAS and the SBS had been involved in the destruction of many communications facilities and, it is estimated, about a third of the mobile Scud launchers. High casualties had been expected. Despite the dangerous terrain, dreadful weather, intelligence mistakes and radio problems, the regiment lost only four soldiers. In recognition of the important role it had played, the regiment received 55 medals for gallantry and meritorious service. General Norman Schwarzkopf, who in the beginning, had doubted the necessity of their presence, also thanked the SAS personally. See also **de la Billière**; **Bravo Two Zero**; **Desert Fighting Columns**; **Iraq**; **Schwarzkopf**.

GULF WAR II On 20 February 1998 a squadron of Australian SAS Regiment (SASR) consisting of 110 men were deployed by Prime Minister

Howard to Kuwait where they are presently undertaking reconnaissance missions, as well as search and rescue duties which would involve travelling into Iraq to extract downed pilots should conflict begin again. The SASR took with them a range of modern-day Special Forces equipment including Light Strike Vehicles and trail bikes. Twenty members of the New Zealand SAS are known to have joined their Australian counterparts.

GULF WAR INCIDENT One battle took place during the early hours of 9 February, when a three-man team from A Squadron was carrying out a CTR (close target recce) on an Iraqi communications installation. The team was commanded by the SSM (squadron sergeant-major). The SSM was standing on the back of a 'Pink Panther', observing through the MIRA (Milan Infra-Red Attachment). The team had already cut their way through the barbed wire which surrounded the installation, leaving one Pinky at their entry point to act as cover. Moving further into the Iraqi position, the SSM realized that the place was far bigger then he had originally thought. Making a snap decision, he concluded their only alternative was to brass it out and drive through the Iraqi position as quietly as possible, hoping that the dark would conceal their identity. Suddenly a soldier stepped out in front of the Land Rover and made a vain attempt to stop it – he was shot. Seconds later, the Land Rover was under fire from all directions. The SSM was hit in the first burst. A round had gone through the top of his knee, throwing him into the back of the vehicle. At the same time the driver shot forward, accelerating hard, hoping to burst through the position. He had just driven through the camp gates, when their luck ran out. Just 300m (327yds) from the camp the Land Rover lurched to a sudden halt as it crashed hard into a tank ditch. Seconds before, the SSM had raised himself, hoping to get the rear gun into action. The sudden stop threw him over the roll bar, where he landed, half on the laps of the passenger and driver and half on the bonnet. His wounded leg was lying twisted on his chest. The other two men immediately made to escape, dragging the SSM between them. They did not get far; the damage from the bullet and the vehicle crash had left the SSM in a critical condition. After climbing a slight rise, the three hid among some rocks. Here they tried to staunch the flow of blood coming from the SSM's leg wound. Slipping in and out of consciousness, the SSM ordered the other two to leave. One of them asked if he should finish off the SSM as capture by the Iraqis would mean torture and possibly death. It was a tempting offer, but the SSM declined, willing to take his chances. Alone, the SSM fell unconscious once more only to be woken by Iraqi soldiers who took him prisoner.

Surprisingly the SSM was fairly treated by an Iraqi civilian doctor, who did a wonderful job of repairing the damage to the injured leg.

Eventually he was treated in hospital, while his interrogation continued. One day, the two interrogators were standing by his bed deliberating about a question to ask him; as they turned to speak he pre-empted the question, giving away the fact that he spoke fluent Arabic. Despite protests from the medical staff the two interrogators ripped the drips from his body and gave him a beating. He survived the ordeal and still serves in the SAS.

GURKHAS The Brigade of Gurkhas was established as an integral part of the British Army after the partition of India in 1947. They moved to the Far East in 1948 and formed 17 Gurkha Infantry Division in Malaya, and served continuously throughout the twelve-year Malayan Emergency. They saw active service in Brunei from 1962 and during the 'confrontation' with Indonesia: four years of continuous operations from 1962 to 1966. They acted in conjunction with the SAS throughout the Malayan campaign where they were used as a QRF (Quick Reaction Force). They also took on independent actions against the Indonesians; in one such operation in November 1965 Corporal Rambahadur Limbu won the Victoria Cross.

GUTHRIE, LIEUTENANT-GENERAL CHARLES Joined the SAS in 1965 from the Welsh Guards, and served with G Squadron as a troop commander. Although he never returned to Hereford after his tour, he was an ardent supporter of the SAS throughout his rapid rise in the military hierarchy.

H

HABASH, GEORGE Born in Lydda, Palestine, in 1925 George Habash was the son of a wealthy grain merchant. His family were practising Christians and followed the Greek Orthodox faith. Habash attended the American University in Beirut where he studied to be a doctor of medicine. In May 1948 the British Army withdrew from Palestine and within a few months his family were forced to flee, to become refugees in Jordan. Habash graduated from his studies in the early 1950s and set up a clinic for the poor in Amman with a fellow doctor and Greek Orthodox Palestinian, Dr Wadi Haddad. Over the next few years Habash became so embittered that he decided to follow Marxism. An arsenal of guns replaced his medical equipment and he established the Popular Front for the Liberation of Palestine (PFLP), determined to liberate Palestine and inform the world about its people's problems.

In 1968 he was arrested and imprisoned by the Syrians for planning to overthrow the regime there. During his imprisonment Dr Wadi Haddad, Habash's friend and co-conspirator, devised an escape plan to rescue Habash from the high-security prison. The plan was a great success and resulted in increased interest in the newly formed PFLP, swelling the number of active members to 3,500 and winning the support of many ordinary Palestinians.

Together, George Habash and Wadi Haddad were responsible for creating the international alliance that brought the first campaigns of terror to Europe and the Middle East in the early 1970s. It was as a result of this violence that units such as the anti-terrorist teams came into being.

HADDAD, WADI The son of a teacher and born in Palestine, in Safad in Galilee, just before World War II, by the age of nine he had become a refugee. Haddad joined George Habash in his formation of the PFLP and became a violent and revolutionary partner in the organization. Haddad was responsible for, amongst other acts, the Entebbe and Mogadishu hijacks.

'HAFT', OPERATION The code-name for a small operation which took place between 8 July and 11 August 1944, when seven men from 1 SAS were dropped into the Mayenne-Le Mans area of northern France. The objective was to report on German troop movements and locations, identify targets for Allied bombers and make contact with local Maquis forces. All the aims were achieved before the mission ended.

'HAGGARD', OPERATION 'Haggard' was one of those SAS missions which suffered from the speed of the Allied advance from the Normandy bridgehead following the D-Day landings. It involved 52 members of B Squadron, 1 SAS, under the command of Major Lepine, later reinforced by a jeep troop from 3 SAS. Its primary aim was the establishment of a base south of the River Loire between Nevers and Gien, from where harassing operations against the Germans could be launched. In late July 1944, when the operation was earmarked to commence, this made sense. But SOE (Special Operations Executive) had the drop delayed because its agents were operating in the area. So when the drop did take place – on 10 August – American forces were already occupying the area. The SAS men were therefore dropped near Villequis to monitor the two main roads leading east from Bourges. Once on the ground the SAS soldiers patrolled aggressively, but in truth there were few pickings as the Americans were getting close and there was little German traffic. 'Haggard' was over by 23 September, when the men were ordered north to link up with the 'Kipling' party.

HAHO (HIGH ALTITUDE HIGH OPENING) HAHO is a method of air insertion where the parachutist exits the aircraft at a height of up to 9,120m (30,000ft) and opens his parachute immediately. Using a RAM air parachute the parachutist can then glide for several kilometres; this allows the SAS to infiltrate undetected across borders or major enemy concentrations. GPS (global positioning system) can be used in flight to track the individual's position in relation to the Earth's surface and the landing zone.

In the early 1980s the SAS dropped a team of free-fallers off the south coast of England using the HAHO principle, all of which made it into France.

HALO (HIGH ALTITUDE LOW OPENING) In a HALO drop, the parachutes do not open until approximately 760m (2,500ft) above the ground. This requires the parachutist to free-fall for most of the way, a method of infiltration that is fast, silent, accurate and tends to land the team in the same spot. The speed of descent in free-fall is fast, but may vary slightly with each individual and the position he holds. For example, in a normal 'delta' position, he will descend at a rate of 192km/h (120 mph), but in a 'tracking' position this may well increase to 280km/h (175mph).

HAMILTON, CAPTAIN JOHN   Commanded Mountain Troop of D Squadron during the Falklands War. He and his troop were initially involved in the recapture of South Georgia and the raid on Darwin, designed to create a distraction while the main amphibious landings took place at San Carlos Bay, East Falkland. He also led the operation to sabotage the Pebble Island airstrip. Towards the end of the war, on 10 June, a patrol led by Captain Hamilton was spotted close to Port Howard, on West Falkland. The four SAS men desperately tried to fight their way out and as two withdrew, Hamilton and his signaller gave covering fire. During this time Hamilton was hit, but continued to provide supporting fire. Some time later the overwhelming force of Argentinians killed Captain Hamilton and captured his signaller; but he had won sufficient time for the rest of his patrol to escape. Captain John Hamilton was awarded a posthumous Military Cross.

HAMILTON SMITH, CAPTAIN MARTIN – AUSTRALIAN SAS REGIMENT (SASR)   The first commander of the Tactical Assault Group (TAG), Captain Martin Hamilton Smith, together with Sergeant Leigh Alver, trained with the SAS anti-terrorist team in late 1979.

HAMMOCK   A form of canvas bed derived from those used at sea by early sailors and adapted for use in the jungle. The modern military hammock can be slung between two trees in the traditional fashion, or formed into a more permanent pole bed. The advantages of the hammock are many, not least for lifting the soldier off the jungle floor, which although comfortable is crawling with biting insect life. Early hammocks were made from discarded parachute panels, which were folded and secured by the rigging lines. The modern military version is designed to be small, robust and quick to erect. When made into a pole bed and covered with a basha sheet it forms a comfortable and waterproof dwelling. The hammock can also be used as an emergency stretcher.

HANGAR   'The hangar' was a location in Northern Ireland that housed members of 14 Intelligence and Security Unit together with a troop of SAS. The hangar was large enough to provide cover for the twenty Portakabins and several caravans that were used to house all the operatives. In addition to this accommodation there was a command centre with operations room, briefing room and armoury. There was also a large gym area, dining-room and social club. The hangar is no longer used by the SAS.

HANGI   The Hangi is a development of the tropical fire pit cooking method which the SAS use on survival training. It is particularly useful when no food containers are available. A hole, 60cm (24in) deep and of similar diameter, will accommodate enough food for a small group. A pyramid fire incorporating fist-sized stones is built over the hole and set alight. It is allowed to burn until the heated stones fall to the bottom of the hole. Food is then wrapped in large clean leaves and the parcels placed on the hot stones. The pit is covered with branches, foliage and a layer of earth. This will retain the heat in the hangi, and during the next 3 to 4 hours the food will be cooked.

HARD DOG SECTION   The hard dog section is a part of the airport police stationed at Heathrow Airport, so called because of the huge beasts they keep there. In the early days when hijacking took priority, the SAS spent a great deal of time at airports and during this period built up a good working relationship with the dog section. The handlers visited Hereford on a regular basis; likewise they hosted the SAS on tours around the capital's main airport and took part in several exercises.

HARD ROUTINE   An attitude adopted during the Malayan Campaign, which takes its meaning from self-imposed discipline. Soldiers were often required to live for months in the jungle carrying much of their daily requirements in a bergen. Additionally they were constantly aware that they could confront the enemy at any moment. Living in such an environment, where the clothes rot off your back, eating the same meagre rations day after day, moving through thick jungle, always talking in whispers, requires exceptional self-discipline which, in the SAS, is referred to as 'hard routine'. The ability to apply this self-discipline remains the backbone of the SAS mentality.

'HARDY', OPERATION   This was the first sizeable mission mounted by 2 SAS in France in 1944. On the night of 27 July, 55 men and 12 jeeps were dropped by parachute into eastern France to establish a base on the Plateau de Langres, northwest of Dijon. The commander of the SAS party was Captain Grant Hibbert, whose orders were to establish a secure supply dump and collect intelligence regarding German activities. At first there was to be no offensive action against the enemy. Intelligence was collected, and in August Operation 'Hardy' was joined by Major Roy Farran's 'Wallace' group.

HARRISON, CAPTAIN DERRICK   Originally of the Cheshire Regiment, Harrison joined the Special Raiding Squadron and took part in the campaigns in Sicily and Italy. In France in 1944 he took part in Operations 'Kipling' and 'Houndsworth'. During 'Kipling' he fought an intense action at the village of Les Ormes, his subsequent account of which provides an interesting insight into how SAS soldiers conducted themselves behind enemy lines in World War II. Harrison's force consisted of two jeeps: 'The Union Jacks on our jeeps jerked into life as we accelerated into the village square. In the road stood a large German truck and two staff cars, blocking the way through. A crowd of SS men in front of the church dashed for cover as I opened up with my machine guns, and as the vehicle burst into flames, I saw some of the Germans fall. But now I was in trouble. My jeep had come to a sudden halt, my Vickers [machine gun] jammed and the Germans were firing back ... I had grabbed my carbine and was now standing in the middle of the road firing at everything that moved; Germans seemed to be firing from every doorway. I felt my reactions speed up to an incredible level. It was almost as if I could see individual bullets coming towards me as I ducked and weaved to avoid them. All the time I was shooting from the hip, and shooting accurately.' Amazingly, Harrison managed to get out of the village in the other jeep, leaving 60 Germans dead and wounded and one truck and two staff cars destroyed behind him. He won a Military Cross for his actions.

'HARROD', OPERATION Code-name for a mission conducted by 85 men of 3 French Parachute Battalion (3 SAS) between 13 August and 24 September 1944. The force was commanded by Commandant Conan (the leader of 3 SAS), and was part of a wider SAS strategy to support General George Patton's US Third Army in its drive to the German border. Conan's men were parachuted into the area around Saône-et-Loire in central France, their task being the disruption of enemy movements and the bolstering of local Maquis units. Though German opposition resulted in the French SAS soldiers losing six killed and eleven wounded, they destroyed a number of bridges, roads and railway lines.

HART, MAJOR L.E.O.T. 'PAT' A regular officer with the Rifle Brigade, Hart became SAS brigade major in charge of administration in 1944–45, and when the SAS was reformed after the war Hart became second-in-command of the regiment, which at that time was a territorial unit. He wrote a detailed report in November 1951 which raised the issue that there was no co-ordinating or supervisory arrangements for it. In particular he was eager for the regimental headquarters to have an officer of sufficient rank who could 'ensure that the SAS is accepted and understood as a permanent and valuable part of the Army'. It was three years before the majority of the recommendations were grudgingly accepted by the War Office.

HARVEY, COLONEL KEN – RHODESIAN 1ST SAS REGIMENT On 24 March 1945 nineteen-year-old Lieutenant Ken Harvey of 3 Squadron, 2 SAS Regiment, commanded by Major Roy Farran, was a member of a combined force of SAS and partisans which attacked the headquarters of the German LI Corps located in two villas at Albinea, in the Po Valley below the foothills of the Apennines in northern Italy. Farran's force was organized into three groups. Harvey was the commander of one, comprising ten SAS and twenty partisans, whose objective was the Villa Calvi which provided accommodation for the corps' chief-of-staff, Oberst Lemelson, and the headquarters' operations room. One of the other groups was responsible for attacking the nearby Villa Rossi which was the home of the corps commander, Generalleutnant Hauk, while the third group was to take up a blocking position to prevent troops from the nearby garrison from intervening.

Having advanced across open ground from a farm where it had laid up during the previous day, Farran's force succeeded in reaching its assault positions undetected. Lieutenant Harvey's group made its way to the front of the Villa Calvi where it attempted to blow in the main door with a rocket launcher, which misfired. There was no time for a second attempt as four enemy sentries appeared and Harvey was forced to kill them with his Bren gun. A major firefight ensued and, under covering fire from the partisans, Harvey and his SAS group stormed the building, clearing the ground floor and killing four Germans, including the chief-of-staff, in the process. Harvey narrowly escaped being shot; he was saved by the swift reactions of one of his NCOs, Sergeant Godwin. An attempt to gain the upper floor was unsuccessful, with the Germans rolling grenades down the stairs, and so Harvey and his men set the villa ablaze, rapidly evacuating the building as it caught fire. Shortly afterwards, Lieutenant Harvey and his men joined the rest of Major Farran's force as it withdrew to the mountains.

Thirty years later Ken Harvey, who was awarded the Distinguished Service Order for his gallantry and leadership during the raid on the German headquarters, was paid the signal honour of being appointed Honorary Colonel of the Rhodesian 1st Special Air Service Regiment.

HATTON ROUND The Hatton round is a 12-bore cartridge with a bullet head made of a soft material that disperses its kinetic energy on impact, and which is used primarily to remove the hinges and locks from a door. The SAS will employ Hatton rounds by firing them from a Remington shotgun to ensure rapid entry during an anti-terrorist assault. The muzzle of the shotgun is placed directly against the hinge or locks and fired; this allows for most doors to be opened without any harm to hostages who might be on the other side.

HAUNTED HOUSE Situated in Brunei, the 'Haunted House' became well known during the Borneo Confrontation campaign as the location for the SAS squadron based there. Its name comes from the reputed presence of the ghost of a young girl murdered by the dreaded Kempeitai, the Japanese secret police, who were housed in the building during the occupation of Brunei in World War II. Located behind the Sultan's palace, the house was large enough to accommodate the squadron headquarters and its administrative element, and provided facilities for patrols returning from operations. The ghost's presence played a major part in the security of the SAS base.

HAWKINS, SERGEANT JOHN   A patrol commander during the Jebel Akhdar campaign in Oman. His nine-man strong patrol ambushed an enemy force of 30 Arabs, waiting until they were only metres away. His coolness accounted for the patrol leaving twelve of the enemy dead. He was awarded the Distinguished Conduct Medal for his actions.

'HEADSHED'   SAS slang for the group of senior or administration officers that controls the SAS.

HEALY, SERGEANT PETER – AUSTRALIAN SAS REGIMENT (SASR)   On the afternoon of 18 July 1966, Sergeant Peter Healy was the commander of a patrol of 3 Squadron SASR inserted in the area of the Nui Dinh Hills in the western part of Phuoc Tuy Province in South Vietnam. Its task was to locate and destroy observation posts and radio outposts belonging to North Vietnamese Army (NVA) units in the area. At 11:45 hours on the following day the patrol came across a platoon position from which the sound of voices could be clearly heard. Having withdrawn some 300m (327yds), Sergeant Healy contacted 3 Squadron's base and requested an air strike. The patrol then withdrew to a distance of 1,000m (1,090yds) from the camp, and during the late afternoon the area was bombed.

At 18:30 hours the patrol approached the camp and on entering it opened fire on a tent containing two Vietcong (VC) who were killed. Other VC in another tent were shot and wounded as the patrol withdrew, concerned that an enemy force was following it. The patrol was extracted at 08:30 hours on the following morning and a second air strike was called in on the camp.

'HEARTS AND MINDS'   A tactic that is integral to the way the modern SAS fights, 'hearts and minds' was a term originally coined by General Sir Gerald Templer, the Military High Commissioner in Malaya during the Malayan Emergency. The term was used in June 1952, when Templer was asked whether he had sufficient soldiers for the job. He replied: 'The answer lies not in pouring more soldiers into the jungle, but rests in the hearts and minds of the Malayan people.' Templer took measures to win over the Malayans, with such policies as building forts in the jungle and gaining the confidence of the indigenous aboriginal tribes. From 1953 the SAS participated in the building of these forts, and lived with the aborigines, learning their language, customs and ways of life. It soon became clear that medical facilities, however primitive, were integral to winning the trust of the locals (it is important to note that aid of any kind had to be real and beneficial; in no way were local people treated patronizingly). Thus SAS soldiers started to acquire midwifery and veterinary skills. A simple aspirin could cure a toothache and make a friend for life. However simple this may seem, it worked in the jungles of Malaya, Borneo and in the deserts of Oman. The benefits of 'hearts and minds' were many, not least the intelligence gained from the locals among whom the SAS soldiers lived. Of course living with locals could be infuriating, and SAS soldiers had to learn the qualities of patience and tact. But the rewards were incalculable.

HECKLER & KOCH   Three former Mauser employees, who used their skills to develop a new type of sub-machine gun, founded Heckler & Koch in 1947. The company had its first big break when, in 1959, the West German Army adopted their Gewehr 3 (G3) assault rifle. The MP5 sub-machine gun was developed from the successful G3 rifle and shares many similar characteristics. Unlike most other sub-machine guns, the MP5 fires from a closed and locked bolt, using the same delayed blowback action as the G3. This makes the weapon expensive to produce, but the increased safety and accuracy compensate for this. Heckler & Koch now have factories world-wide, and their weapons are used in over 50 countries.

HECKLER & KOCH G3   *Specification* Calibre: 7.62mm; Length: 102.5cm (40in); Weight: 2kg (4.4lbs); Magazine: 20-round, box; Muzzle velocity: 790m (861yds) per second.

The Gewehr 3 has its origins in a Mauser design which, curiously, found its way through Spain, Holland and eventually back to Germany, where Heckler & Koch took on the task of perfecting the G3 into the weapon we know today. The weapon is robust and reliable which is why so many armies around the world have chosen it as the standard infantry weapon. The G3/SG1 comes with a telescopic sight and bipod and has an adjustable hair-trigger which the SAS anti-terrorist teams use for sniping.

HECKLER & KOCH MP5   *Specification* Calibre: 9mm × 19 Parabellum; Weight: 1.1kg (2.5lbs); Muzzle velocity: 400m (436yds) per second; Magazine capacity: 15- or 30-round, box.

The weapon of choice for many of the world's anti-terrorist units, including the SAS. It was the weapon used during the Iranian Embassy Siege. Its closed bolt mechanism makes it the most accurate sub-machine gun currently on the market. However, these weapons are not cheap. There are various versions of the MP5, including one with a telescopic metal stock and another with a short barrel.

HECKLER & KOCH PSG1 SNIPER RIFLE   *Specification* Calibre: 7.62mm × 51 NATO standard (.308 Winchester match); Weight: 4kg (9lbs) with sight; Muzzle velocity: 820m (894yds) per second; Magazine capacity: 5- or 20-round, box; Range: 1,000m (1,090yds).

Heckler & Koch produce a range of sniper rifles, all adapted from the basic G3 model. The type considered the most accurate is the semi-automatic Prazisionsschutzengewehr 1 (or PSG1). This weapon has silenced working parts, a heavy barrel, adjustable butt and trigger and a ×6 zoom telescopic sight. It is in use with German Special Forces and police, as well as other police forces world-wide.

HEDGEHOG   Fire bases constructed and used by the RAF Regiment in the early 1970s to protect the airfield close to Oman's southern capital of Salala. A mortar tracking system called 'Green Archer' was used to help pinpoint the rebels' positions when the airfield was attacked. Before the sultan's forces became established on the Jebel Massive that overlooked the air base, the Hedgehogs were the only lines of defence for the airfield (see Dianas). Soldiers of the RAF Regiment manned the Hedgehogs.

HERCULES   See C-130.

HEREFORD   A cathedral city situated on the Welsh borders, which has been home to the SAS since the early 1960s. Many of the soldiers have married local girls, whose sons have also joined the regiment. The city suffered a double tragedy during the Falklands War, when a helicopter full of SAS troops crashed into the sea killing 22 men, while a few days later, HMS *Antelope*, Hereford's adopted ship, was destroyed by Argentinian aircraft. The city was devastated and joined in prayer; the cathedral remained open to all denominations.

HEREFORD BRANCH OF THE SAS ASSOCIATION   The Hereford Branch of the SAS Association serves to preserve the relationship between serving and retired members of the regiment. It also provides welfare to those who find themselves in difficulty. Full membership is open to all former and serving 'badged' members of 22 SAS, and invited members from L Detachment, 264 SAS Signals Squadron and other members who have worked with the SAS in a long-term support role. In addition to full membership, the association also admits associate and honorary members.

HEROS LOKOS   See Sacred Squadron.

HIDE   Name used to describe an IRA arms cache, and also used when talking about an SAS observation position.

HIGH EXPLOSIVES   The SAS use a wide range of explosive devices, most of which are tailor-made for a particular task. Where precision cutting is required, a few grammes of Blade explosive or the equivalent will be used, while a bridge demolition will require many kilos of PE4 plastic explosive. An SAS demolitionist will rely on the accurate positioning of an explosive charge rather than the quantity used.

Modern high explosives are fairly safe to handle; they can be dropped, jumped on and even set on fire, although burning more than 9k (20lbs) is likely to produce enough heat to cause detonation. Handling plastic explosive is a little like playing with children's plasticine and it can be moulded in a similar way. For the most part, the SAS still use PE4, which is white in colour and odourless, unlike its predecessors.

To activate high explosives a detonator is required. This device comes in two types: electrical and non-electrical. A detonator is a small aluminium tube about 250mm (10in) long and half filled with a substance known as PETN. The non-electrical detonator is open, ready to receive a length of safety fuse, while the electrical detonator has two wires protruding from it. When a detonator is pushed into plastic explosive and the fuse is lit, or the wires are connected to a battery, the detonator is activated. The speed of a detonator is around 5,776m (19,000ft) per second; this jump-starts the explosive, which in the case of PE4 explodes at around 7,296m (24,000ft) per second – sharp enough to cut steel. High explosive becomes dangerous to handle only when a detonator and initiation device is connected.

HILL, LIEUTENANT MICHAEL SINCLAIR During the Malayan Emergency, Hill was one of Mike Calvert's officers and made his name by leading a patrol which stayed in the jungle hunting down Communist Terrorists (CTs) for a total of 103 days. This is believed to be the longest jungle patrol ever, to the extent that the members forgot which day it was. It was also an indication of what the SAS could do with the right training and personnel.

HINDSON, SECOND-LIEUTENANT BILL – AUSTRALIAN SAS REGIMENT (SASR) In South Vietnam on 9 August 1967 Second-Lieutenant Bill Hindson's five-man patrol was inserted at around midday into thick jungle in an area 4km (2.5 miles) southeast of Thua Tich, in the northeastern part of Phuoc Tuy Province to carry out a reconnaissance mission. From the very start of the operation it became apparent that there were a number of Vietcong (VC) in the area, at times as near as 15m (16yds) away. On the following day four VC were sighted and a number of shots were heard. At 10:15 hours on 11 August a large force of 63 VC, preceded by two scouts, moved carefully down the track near the patrol's position. At 12:55 hours the patrol moved out, having passed the information about the enemy force over its radio, and proceeded to cross the track. As the lead scout, Lance-Corporal Alan Roser, stepped on to it, a VC appeared about 20m (22yds) away. Roser engaged him and then switched his aim to a light machine gun which opened fire on the patrol. Second Lieutenant Hindson also engaged the enemy, standing his ground instead of adopting the normal 'shoot and scoot' contact drill.

During the firefight, however, the patrol signaller, Private Noel de Grussa, was seriously wounded in the left thigh and unable to walk. Under covering fire from Hindson the patrol withdrew, carrying de Grussa to a spot where the medic, Private Gerry Israel, was able to apply emergency medical treatment to his wound. Carrying de Grussa, the patrol then moved off again, while Hindson covered their rear. Shortly afterwards, he activated his URC 10 radio beacon and the signal was picked up by an airborne forward air controller in the area. Within 45 minutes US Air Force A-1 Skyraiders and F100 Super Sabres were overhead and carrying out air strikes on the VC who were approaching the patrol's location. Helicopters of 9 Squadron Royal Australian Air Force also arrived, accompanied by helicopter gunships which laid down suppressive fire as the patrol was winched up through the jungle canopy. The enemy were so close that they were engaged by the door gunner of the winching helicopter and by Second-Lieutenant Hindson as he ascended. Nevertheless, the extraction was successful and the patrol arrived back at 1 Squadron's base at 14:40 hours.

HITLER'S COMMANDO ORDER   In response to the many raids and sabotage missions carried out by British commandos in North Africa, Hitler issued a directive in October 1942. This stated: 'I therefore order that from now on all opponents . . . in so-called Commando operations . . . are to be exterminated to the last man in battle or flight. Even should these, on their being discovered, make as if to surrender, all quarter is to be denied on principle.' This obviously gave local commanders licence to execute any captured Commandos, including SAS, and during the French campaign in 1944 the Gestapo in response to the order executed several SAS soldiers. For example, during Operation 'Bullbasket', 31 British servicemen were murdered by the Germans. Some German commanders, such as Rommel, chose to ignore the order. After the war Major Eric Barkworth and a small team carried out a series of extensive examinations into war crimes against SAS soldiers, which resulted in several of the perpetrators being hanged.

HMS *ANTELOPE*   Hereford's adopted Royal Navy ship hit by an Argentinian bomb during the Falklands War on 23 May 1982.

HMS *FEARLESS*   A Royal Navy command and communications ship with which the SAS has been involved on several operations and training exercises.

HOOLIGAN BAR   The 'Hooligan bar' was designed in America for the express purpose of removing windows. Basically, it is a one-metre metal bar with various attachments. Two or three blows with the bar will take out most of the window; then the hooks are used to pull out the debris, or used as leverage on sash-type windows.

HOSTAGE RESCUE, GULF WAR One of the first roles considered for the SAS in the Gulf was that of hostage rescue, aimed at releasing those civilians who had been taken prisoner in Kuwait before being transported by the Iraqis back to Baghdad. Saddam Hussein used some of the hostages as a human shield around various military installations. Fortunately most of the hostages were released before the main invasion began.

'HOUNDSWORTH', OPERATION For nearly three years during World War II, the role of the SAS was misunderstood by Supreme Headquarters Allied Expeditionary Force (SHAEF). On the eve of the D-Day landings in June 1944, SHAEF initially wanted to drop SAS parties to prevent German reinforcements from reaching the front. This would undoubtedly have resulted in the decimation of SAS units. Fortunately, the lack of aircraft available for transport forced the abandonment of the plan. However, the SAS did manage to mount other missions more suited to their talents, of which 'Houndsworth' was one.

The operation involved A Squadron, 1 SAS, under the command of Major Bill Fraser. His task was to establish a base in the densely wooded country to the west of Dijon. His orders were to disrupt German communications, cut railway lines and assist local Maquis units. The advance party dropped on the night of 5 June, and included Johnny Cooper and Reg Seekings. Despite flying in foul weather and dropping blind (Cooper hit a stone wall on landing and knocked himself unconscious), the party managed to assemble and release carrier pigeons carrying intelligence (though they never reached England).

After making contact with the local Maquis, a landing strip was made ready to receive more supplies and reinforcements. Bill Fraser was the first to arrive, with two sticks following, led by Captains Wiseman and Muirhead. The 'Houndsworth' base eventually numbered 18 officers and 126 other ranks, and nine jeeps. For the next three months the SAS force repeatedly cut the railway lines around Dijon. Of course, such a force, combined with varying numbers of Maquis, did not go unnoticed, and the enemy soon moved into the area to deal with them. The opposition consisted of Russians in the service of the Germans, together with the despised Milice (Fascist militia). The major enemy garrison was at Château Chinon, and in early July the German-officered Russians began a campaign of intimidation in the local villages, taking hostages and burning property. They took a number of Maquis sympathizers from Montsauche, and transported them towards Château Chinon and almost certain torture and execution.

Alec Muirhead's troop and the Maquis set an ambush for them, however, at a site with forest on one side and open country on the other. Johnny Cooper was one of those who took part in the ambush: 'The first three-tonner crammed with soldiers drew level with the wood pile and over came two plastic bombs. One hit the bonnet and the other the rear of the vehicle. Pandemonium among the occupants. Many were killed by fire from the Maquis as they fled across the road towards the open fields. Our Brens opened up with devastating effect and many of the Russians retreated back to the ditch, which was in Reg's sights. It was a massacre. Three trucks were set on fire, the hostages were released unharmed from two civilian cars, but the German light vehicle bringing up the rear managed to turn round and make off.' In retaliation for this attack the Germans executed thirteen hostages from the village of Montsauche and burned the place.

'Houndsworth' continued its operations: in one spectacular incident a plant manufacturing synthetic petrol near Autun was destroyed by a mortar attack in early August. By the beginning of September A Squadron, having continued to hit the enemy at every opportunity, in conjunction with Maquis units, was exhausted, and the decision was taken to replace it with C Squadron. The latter arrived on 6 September.

'Houndsworth' had been a great success: 22 railway lines had been cut, 200 Germans killed or wounded, and 30 bombing targets reported.

HOUSE OF HORRORS A specially constructed building used for shooting practice by the American Delta Force. The 'House of Horrors' is the equivalent to the SAS's 'Killing House' inasmuch as it is divided into different rooms, presenting a variety of targets to shoot at with varying degrees of difficulty.

HOWARD, LIEUTENANT-COLONEL NEVILLE A well-liked and much respected member of the SAS who, despite his slight physical stature, proved to be an excellent leader of men. He joined the SAS in 1968 as Troop Commander of 22 Troop (Mountain), having arrived from the Coldstream Guards. He returned for a second time in 1973 as squadron commander of G Squadron, and was eventually made commanding officer of 22 SAS in 1982. He was affectionately known as 'Belt Kit' due to the vast variety of extra knives and utensils he carried around his belt, with which he could handle any situation.

'HOWARD', OPERATION This was a jeep-mounted SAS operation comprising B and C Squadrons, 1 SAS, commanded by Lieut-enant-Colonel Paddy Mayne. The party left Tilbury Dock on 6 April 1945 and arrived at Nijmegen in Holland the next day. Mayne's task was to carry out reconnaissance ahead of the Canadian 4th Armoured Division's advance towards Oldenburg in northwest Germany. There were 40 jeeps in all, which travelled in two columns, though the going was slow through terrain containing many rivers and dykes.

During the advance B Squadron was caught in an enemy ambush, and it was during this action that Mayne won his fourth DSO. Though managing to fight their way out of one ambush, the 'Howard' party soon found itself being ambushed again and again. This inflicted a steady toll of casualties, forcing the SAS soldiers to pull back to refit. It was soon clear that the mission could not continue, and so after reaching Oldenburg on 3 May the SAS soldiers were withdrawn to Belgium. 'Howard' was only a partial success; there were too many enemy troops concentrated in its patrol.

HS125 A seven-seater private jet, which was used by Lieutenant-General Sir Peter de la Billière during the Gulf War. It proved to be invaluable prior to the main conflict, allowing the general to travel swiftly around the Gulf States.

HUEY – UH-1H IROQUOIS *Specification* Length: 12.77m (13yds); Height: 4.41m (5yds); Weight: 2,363kg (2.3 tons); Speed: 205km/h (127mph) max; Range: 800km (496 miles).

The Bell Huey was first delivered to the US Army in 1959 and became synonymous with supporting troops in Vietnam. The aircraft is known for its distinctive rotor-chopping sound and its ability to take severe punishment. Universally known as the Huey, the Utility Helicopter 1 is officially called the Iroquois. Its double doors on either side make it easy for soldiers to disembark rapidly, or allow up to six men simultaneously to repel while in the hover.

It has been used as the vehicle of many SAS operations, and during the Oman War it provided the main method of airborne evacuation of casualties, often flying directly into the battle. The Huey is still in service with many armies around the world.

HUGHES, SERGEANT W.J. 'TAFF' Attended Selection in October 1972, having served with the Welsh Guards. He was retained by the regiment for his excellent skills in accounting and equipment procurement, serving with G Squadron as their 'store man'. Over the years he proved to be one of the best supportive soldiers in the regiment's history. Always with the squadron, his loyalty and dedication to duty were second to none. He was killed on 19 May 1982 when the helicopter he was travelling in crashed during a ship-to-ship cross-decking operation.

HUNGERFORD Two Range Rovers of the SAS anti-terrorist team happened to be in the vicinity of Hungerford, Berkshire, in August 1987 when they heard on the radio that a gunman had gone berserk, killing several people. All anti-terrorist team vehicles carry multi-band radios to communicate with every police force. As the team never move their vehicles without full anti-terrorist equipment, the senior NCO decided to divert and offer any assistance that the police might deem necessary. This included the use of firing CS gas into the building where the gunman, Michael Ryan, was holed up. The police, however, turned down the offer of help and the SAS made their way back to Hereford.

HYLANDS HALL   The estate near Chelmsford, Essex, was the home of the SAS Brigade during the winter of 1944–45, and was indeed to be the final home of the SAS during World War II. After the deployment to Norway, the brigade returned to Hylands to be disbanded.

I

IBAN TRIBESMEN Also known as the Sea Dyaks, these indigenous people of Sarawak in Borneo were employed by the British in both Borneo and Malaya. Their skills in jungle warfare and tracking were very useful to the British forces, especially the SAS, who were taught many jungle skills by the Iban. Traditionally a head-hunting tribe, they befriended the SAS in the war against the Indonesians. They lived in bamboo huts raised off the ground by stilts and known as 'long houses'. SAS patrols used 'hearts and minds' campaigns to win over these fierce tribesmen. In the early days not all the villages could be trusted. However, once won over, the Ibans proved to be a most excellent source of information on Indonesian movement.

ILRRPS (INTERNATIONAL LONG RANGE RECONNAISSANCE PATROL SCHOOL) The ILRRPS is located at Weingarten, near Ravensberg in southern Germany. One half of the school houses the training depot for the German ILRRPS's units, while the other half is given over to the International Wing. The International Wing, although under the overall control of the German ILRRPS Commandant, is commanded by an SAS lieutenant-colonel. The staff and students come from a dozen different nations, with a strong contingent of SAS instructors. The school specializes in long-term reconnaissance patrol techniques, including survival skills, evasion and signalling, and courses which are beneficial to jet pilots and Special Forces units. Special courses covering infiltration and stay-behind techniques are also run for members of the territorial SAS.

Employment at the school is normally a two-year assignment for the SAS instructors and is one of the rare postings where an SAS soldier may choose to take his family.

IMAM In November 1958 the Imam of Oman, Ghalib bin Ali, established a theocratic state and sought to overthrow the Sultan of Oman, Said bin Taimur. The rebels were well entrenched in the mountainous plateau of Jebel Akhdar in the north of the country. The

Imam was supported by his brother and about 100 followers. Additionally Sheikh Suleiman bin Himyar, a powerful tribal chief who had disagreed with the sultan, backed the rebels. The local army was no match for the rebels and the sultan requested assistance from Britain. A detachment of Life Guards, equipped with Ferret armoured cars and supported by fighter aircraft flying from Khormaker airport in Aden, were committed. At the same time units of the SAS were ordered to Oman from Malaya.

INDIVIDUAL SAS SKILLS   Individual skills are learnt in order that a basic four-man patrol can operate independently. Medics are highly trained and are capable of sustaining life until the casualty can be evacuated. The role of the medic is also important in any 'hearts and minds' campaign. The signaller will be required to communicate using sophisticated radio equipment; his job is to keep the patrol in touch with base and request any extraction or assistance. Linguists are required to converse with the local inhabitants and help with translation for the medic. At least one man will be demolitions trained, a skill required when the patrol is tasked with attacking an enemy installation.

More specialist skills such as forward air control, high-speed driving and even lock-picking are normally taught after the individual and troop skills have been acquired. The soldier can request individual skills, especially if he has a flair for the subject, but the squadron commander will ensure that there is an equal balance of skills within the troop.

INGRAM MODEL 10   *Specification* Calibre: .45 ACP or 9mm × 19 Parabellum; Weight: 1.15kg (2.84oz); Muzzle velocity: 280m (305yds) per second; Magazine capacity: 16- or 32-round, box; Rate of fire: 1,145 per minute.

Also known as the MAC 10 after the original promoter of the weapon, Military Armaments Corporation, this model was designed by Gordon B. Ingram in the United States. The weapon has a high rate of fire, which can compromise its control and accuracy. This problem was solved by adding a suppressor that is covered in heat-resistant material, allowing it to be used as a fore-grip, enabling greater control over the weapon. The SAS trialed the Ingram in Northern Ireland during the early 1970s where it met with some approval. Unfortunately, the Heckler & Koch MP5 appeared on the scene and completely eclipsed it. Since its fall from military favour the weapon has become a firm favourite with the drugs cartel.

'INHIBIT', OPERATION   On 17 December 1978 Lieutenant Rich Stannard and his troop of C Squadron of the Rhodesian 1st SAS Regiment (RhSAS) parachuted into southeastern Mozambique to carry out an ambush operation against ZANLA terrorists and FRELIMO troops who were travelling by road up to Malvernia, a town on the southern part of

Rhodesia's border with Mozambique. Having been dropped a considerable distance from their intended drop zone, it took them two nights to reach their intended ambush area. Putting out two two-man early warning groups in each direction along the road, Stannard proceeded with positioning his killer group. One of the early warning groups had, however, only just reached its position when 40 ZANLA terrorists appeared. The commander, Sergeant Dale O'Mulligan, signalled the killer group but the latter was caught unprepared and forced to let the guerrillas pass by unmolested.

Throughout that day the troop lay in its ambush positions but no further targets appeared. Lieutenant Stannard's principal concern was the shortage of water among his men and he gave serious consideration to the idea of carrying out a silent attack on some buildings at a nearby railway siding, killing the occupants and replenishing his troop's water supplies. However, this problem became of secondary importance when, at 05:30 hours on the following morning, with the early warning groups having taken up their positions once more, another group of 80 ZANLA terrorists approached along the road.

This time there was no mistake: on Stannard's signal, Sergeant Billy Gardner initiated the ambush and a withering hail of fire, augmented by several fragmentation and white phosphorous grenades, was directed at the guerrillas. Seventeen bodies were found after the troop ceased fire and went forward to search the dead; a further 28 died subsequently in the bush, making a total kill count of 45. This was increased shortly afterwards to 47 when two more terrorists approached along the road and were summarily despatched. Unfortunately, the troop also suffered one casualty as a corporal, Mo Taylor, had been killed.

IPOH This main town in northwest Malaya was such a stronghold of the Communists during the Malayan Emergency that insurgents of a supposedly clandestine organization paraded openly though the streets. For this reason Ipoh became the location of the Malayan Scouts' first operation, which took place in November 1950 under the leadership of Major 'Mad Mike' Calvert. His strategy was to place fourteen-man teams in the jungle with a base camp and a radio. Three- or four-man patrols would then be sent off to hunt for groups of terrorists and either kill them themselves, or direct air strikes. This policy was a success, for Communist activity soon decreased markedly. In this way Ipoh was important for two reasons: for striking at a Communist centre, and proving the worth of Mike Calvert's Malayan Scouts.

IRA (IRISH REPUBLICAN ARMY) A terrorist organization formed in 1919 and dedicated to the cause of Irish Nationalism and the end to British rule in Ireland by any means possible, even using violence – 'the bullet and the bomb'. During civil rights disturbances in Northern Ireland in 1969 a division within the ranks of the IRA appeared. The old leadership wanted a more peaceful solution to the problem, but the Provisionals, hard-liners from Belfast, believed that violence was the only way to free Northern Ireland. This hard-line group gained the upper hand and became known as the Provisional Irish Republican Army (the PIRA or the Provos).

The IRA is organized along military lines. Twelve Army Executive Members oversee all its actions and have the power to elect the seven members who make up the Army Council. Next in the command structure are the General Headquarters staff who act upon those decisions made by the Council. Orders are despatched from here to the Northern and Southern Commands of the IRA which are made up of brigades, battalions, companies and finally the smallest operating entity, the Active Service Unit. The IRA has only about 50 full-time soldiers to undertake its work, despite the impressive sounding nature of its organization. These soldiers, however, are well-trained, well-armed, well-disciplined and very resourceful, as well as being heavily financed by their supporters, especially those in the United States. They also have a number of volunteers who provide logistical support.

Although most of the IRA's activities have taken place in Northern Ireland, they have brought violence to the mainland of Britain and Continental Europe. The terrorists also successfully attacked the British Government by bombing the Grand Hotel in Brighton in October 1984, when Margaret Thatcher and most of the Cabinet were staying there for the Conservative Party Conference. Other bomb attacks and killings have involved civilians totally unconnected with either the government or any of the security services. These attacks include the Birmingham pub bombings in 1974 and the Enniskillen massacre on Remembrance Day 1987.

Recent talks of peace and ceasefires have given the people of Northern Ireland and Britain renewed hope that there is a way to end the violence. Unfortunately for the civilians of Northern Ireland, this is an unlikely dream, for if the PIRA ever does give up its weapons, another hard-line group is bound to retrieve them and carry on the struggle.

IRANIAN EMBASSY SIEGE   More than any of their previous actions, the siege at the Iranian Embassy in London brought the SAS into the public eye. For the first time the black-clad men of the anti-terrorist team were seen in action. At 11:25 on the morning of Wednesday 30 April 1980 six armed gunmen took over No. 16 Princes Gate, the Iranian Embassy, in London's Kensington. As they took control of the embassy, they seized 26 hostages including the British policeman who had been on duty at the entrance. The police were on the scene almost immediately, a swiftness initiated by the captured policeman, Trevor

Lock, who had managed to alert his headquarters before being taken by the terrorists. D11 marksmen soon surrounded the building and the siege negotiating plans were put into operation.

By 11:47 Dusty Grey, an ex-D Squadron SAS man who now worked with the Metropolitan Police, was talking to the commanding officer and the anti-terrorist team in Hereford. His information contained the briefest details, but it was enough to alert the regiment. Although the SAS had prior warning, there could be no move without official sanction from the Home Secretary. Despite this, it made sense for the SAS to plan ahead, and positioning the anti-terrorist team closer to the scene could save time. So around midnight on the first day, most of the team had made their way to Regent's Park Barracks, which had been chosen as a holding area. From here information could be assembled by the regiment's intelligence cell, and assessed.

By this time the terrorist leader, Oan, had secured the hostages and made his demands. The line taken by the terrorists was hard but fair, and despite several threats to blow up the embassy and kill the hostages, by Thursday 1 May they had released a sick woman.

Later that night, under the cover of darkness, three vans pulled up in a small side street by Princes Gate. Men carrying holdalls quickly made their way into No. 14, two doors down from the siege. Within minutes they had laid out their equipment and made ready for an IA – immediate action. At first this was very simple; if the terrorists started shooting, they would run to the front door of the embassy and beat their way in – a slow and primitive method, but better than doing nothing until a clear defined plan could be organized.

By 06:00 on the morning of Saturday 2 May, the situation inside No. 16 was getting very agitated. Oan, also the spokesman, rang the phone line which had been set up between the embassy and No. 25 Princes Gate and which now housed Alpha Control (main forward control point) and the police negotiator. Oan's main criticism was that the media had not broadcast news of the siege. By late afternoon on the same day Oan was allowed to make a statement which was to be broadcast in the next news bulletin. In return for this two more hostages were released, one of whom was a pregnant woman. The trouble was that Oan would not release the hostages before the statement was read out; likewise, the police wanted the hostages first. In the end a compromise was reached and the broadcast went out at 21:00.

Two hours later eight members of the SAS team had climbed on to the rear roof of No. 14 and were making their way, amid a jungle of TV antennae, to No. 16. Two of the men made their way directly to a glass skylight and, after some time managed to get it free. It opened directly into a small bathroom on the top floor of the Iranian Embassy, and provided an excellent entry point. Meanwhile, other members secured abseil ropes to the several chimneys and made ready for a quick descent to the lower floors where they could smash their way in through the windows.

By 09:00 on Sunday morning things seemed to be heading for a peaceful settlement. Oan had agreed to reduce his demands, and at the same time Arab ambassadors had attened a COBRA Committee meeting in Whitehall. The meeting was chaired by William Whitelaw, the Home Secretary, who had responsibility for the whole operation. He was aware the SAS team now had access to the embassy. COBRA was also aware that a basic plan had been formalized. This plan involved attacking all floors simultaneously, with clearly defined areas of demarcation to avoid overshoot. Mock-ups of the floor layouts were constructed at Regent's Park Barracks in order that the SAS could practise.

The police, who had adopted a softly-softly negotiating approach, managed to drag the siege out for several days – time that was desperately needed for the SAS to carry out covert recces, study plans, and more importantly, locate the hostages and terrorists within the embassy building. A major break was the debrief of released hostage Chris Cramer.

By the sixth day of the siege (5 May) the terrorists were becoming frustrated and the situation inside the embassy began to deteriorate. All morning threats were made about executing hostages and at 13:31 three shots were heard. At 18:50 more shots were heard, and the body of the embassy press officer was thrown out. Immediately the police appeared to capitulate, stalling for time. A handwritten note transferring control from the police to the SAS was then passed, and SAS plans to storm the embassy were advanced. Shortly after, while a negotiator from Alpha control talked to Oan, the SAS moved in. Oan heard the first crashes and complained that the embassy was being attacked. For the SAS assault team the waiting was over, and the orders were given guaranteed to send their adrenalin pumping: 'Go Go Go!'

At 19:23 p.m. eight men abseiled down to the first-floor balcony. The assault came from three directions, with the main assault coming from the rear. Frame charges blew the windows. Stun grenades were thrown in, and the SAS went into action. Systematically the building was cleared from the top down, room by room. The telex room on the second floor, which housed the male hostages and three of the terrorists, was of utmost priority. Realizing that an assault was in progress, the terrorists shot and killed one hostage and wounded two others before the lead SAS team broke into the room. Immediately they shot the first two gunmen that were visible; the third hid amongst the hostages and was not discovered until later. As rooms were cleared, hostages were literally thrown from one SAS soldier to another, down the stairs and out into the back garden. They were laid face down on the ground while a search was conducted for the missing terrorist. They were then released into medical care.

Breaking the siege took just seventeen minutes. The SAS took no casualties, other than one man who got caught up in his rope harness and was badly burnt. Of the six terrorists, five had been shot dead and one taken prisoner. Once the embassy had been cleared, and all the terrorists and hostages had been identified, control was handed back to the police. See also Anti-terrorist Team; CRW; Stun Grenade.

IRAQ　On 2 August 1990 Saddam Hussein of Iraq began his invasion of neighbouring Kuwait at 02:00 hours local time (23:00 1 August GMT), by unleashing 100,000 soldiers on Kuwait. As a direct result of this action the United Nations sanctioned Coalition forces to go to war. By January 1991 three squadrons of SAS A, B and D plus 17 civilians from the reserve squadron, the largest British Special Forces group ever, were preparing to enter Iraq and remain there until the war was over.

IRIAN JAYA　On 29 July 1977 the Australian Department of Defence was informed that an Royal Australian Air Force (RAAF) helicopter, flying in support of a survey operation, had crashed in the jungle-clad mountains of Indonesian Irian Jaya. The pilot had been killed and four passengers injured, two seriously. The Indonesian Government readily agreed to a request that Australian forces should co-ordinate and carry out the rescue operation. Soon afterwards the Australian SAS Regiment (SASR) was tasked with providing a party to be inserted into the area and provide medical assistance and evacuation for the injured. A party under the unit's medical officer, Captain John McLean, was flown in on an RAAF C-130 to Wamena, and from there to the crash location in an RAAF helicopter which winched it down to the crashed aircraft.

Meanwhile there was concern that Irian Jayan guerrillas of the local liberation movement might appear on the scene and attempt to remove equipment. Accordingly, a second party of eleven SASR under Captain Jim Wallace, accompanied by six engineers and two RAAF ground staff, was also inserted to provide protection until the arrival of Indonesian troops. The operation was hampered by bad weather and it took several attempts before the body of the pilot was finally recovered and the operation concluded on 8 August.

'IRON FOX', OPERATION　At the end of July 1971 the 1st Australian Task Force mounted Operation 'Iron Fox' against Vietcong (VC) and North Vietnamese Army (NVA) positions which spanned the western border of Long Khanh Province. The 3rd Battalion Royal Australian Regiment (3 RAR) established blocking positions while the 4th Battalion (4 RAR) succeeded in trapping a large number of VC and

NVA in a bunker complex from which some succeeded in slipping away. Cut-off groups to block the escaping enemy were provided by 2 Squadron SAS Regiment (SASR), which had previously provided intelligence for the operation. One of these was a ten-man patrol commanded by Sergeant Paul Richards, which detected indications of an enemy camp 10km (6 miles) southwest of the Allied operational base designated 'Black Horse' and located just west of a main road called Route 2.

While moving up to reconnoitre the area to confirm the existence of the camp, the patrol was seen by a VC sentry, whom they shot and wounded. The patrol subsequently withdrew and shortly afterwards directed a helicopter gunship strike and an artillery fire mission on to the area. On the following day, accompanied by a guide from Sergeant Richards' patrol, A Company 3 RAR carried out a follow-up operation and sweep of the area. It located the camp which was found abandoned and proved to be a hospital complex, complete with operating theatre and sixteen bunkers, manned by C24 Convalescent Company of the 274th Regiment. Already badly damaged by the gunship strike, the entire complex was destroyed by 3 RAR before it withdrew.

ISOLATION Prior to many operations SAS troops will be placed in isolation. Once there, they will be briefed on their mission, after which they will plan and prepare accordingly. If several patrols are used for the same operation within the same area, to avoid knowledge of each other's missions they will be separated even to the extent of staggering meal times. Isolation can last for several days, and serves primarily as a security measure. Only those involved will know their target, rendezvous and pick-up points etc. The word isolation also refers to a practice carried out during resistance to interrogation training.

J

'JAGUAR', OPERATION Launched to establish a firm base on the Jebel Dhofar, beginning in October 1971. The senior Qadi (religious leader) had given dispensation to all Arabs fighting during the religious period of Ramadan, which is normally a time of fasting. Two full squadrons of SAS, together with their Firqats, spearheaded the operation. One squadron infiltrated at night by climbing the Jebel while the other squadron was helicoptered in the next morning. Additionally, several companies of the Sultan's Armed Forces (SAF) and various support units also took part. Colonel Johnny Watts, a brilliant commander who, above all, had the respect of his men, led the whole force. Watts had a quick, decisive mind, yet he would not commit the SAS without committing himself. He was no stranger to the battle front and could often be seen running forward with one gun group or another, carrying boxes of ammunition and shouting orders as he did so.

The first night on the Jebel saw only light long-range sniping from the Adoo, but by next morning, when the bulk of the force had split into three battle groups, the enemy made close contact. The first week of Operation 'Jaguar' saw almost continual fighting as one or other of the battle groups were confronted by the enemy.

JALO An oasis in Libya, some 240km (148 miles) south of Benghazi (see Raid on) at the western edge of the great sand sea. Originally a French Foreign Legion outpost, it became home to the LRDG (Long Range Desert Group) and the SAS during the North African campaign of World War II. It changed hands several times during Rommel's push but was finally taken from the Italians on 25 November 1941. With the aid of LRDG transportation the SAS launched many of their raids against the German airfields.

JEAPES, MAJOR-GENERAL TONY Originally commissioned into the Dorset Regiment, Jeapes joined the SAS as a lieutenant in 1958, serving in the Oman Campaign of 1958–59, and was awarded the Military Cross. He served with the SAS for 19 years, with only short breaks to attend the Army Staff College and the National Defence College. He commanded 22 SAS from 1974 to 1977 and received an OBE in 1977. His book, *SAS Operation Oman*, where he served as a squadron commander in 1971, is an unprecedented historical account of the war.

JEBEL AKHDAR   Jebel Akhdar is the high plateau amid a mountain range situated in northern Oman, close to the settlements of Nizwas and Saiq. It is an area which, in 1957, was declared by rebel tribesmen an independent region from the Sultanate of Oman. British help to the beleaguered sultan included men of A and D Squadron 22 SAS.

JEBEL MASSIF   The Jebel Massif is a mountain that rises steeply from the plains of southern Oman to overlook the metropolis of Salalah and the Indian Ocean beyond. At its highest point the mountain plateau is covered with grass and trees, providing homes for birds and other wildlife. In places it is cut with steep-sided gorges that are more akin to the Grand Canyon than the desert. To the north the vegetation fades out to nothing, leaving only rock and sand. To the east and west, buried in the steep-sided gorges, there are developments of small villages with terraced fields. In the greener regions, especially after the monsoon season, it is a place of great beauty.

SAS soldiers' first sight of this impressive feature was on landing at RAF Salalah during the Oman War; the majority of fighting took place there.

JEDBURGH TEAMS   These were specially trained formations whose task was to parachute into occupied France after the D-Day landings to liaise with Maquis units. They usually comprised an American, a British and a French officer or NCO. Once on the ground the Jedburgh teams organized Maquis units, established drop-zones and instigated attacks on German forces. There were 86 Jedburgh teams in total, all controlled by Headquarters Special Forces, and they often dropped with SAS parties into France in 1944.

JEFFERY, LIEUTENANT-COLONEL MIKE – AUSTRALIAN SAS REGIMENT (SASR)   Assumed command of the SAS Regiment (SASR) on 7 January 1976. Commissioned into the Royal Australian Regiment (RAR) from Royal Military College Duntroon in December 1958, he had joined 1st SAS Company in the following year and remained with the unit until 1962. He subsequently served with 2 RAR and 3 RAR in Malaya before being appointed ADC to the Chief of General Staff. Thereafter he returned to the SAS, serving as operations officer at Headquarters SAS in the Far East until returning to the SASR as adjutant. Following tours as a company commander in the 1st Battalion Pacific Islands Regiment (1 PIR) and 8 RAR in Vietnam, he attended the British Army's Staff College before assuming command of 2 PIR.

Under Jeffery, the SASR developed its capability to conduct surveillance operations in Northern Australia. A number of exercises were conducted which proved that the regiment had a viable role to play in the defence of Australia, namely surveillance, monitoring and reporting of enemy coastal landings and any advance inland, assisting in hindering the latter through direction of air strikes.

On 22 October 1977 Lieutenant-Colonel Jeffery handed over command of the SASR to Lieutenant-Colonel Reg Beesley. His next posting was SO1 Joint and Special Warfare in the Directorate General of Operations and Plans, but shortly afterwards he was promoted to the rank of colonel and appointed to the newly created post of Director Special Action Forces (DSAF). In that post he continued to develop the concept of regional surveillance forces for deployment in Northern Australia. At the same time he played a major role in the planning and development of the SASR's counter-terrorist capability.

JELLICOE, EARL GEORGE   One of the early members of the SAS, Jellicoe was the son of the famous World War I admiral who fought at the Battle of Jutland on 13 May 1916. In June 1942 during a raid against Heraklion airfield on Crete, he and his party managed to destroy 21 enemy aircraft. His tenure with the SAS effectively ended in March 1943 when he was given command of the Special Boat Squadron (SBS). He led this unit until January 1945, when he was sent to the British Army's Staff College.

JOC   An acronym for Joint Operations Centre. The JOC includes representatives from the armed forces (including the SAS), the Foreign Office, the Home Office and all the intelligence services. It has the authority to send the SAS on operations, both home and abroad, as it did with their observation of IRA terrorists in Gibraltar in 1988. The JOC is based at the British Ministry of Defence in London.

'JOCKWORTH', OPERATION   On 15 August 1944, 57 men of 3 SAS led by Captain Hourst dropped into southeast France between the Rhône and Loire rivers. Their aim was to interrupt enemy movements and organize Maquis forces. The mission lasted until 9 September, during which time the French soldiers achieved considerable success. They were the first Allied troops to enter Lyons, where they engaged in house-to-house fighting.

'JOINING THE EXIT CLUB'   Meaning to be killed or about to be killed.

JONES, LANCE-CORPORAL DAVID   A member of 14 Intelligence and Security Unit enlisted from the Parachute Regiment who was killed in Northern Ireland on 17 March 1978. He and another member of the unit were mounting a covert surveillance operation near the village of Maghera, County Londonderry. Three men approached them in combat dress and Jones, thinking they were members of the Ulster Defence Regiment, stood up and issued a warning. The men, who were in fact terrorists, acted fast and Jones was unable to protect himself as they fired, hitting him in the stomach and also wounding his companion. However, Jones did manage to fire his weapon, wounding one of the terrorists, before he fell. The wounded man was eventually captured after a long search with dogs and was identified as Francis Hughes, a member of the IRA. Jones died the next day from his wounds.

The whole unfortunate incident meant that lessons had to be learnt: not only did communications between the Army, police and SAS need to improve, but also operatives needed to be more cautious and react more quickly in such situations. All of these problems were soon addressed and rectified.

'JONQUIL', OPERATION   One of the most disastrous SAS missions in World War II. The idea was sound enough: the rounding-up of large numbers of Allied prisoners-of-war (PoWs) who were wandering around the Italian countryside after Italy's surrender.

Beginning in October 1943, the plan involved four airborne parties from B Squadron, 2 SAS, landing between Ancona and Pescara on Italy's Adriatic coast to be guides for the PoWs. Fishing vessels were assembled for transportation, but a German attack at Termoli on 5 October meant they had to be moved back to Bari (the Germans had also taken a number of fishing vessels). For their part the PoWs made it to the beaches, but due to lack of communication they arrived to find no boats, or the boats arrived and there were no prisoners. The whole mission was a fiasco, and all those involved were very disappointed.

JSIU (JOINT SERVICES INTERROGATION UNIT)   A section of the Intelligence Corps, JSIU have their headquarters at Ashford in Kent. JSIU provide the interrogators during the escape and evasion phase of SAS Selection, and similar exercises with which the regiment is involved. They also provide interrogation teams that are attached to an SAS unit, especially when the theatre of operation is new and intelligence is limited.

In theory the Geneva Convention (1949), the rules of which have been ratified by most major powers, protects all SAS soldiers from physical harm if captured. As far as the British Army is concerned, the rules governing the Convention are laid down in 'Regulations for the Treatment of Prisoners-of-War' and in 'Manual of Military Law' part III. Although JSIU plays a vital part in the training of SAS soldiers during resistance to interrogation training, there is little admiration for their efforts.

JUNDIE Word used by the SAS to describe an Arab soldier; the term 'raghead', referring to their custom of wearing a shamagh, is used in a similar way.

JUNGLE TRAINING Jungle training is an important requirement for the SAS as they are often committed to operations in tropical regions. Surviving in the jungle is not easy: patrolling and operating in secret requires special skills. SAS jungle skills are designed so that a small team is able to operate, fight and survive in a hostile environment. Moving from place to place in the jungle is slow and laborious, and there are hidden dangers all around, not just from the enemy, but from a host of different insects, animals and the jungle itself.

In SAS Selection, the jungle phase takes place twice a year, at the Jungle Training School at Tutong, Brunei. The school is run by experts from several nations, including several instructors from SAS Hereford, and the six-week training periods are run from March and September. The SAS has a saying that 'the jungle is a great equalizer of men', meaning each soldier must find his own way of coping with the jungle environment. Many find the closeness of the forest and dense foliage very claustrophobic, while others enjoy the challenge, seeing it as an adventure playground.

Everything in the jungle is growing or dying together. There are a million smells and thousands of bird and animal sounds. Jungle training involves learning jungle navigation and patrolling techniques where candidates are required to find their way through thick, dense foliage on steep-sided hills and over the most rugged terrain. The threat of coming face to face with the enemy is ever present, so close-quarter contact drills and techniques of preparing a quick ambush are an integral part of the training. Jungle training is a tough discipline, which relies on the use of hand signals, the minimum amount of noise possible, slow movement and testing routine.

The SAS will often be requested to undertake missions in any one of the world's jungles, all of which differ greatly in the risks they pose. In the Far East, Malaysia and Brunei the jungle is reasonably safe, but in South America, in particular Belize, it is particularly dangerous with an enormous number of hazards. Here even some of the trees contain an acid-type sap.

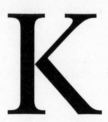

K

'K-CAR' An Alouette III helicopter adapted by the Royal Rhodesian Air Force for use as a gunship, being fitted with twin 20mm cannon. Flown by a crew of two, it was in some instances also used as an airborne command post. It was thus fitted with the necessary radio communications equipment to enable the commander of an operation to communicate with his troops on the ground, and with other aircraft.

KABRIT A small Egyptian village about 160km (100 miles) from Cairo, on the edge of the Great Bitter Lake, where David Stirling established his first training camp in July 1941. With no tents or supplies, Stirling, true to form, decided to 'borrow' them from a nearby New Zealand camp. The subsequent raid can be called the SAS's first raid and was entirely successful. Once up and running, Kabrit became the scene of intensive training to prepare the men for the real thing.

KALABIT A head-hunting tribe from Borneo who lived for the most part in the higher regions. They became very friendly with the SAS during their time there, and always treated them with the greatest of kindness. It was through the Kalabit that the SAS soldiers first learnt most of their basic Malay and the customs of individual tribes.

KAS ENTERPRISES A private security business, formed by David Stirling in 1986, that operated from offices at No. 22 South Audley Street, central London. Stirling, who was the founding father of the SAS, employed Ian Crooke, who had previously been commanding officer of 23 SAS, as managing director. KAS Enterprises became involved in what was known as 'Project Lock', whereby the company would help solve the problem of rhino and elephant poaching in Africa. However, the intelligence-gathering activities of KAS led opposition groups to believe that they were trying to destabilize certain black African states, using ex-SAS mercenaries. Stirling sued for libel and won, but the damage had been done and the company was wound up.

KEALY, MAJOR MIKE   Led the defence at the Battle of Mirbat in Oman, against overwhelming odds on 19 July 1972. A captain at the time, his command of his men, and his actions during the battle, earned him the Distinguished Service Order. In February 1979, having returned to the regiment, Major Kealy decided to attempt the endurance march during the SAS Selection course. His aim was to prove to himself that, at the age of 33 and after some years away from the SAS, he could still manage the weight and distance in the allotted time. He set off in driving rain, against which he had not thought to carry protective waterproofs, and moved at a strong pace. Higher up the mountain the rain had turned to snow, and this, combined with the wind, continued to lower Kealy's body temperature. Around 10:00, some eight hours into the march, two members of Selection stumbled across Major Kealy partially covered with snow in a sitting position – he was barely alive. Although the alarm was raised shortly after midday, due to the appalling weather Major Kealy was not recovered until 04:30 the next day, by which time he had died from hypothermia.

'KEENI-MEENI'   Swahili term meaning 'snake in the grass', given to the dangerous and covert operations carried out by certain members of the SAS against rebel forces in Aden in the mid-1960s. This undercover work proved to be well suited to the men of the regiment, especially the Fijians, who were able to pass themselves off more easily as Arabs. Some of the techniques learned on 'Keeni-Meeni' operations were later applied to other counter-insurgency work.

The initial aim of the Keeni-Meeni teams was to get rid of several Yemeni assassins operating in the Sheikh Othman area of Aden. These assassins were targeting British Special Branch officers and their informers. This work was new to the SAS and although they collected a fair amount of intelligence they only succeeded in killing two assassins.

'KEYSTONE', OPERATION   This mission was intended to disrupt enemy movements south of the Ijsselmeer, Holland, and commenced on 3 April 1945, when an advance party landed to secure a drop-zone and link up with the local Resistance. The operation was led by Captain Henry Druce, who commanded a jeep-mounted squadron from 2 SAS. The advance party landed safely, though the radio smashed, and so a second unit was unable to make contact and had to return to Britain. The jeeps and their crews were dropped on 11 April, though follow-on drops were not made due to bad weather conditions. Druce himself could not drop, and so he and his jeeps were forced to drive through enemy territory to reach the forward group on 18 April, when the whole squadron drove northeast to join the Operation 'Archway' teams. In summary, 'Keystone' achieved some results, though overall the mission was a disappointment.

KILLING HOUSE The 'Killing House' is the name given to a flat-roofed building in the grounds of Stirling Lines. This structure was designed and built with the express purpose of perfecting the individual shooting skills of the SAS, and for training in room combat. Weapon training starts from the very basics of pistol work, and encompasses all the problems of movement and weapon stoppages, moving right through to the famous SAS 'double tap'.

Another well-practised skill in the 'Killing House' is the snatch. This is a drill that is practised as part of the anti-terrorist hostage-rescue scenario. Visiting VIPs could often find themselves used as hostages waiting to be extracted. This requires sitting in a 'hot' seat while black-clad figures burst into the darkened room firing live rounds at targets positioned a few centimetres away.

The inner rooms can be set out in any number of different ways to represent a likely hostage situation. Due to an accident in 1986, when a sergeant was killed during room combat training, live hostages are now rarely used. Since then 'terrorists' and 'hostages' are separated into two rooms, connected by a camera system. What takes place in one room is relayed on to a life size wrap-around screen in real time in the other, and vice versa. The assault team fire at the images of the 'terrorists', but in reality they are firing at bullet-absorbent walls. Not only is the system safer, but it also allows the whole exercise to be videotaped and replayed later for evaluation purposes.

'KIPLING', OPERATION This mission into France was designed to aid the Allied airborne landings which were due to take place in the Orleans Gap in August 1944. The SAS party, 107 men and 46 jeeps of C Squadron, 1 SAS, began their mission on 13 August, when an advance party under Captain Derrick Harrison dropped into the area west of Auxerre.

Having landed successfully and established a base, the SAS were then informed that the airborne landings had been cancelled. A change in tactics was therefore required. At this time the situation was very fluid, with the Allies penetrating deep into German-held areas. Patton's US Third Army was nearing Reims, while other Allied units were pushing north following the 'Dragoon' landings in southern France. The 'Kipling' party therefore took advantage of the confusion among the Germans to launch a series of daring attacks. Harrison himself attacked the village of Les Ormes, and ran straight into Waffen-SS troops who were in the process of executing suspected Maquis. In a savage firefight Harrison's two jeeps set the German vehicles on fire, though they were then forced to retire, leaving one damaged jeep behind. For this he won the Military Cross.

The SAS suffered fuel shortages because supply drops were erratic. Nevertheless, the 'Kipling' party still managed to mount a number of successful patrols. Some of the latter joined the French First Army and took part in the surrender of Autun with its garrison of 3,000 Germans. By 26 September 'Kipling' was over, and the SAS soldiers were at Cosne in central France partaking of a well-earned rest.

KLEPPER CANOE   A two-man collapsible canoe used by both the SAS and SBS. This German-designed canoe, which proved to be much lighter that the previously used Cockle II, came into service in the 1950s and remained in use until the mid-1980s. Despite its primitive design – the frame is made from hardwood mountain ash and Finnish birch, while the deck is covered with self-drying cotton woven with hemp, and the hull material has a core of polyester cord surrounded by rubber – it is ideal for clandestine insertions on to hostile coastlines. It can also be carried ashore and camouflaged by its crew. The canoe's skin is loose fitting until 'airsponsons', which run under each gunwale, are inflated. It measures 5.2m (5.5yds) long, 89cm (34in) wide and 61cm (23in) deep. It will pack into a bag 69cm × 58cm × 20cm (26in × 22in × 8in).

KMS   The initials KMS are taken to mean 'Keeni-Meeni Services', and represent a private security organization formed in 1974 by David Walker, as an offshoot of Controlled Risks. Major Walker, who had previously served with the SAS, staged a management buy-out of KMS in 1977. The company prospered, mainly with contracts to supply military instructors and equipment to Oman, and training work in Sri Lanka which helped to combat the Tamil Tiger guerrillas. Shortly afterwards, KMS became involved with the Oliver North affair in the United States which undid much of the original good work.

KOREAN WAR   This conflict started on 25 June 1950. The United Nations Supreme Commander, General Douglas MacArthur, requested that the SAS be sent into Korea and M Squadron, a detachment of 21 SAS (the Territorial Army unit made up of volunteers with experience from World War II), was prepared for service. However, in November of that year the Chinese entered the war and it was no longer deemed politically acceptable to engage in behind-lines operations. Instead, the detachment was sent to Singapore and from there to Malaya, where it joined forces with the Malayan Scouts.

KREMLIN   Name given to the old wooden building that served as the regimental headquarters of 22 SAS in Bradbury Lines. Security around the 'Kremlin' was stepped up in 1970 by placing a twelve-foot fence around the whole of the section. The importance of the name faded a little once the new barracks was built and renamed Stirling Lines.

KUFRA   The site of an oasis in North Africa which was used by the SAS as a staging post during its campaign in the desert in 1941–43.

L

L2A3 STERLING SUB-MACHINE GUN *Specification* Calibre: 9mm × 19 Parabellum; Weight: 1.2kg (2.72lbs); Muzzle velocity: 293–310m (319–338yds) per second; Effective range: 200m (218yds); Magazine capacity: 30-round, box.

This simple weapon is both robust and reliable, with the original design dating back to the Sten of World War II. It was in use with the SAS and SBS during the 1960s and 1970s, and the single-shot version was used by the British police force. Although no longer used by the British Army it can still be found in many countries, especially Chile who still manufacture a modified pattern of the Sterling.

L34A1 STERLING A 'silenced' version of the L2A3.

L42A1 SNIPER RIFLE *Specification* Calibre: 7.62mm × 51 NATO standard; Weight: 2kg (4.43lbs); Muzzle velocity: 838m (913yds) per second; Magazine capacity: 10-round, box; Sight: × 4.

The L42A1 is basically an improved version of the British Lee Enfield rifle, one of the toughest and most reliable battle rifles of World War II. Although now surpassed by the latest high-tech rifles, it gave good service to the SAS throughout the Middle East and the Falklands conflicts. Today it is still used by the British police force and is known as the Enfield Enforcer.

LABALABA, CORPORAL SAS soldier from Fiji who was killed while bravely engaged in the Battle of Mirbat against the Adoo in July 1972. He was already an experienced veteran of SAS operations, including 'Keeni-Meeni' in Aden and missions in Borneo. For his sense of duty and bravery at Mirbat he was 'Mentioned in Despatches'.

LAND ROVER *Specification* Length: 4.5m (15ft); Width: 1.89m (2yds); Weight: 3,400kg (3 tons); Engine: 3.5 litre V8 diesel.

The Land Rover has been in use with 22 SAS since it first came into being in 1948. It is a tough and reliable vehicle, adaptable to most terrain and capable of carrying a good payload. For many years the regiment used a special 'Pink Panther' version which came to epitomize the SAS. More recently, especially in the Gulf War, the regiment used the existing Land Rover 110, modified with extra stowage and weapons-mounts, including smoke-dischargers mounted on the front and rear bumpers. Land Rover now produce a Special Operations Vehicle, based on the 110 used by the SAS, and retaining many of its special features and modifications. The result is a long-wheelbase, all-terrain, weapons platform capable of supporting a wide variety of weapons, such as the Milan anti-tank missile, Mark 19 grenade launcher, and .50 heavy machine gun.

LANE, CORPORAL MICHAEL 'BRONCO'   Reached the summit of Mount Everest in April 1976 along with Sergeant John 'Brummie' Stokes. During the descent, both men suffered frostbite and lost several toes. Later, Lane was awarded a Military Medal for his services in Northern Ireland.

LANE, TROOPER STEVEN 'LEGS', MM   'Legs' Lane joined the SAS in February 1990 having served with 9 (Parachute) Squadron Royal Engineers. He was one of the eight members of the ill-fated patrol 'Bravo Two Zero'. After the group had split, he and two others were confronted by a wide river. By this time Bob Consiglio had been shot and killed and they were out of ammunition, leaving them no choice but to swim. The water was bitterly cold and proved to be the last ordeal for Legs. 'Dinger', the other surviving member, dragged him from the water to a small pump-hut, where Legs lay totally exhausted. At this stage 'Dinger' was captured by local Iraqis and handed over to the army. Legs was last seen by other patrol members lying on a stretcher. He had died from exposure and hypothermia.

'LARKSWOOD', OPERATION   This was one of the SAS operations carried out towards the end of the war in Europe, when Special Air Service units were being used more as regular infantry than as a Special Forces formation. As a result, it suffered accordingly. The mission was carried out by two Squadrons of 5 SAS, the Belgian SAS, led by Captain Blondeel, who acted as reconnaissance troops for the Canadian II Corps and then the Polish Armoured Division. The SAS party was equipped with 40 jeeps, but the terrain contained many dykes and canals, which made the going heavy. The SAS captured a number of bridges and pushed into Germany, but the terrain and enemy resistance took a heavy toll. Blondeel forged on, carrying out reconnaissance duties for the Polish Armoured Division until the end of the war.

LASER AIMING SYSTEMS   These laser devices can be fitted to most weapons to assist in target acquisition. They are especially used by the SAS in counter-terrorist and hostage rescue operations, where accurate aim in low light conditions is essential. There are many models available, most of which can be fitted to just about any weapon. However, they all work on the same principle: the operator of the weapon points it at the target and a small laser light or beam will light up where the bullet will hit.

Other laser sighting systems are only visible with night-vision goggles or infra-red sensitive equipment. These systems are used by counter-terrorist snipers, and in both jungle warfare and in the field. One laser system, International Technologies AIM-1DLR long-range laser, projects a beam up to a range of 3km (2 miles). However, this beam also needs night-vision goggles in order to see it.

LASER RANGEFINDER *Specification* Weight: 1kg (2.2lbs); Range: 10km (6 miles); Field width: 7 degrees; Magnification: ×7.

The laser rangefinder is about the size of a pair of 7×50 binoculars and gives the range of a target; it is accurate to 5m (5.5yds) up to a range of 10km (6 miles). The SAS and British armed forces use the SIMRAD LP7 to give an accurate range for direct-fire weapons. The rangefinder is particularly effective for Mortar Fire Controllers (MFC) or artillery Forward Observation Officers (FOO). The range is displayed in the eyepiece and there is an indication if more than one target has been detected, with a minimum range control cutting out unwanted reflections. The monocular on the LP7 has a ×7 magnification and is combined with the optical receiver, which allows a four-digit LED (light emitting diode) display to be observed through the left eyepiece, which is superimposed on the picture seen in the right eyepiece.

LASER TARGET DESIGNATOR *Specification* Weight: 2.7kg (6lbs); Range: 300–9,000m (327yds–5.5 miles) approx; Field view: 3 degrees; Magnification: ×10.

Laser target designators allow SAS soldiers to deliver airborne ordnance, such as Paveway and Pavetack Laser-Guided Bombs (LGBs), on to ground targets with very high accuracy. This eliminates the need for deep penetration patrols to expose themselves on target, and avoids the need to carry around the heavy weight of explosive equipment required to destroy a large target. Despite what has been previously written, laser target designators were not used by the SAS with any great success during either the Falklands War or the Gulf War. However, they have been used in Bosnia, painting targets for Sea Harriers to attack once NATO had launched an air campaign against Serb positions. The Pilkington LF25 designator is lightweight and can be carried by a soldier in its transit case or in his bergen, and can designate targets up to 10km (6 miles) away.

LASSEN, MAJOR ANDERS One of the most famous members of the SAS, who was also a member of the Special Boat Squadron (SBS).

Lassen, a Dane, joined the British Army at the beginning of World War II and participated in commando training before joining the specialist Small Scale Raiding Force. In May 1943 he was in the Middle East as part of D Squadron, 1 SAS, which became part of the Special Boat Squadron. His fighting qualities came to the fore, and Lassen was soon recognized as being an exceptional soldier, ideally suited to elite forces operations, where quick decisions and raw courage are often called for, combined with ice-cool nerves. He took part in a number of SBS missions, such as the raids against Crete and Simi in June 1943, while in 1944 he fought in Italy, the Adriatic and Greece. It was in 1945, though, that he entered SAS legend. Fighting around Lake Commachio, he was killed attempting to destroy a number of German pill-boxes. Before he died he had captured or killed a large number of Germans, and his presence had even affected enemy strategy in the area. For this and his other actions he was awarded a posthumous Victoria Cross.

LAST LIGHT A significant time of day for any SAS soldier as it traditionally represents a time when an enemy will attack. With the advancement in night-fighting aids, however, the last-light stand-to has lost some of its importance.

LAW 80 LIGHT ANTI-TANK WEAPON *Specification* Launcher length: 150cm (4.7ft); when ready to fire; Weight: 4.5kg (10lbs); Warhead diameter: 94mm (3.6in); Warhead type: HEAT (High Explosive, Anti-Tank); Effective range: 20–500m (22–545yds).
    A British derivative of the American 66mm weapon, this disposable, one-shot missile launcher is capable of destroying most targets. It is only 1m (1.09yds) long (collapsed), and its light weight means that it can be carried in addition to a soldier's kit and personal weapon. It is reliable and easy to use, requiring little preparation. It contains a spotting rifle which fires tracer rounds to enable aim correction before the main round is released. This rocket launcher was used by the SAS in the Gulf War.

LAW ROCKET, 66MM *Specification* Warhead diameter: 66mm (2.5in); Weight: 1.5kg (3.45lbs); Length: 878mm (34in) unextended; Range: 220m (239yds); Velocity: 200m (218yds) per second.
    The 66mm LAW rocket is capable of penetrating 275mm (10.5in) armour and is extremely effective, as was demonstrated in the Falklands War. Although designed for use against tanks, the SAS have used it successfully against caves, bunkers, and other enemy fortified targets. In an unconventional method, the SAS used batches of the 66mm rockets to protect the outer limits of the 'Diana' defences during the Oman War. The firing mechanism of the rockets was rewired so they could be triggered electrically from a distance.

The 66mm is a complete weapon system consisting of a lightweight, shoulder-fired launcher and HEAT (High Explosive, Anti-Tank) rocket. The weapon comes pre-loaded and is basically a single shot, disposable launcher. It is a rugged, reliable and lightweight anti-tank weapon weighing 1kg (2.2lb) which, when fully extended, is 980mm (38in) long unextended. The launcher requires no maintenance, as the outer tube serves to protect the weapon once removed from the transit packaging.

The weapon is prepared for firing easily and quickly, by simply removing the front and rear covers, and extending the rear section, which contains the rocket. Extending the rocket also allows the spring-loaded sights to pop-up. They are marked for range and movement and have luminous spots for night firing. The effective range is little more than 200m (218yds) although the sight is graduated up to 350m (381yds). No zeroing of the sight is necessary.

Like all such rockets, there is a back-blast danger area, which must be clear of friendly troops, equipment or close, solid obstacles. Once fired, the launcher tube may be discarded, although it is common, time permitting, to destroy it.

LAYFORCE This unit, commanded and named after Brigadier-General Robert Laycock, was a commando brigade attached to General Wavell's Middle Eastern Army. An impressive force on paper, it comprised 2,000 men of 7, 8 and 11 Commandos who arrived in the Middle East on 11 March 1941.

In December 1940 David Stirling was serving with No. 8 Commando and had not yet presented his ideas for raising the unit which would become the SAS. Though Layforce had been formed to exploit the results of Major-General O'Connor's success against the Italian Tenth Army between December 1940 and February 1941, the appearance of Rommel and his Afrika Korps in North Africa meant it was split up into three units. One, under Laycock, fought in Crete, another was based around Tobruk, on the Libyan coast, and the third was sent to Syria where it took part in a number of raids on the Cyrenaican coast.

They were singularly unsuccessful because they were too large and unwieldy, but they did prompt Stirling to devise new methods of hitting the enemy hard. He was convinced the answer lay in independent small-sized teams; and he would be proved right. Layforce itself was disbanded as the men and materials were needed elsewhere.

LAYFORCE II Two specialist raiding units, Forfar Force and 12 Commando, were disbanded in November 1942 and the job of deception raids passed to Layforce II. The force was drawn largely from French commandos of 10 Commando, a polyglot unit of Britain's Allies from overseas, commanded by General Laycock's brother, Major Peter Laycock. Combined Operations Headquarters planned 44 deception raids for Layforce II but only seven were ever carried out. This was mainly due to the high cost in lives lost. In some cases, men were sacrificed for sand samples and details of minefields that were never used in future planning. A series of sea-borne raids was carried out in December 1943 at Gravelines, to the west of Dunkirk, and around the cliffs near St Valery. The raids ended in disaster and whilst some managed to escape, two men drowned and two more were captured. The purpose of these raids was to collect useful intelligence, but others saw it as a diversionary tactic to deceive the Germans about the forthcoming landings.

L DETACHMENT This was the original name of the Special Air Service in July 1941, or to be more precise L Detachment, SAS Brigade. HQ Middle East dreamed up the name in an effort to convince the Germans that they had formed a whole new airborne brigade. Whether the ploy worked or not is unknown, but the reality was that L Detachment comprised 67 men who had been recruited from Layforce. This 'brigade' had no weapons, no tents and no supplies.

LEA, LIEUTENANT-GENERAL GEORGE Became commander of 22 SAS in 1955, when the regiment was involved in Malaya. He brought a new sense of discipline and professionalism to the SAS, getting rid of officers he thought unfit for such a role, and bringing in some new ones whom he considered bright and dynamic. One of these officers was Peter de la Billière.

LEAD SCOUT The man who takes up the lead position in a four-man patrol's line of advance. Also called the 'point', it is a responsible role requiring alertness to any possible enemy activity or traps, while navigating the patrol to its objective. Due to the fact that lead scouts are often the first point of contact with enemy forces, they are usually armed with a weapon capable of substantial firepower such as a light machine gun, a semi-automatic shotgun or a rifle fitted with a grenade launcher. Patrol commanders will usually select their most experienced man for the position of Lead Scout.

LETTS, CAPTAIN ROBIN In 1965, during the Borneo Confrontation, Captain Robin Letts of D Squadron and his patrol were given the task of collecting information on the Indonesians' communication routes. In order to do this, the patrol had to infiltrate several kilometres across the border, before they eventually found a good observation post (OP). Their journey, which began on 17 April, took six days and involved slow and silent movement through deep jungle and swamp. They finally established an OP overlooking a bend in a tributary which ran into the River Sentimo: it had good visibility, about 60m (65yds) in either direction. From their well-concealed hide they watched several enemy boats pass downstream; all contained armed soldiers. Knowing he had struck lucky, Letts sent a message back to base seeking permission to engage the enemy as and when the opportunity presented itself.

A day later such permission had still not been received, but Letts decided to engage the enemy at the next possible opportunity. The river, which served as a road through the jungle, was a main supply route for both men and equipment.

By dawn on 28 April, Letts moved forward to a pre-arranged ambush site, which was chosen mainly due to the boats coming closer to the bank in order to negotiate the river bend. It also allowed him to take on two boats at the same time. He also worked out a good escape route, knowing that once he had made contact with the enemy, the patrol would be forced to flee back to the safety of the border. At 09:15 a boat with three soldiers in it came into view; this was followed by a second boat and a further three soldiers. Letts gave the signal to stand-by, only to pause as a third boat containing more soldiers appeared. To make matters worse, the second boat crashed into the bank and stopped while the others made their way around the river bend. At this stage Letts could wait no longer as he stood to initiate the ambush. Unfortunately, the movement was seen by the enemy and one of them stood up in the boat, gun in hand ready to fire. The man posted at left-hand stop saw this and fired, hitting the Indonesian soldier in the chest and knocking him into the water. The next second the whole patrol opened up at close range on all three boats. In the panic almost all the soldiers lost their balance and fell into the water, some injured and some trying hard to make it to the river bank.

It was thought that the Indonesian soldiers had been practising anti-ambush drills, for seconds after they had thrown themselves in the water they emerged on the bank, some with their weapons. Luckily Letts' patrol remained calm and quickly foiled any possibility of a counter-attack. Then, just as the action was about to end, another boat appeared, but the sound of gunfire had warned the enemy who were now trying to bring their boat into the bank. The patrol fired but they backpaddled frantically, disappearing back out of sight. Letts now decided it was time to leave, a quick count showing they were leaving eight dead Indonesian soldiers behind in an ambush that had taken only three minutes.

Now they were running, there was no point in trying to hide and the Indonesians were in hot pursuit. Crashing through the jungle at speed, with mortar bombs from the enemy continually raining down on them, Letts' patrol covered the distance back to the border in just over twelve hours. Shortly after, they were picked up by helicopter and returned to base. Letts was awarded the Military Cross.

LEWES BOMB   A bomb designed during World War II by Lieutenant 'Jock' Lewes for the express purpose of destroying aircraft. The bomb was basically a mixture of plastic explosive (TNT 808) thermite and diesel oil. The bombs were attached to the aircraft normally on or near the engine and initiated by a time pencil and detonator. The time pencils operated by crushing a small glass vial of acid which was encased in a soft copper case. This acid dissolved a thin wire which held back the firing pin poised over a detonating cap. The strength of the acid and the time it took to eat through the restraining wire determined the delay time. They were very inconsisent with most time pencils, having a 50 per cent error.

LEWES, LIEUTENANT JOHN 'JOCK' STEEL One of the originals of L Detachment, Lewes volunteered for the SAS while a member of Layforce's No. 8 Commando. He took part in the early SAS operations in North Africa, but it was his training programme that was instrumental in moulding the ethos of the SAS, as Johnny Cooper states: 'Jock instilled into us that the end product of our training was for us to become independent in every war, operating either alone or in very small groups. We would have to develop an ingrained self-confidence in our ability to navigate across featureless terrain without any back-up whatsoever and using maps that gave little or no detail. We would have to survive on minimum sustenance and to control the use of food and water during the hot periods of the day, using the cover of darkness for offensive activity.' These words could have been written by a modern SAS soldier talking about today's missions. Lewes was killed when his vehicle was strafed by an Italian aircraft after taking part in a raid against Nofilia airfield on 26 December 1941. As well as his training programme, Lewes invented the Lewes bomb.

LIFE-LINE A standard piece of SAS equipment first issued in the 1970s, and used primarily as a 5m (5.5yds) safety line for crossing rivers. The line is made from olive drab 15mm (.5in) climbing tape with a loop stitched at either end, to which a metal screw-gate karabiner is attached. Several lines can be fixed together, as required.

LIGHT ORDER Normally means just weapon and belt equipment. If a patrol is required to do a close target recce or just take a look around, prior to entering a lying-up position (LUP), several members, normally two in a four-man patrol, will stash their bergens and move in light order.

LI HAK CHI In December 1956, during the Malayan Emergency campaign, the New Zealand SAS Squadron under Major Frank Rennie commenced an operation to hunt down a notorious Communist Terrorist (CT) leader named Li Hak Chi whose group of 24 terrorists was based deep in the jungle-covered mountains of the state of Negeri Sembilan. Having reconnoitred a sector where Li Hak Chi was known to be active, the squadron established a number of ambushes on routes used by his group. Ten days later two CTs entered an ambush area and one terrorist, a courier, was killed while the other escaped. Three days later another ambush claimed a second courier. The squadron spent thirteen weeks in the area until March 1957, when it was extracted for a brief period of rest and recuperation before returning to Negeri Sembilan to continue its hunt. The following four and a half months were spent patrolling the area whose rugged terrain took its toll, with one member of the squadron, Corporal 'Buck' Buchanan, dying of heat exhaustion.

On 12 April 1957 the squadron was about to leave for another period of rest and recuperation in the capital, Kuala Lumpur, when information was received from Special Branch that Li Hak Chi had come out of hiding to collect food from a cache and, with four of his terrorists, was back at his base. The squadron deployed immediately to intercept him. A patrol under Corporal Huia Woods, a highly skilled tracker, was despatched to follow the CTs while an ambush group, commanded by Sergeant Noel O'Dwyer, was positioned on a ridgeline thought to be one of two likely routes. Another ambush, under Lieutenant Ian Burrows, was established on the alternative route which was longer and followed lower-lying terrain through very dense jungle. By the fourth day of the operation Corporal Woods' patrol had succeeded in closing the gap with Li Hak Chi's group which was taking the lower route. At dusk, two CTs entered Lieutenant Burrows' killing area and were eliminated. A few minutes later, another group approached but fortunately the patrol held its fire as it could not positively identify its targets in the failing light: the second group was in fact Corporal Huia Woods' patrol.

On the following day one of the two bodies was identified by Special Branch as being that of Li Hak Chi. The other was his personal bodyguard, Ah Song. The New Zealand SAS Squadron remained in Negeri Sembilan until October, continuing its operation against the CT group which, having lost its leader, ceased to be a threat. During the last week of the operation, four CT members surrendered to the security forces.

LILLICO, SERGEANT EDDIE 'GEORDIE'   Involved in many of the 'Claret' cross-border raids in Borneo. In February 1966 Lillico and his men from D Squadron were attacked and he was wounded in the legs. Despite the seriousness of his injuries, Lillico spent the next couple of days crawling through the bush to reach a helicopter rendezvous. He is one of the longest serving members of 22 SAS, much respected for his devotion to military training especially in SAS techniques. He was awarded the Military Medal.

LILLICRAP, SERGEANT BILL – 4 TROOP NZSAS   On 29 October 1969 Sergeant Bill Lillicrap was commander of a twelve-man patrol of 1 Squadron SAS Regiment, including six men of 4 Troop New Zealand SAS, which was inserted into an area in the far northeast of

Phuoc Tuy Province, some 7km (4 miles) west of Nui May Tao. Together with another patrol operating in an adjacent area under Sergeant Fred Roberts, it was to ambush a Vietcong (VC) supply route along which guerrillas of the VC's 84th Rear Services Group, escorted by North Vietnamese Army (NVA) troops, were expected to be bringing supplies. On the morning of 31 October, Sergeant Lillicrap's patrol found a track and some time later spotted a group of fourteen VC, comprising five armed men and nine porters, moving eastwards along it.

On the following morning, 1 November, the patrol established an ambush on the track and at 09:40 hours heard the sound of detonating Claymore mines from the direction of Sergeant Roberts' patrol's area 3km (2 miles) to the northeast. No further enemy appeared until 08:30 hours on 3 November when the Australian element of the patrol, under Corporal Joe van Droffelaar, which was deployed on the right flank of the ambush, observed five VC advancing towards it. Corporal van Droffelaar initiated the three Claymores in front of his patrol's position, followed almost immediately afterwards by Sergeant Lillicrap who fired twelve more sited in the main ambush killing area. Heavy fire was by then being brought to bear by an NVA force which was subsequently estimated to be of platoon strength.

The NVA troops then mounted a strong attack and Sergeant Lillicrap's group moved round to cover Corporal van Droffelaar's. Using fire and movement, the two groups withdrew from the ambush area as they heard further NVA troops approaching the area. Sergeant Lillicrap activated his URC 10 radio beacon and his signal was picked by a South Vietnamese Air Force OH-1 Bronco ground support aircraft which, having passed on a request for extraction, then attacked the ambush area with napalm after directions from the patrol. This succeeded in driving the NVA off and at 11:10 hours the patrol was extracted by helicopter.

LINGUIST The role of the linguist is vitally important when communicating with natives of an operational area. The ability to speak the native tongue enables the patrol to develop a good relationship with the locals, especially during a 'hearts and minds' campaign. It is also beneficial to have someone with a good working knowledge of the local language when interrogating prisoners-of-war.

Most SAS soldiers are actively encouraged to take a language course during their years at Hereford. Most courses are conducted at the Army School of Languages in Beaconsfield, although some languages are taught at Hereford. A language course is usually followed by a visit to the respective country, enabling the student to practise what he has been taught.

LO (LIAISON OFFICER) The SAS will establish a liaison officer in countries and with organizations of long-term interest to it, such as

Northern Ireland, Brunei, MI5 and other security services. The aim of the liaison officer is to monitor activity and find future work for the SAS. In Northern Ireland, SAS liaison officers were located with the regions' Tactical Control Group (TCG) where they would act as the eyes and ears of the regiment, working in co-ordination with the RUC Special Branch.

LONG BAWAN   On 12 June 1965, during the Borneo Confrontation campaign, a patrol of 1 Squadron Australian SAS Regiment under the Squadron Sergeant-Major, WO2 Alex Thompson, was inserted on the border between Sarawak's Fifth Division and Indonesian Kalimantan. Its mission, under the auspices of Operation 'Claret', was to penetrate up to 10,000m (6 miles) into Indonesian territory and reconnoitre an airfield at Long Bawan, determining its defences and the type of aircraft using it. Unfortunately the patrol failed to locate the airfield but observed a number of Indonesian troops in a nearby village. The patrol had, however, been spotted earlier and shortly afterwards a group of the enemy appeared some 20m (21yds) from its position and deployed into line for an assault. Forced to abandon its packs, the patrol withdrew in haste and made its way back to the border.

On 1 July WO2 Thompson led another patrol back to Long Bawan to complete the task of reconnoitring the airfield. At 12:00 hours on 5 July the patrol moved into a lying-up position (LUP) with a view to carrying out its reconnaissance task after nightfall. Shortly afterwards, however, an Indonesian force approached the patrol's position and it rapidly became apparent that it was tracking Thompson and his men. Opening fire at a range of 4m (4yds), the patrol killed the leading two enemy but the remainder deployed rapidly for an assault, with a second group carrying out a flanking movement. Once again, Thompson and his men had to abandon their packs, which had been cached earlier, and withdraw rapidly to the border.

'LONG DRAG'   'Long Drag' or 'Endurance' is the final march of Test Week for those attending SAS Selection. It is a 64km (40 mile) march over the Brecon Beacons with a 55kg (121lbs) bergen in 20 hours. Students start around midnight, with little or no sleep between the previous days march and 'endurance'. The distance, route and weight all combine to make this the hardest of all tests that those wishing to join the SAS must face.

LRDG (LONG RANGE DESERT GROUP)   Like so many ad hoc British units that came into existence during World War II, the Long Range Desert group (LRDG) was the product of a group of eccentric individuals. During the 1920s and 1930s, Major Ralph Bagnold, Royal Corps of Signals, and a group of friends had undertaken a series of desert journeys which had resolved the not inconsiderable problems of living in and travelling through the desert. His studies resulted in a paper advocating the formation of a military desert reconnaissance force; not unsurprisingly GHQ Middle East rejected the idea.

The High Command reconsidered their decision when Italy declared war on Britain in June 1940 and they were suddenly in need of intelligence regarding Italian dispositions in North Africa. The Provisional War Establishment of the Long Range Desert Group (LRDG) was authorized in July 1940, originally for 11 officers and 76 men. In November 1940, though, this number was increased to 21 officers and 271 men, though by March 1942 the LRDG numbered 25 officers and 324 men. Operating in open-topped Chevrolet trucks, the LRDG carried out reconnaissance, intelligence gathering and courier duties. These tasks involved long drives across the featureless desert terrain, followed by observation of enemy posts and convoys. There were also raiding activities, which forced the Italians to divert troops from the front to safeguard their rear areas. The SAS used LRDG trucks for transport from late 1941 until early 1942, though Stirling's men caused problems for the LRDG because they provoked greater enemy reaction, which meant more enemy patrols.

The LRDG was withdrawn to Cairo to regroup in March 1943, and undertook operations in Greece, Italy and Yugoslavia. Like many specialist units, the LRDG was disbanded at the end of the war.

LONG RANGE RECONNAISSANCE PATROL (LRRP) WING

During early 1968 the Australian Army Training Team Vietnam (AATTV) established the Long Range Reconnaissance Patrol (LRRP) Wing at a training camp at Van Kiep near Baria, the capital of Phuoc Tuy Province in South Vietnam. Its role was to train the Army of the Republic of Vietnam (ARVN) troops in LRRP, skills with the ultimate objective of forming an ARVN/LRRP unit for operations in Phuoc Tuy Province, under the command of 1st Australian Task Force. Instructors were all former members of the Australian SAS Regiment (SASR), with the exception of the first Chief Instructor, Captain Stan Krasnoff of the Royal Australian Regiment, who was later replaced by Captain Doug Tear, who had previously served in 2 Squadron SASR. Among those who were instructors in the LRRP Wing were Warrant Officers Roy Weir, John Pettit, Kevin Mitchell, Shorty Turner, Sonny Edwards, Merv Cranston, Ola Stevenson, Tom Hoolihan and Sergeant Bob Broadhurst.

By July 1968 the LRRP Wing was commencing the conduct of patrols, comprising students commanded by their instructors, under the auspices of 2 Squadron SASR. On 28 July two patrols, commanded by Warrant Officers Turner and Edwards, were together when they were attacked by a force of ten Vietcong (VC). One of the enemy was killed in the ensuing firefight but, when twenty more VC were observed approaching, both patrols withdrew and were subsequently extracted. Thereafter the SASR squadrons based at Nui Dat continued to include LRRP Wing patrols within their own patrol programmes.

LOUGHALL, COUNTY ARMAGH A classic SAS operation, which took place in Loughall, Northern Ireland, on Friday 8 May 1987. Intelligence had been received to indicate that the police station at Loughall was to be attacked by the method used the year before in County Armagh. That incident had taken place in April 1986, when a mechanical digger (JCB) had been packed with explosives and driven into the RUC station at the Birches. It had caused widespread damage. A report that another JCB had been stolen in East Tyrone gave rise to the suspicion that an identical IRA operation was being planned. All efforts were made to locate the digger and identify the target. After intensive covert searching, the weapons and explosives were located. Subsequently, the digger was also located in a derelict building on a farm some 15km (9 miles) away.

Surveillance by E4A provided more information and eventually the target was assessed as the RUC station at Loughall. This station was only manned part time and consisted of one principal building running parallel to the main road, surrounded by a high wire fence. The time and date of the attack was eventually confirmed through intelligence received.

Two of the IRA activists were named as Patrick Kelly and Jim Lynagh, who commanded the East Tyrone active service unit. When masked men stole a blue Toyota van from Dungannon, Jim Lynagh was spotted in the town, which suggested that the van was to be used in the Loughall attack. Not long after the observation post (OP) reported that the JCB was being moved from the derelict farm. At this stage the SAS, who had been reinforced from Hereford, took up their ambush positions. It was reported that some were in the police station itself, but this was not true – instead most of the main ambush party was hiding in a row of small fir trees which lined the fence on the opposite side to the station. Several heavily armed stops were also in position, covering all avenues of escape.

At a little past 19:00. the blue Toyota van drove down the road in front of the police station. Several people were seen to be inside. A short time later it returned from the direction of Portadown, this time followed by the JCB carrying three hooded IRA terrorists in the cab. Declan Arthurs was driving, with Michael Gormley and Gerald O'Callaghan riding shotgun. The bucket of the JCB held rubble in which was concealed an oil drum filled with explosive. As the blue van charged past the station the JCB slammed through the gate. One of the two terrorists riding shotgun, although it was not clear which one at the time, ignited the bomb and all three made a run for it. Back at the van, several hooded men jumped clear and started to open fire in the direction of the RUC station. At this stage the SAS ambush was activated.

The sudden hail of SAS fire was terrifying. All eight members of the IRA fell under the hail of bullets. At the height of the firefight the bomb exploded, taking with it half the RUC station and scattering debris over all concerned. As the dust settled, the SAS closed in on the bodies. At that moment a white car entered the ambush area with its two occupants dressed in blue boiler suits similar to those worn by the IRA. They were unfortunately mistaken for terrorists, especially when, on seeing the ambush in progress, they stopped and started to reverse. One of the SAS stops opened fire, killing one of the occupants and wounding the other. It later transpired that the dead motorist, Antony Hughes, had nothing to do with the IRA. Several other vehicles and pedestrians soon appeared on the scene, but by this time the situation had been stabilized.

Loughall was one of the most successful operations ever mounted against the IRA, but their retaliation was savage. On Remembrance Day 1987, a huge bomb was detonated during the ceremony in Enniskillen, killing eleven and injuring more than sixty.

'LOYTON', OPERATION Carried out by 91 men of 2 SAS in the Vosges mountains, eastern France, under the command of Lieutenant-Colonel Brian Franks, this mission was detailed to collect intelligence regarding German rail and road movements, strike at enemy installations and co-operate with the local Maquis (which was problematic at the best of times). The advance party, together with a Phantom patrol and Jedburgh team, were dropped on the evening of 12 August 1944, with subsequent drops taking place in the days which followed. Unfortunately the Germans had placed large numbers of troops on the crests of the Vosges mountains and the east bank of the River Moselle. The SAS party thus dropped into a veritable nest of vipers (to make matters worse the Gestapo were also in the area, at Nancy and Strasbourg, and both locations had anti-partisan units).

The SAS men had to contend with large numbers of enemy troops and traitors within the Maquis. There were also a number of reprisals against local villages in response to SAS successes. The male population of Moussey, for example, was rounded up and packed off to concentration camps. Of the 210 men between the ages of 16 and 60 who were taken, only 70 returned. Franks brought the operation to an end on 9 October, by which time two SAS soldiers had been killed and 31 captured (all of whom were shot by the Gestapo). The lack of supplies had brought the mission to an end.

LS/LZ LS is the abbreviation for Landing Site, a location were troops are infiltrated by helicopter and actually placed on the ground. LZ or Landing Zone is an area where troops will normally land after being dropped by parachute.

LUCY-SUR-YONNE   Lucy-sur-Yonne was the scene of a fierce engagement in July 1944, involving members of A Squadron 1 SAS on Operation 'Houndsworth' in the area south of Dijon in France. The squadron's 3 Troop, commanded by Captain Roy Bradford, was due to move to a new base in the area of Fort des Dames, and two days earlier Bradford had sent ahead an advance party of two men, Sergeant Jeff Duvivier and Trooper Ball, to reconnoitre the area. Late in the evening of 19 July, he set off from the SAS base at Chalaux in a jeep to join up with them. He was accompanied by Sergeants 'Chalky' White and 'Maggie' McGinn, who were the vehicle's front gunner and driver respectively, and Trooper Devine who was manning the rear guns. Also in the vehicle was a member of the Maquis, Jacques Morvillier.

Travelling all night, Bradford and his men had reached the village of Lucy-sur-Yonne at 08:00 hours when they suddenly encountered two Germans, an officer and a sergeant, walking towards them along the road. Sergeant White opened fire with his Vickers K guns but almost immediately afterwards the jeep came under fire from about 150 enemy troops in a convoy of seven trucks parked nearby. Without hesitation, Sergeant McGinn accelerated past the convoy while Sergeant White and Trooper Devine brought their guns to bear at point blank range. An enemy machine gun at the rear of the convoy, however, opened fire in response. Devine was killed. At the same time Captain Bradford was hit in the arm and shortly afterwards was hit by a burst of machine gun fire which killed him and severely wounded Jacques Morvillier. Sergeant White was also badly wounded but nevertheless continued to operate his guns, changing magazines despite a shattered left hand and wounds to one of his shoulders and legs.

Sergeant McGinn, meanwhile, was unhurt and managed to coax the jeep, which was severely damaged, round a corner out of sight of the enemy. Seeing that Captain Bradford and Devine were dead, he dragged Sergeant White and Morvillier from the vehicle and, pulling them through a hedge, hid them in a nearby wood. Shortly afterwards, enemy troops appeared and the three men watched them search the jeep and two bodies. After dusk had fallen, Sergeant McGinn helped the two wounded men to move away from the area to avoid any subsequent search by the enemy, but it became apparent that they would not be able to travel any distance. The following day, he swam the River Yonne and purloined a boat with which he ferried Sergeant White and the Frenchman across. The three men hid in an orchard until the evening when Jacques Morvillier made contact with the Maquis who rescued them after dusk.

LUMBIS   On 4 June 1965, during the Borneo Confrontation campaign, a patrol of 1 Squadron Australian SAS Regiment under Corporal John Robinson carried out a reconnaissance of the area of Lumbis, situated

10,000m (6 miles) inside the border of Indonesian Kalimantan, where the presence of 150 Indonesian troops had been previously reported in the villages there. Robinson and his lead scout, Private Bob Stafford, spent two days carrying out a close reconnaissance of the area, determining that there was a force of twenty enemy in the village of Kamong. As a result of Robinson's subsequent report and those of other patrols covering the area, the commander of Central Brigade, Brigadier Harry Tuzo, decided to mount an attack on Lumbis. Corporal Robinson and his patrol were tasked with acting as guides for the assault force.

On 21 June, B Company 2nd Battalion 7th Duke of Edinburgh's Own Gurkha Rifles, together with a section of two 81mm mortars and Corporal Robinson's patrol, were inserted by helicopter into Saliliran, 5,000m (3 miles) inside the border of the Malaysian state of Sabah, and three days later, on the afternoon of 24 June, reached a location near Lumbis. While the mortar section established its baseplate position, Corporal Robinson's patrol went forward and carried out a reconnaissance of the enemy positions, confirming that there were still enemy in Kamong.

At 04:00 hours on the following morning, B Company took up its positions and at 09:00 hours opened fire as the Indonesian garrison was assembling for its breakfast. Half a dozen enemy were killed in the first burst from the company's eight general purpose machine guns and soon afterwards its two 81mm mortars scored direct hits on one of the buildings housing the enemy. The Indonesians responded with a 60mm mortar, which was knocked out shortly afterwards by one of B Company's mortars, and a 12.7mm heavy machine gun which resisted all attempts to silence it. Fifty minutes later, B Company ceased fire and withdrew with Corporal Robinson's patrol to the border, which was reached before last light. It was subsequently reported by Border Scouts that the Indonesians had strengthened their defences at Lumbis but were no longer patrolling the area, preferring to remain within the relative safety of their positions.

LUP A lying-up position is a position to hide by day or night. The LUP is chosen with care and the SAS pride themselves on the choice of site and construction of their LUPs. The site is normally defensive, well camouflaged with several bug-out routes should the patrol need to run. There will always be a sentry to give early warning of approaching enemy. The LUP routine will consist of eating, cleaning weapons, sending Sit Reps (situation reports) and sleeping.

M

M1 CARBINE *Specification* Calibre: 30 Carbine (7.62mm × 33); Weight: 1kg (2.36lb); Muzzle velocity: 600m (654yds) per second; Magazine capacity: 15- or 30-round, box.

First produced in the US in 1941 by Winchester, it quickly became popular with US Special Forces, especially in the Pacific campaigns. It incorporated a new type of gas operation, now known as short-stroke piston operation. Its use continued after World War II, and it also found popularity with the British forces in Malaya. There were different types of M1s, the most common being the M1A1 semi-automatic. In addition, a fully automatic version, the M2, was also used. Today the weapon is largely obsolete, although it still can be found in second line service in South America and Asia.

M SQUADRON A volunteer force for service in Korea, made up from soldiers with war-time experience from 21 SAS and the Z Reserve (TA). When the political situation in Korea changed with the entry of China into the war, the force, which by this time was well organized and equipped, was diverted to Singapore where it joined up with the Malayan Scouts.

M203 40MM GRENADE LAUNCHER *Specification* Calibre: 40mm (1.5in); Weight: 0.7kg (1.63lb); Muzzle velocity: 75m (81yds) per second; Range: 400m (436yds).

Designed by the AAI (American Armaments Industries) Corporation and manufactured by Colt, the M203 was designed as a grenade launcher that could either be fitted to an M16 rifle or used as a weapon on its own. It is a single shot, breech-loading weapon which works like a pump-action shotgun. Newer versions are designed to fit any assault rifle. The M203 is widely used by the SAS and other Special Forces, and was to prove its worth during the Gulf War.

M60 GENERAL PURPOSE MACHINE GUN *Specification* Calibre: 7.62mm × 51 NATO standard; Weight: 5kg (11.1lbs), 8kg (17.9lbs) with tripod; Muzzle velocity: 853m (929yds) per second; Magazine capacity: belt-fed.

This American general purpose machine gun has been in service with the US Army since the Vietnam War, despite having many problems. Although a powerful weapon, it was awkward to use with its permanently attached bipod. Also, when the barrel had to be changed, asbestos gloves were needed as it became so hot. The Minimi has now replaced it in the light machine gun role. It is still produced by the manufacturers as the M60E3, a version of the M60 re-designed by the US Marine Corps, in which many of the design faults have been ironed out, resulting in a much more acceptable weapon. The M60 has been used by the IRA in Northern Ireland against the SAS.

M79 GRENADE LAUNCHER *Specification* Calibre: 40mm (1.5in); Weight: 2.95kg (7lb); Muzzle velocity: 76m (82yds) per second; Range: 350m (381yds).

Also called the 'bloop gun' because of the sound it makes when fired, this predecessor of the M203 grenade launcher saw extensive service with US forces in Vietnam. Although it has a high trajectory, it can be very accurate in the right hands. It is now in use mainly in Korea and several other Asian and South American countries. It was a weapon widely used by the SAS during the Oman War and remained in service until the M16 arrived with the M203 attached.

MAIDA BARRACKS – AIRBORNE FORCES DEPOT Located at Maida Barracks, Aldershot, the Airborne Forces Depot was the scene of the first Selection course for 22 SAS, conducted by Major John Woodhouse towards the end of 1952. Since 1950 the depot had also acted as a holding and training unit for personnel joining M Squadron 21 SAS, originally destined for operations in Korea but subsequently deployed to Malaya, and thereafter for volunteers for D Squadron Malayan Scouts (SAS). By 1955, 22 SAS had established its own Selection and training wing at Dering Lines in Brecon.

MALAYAN EMERGENCY, 1948–60 Prior to World War II, Malaya, with its population of Malays, Indians and Chinese, was ruled by the British. Following the war and the Japanese occupation, the British planned to reorganize the peninsula into a federation, a move which angered the Chinese minority, which led to revolt. In June 1948 Chin Peng, secretary-general of the Malayan Communist Party (MCP), issued orders for its members to take up positions throughout Southeast Asia. The MCP had been established in 1930 and drew the majority of its members from the Chinese in Malaya, where they represented one third of the population. They distributed the supplies stored after World War II and collected money from the Chinese population via the Min Yuen (Masses Movement).

A spate of murders and sabotage ensued, much of which was aimed at isolated police posts and the rubber plantations in the interior. On 16 June 1948 the murder of three European planters resulted in the British authorities proclaiming a State of Emergency throughout Malaya. But the British were slow to respond due, in the main, to the death of Sir Edward Gent, the High Commissioner of Malaya, in an air crash. It was not until September 1948 that his successor, Sir Henry Gurney, was appointed, giving the rebels plenty of time to establish themselves. Also, in February 1949, and in an attempt to increase its popularity, the MCP changed its name to the Malayan Races Liberation Army (MRLA).

Lieutenant-General Sir Harold Briggs was appointed Director of Operations in Malaya in April 1950 and, based on a report by Lieutenant-Colonel Mike Calvert about the growing violence, established the 'Briggs Plan'. On 6 October 1951, Sir Henry Gurney was murdered in an ambush at Fraser's Hill. One month later Lieutenant General Briggs was forced to retire on account of his ill-health, yet despite these set-backs the fight against the Communists continued. In February 1952 General Sir Gerald Templer was appointed as High Commissioner and Director of Operations, a combination of the primary civil and military posts. At this stage, Lieutenant-Colonel Calvert had developed the special counter-insurgency force known as the Malayan Scouts, using them in the jungle to attack the enemy.

By the following March, 423,000 Chinese squatters had been forcibly resettled in 410 'New Villages' all carefully guarded and strictly controlled, particularly where food supplies were concerned, making it impossible for the rebels to access their main source of money, information and new recruits. As a result, the remaining Malay Chinese fighting in the jungle turned against the Communists and some 1,097 insurgents were killed during the rest of 1952. Moreover, General Templer instigated a 'hearts and minds' campaign, promising the inhabitants of Malaya early independence and granting all foreigners born in Malaya full citizenship.

In July 1955, following a general election, Tunku Abdul Rahman was elected to form a government as Chief Minister of the Malayan Federation. Two years later Malaya became an independent sovereign state, and with Tunku Abdul Rahman as prime minister, the emergency was finally declared over in 1960.

MALAYAN RACES LIBERATION ARMY (MRLA) Military wing of the mainly Chinese Malayan Communist Party (MCP). They ran a terrorist campaign against the British in Malaya from 1948 to 1960. During World War II, Britain had encouraged and armed the MCP Malayan People's Anti-Japanese Army (MPAJA) to fight the Japanese occupiers. After the war a substantial number of weapons were hidden and later used against the British.

The MRLA, headed by Chin Peng, wanted an end to British rule in Malaya and to redress the balance of power in the country in favour of the Chinese. The guerrillas operated from camps on the edges of the deep jungle, which covered three-quarters of the country. At its height in 1951, the MRLA had 8,000 guerrillas aided by approximately 60,000 Min Yuen (Masses Movement) who conducted their operations from the villages and squatter camps. They provided food, money and intelligence for the guerrillas. More help, either given freely or under pressure, was provided by the rural Chinese, numbering approximately 500,000.

Following the successful implementation of the 'Briggs Plan', the Communist Terrorists (CTs) moved deeper and deeper into the dense jungle with the security forces, including the SAS, following them in hot pursuit. Because of operations directed by the security forces and the social and economic policies of British administration, plus the plans for accelerated independence, the MRLA had, by the middle of 1958, been reduced to about 1,000 men. Although they were determined fighters, the guerrillas did not manage to convince the mainly non-Chinese villagers that they would benefit under Chinese Communist rule. The 'hearts and minds' policy waged by the administration in urban areas and by the SAS in the jungle area encouraged this belief and led to the British victory over the MRLA.

MALAYAN SCOUTS British unit founded by Lieutenant-Colonel Mike Calvert, which was one of the forerunners of today's 22 SAS. It was formed as a counter-insurgency unit to fight the Communist guerrillas in Malaya; the original recruits of A Squadron came from local volunteers, some of them with SOE (Special Operations Executive) experience in World War II. The men of A Squadron were trained at Johore to live and fight in the jungle in groups of three or four, in order to track and ambush guerrilla forces and to direct air strikes. They were also instructed to pursue a 'hearts and minds' policy with the native peoples.

Almost immediately the Malayan Scouts were called upon to tackle the problem of open rebel insurgency in Ipoh. Despite a lack of discipline at times, probably caused by the short training period, they had some success in subduing guerrilla activity.

A Squadron was soon joined by B Squadron, made up of men from a temporary unit called M Squadron. This squadron, consisting of members of 21 SAS and other World War II Special Forces reservists, had originally been intended to serve in Korea. However, political measures demanded that they instead be stationed in Singapore. From there they were despatched to Malaya. Unlike their counterparts in A Squadron, the men of B Squadron showed more of a sense of discipline and professionalism. C Squadron was added after Calvert visited Rhodesia and raised some more volunteers from there.

In 1951, Calvert was replaced by Lieutenant-Colonel John Sloane. Together with his officers John Woodhouse and Dare Newell, he managed to instil a greater sense of discipline and professionalism into the Scouts. By 1952, the Scouts were proving to be very successful in their operations and the way was now open for the formation of 22 SAS the same year.

MALVERN The first real barracks after the formation of 22 SAS located at Merebrook Camp, Malvern, Worcestershire. The regiment remained there until the early 1960s, after which they moved to the old Royal Artillery Barracks in Hereford.

'MAPLE', OPERATION Code-name for the mission undertaken on 22 January 1944 by 2 SAS to support the Allied landings at Anzio, Italy. Divided into two groups, 'Thistledown' and 'Driftwood', the aim of the mission was to cut the rail communications to the north of Rome and on the Italian east coast. 'Thistledown' included parties of four men assigned to destroy railway lines around Terni and Orvieto. The second group, 'Driftwood', was made up of two four-man parties ordered to disrupt the Urbino-Fabriano and Ancona-Rimini lines.

All parties landed at their targets by parachute on 7 January and the designated lines of 'Thistledown' were successfully destroyed (although one of the lines had already been bombed by the RAF). Yet despite the success of the attacks all the men were captured.

Unfortunately the whereabouts of the 'Driftwood' party remained a mystery with not a single member of the party arriving at the beach evacuation rendezvous. It is speculated that they may either have drowned, or been captured and killed. A reinforcement party named 'Baobab' was ordered to join the 'Driftwood' group but bad weather delayed their departure until the end of January.

MAQUIS Of Corsican origin, the word 'maquis' translates literally as scrub or bush, but in 1942 it was the name given by the French to the many men who left their homes to live in makeshift camps in the woods and forests. This was to escape compulsory labour enforced by the Germans in the occupied countries of Western Europe.

Prior to the D-Day landings on 6 June 1944 the British Special Operations Executive (SOE) and the American Office of Strategic Services (OSS) had tried to recruit the Maquis on sabotage missions behind German lines but without a great deal of success. The SAS also had several problems with the Maquis whose loyalties were divided between the supporters of General de Gaulle's Free French and the Communists. The Communists despised de Gaulle, saying he was little more than a British and American stooge to be employed only until he outlived his usefulness and then discarded. Many of the Maquis preferred to spend their time amassing weapons for use against de Gaulle's supporters when the war was over rather than obeying orders to kill the Germans.

However, after D-Day the SAS began to nurture good relationships with the Maquis and many groups parachuted into France to aid the Resistance groups and establish operating bases. The SOE disliked the fact that the SAS were arming and organizing Resistance groups especially since they had their own Jedburgh teams to carry out the same jobs and regarded the Maquis groups as their own concern. Despite these difficulties, improved co-operation developed between the SAS and the Maquis, who were a well-organized and highly motivated group with extensive local knowledge which was invaluable for planning raids. Unfortunately, there were some members of the Maquis who compromised the sensitive nature of the work carried out by the SAS. Although joint operations did occur, like Operation 'Wallace', in which the Maquis and the SAS launched a joint attack on German forces at Chatillon, often the SAS commanders preferred to operate without the Maquis. For example, Operation 'Houndsworth' was a mission where the SAS helped to beat off an attack on a Resistance camp without them.

'MARBLE ARCH'   In World War II, 'Marble Arch' was the name given to an Axis airfield in North Africa, so called because of a nearby arch erected in the desert by Mussolini to mark the border of Tripolitania. Led by Major Bill Fraser, the airfield was raided by an SAS party on 24 December 1941. When they arrived at the airfield they found it deserted and so returned to the rendezvous with Long Range Desert Group (LRDG) to wait. In fact a LRDG patrol had been despatched to meet them but had mistakenly arrived at the wrong rendezvous. After waiting for a whole week, Major Fraser and his four men set off to walk back to the British lines, but their journey turned into an eight-day nightmare across the desert. They ran out of water, hijacked a German staff car and covered an astonishing 320km (198 miles) before reaching safety.

'MARDON', OPERATION   During the final quarter of 1976 a large number of terrorists entered Rhodesia in the wake of peace talks held in Geneva between the Rhodesian Government and the black nationalists represented by the Patriotic Front. At the same time, Operation 'Mardon' was launched to pre-empt a major invasion of northern and eastern Rhodesia by ZANLA guerrillas. It comprised a two-pronged attack into the northern Tete and southern Gaza provinces of Mozambique. Targets in Tete Province were allocated to C Squadron Rhodesian SAS (RhSAS) and the Rhodesian Light Infantry (RLI), who approached their initial objectives on foot. Thereafter they were transported by some 80 vehicles which carried them on to their subsequent targets. Also taking part were the Grey Scouts, a mounted unit whose horses carried

81mm mortars and bombs on their backs. C Squadron and the RLI attacked a number of camps, killing a large number of terrorists and capturing large quantities of weapons and ammunition. Casualties were light, amounting to two men killed and one wounded.

The force withdrew after reaching a point deep in Tete Province, but a few days later the RhSAS and RLI returned to Mozambique, attacking a camp at Mavue and killing 30 terrorists. During the following month they also attacked a bunker complex at Rambanayi, only a few kilometres from the Rhodesian border, and found that it was occupied by Tanzanian and FRELIMO troops in addition to ZANLA terrorists. A fierce battle ensued and the enemy eventually had to be burned out of their positions. During the withdrawal C Squadron lost two men, Lieutenant Bruce Burrell and Trooper Enslin van Staden, who stepped on a landmine.

'MARIGOLD', OPERATION An unsuccessful mission in Sardinia by a joint SAS/Special Boat Section (SBS) party. On 30 May 1943 eight SAS and three SBS men landed by submarine under cover of darkness with the aim of recovering a prisoner. However, they were surprised on landing by the enemy and a short firefight ensued, but the party escaped and made it back to the submarine by dinghy, without loss of life.

MARINE ASSAULT ACCESS SYSTEM (MOBY) The marine assault access system has been designed to provide anti-terrorist personnel with the means to gain access from the water to elevated marine structures (such as oil rigs) and sea vessels. The system, which raises a flexible ladder and grapple, is particularly suitable where silence and stealth are of paramount importance. The device is compact, extremely portable and has proven operational advantages unsurpassed by any other existing equipment. One diver easily deploys the device to the target, and its compact design allows mobilization within seconds, together with easy manoeuvrability during operation. The system is used by both the SAS and SBS when quick access is required and traditional ladder or grappling hook systems are not feasible.

MARK 19 40-MM AUTOMATIC GRENADE LAUNCHER *Specification* Calibre: 40mm; Weight: 15kg (34lbs); Muzzle velocity: 240m (261yds) per second; Range: 1,600m (1,744yds); Rate of fire: 325–327 rounds per minute.

This grenade launcher is belt fed and mounted, leading to it actually being designated a machine gun. The later models have overcome the earlier problems of reliability and now provide a real source of heavy firepower at a low cost. The rounds are effective against personnel or light armour and are unusual in that each link stays with the cartridge and is ejected with it. Its versatility means that it can also be used mounted on vehicles and used with day, night and laser sights. The SAS used this weapon during their missions in the Gulf War.

MARS & MINERVA A regimental magazine which, until recently, featured many historical events of the SAS, especially World War II actions. The magazine has ceased to exist in its old form.

'MARSHALL', OPERATION This was a very successful mission handled by 32 men of 3 French Parachute Battalion (3 SAS) who were parachuted into the Corrèze area of France.

It took place between 11 and 24 August 1944, and the purpose of the raid was to interfere with enemy troop movements and stiffen the local Resistance. The party, led by Captain Wauthier, carried out many daring attacks on the Germans including one on a 300-strong SS unit.

MARTUBA This was an Axis airfield in North Africa during World War II. The SAS planned to attack it at night on 13 June 1942. It was part of a bigger Special Air Service operation to help a British convoy trying to reach Malta. The party, which was made up of Free French volunteers driven by Special Interrogation Group staff, were dressed up as Germans and drove enemy vehicles which had been captured. They were betrayed by an ex-Afrika Korps soldier who was part of the group (which was also going to attack Derna airfield). Only two of the party escaped.

MASSEY, BRIGADIER ANDREW Joined the SAS as a troop captain in 1971 and was the officer responsible for devising the outline concept of the British anti-terrorist team. During the Gulf War, having been promoted to Brigadier, Massey served as Deputy Director Special Forces. It was he who gathered A, D and B Squadrons, the strongest concentration of SAS troops since World War II, and announced Schwarzkopf's decision to use them inside Iraq. Brigadier Massey was well respected by his soldiers and renowned for his personal approach when addressing his men.

MAYNE, LIEUTENANT-COLONEL 'PADDY' BLAIR One of Stirling's first recruits into the SAS. The nickname 'Paddy' came from his Irish ancestry, and before the war he was well known for his accomplishments in the world of sport. In battle he possessed qualities of leadership which set him apart from most men, with a reputation built on his personal bravery, which at times was characterized as reckless and wild.

Mayne joined L Detachment SAS Brigade on its formation in July 1941 and played a major role in operations during the North African campaign. On the unit's expansion as 1st SAS Regiment (1 SAS), he commanded A Squadron, and during this period was awarded the DSO. After David Stirling's capture on 27 January 1943, Mayne was promoted to Lieutenant-Colonel and assumed command of the regiment until its reorganization into two separate units, the Special Raiding

Squadron (SRS) and the Special Boat Section (SBS). Mayne subsequently commanded the SRS throughout its operations in Sicily and Italy and by the time the campaign ended he had been awarded a bar to his DSO.

In March 1944 the SRS returned to England where it was expanded and reverted to its previous designation of 1 SAS, joining the newly formed SAS Brigade. Lieutenant-Colonel Paddy Mayne continued in command of the regiment during operations in France, the Low Countries, Scandinavia and Germany, subsequently being awarded two more bars to his DSO. On 1 October 1945 the SAS were disbanded and shortly afterwards Paddy Mayne was demobilized and returned to civilian life. Ten years later, on 15 December 1955, he was killed in a traffic accident in Newtownards, Northern Ireland.

McALEESE, PETER Enlisted in the Parachute Regiment in 1960 and a year later volunteered for service with 22 SAS Regiment. Posted to D Squadron and subsequently seeing action in Aden and Borneo, he became one of the most colourful soldiers the regiment has ever produced. In 1969 he left the Army and returned to civilian life. In 1975, however, he was recruited as a mercenary to fight with the FNLA guerrillas against the Cuban-backed forces of the MPLA government in Angola. A year later he returned to Britain, but shortly afterwards went back to Africa where he joined C Squadron Rhodesian SAS, subsequently 1st SAS Regiment, with which he served until 1980, taking part in a large number of cross-border operations into Mozambique.

Rhodesia having fallen to the Communist government of Robert Mugabe, McAleese left for South Africa where he joined the 44th Parachute Brigade in which he reached the rank of warrant officer. He was soon on active service again, returning to Angola on cross-border operations against the guerrillas of SWAPO (South West Africa Peoples Organization). Eventually he retired and returned to Britain in 1986, but shortly afterwards made his way to Africa once more, working in Uganda in the employment of a security company. Subsequently he travelled to South America and Colombia where he was hired to lead an attack on a Communist terrorist base deep in the jungle. The operation was, however, aborted but McAleese's employers then contracted him to mount an operation to assassinate Pablo Escobar, the head of the Cali drugs cartel. McAleese assembled and trained a twelve-man force to carry out the operation but disaster struck en route to the target in helicopters. Flying in mist, one of the aircraft struck a mountainside and the operation had to be aborted. Thereafter McAleese returned to Britain where he has since been employed in the security industry.

McAULIFFE, CORPORAL MICHAEL 'MAC' Joined the SAS from the Guards Independent Parachute Company in 1966 and was posted to G Squadron's Mountain Troop. An outstanding climber, Mac was one of the first men to climb the formidable pillar known as 'The Old Man of Hoy' in 1969. In January 1975, during the attack on the Shirshitti caves in Oman, McAuliffe was shot in the arm while acting as fire controller (MFC) to a battery of mortars. He had taken over the position just two hours earlier from the previous SAS MFC who had also been shot. Two months later he was driving a Land Rover from Ravens Roost to Point 825 when he hit a landmine resulting in severe injury to the front of his skull which forced him to be invalided out of the regiment. He died at home in Hereford several years later. The circumstances of his death as described by Sir Ranulph Fiennes in *The Feather Men* are completely fictitious.

McFARLANE, LIEUTENANT-COLONEL IAN – AUSTRALIAN SAS REGIMENT (SASR)   Assumed command of the SAS Regiment on 26 January 1972. Commissioned into the Royal Australian Regiment (RAR) from Royal Military College Duntroon in 1954, he was posted to 1st SAS Company as a platoon commander in July 1962, and subsequently served as company second-in-command. Thereafter, he served as a company commander in 4 RAR in Vietnam and as an instructor at the Australian Army Staff College before taking command of the SASR.

McFarlane assumed command at a difficult time for the SASR. For some reason the regiment was not popular among the higher echelons of the Army, this being manifested in part by the fact that officers were frequently discouraged from volunteering for service with it. Furthermore, the operational commitment in Vietnam had ended and the regiment reduced in size with the disbandment of 2 Squadron. McFarlane concentrated on retraining the regiment in specialist skills and the two Sabre Squadrons thus concentrated on reintroducing and developing their free-fall parachuting, diving and small boat handling, long range mobility and climbing skills.

At the beginning of 1973 Lieutenant-Colonel McFarlane formed the Unconventional Warfare Wing, under Captain Tony Tonna, to produce special mission teams along the lines of the US Army's Special Forces A-Teams. The SASR, however, was still searching for a new role and in August 1973, in an attempt to define it, McFarlane submitted a paper on the employment of Special Forces in the defence of Australia. He proposed that the regiment should be used for long and medium range reconnaissance, counter-guerrilla operations and counter-terrorist support for Australian law enforcement agencies. On 10 December 1973, Lieutenant-Colonel McFarlane handed over command of the SASR to Lieutenant-Colonel Neville Smethurst.

McKENNA, CAPTAIN 'BOB'   During early 1979 the Rhodesian 1st SAS Regiment (RhSAS) and Mozambique National Resistance (MNR) mounted a joint operation designed to strike a major blow at the

FRELIMO government of Mozambique. On the night of 23 March a combined force of RhSAS and MNR infiltrated the area of Beira, their target the large fuel depot of forty huge storage tanks which lay just outside the port. Disguised as FRELIMO troops, they waded through mangrove swamps, riverbeds and slippery, muddy terrain before moving through the back streets of the city to their objective. The commander of the operation, Captain Bob McKenna, led the main group to its positions while Lieutenant Pete Cole headed off with a smaller group to lay charges on a nearby electricity pylon. Captain Colin Willis, meanwhile, was leading a third group to place an explosive charge on a fuel pipeline which led from the depot to the wharfs where tankers off-loaded oil.

Lieutenant Cole and his men completed their task without any problems and rejoined the main group. Captain Willis's party, having placed and armed the explosive charge on the pipeline were, however, delayed in reaching their firing position because of the proximity of FRELIMO troops, including a 37mm anti-aircraft battery which was located near the pipeline. It was not until 23:45 hours, fifteen minutes after the attack was scheduled to begin, that he was able to report by radio that his men were in position. On receiving Captain Willis's signal, Captain McKenna initiated the attack by firing an RPG-7 grenade at the huge tank in front of him, joined a split second later by the rest of his force who let fly a barrage of rockets and armour-piercing tracer ammunition. Within seconds, tanks were exploding and the depot was ablaze, with the flames being fanned by the wind. The FRELIMO guards thought that they were under attack from the air and the anti-aircraft battery began firing indiscriminately into the air.

The RhSAS and MNR withdrew, their mission accomplished. However, they were seen as they did so and, realizing what had happened, the FRELIMO anti-aircraft battery opened fire on them. Fortunately, it was unable to depress the barrels of its guns sufficiently and so its shells passed harmlessly overhead. Unfortunately other FRELIMO fire was effective, and one MNR guerrilla was killed and a Rhodesian soldier wounded. Nevertheless the force succeeded in making good its escape and shortly afterwards the explosives on the pipeline and pylon blew up, cutting off Beira's electricity supply and preventing the passage of oil from the tanker wharfs. A major economic blow had been inflicted on FRELIMO and the reputation of the MNR further enhanced.

McKENNA, SEAN A hardened member of the IRA who was arrested by an SAS team sent over the Irish border on the night of 11 March 1976. Two SAS men dressed in civilian clothes apprehended him at his rented cottage and, with another soldier, walked him back over the border to where the RUC was waiting. His fear of the SAS was such that he told everything he knew without being asked a single question. At his trial, it was alleged that McKenna had been found in a drunken state north of the border. Whatever, he was found guilty on 25 different charges and received a total sentence of 303 years. The fact that he was arrested when he could have so easily been assassinated without any witnesses shows that the SAS were not operating a shoot to kill policy.

McLEAN, TROOPER TOM   Famous for rowing single-handedly across the Atlantic in 1969. A most amazing character, he took up the challenge for a bet, used Army rations and simply rowed his heart out. After 72 days at sea he hit the coast of Ireland near Blacksod in County Mayo. He repeated the feat in 1982, but this time established another record by crossing the ocean in the smallest recorded vessel, the *Giltspur*, which was only 3m (9.8ft) long.

McLEOD, GENERAL RODERICK 'RODDY'   General McLeod was in charge of the SAS Brigade for operations in northwest Europe in January 1944, prior to D-Day. He worked extremely hard to turn the brigade into a top force, but had disagreements with his superiors who did not understand the true military role, strategic rather than tactical, of the SAS. McLeod struggled to find fitting missions for the brigade to stop its early disbandment. He left in March 1945 and became Director of Military Operations in India. He was replaced by Brigadier Mike Calvert.

McNAB, ANDY   The pseudonym of the SAS soldier and author of the book *Bravo Two Zero*.

MCR 1   A World War II radio which was designated the MCR 1 and nicknamed the 'biscuit receiver' due to its resemblance to a Huntley & Palmer biscuit tin. It was arguably the best small radio developed at the time and capable of operating for up to 30 hours on a set of batteries.

M DETACHMENT   Commanded by Captain Fitzroy Maclean, M Detachment was made up of 150 volunteers from the Special Boat Section (SBS) trained in parachuting and other infiltration techniques. It was raised in the autumn of 1942. General Headquarters in Persia and Iraq had created an SAS-type force to counter the threat that the Germans would break through to Persia to seize important oilfields.

   M Detachment's first task was to kidnap General Zahidi, a Persian officer believed to be in constant contact with the Germans and planning a pro-Axis coup. However, the enemy threat to Persia receded following defeats at both El Alamein and Stalingrad. M Detachment was subsequently requested to train with the Special Boat Section at Athlit in Palestine before moving to the Lebanon. After this, the unit was involved in no further action and Captain Maclean was chosen as commander of a military mission to help Tito's Yugoslavian partisans.

MEDIC PACK   Each SAS patrol will carry a medical pack which, depending on the area of operation, will be prepared for the medic by the Regiment Medical section. SAS medical packs are designed to provide unit patrol medics with the capability of dealing with severe wounds and injuries, including those caused by blast and bullets, and of providing emergency life-support for casualties until such time as they can be moved from the operational area to a hospital. The pack includes: resuscitation, ventilation and aspiration equipment; intubation equipment; intravenous administration kits; dressings; tracheotomy and crico-thyrotemy kits; burns treatment kits; instruments; limb immobilization equipment and anti-shock suits, together with a wide variety of drugs and medications to cover most emergencies.

MEDICS   SAS medics are highly trained personnel who undergo an internal course at Hereford prior to attending one of several hospitals where they carry out practical work on real patients. The ability to carry out life-saving first aid and deal with most medical situations is of enormous value to a four-man patrol operating and cut off behind the enemy lines. In many cases an injured soldier will have no prospect of skilled assistance and the patrol medic will be responsible for his well-being. SAS medics train to deal with everything from childbirth to massive gunshot wounds.

'MELON', OPERATION   In November 1977, acting on information gleaned from radio interception, C Squadron Rhodesian SAS (RhSAS) mounted an operation, code-named 'Melon', to ambush a convoy of six ZANLA trucks travelling from the port of Maputo via the FRELIMO garrison town of Mapai in Mozambique's Gaza Province to Rhodesia's southeastern border region. The convoy's cargo would be a number of terrorists, including some ZANLA commanders.

On the evening of 1 November fifteen men of A Troop, under Captain Colin Willis, landed on to a drop-zone 120km (74 miles) inside Mozambique. After marching 15km (9 miles) they reached their ambush area at 10:00 hours the following morning and commenced mining the road. Shortly afterwards two FRELIMO soldiers, accompanied by a ZANLA guerrilla, approached and were shot dead by one of the early warning groups. Fearing that they had been compromised, Captain Willis and his men finished laying their mines and Claymores before moving off rapidly to avoid any follow-up by FRELIMO.

During the early evening, having travelled only 4km (2.5 miles), they heard the sound of vehicles followed by a massive explosion as their landmines and Claymores detonated. A split-second later they heard another as a truckload of ammunition in the leading vehicle also exploded. Returning to the road, the Rhodesians requested an air strike on the remainder of the FRELIMO force which had halted in the area for the night. Royal Rhodesian Air Force (RRAF) Hunters struck just after first light, wreaking havoc during an air-to-ground action which lasted five hours. The RhSAS, meanwhile, made themselves scarce and, despite an aggressive follow-up by FRELIMO troops, succeeded in making good their escape.

Captain Willis and three of his men later returned to the ambush area to assess the extent of the damage, and discovered that the patrol and the RRAF had inadvertently taken on the headquarters of FRELIMO's 4th Mobile Brigade which, under Russian advisers, was making its way to Mapai to establish close support for ZANLA terrorist groups operating in Rhodesia. FRELIMO had suffered 50 casualties, and a large number of new Russian-supplied vehicles, together with a huge amount of weapons and equipment, had been destroyed.

MELOT, MAJOR BOB An accomplished linguist who spoke Arabic fluently, Major Melot was involved with British Intelligence and became an early recruit to the SAS during World War II. He took part in raids on Benghazi (see Raid on) in North Africa in September 1942 and was wounded in the ensuing action. Later he fought with the Special Raiding Squadron at Termoli, Italy, and co-ordinated operations in northwest Europe as 2 SAS's intelligence officer.

MEXE SHELTER Now obsolete, the MEXE shelter was used by the two Territorial Army units, 21 SAS and 23 SAS, when they were deployed in the forward observation or 'hide role' in Germany during the days of the Cold War. Designed to accommodate a patrol of four fully equipped men for a period of several weeks, it was installed underground. An excavation was dug out for it, and the soil and turf were replaced thereafter to provide protection and camouflage. The main components comprised a steel frame, which had a load-bearing limit sufficient to support a vehicle crossing the ground above, a prefabricated hatch unit which provided entry to the shelter and a special skin. Once assembled, the frame was covered with the skin manufactured from special composite fabric which was both waterproof and NBC (nuclear, biological and chemical) agent-proof. The latter property also stopped scent permeating through to the surface of the ground thus preventing tracker dogs from detecting the presence of the occupants.

MFC (MORTAR FIRE CONTROLLER) The SAS train a number of MFCs, which are used whenever they are in an operational forward base and where mortars are used for defence. Most SAS soldiers are trained to operate the 81mm mortar and will work under the directions of the MFC. It is the MFC's job to plot the enemy objective, converting it to a bearing and elevation from which the mortar is capable of hitting the target. The 81mm mortar was extensively used during the Oman War where SAS MFCs were used to control fire from a battery of six mortars manned by Baluchi soldiers.

MI5 Stands for Military Intelligence Department 5. It is also known as the Security Service and deals with any threats to Britain's national security, especially through terrorism and espionage. MI5 works on close terms with the SAS in Northern Ireland, with both organizations sharing intelligence material with each other and acting upon it if necessary. It has representatives in the Joint Operations Centre (JOC), which authorized an SAS team to go to Gibraltar to observe and arrest three IRA terrorists in 1988.

MI6 Military Intelligence Department 6. Also known as the Secret Intelligence Service (SIS), this organization is responsible for gathering intelligence. Like MI5, it works closely with the SAS in Northern Ireland where it runs a network of undercover operatives. Divisions between MI5, MI6 and the RUC created many problems for British forces in Northern Ireland in the mid-1970s, and information was often not shared when it should have been. This led to a situation which could only benefit the IRA.

MICROLIGHT AIRCRAFT In the mid-1980s the SAS carried out field trials on a Microlight aircraft that consisted of a three wheeler trike and a ram-air parachute. The trike had a rear mounted engine with the propeller housed in a protective cage. The pilot would be strapped into an open seat in front of the engine where his right foot would control the throttle. Revving the engine would speed the trike forward, forcing the ram-air parachute that was attached to the trike to act as a wing. The Microlight had a very short take-off and landing, added to which a pilot could be taught to fly in less than a day. Despite the fact that it was almost impossible to stall the Microlight, SAS trials were discontinued after several messy landings.

MILAN, WIRE GUIDED ANTI-ARMOUR MISSILE *Specification* Launcher length: 900mm (35in); Launcher weight: 12kg (27.7lbs); Missile length: 796mm (31in); Missile weight: 1.3kg (2.98lbs); Warhead: High Explosive, Anti-Tank; Range: 2,000m (2,180yds).

The Milan has been in service with the British Army since the mid-1970s. Built by Euromissile, a Franco-German consortium, it is one of the world's leading anti-tank weapons. Milan is simple to fire and has a very high accuracy rate, both by day and night. It can be fired by a two-man infantry team or attached to a vehicle. During the Gulf War the SAS used the Milan mounted on a roll bar attached to one of their open-topped Land Rover 110s. When fired, a small charge forces the missile from the launcher before the main rocket motor ignites. The missile is kept on target by using the optical sight which guides the missile to its target by sending commands and corrections down the command wire. By night the Milan relies on the powerful MIRA night sight which clamps to the top of the weapon.

MINIMI *Specification* Calibre: 5.56mm × 45 NATO standard; Weight: 3kg (6.85lbs); Muzzle velocity: 965m (1,051yds) per second; Effective range: 600m (654yds); Magazine capacity: disintegrating link belt, 200-round, belt or 30-round, M16 type box.

Made by Fabrique National of Belgium, this gas-operated weapon has been chosen as the squad support weapon for the US Forces. With its greater firepower and range capabilities it has proved itself to be the natural partner to the M16. The SAS have also adopted the Minimi, and it proved its worth during the Gulf War in many contact situations, for example, allowing those in the ill-fated patrol 'Bravo Two Zero' to escape.

MIRA (MILAN INFRA-RED ATTACHMENT) A self-contained unit which is attached to the Milan missile. It is extremely sensitive, capable of detecting 'hot' hostile vehicles by both day and night including inclement weather such as fog and mist. The MIRA proved most effective during the Gulf War when the SAS operated mostly at night.

MIRBAT At dawn on 19 July 1972, a large rebel force, about 250 strong, attacked the nine-man SAS garrison at the Port of Mirbat in the Dhofar Province of southern Oman. This was the last great attack by the Adoo in the Oman War and failed only due to a stroke of bad luck: there were two SAS squadrons in Oman at the time, carrying out an end-of-tour hand-over.

At around 05:00 the picket at the top of Jebel Ali, a small hill 1,000m (1,090yds) to the north of Mirbat and halfway towards the Jebel Massive, was being manned by a section of DG (Dhofar Gendarmerie). Jebel Ali provided a dominating feature that protected the town and the surrounding coastal area. The DG were the first to be killed. Stealthily at first, the Adoo cut the throats of those still asleep then, as the alarm was raised, the Adoo opened up with small arms. Those in the SAS HQ, the BATT House, heard this exchange of fire. The commander, Captain Mike Kealy, and his men observed the fire coming from Jebel Ali and the waves of men advancing towards the fort.

Captain Kealy shouted orders for the 81mm mortar to open fire in support of the Jebel Ali, while the rest of the SAS took up their positions behind the sand-bagged emplacements and awaited confirmed targets. As a safeguard the signaller was ordered to establish communications with SAS Headquarters at Um al Quarif. The SAS Fijian soldier, Corporal Labalaba (right), left the house and ran the 500m (545yds) to the DG fort, where he manned an old World War II 25-pounder artillery piece.

By 05:30 there was enough light for Kealy to make out the silhouette of the gun position and fort. Suddenly, a vast amount of small arms fire started pouring into the town. Through the mist, figures could be seen approaching the perimeter wire from the direction of Jebel Ali – the Adoo were attacking in waves. In answer, both SAS machine gun bunkers opened up, at the same time the 81mm mortar added its fire-power. In the gun-pit by the DG fort, the 25-pounder sent shell after shell into the massing enemy. The battle flowed back and forth, then a radio message came through on the Tokki from Labalaba, stating that he had been hit in the chin while operating the gun. A man of such stature is not given to reporting such trivia, and those at the BATT House suspected he was badly injured. Immediately Captain Kealy sent Labalaba's countryman, Takavesi, to his aid. The machine gunners provided supporting fire from the roof of the BATT House as they watched Takavesi run the gauntlet of tracer bullets and exploding shells, diving headlong into the gun-pit. He found Labalaba firing the big gun on his own. He gave no indication that he was injured, but simply indicated the unopened ammunition boxes, and the desperate need to keep the gun firing. Much of the Adoo attack was now directed against the gun. Takavesi left the pit to solicit help from the DG fort a few metres away. As the rounds zipped past his head, he banged on the fort door until, at last, he was heard. The first man to appear was the Omani gunner and Takavesi grabbed at him. Together both men raced back to the gun-pit; as Takavesi cleared the sandbags, the Omani gunner fell forward as a bullet hit him in the stomach.

It was now light enough to see groups of men near the outer perimeter fence that covered the three open sides of the town. Behind them wave after wave could be seen advancing towards Mirbat in support. Abruptly, several rockets slammed into the DG fort, causing great chunks of masonry to be blown from the ancient wall. From the BATT House roof a new threat could be seen. The Adoo had breached the perimeter wire. Men could be seen all along the wire, but the main breakthrough seemed to be in front of the fort. Once inside the perimeter, the Adoo advanced on the fort and gun position in large numbers. The gun, now levelled directly at the wire, fired at point blank range into the charging figures. Takavesi was hit but he continued to fire. Labalaba made a quick grab for a small 60mm mortar that lay close by. He almost made it; then a bullet took him in the neck and he fell dead.

Communication with the gun-pit had been lost and Captain Kealy decided that he and an SAS medic, Trooper Tobin, would give assistance. Before they left Kealy contacted Um al Quarif, informing them that air cover was desperately needed and requested a chopper to evacuate Labalaba. Additionally, if the firefight continued at its present rate, further ammunition would be required.

Most of those mustered to form a relief in Um al Quarif were from the newly arrived G Squadron; they were already dressed and equipped for the firing range. It took about five minutes for 22 of them, under the command of Captain Alastair Morrison, to get together an impressive array of weapons, among them eight GPMGs and several grenade launchers. When this group hit trouble the enemy was going to know about it. The total ammunition count for the reinforcements was in excess of 25,000 rounds.

Back in Mirbat, Captain Kealy and Trooper Tobin worked their way forward to the gun-pit. As they approached the fighting increased and both ran for cover. With a final dive Tobin rolled into the gun-pit; Kealy was about to follow, but realizing there was not enough room, and tripping over the dead body of a gendarme, he threw himself headlong into the sandbagged ammunition bay.

Trooper Tobin could not believe the mess. Labalaba lay face down and very still, Takavesi sat propped against the sandbags, SLR still in hand. Assessing the priorities Tobin quickly set up a drip on the seriously wounded Omani gunner. Takavesi was severely hit in the back, but despite the loss of blood he continued to fight, covering the left side of the fort. The firefight was reaching its height and the Adoo made a real effort to overrun the gun. As Kealy concentrated amid the mayhem, he saw Adoo close by the fort wall; several grenades were thrown and bounced by the lip of the gun-pit before exploding. An Adoo appeared at the side of the gun-pit but Kealy cut him down. In the pit Tobin reached over the inert body of Labalaba. Realizing there was little he could do he made to move away when a bullet hit him in the face; he fell by the side of the big Fijian, mortally wounded. The gun-pit seemed done for when suddenly there came an almighty explosion – Omani air force jets had arrived. Firing heavy cannon, the first two jets made pass after pass, driving the Adoo back into a large wadi outside the perimeter wire, before finally dropping a large 500kg (1.100lb) bomb into where the Adoo had taken refuge.

The G Squadron relief force had already loaded themselves into three helicopters and were rapidly heading down the coast. Due to the low cloud they were dropped off to the south of Mirbat and instantly made contact with an Adoo patrol that was covering the rear. The Adoo, consisting of one older soldier and three youths, were cornered in a cave and refused to surrender. Several 66mm Law rockets slammed into the entrance, followed by fire from several GPMGs. The Adoo picket was quickly eliminated.

With the jets taking the sting out of the Adoo, Kealy had time to crawl forward and examine the gun-pit. He could see that the Omani gunner was still alive and so was Tobin, although his wound looked horrendous. Takavesi lay listless against the sandbags, his whole body seemed covered with blood – but he smiled. Then the SAS relief force arrived. Although several of the choppers had been hit, they continued to ferry in more reinforcements, extracting the wounded in return. Trooper Tobin and the Omani gunner, both seriously wounded, were 'casevaced' on the first available flight. Takavesi, who suffered wounds from which a normal man would have died, walked calmly to the chopper without assistance. Three young Adoo prisoners, who had been captured and held in the BATT House, were also sent back for interrogation. Meanwhile the relieving force commander, Alastair Morrison, re-organized Mirbat's defences and, with the aid of two Land Rovers, started to collect the dead and wounded Adoo. The final count of dead Adoo was 38; they had suffered a defeat from which they would never recover. See also Adoo; BATT; Dhofar; Kealy; Labalaba; Takavesi; Tobin.

'MISSED COMMS' The SAS have a strict procedure with regard to failed communications. Patrols, both in peacetime and on operations, are required to report in several times a day. If one call is missed it is deemed to be for some simple reason such as a defective radio or poor communications area, and a 'missed comms' note is made. If two calls are missed efforts are made to contact the patrol, with the base signaller reporting the matter to his superiors. After three missed calls, depending on operational circumstances and location, help is despatched to locate the patrol.

'MIXED FRUIT PUDDING' A pattern of mortar fire developed by the SAS meaning 'to fire one high explosive round followed by one white phosphorus round repeatedly'. It was commonly used during the Oman War where white phosphorus was extremely effective. The standard fire command would be: 'Ten round mixed fruit pudding.'

MOBILITY TROOP Mobility Troop operates using a wide variety of vehicles, of which the SAS Pink Panther ('Pinky') is the best known. The current vehicle is the Land Rover 110 which comes fitted with a variety of armaments including GPMGs, .50 calibre machine gun, and Mark 19 40mm grenade launcher. They are all fitted for long range and heavy engagements. Additional weapons include 80mm mortars and Milan missiles. Other vehicles used by Mobility Troop include KTM 350 and Honda 250 motorbikes. Courses for members of Mobility Troop cover several weeks, with the REME (Royal Electrical and Mechanical Engineers) doing basic mechanical fault-finding and emergency mainten-ance. Training in cross-country conditions can vary from those in the UAE (United Arab Emirates) to the deserts of North America.

MOD POLICE Ministry of Defence Police force, also known affec-tionately as 'Modplod', is responsible for the protection of Stirling Lines and the Pontrilas training area. The MoD police took over security of the

SAS camps in the late 1980s, prior to which the SAS provided its own camp guards. Some of the MoD police are armed and in an emergency are backed up by an SAS armed piquet.

MONTE CASSINO   Monte Cassino was the code-name given to a large ZANLA base reported to be in the area of Chimoio, in Mozambique's Manica Province, and accommodating 2,000 ZANLA terrorists. Its location was, however, unknown and the task of pinpointing it was given to an eleven-man patrol of A Squadron of the Rhodesian 1st SAS Regiment (RhSAS), under Lieutenant Andrew Sanders, accompanied by four members of the Mozambique National Resistance (MNR). Its task was to locate the camp and thereafter ambush a track in its vicinity to snatch a senior member of the ZANLA High Command. The patrol was inserted before last light on an evening in October 1979 and reached the suspected area of the camp by the afternoon of the following day. While the SAS established a lying-up position (LUP) and kept watch on a nearby road, the four MNR guerrillas made contact with local people who confirmed that the camp was 5km (3 miles) away.

Unfortunately the following morning a ZANLA patrol approached the LUP and encountered one of the SAS early warning groups. After evacuating the LUP, which was by then under fire from enemy mortars, the patrol headed down to the road in the direction of the camp, in the hope of engaging any opportune targets. Shortly afterwards, two Toyota Landcruisers approached and the patrol opened fire, destroying both vehicles and killing the occupants. Requesting extraction, the patrol withdrew and moved to a landing zone about a kilometre from the ambush area. While waiting for the helicopters, however, a ZANLA follow-up force arrived and, after a short but fierce battle, the patrol was forced to withdraw. Under mortar fire, and with the enemy in hot pursuit, the patrol ran for a kilometre to another LZ where it was extracted under fire.

Intelligence reports subsequently revealed that the occupants of the two Landcruisers had included three Russian advisers, one a general. Aerial reconnaissance showed that the ZANLA base was massive, covering 100 sq km (40 sq miles) and comprising five separate heavily defended camps accommodating over 12,000 guerrillas. It was subsequently attacked by the Rhodesians from the ground and air, and was taken after a two-day battle.

MOOR PARK   A suburb of northwest London and the home of the SAS Brigade's HQ during operations in northwest Europe in 1944.

MORO, Aldo. In March of 1978 the Italian Red Brigade kidnapped the leading Italian Christian Democrat politician Aldo Moro. The attack on his car and escort in a busy street was carried out with military

precision. His car was blocked and several automatic weapons opened
fire; two of Aldo Moro's bodyguards were killed at the scene. Moro
himself was whisked away and held for 54 days, during which time the
Italian Government refused to give in to the terrorists' demands.
Eventually on 10 May Moro's body was found in the boot of a car,
parked in a Rome street. He had been shot in the head. During the 54
days of Moro's captivity it is known that several SAS units were
operating in Northern Italy.

MORRISON, MAJOR ALASTAIR, OBE MC   Joined the SAS 1968
from the Scots Guards, and originally commanded G Squadron's Mobility
Troop. Shortly after, due to a problem with the squadron commander, he
was made acting squadron OC and commanded the fighting unit that
went to the relief of Mirbat. In 1977 while second-in-command of 22 SAS
he and Sergeant Barry Davies were sent to Mogadishu by the British
prime minister to assist the German GSG9 in the storming of the
hijacked aircraft LH181. Major Morrison left the SAS in 1979 after
which he worked for the German arms manufacturer Heckler & Koch
prior to setting up Defence Systems Limited (DSL).

MORTAR 51MM   *Specification* Calibre: 51mm; Barrel length: 104cm
(40in); Weight: 3kg (6.82lbs); Bomb: 920g (29.5oz) high explosive,
smoke and illuminating flare.

The 51mm mortar is manufactured in Belgium by FN Herstal and has
been adopted by the British Army to replace the older 2-inch mortar.
The weapon is a simple tube with a self-cocking trigger and a simple
spirit-level range sight. A bomb is slipped down the barrel and the firer
adjusts the alignment by sight before pulling down on the lanyard
attached to the trigger. The weapon is simple but very effective,
especially at short ranges.

MORTAR L16 81MM   *Specification* Calibre: 81mm; Barrel length:
128cm (50in); Weight; 16kg (36.6lbs); Weight of bomb: 1.8kg (4.2lbs);
Types of bomb: high explosive, illuminating, smoke, practice and guided
anti-armour; Maximum range: 5,650m (6,158yds).

The standard infantry mortar of the British Army. Sturdy and
portable, with a good rate of sustained fire, the 81mm performed well
in the Oman War, providing fire support when the British Army Training
Team (BATT) became short of artillery. Most SAS outposts would have
a mortar as their main support weapon, which they would also use on
some of the larger patrols. Their favourite trick, one not recommended
by the Army, was to pour a pint of petrol down the barrel to increase
the range. This somewhat unorthodox method of firing the mortar
achieved the desired results, but also proved expensive as it destroyed
the mortar baseplate.

'MOSES', OPERATION   Under the command of Captain Simon, 47 men of 3 French Parachute Battalion (3 SAS) successfully completed 'Moses' between 3 August and 5 October 1944. The team was tasked with destroying enemy communications in the area around Poitiers, southwestern France, a mission which resulted in significant casualties among the enemy. In one incident alone over 400 enemy vehicles were destroyed when the target was attacked by Allied aircraft.

MOUNT KENT   A position in the Falkland Islands 30km (18 miles) west of Port Stanley, which had been observed by an SAS patrol under Captain Wight for 26 days at the start of the war. At the end of May, D Squadron, under command of Major Cedric Delves, returned to seize Mount Kent, still some 60km (40 miles) behind enemy lines, and despite aggressive Argentine resistance which resulted in a series of night firefights, held it for several days until reinforced by 42 Marine Commando.

MOUNTAIN TROOP   Responsible for all aspects of mountaineering and skiing. Training for the troop takes several forms. At times the whole troop may embark on a rock-climbing course where new members, with no previous experience, will be taught the basics of rock climbing and abseiling techniques. Depending on length of service and aptitude, many individuals will attend courses in Europe, with a select few attending the German Alpine Guides course. This course is held at the German Mountain Warfare School in Mittenwald and normally lasts a year, with the Germans allowing two SAS personnel per course. The Mountain Guides course is divided into summer and winter mountain skills, and those that qualify return both expert climbers and skiers. Over the past few years the SAS have become highly proficient at mountaineering and skiing, and they now run their own Alpine training course. Additionally, several SAS members have climbed Everest.

Mountain Troop is also responsible for ski instruction. Most troop members will be required to instruct the other squadron members during the annual winter exercises in Arctic Norway. Again, several advanced ski instructor courses are available to the regiment, in both France and Germany.

MOUSSEY   A small valley town near the Vosges mountains of eastern France, 60km (40 miles) south east of Nancy and 16km (10 miles) north of St Die. The town itself is spread out for about a kilometre and a half, with odd houses dotting the roadside. Towards the centre is a church, with a military graveyard, where men from 2 SAS are laid to rest.

The unit parachuted into France in September 1944, landing north of Moussey, near Baccarat. It was to be one of the last drops the regiment made during World War II. Soon after the drop, the group moved to the woods and forest close to Moussey. The local population befriended the unit who, as time went on, provided them with the necessities of life, and help in whatever way they could. The advancing American army, under General Patton, were held up due to lack of supplies. It was a delay the Germans took advantage of, moving reinforcements along the River Meurthe, a few kilometres to the west of Moussey. Numerous raids were carried out on the Germans, which in the end brought retaliation. As a direct result the Germans rounded up the population of Moussey and interrogated them. Not a word escaped their lips and in frustration the Germans sent most of the men to concentration camps. Of the 210 men transported to those horrendous camps, only 70 returned alive. One tenth of the population was killed. Despite this the SAS headquarters, hidden in the nearby woods, was never discovered.

MOZAMBIQUE NATIONAL RESISTANCE (MNR) During 1977 the Rhodesian Central Intelligence Organization (CIO) formed the Mozambique National Resistance (MNR) as part of its efforts to destabilize the FRELIMO government of Samora Machel in neighbouring Mozambique. Training of the initial elements of MNR was carried out at a camp near an abandoned farm situated at Odzi, near Umtali. This was carried out by the CIO, which initially used Portuguese instructors but subsequently replaced them with former SAS officers and NCOs, after objections from the guerrillas. MNR operations in Mozambique began in mid-1978 and in January 1979 the task of training the guerrillas and operating with them was handed over to the Rhodesian 1st SAS Regiment (RhSAS), under the code-name 'Operation Bumper'.

Shortly afterwards, MNR bases were established inside Mozambique. One was located at Gogoi, which was situated some 35km (21 miles) inside Mozambique, while the guerrillas' headquarters was located in the Serra Da Gorongoza mountains of Mozambique's Sofala Province, about three weeks' march from the Rhodesian-Mozambique border.

The RhSAS base for Operation 'Bumper' was at the abandoned farm at Odzi, from which elements of C Squadron, and subsequently B Squadron, accompanied the guerrillas to Gogoi and their headquarters in the mountains. There the Rhodesians helped the MNR to construct defensive positions and facilities such as accommodation, hospitals and storehouses. Rifle ranges were also constructed and instruction given in weapons, marksmanship, tactics and signals. The first joint MNR/ RhSAS operation was a successful attack on a hydro-electric power station at Mavuzi, cutting off electricity to much of Mozambique. This was followed by numerous ambushes and raids on a number of targets, including a telecommunications centre at Monte Xilvuo and the large fuel depot at Beira. One raid, on a FRELIMO-held village at the foot of the Serra Da Gorongoza mountains, yielded a massive haul of weapons, ammunition, food and cattle which was sufficient to last the MNR for a very long time.

The following year the MNR became a major force in Mozambique, becoming increasingly popular throughout the country through its very effective 'hearts and minds' campaign. However, Operation 'Bumper' was closed down in 1980, on the declaration of a ceasefire and the arrival of the Commonwealth monitoring forces, to oversee the election and transfer of power to a majority black government. In February the MNR camp near Odzi was closed and the RhSAS elements withdrawn to the regiment's base at Salisbury. The MNR, however, continued to flourish and remained a thorn in the side of FRELIMO for long afterwards.

MRE (MEAL READY TO EAT)   An American-designed military ration that can be consumed hot or cold. The newer versions contain a special pad to which water is added in order to generate heat. MREs are designed for patrol work and not for long-term consumption. The SAS have tried American MREs but prefer to stick with British SAS rations.

MRLS (MULTIPLE ROCKET LAUNCH SYSTEM)   Used by both the Coalition and Iraqi forces during the Gulf War. They caused problems for the SAS in as much as many of the rockets fell on soft sand and failed to explode yet remained active. The effect was to create a sort of uncharted minefield.

MSR (MAIN SUPPLY ROUTE)   Abbreviation for roads or tracks on which Iraqi troops and mobile Scuds travelled during the Gulf War. The MSRs were known to all attack aircraft pilots, so when SAS troops were able to identify a missile and its support vehicle on the move, they could call in an air-strike. This detection turned their campaign into one of outstanding success. The Iraqis rarely brought their weapons out during daylight hours, preferring to hide until dark. The construction of MSRs varied from graded stone tracks to tarmac roads similar to European motorways, complete with garages and flyovers.

MUNICH OLYMPICS MASSACRE   The 1972 Olympic village had been deliberately planned with the minimum of security, reducing the unpleasant memories of the last time Germany hosted the games in 1936. The Israeli team were billeted in Connollystrasse 31, separated from the public by a wire fence and the odd patrolling guard. A little before 04:30 on the morning of 5 September, a group of young men were seen climbing the fence. Not an uncommon sight; many of the athletes stayed out late in the beer halls of Munich.

However, these were not athletes but members of the Palestinian terrorist group, Black September. Bursting into the Israeli accommodation, seven terrorists opened fire, killing many and taking nine athletes hostage. The Israeli Government, true to its firm policy, declined to cave in and refused to free any Palestinian prisoners or meet the terrorists' demands. In turn, West Germany refused the offer of Israeli troops to counter the problem and decided to attempt a rescue plan of its own.

By 22:00 that same night a grey army bus transferred both terrorists and hostages to the edge of the Olympic village, where they climbed into two helicopters. Next they flew to Furstenfeldbruck, 24km (15 miles) to the west, where they landed in a well-illuminated area. A requested Lufthansa 727 sat on the tarmac a little over 90m (100yds) away, and two of the terrorists left the helicopter to check it out. At 22:44 the first sniper bullet was fired and a fierce firefight broke out. The bolt action rifles of the German police were no match for the automatic fire of the terrorists' AK-47s, and a police sergeant who stepped out from the control tower took a bullet through the head. More police arrived in armoured vehicles and an abortive gun battle to free the hostages followed.

Meanwhile, Israeli diplomats watched helplessly from the control tower of Furstenfeldbruck air base as inexperienced and ill-equipped German sharpshooters failed to kill all the terrorists in the first volley. Three were still alive and they fired their guns and detonated their grenades to kill the handcuffed hostages who were slaughtered as they sat in the helicopters. In the end, the three were overpowered and captured, but not before they had slaughtered all nine hostages.

MUSANDAN PENINSULA In November 1969 British Intelligence in Oman warned that Iraqi-backed forces were training guerrillas in a village off the Musandan Peninsula to the north, and had picked up information on a huge arms shipment due to arrive at the tiny coastal village of Jumla. This arms shipment was to be accompanied by a group of Iraqis of Communist persuasion. British Intelligence interpreted this as the start of a major Communist push into the area to take advantage of the turmoil within Oman.

G Squadron 22 SAS were despatched via Cyprus to the British air base in Sharjah. Without leaving the confines of the airport they were loaded, with their bergens and weapons, on to several 3-ton trucks and driven out into the desert. Later that evening several helicopters arrived and ferried the men over to a camp site on the eastern coast. This had been done for two reasons: firstly the area was similar to the one they would attack, although minus a village; secondly, a Royal Navy minesweeper complete with several rigid raiders manned by the SBS was due to arrive offshore the following day.

The plan was for the SBS to insert the SAS on to the small beaches both north and south of Jumla. This would be done during the hours of darkness and would allow enough time for them to scale the high rocky peaks that towered out of the sea and surrounded the entire village. By dawn, with the SAS in place to stop any enemy running away, a combined force of the local Arab states would assault the village and capture both the dissidents and their equipment. On the surface a sound plan; not only would it protect the Straits of Hormuz, through which half the world's oil passed, but it would stop a major catastrophe in the area. However, this did not happen.

Due to bad weather the whole plan was delayed for 24 hours, but only after the SAS had put to sea. By the time the men were due to leave the minesweeper and load into the rigid raiders most were suffering from acute sea-sickness. However they finally approached the beach in total darkness, with nothing to see other than a few faint lights coming from the village. Immediately the SAS were ashore they started to climb with Mountain Troop members, leading what was a difficult and dangerous assault. They made it, one hour before dawn on 8 December 1970, with the only injury being a broken finger. As the light improved, the main landing force made for the beach at full speed. Several shots awoke the surprised villagers, for whom visitors were, in such a remote area, a rarity. When an officer demanded to know the whereabouts of the Iraqi rebels, they became even more confused. Thanks to an intelligence error the SAS had landed at Gumla, not Jumla as planned. By the time the SAS reached the right village the rebels had gone, as had most of their equipment, and the SAS were pulled back to the British base at Sharjah.

N

NAAFI NUMBERS NAAFI numbers are used by the SAS on operations as a substitute for names. Every soldier will be issued a three-digit number which will identify him during uncoded 'clear' language messages. During a contact the first 'SitRep' (situation report) is normally sent in 'clear', mentioning those soldiers killed or wounded; the number protects their identity. NAAFI numbers are also used as a form of credit against which a SAS soldier may buy beer or essential NAAFI goods such as soap and toothpaste, and the total is billed at the end of the operation.

NADEN, STAFF SERGEANT DAVID Staff Sergeant Naden died on 7 June 1978 in a road accident while serving as a RUC Special Branch liaison officer in Northern Ireland. He was travelling alone from Portadown to Londonderry when his car left the road at Shanalongford Bridge. Naden joined the SAS after serving in the Royal Signals; on passing Selection he was posted to Boat Troop in 'G' Squadron.

NAIRAC, CAPTAIN ROBERT The IRA killed Captain Bob Nairac in May 1977. Nairac was attached to 14 Intelligence and Security Unit (14 Int), although at the time he was working with the SAS detachment located at Bessbrook Mill, South Armagh. A highly intelligent officer, Nairac had been educated at Ampleforth College before attending Lincoln College, Oxford, where he read history. After Sandhurst he joined the Grenadier Guards, before being transferred to 14 Int. Nairac perfected an Irish accent and made a detailed study of the local customs and Republican protocol. He purchased Republican song sheets, which he learnt and would sing in the local border public houses. On one such evening, while visiting the Three Steps Inn at Drumintee 5km (3 miles) from the border, he sang several songs to a packed house. He went to leave around 23:30 and headed for the car park. At his car he was confronted by a number of men curious as to his identification and a fight ensued (Nairac was an excellent boxer). During the scuffle his 9mm Browning pistol fell to the ground, giving away his identity and he was soon overpowered.

Blindfolded and gagged, Nairac was taken first to a house where he tried in vain to escape, after which he was moved by car to a field whereupon he was tortured. Despite being beaten repeatedly to the ground with a fence-post, Captain Nairac refused to talk. In the end he was shot with his own pistol and his body was disposed of, never to be recovered. Some years after his death, information from an eyewitness verified the punishment Nairac had suffered, and the IRA grudgingly acknowledged the man's courage. It was widely rumoured that his body was converted to animal feed.

'NARCISSUS', OPERATION   On 10 July 1943 a 40-man detachment of A Squadron, 2 SAS, landed on the southeast coast of Sicily to take a lighthouse where enemy artillery pieces were suspected of being stored. This would undoubtedly interfere with the planned Allied invasion of the island known as Operation 'Husky'. On reaching the lighthouse they found it to be deserted and so returned to the *Royal Scotsman*, which was lying offshore, having achieved their objective without any loss of life.

NBC (NUCLEAR, BIOLOGICAL AND CHEMICAL)   Up until the Gulf War the SAS paid scant attention to the role of NBC warfare, although it regularly sent soldiers on courses to comply with Army regulations. The wearing of a respirator was more suited to the role of gas assault when used in anti-terrorist work. During the Gulf War, with the high risk of chemical attack always present, the SAS adopted full NBC equipment and drills. Chemical tests were carried out after every Scud raid.

'NEUTRON', OPERATION   During March 1979 an operation code-named 'Neutron' was carried out by the Rhodesian 1st SAS Regiment (RhSAS) to locate and attack a large ZANLA base situated some 15km (9 miles) from the town of Chimoio in Mozambique. At the beginning of March a six-man team of C Squadron, under Lieutenant Rich Stannard, was inserted by helicopter. Having established a firm base and leaving the other four members of the patrol to man it, Stannard and Lieutenant 'Jungle' Jordan spent the following week making their way to Monte Bosse, a mountain overlooking the ZANLA base, from which they could observe the entire area.

During the next few days Stannard and Jordan watched the base, much of which was concealed by thick woods with dense foliage, sending reports to their firm base which relayed them to the RhSAS headquarters in Salisbury. Acting on these, Combined Operations Headquarters decided to mount an air attack. At first light, on 17 March, a combined force of Royal Rhodesian Air Force (RRAF) Canberras, Hunters, and Alouette G-car and K-Car helicopter gunships, bombed and strafed the camp. Two Hunters carried out a second strike on the following day, one of which narrowly escaped being shot down by a SAM-7 missile.

Warned by their firm base that radio intercepts had confirmed FRELIMO suspicions of the presence of Rhodesian forward observers in the area, Lieutenants Stannard and Jordan withdrew from the mountain but were spotted by a group of ZANLA guerrillas shortly after they reached the area below it. As they were being pursued under heavy fire, Lieutenant Jordan was wounded in the lower leg but continued to run; at the same time, Lieutenant Stannard called on his radio for a 'hot extraction'. Two hours later, the two men were extracted.

NEWELL, MAJOR DARE   Veteran member of the SOE (Special Operations Executive) and Force 136 in Malaya. With his fighting and jungle experience, he was a welcome addition to the Malayan Scouts in the 1950s where he assisted Mike Calvert in bringing a new professionalism to the force. He went on to become the regimental adjutant of the SAS and Secretary of the SAS Regimental Association. Awarded the OBE for his services, he died in 1989 aged 71. Dare Newell is best remembered for his unswerving defence against those that would politically attack the SAS and frequently stood his ground against their enemies in Whitehall.

'NEWTON', OPERATION   Under the command of Lieutenant de Roquebrune, 57 men of 3 French Parachute Battalion (3 SAS) undertook this successful mission between 19 August and 11 September 1944. Operating from the Champagne-Burgundy area of central France, they were given the job of reinforcing existing SAS bases designed to put the pressure on retreating German forces, causing the enemy numerous injuries. They often operated in conjunction with advancing US troops.

NEW ZEALAND SAS   In early 1955, as a result of a request from Britain for assistance in the Malayan Emergency campaign, the New Zealand SAS (NZSAS) Squadron was formed under Major Frank Rennie. In December 1955 the squadron arrived in Malaya and, after parachute training, was deployed on operations against Communist Terrorists (CTs). At the end of 1957 the NZSAS Squadron returned to New Zealand and disbanded. In 1959 the squadron was reformed and three years later, in May 1962, a detachment under Major M.N. Velvein was deployed to Thailand, where its two troops assisted US Army Special Forces A Teams in providing training for Thai troops and border police. During the following year the squadron was redesignated 1st Ranger Squadron New Zealand SAS.

From February 1965 to September 1966, during the Borneo Confrontation with Indonesia, four detachments of NZSAS were deployed in turn, on six-month attachments to 22 SAS Regiment. During some eighteen months of active service NZSAS personnel took part in reconnaissance and ambush operations inside Sarawak and across the border in Indonesian Kalimantan, under the auspices of Operation 'Claret'.

In December 1968 a detachment, designated 4 Troop, 1st Ranger Squadron NZSAS was deployed to South Vietnam on attachment to the Australian SAS squadron based at Nui Dat in Phuoc Tuy Province. During the next two and a half years personnel from the squadron were rotated through 4 Troop which carried out 155 reconnaissance or ambush patrols during operations in the province. In February 1971 4 Troop was withdrawn to New Zealand. Subsequently, the 1st Ranger Squadron NZSAS was redesignated the 1st NZ SAS Group and expanded to its current establishment of a headquarters element, two Sabre Squadrons and a training wing. Each of the Sabre Squadrons provides a counter-terrorist team on a rotational basis.

Like its British and Australian counterparts, the current NZSAS has a major counter-terrorism role, as well as supporting the country's regular forces in times of war. It still maintains its strict Selection procedure and high standard of training, and regularly conducts exchange training with the Australian and British SAS. The squadron is currently based at Papakura Military Base, and has a strength of five troops and a headquarters group.

'NIMROD', OPERATION   The code-name used for the SAS operation at the Iranian Embassy Siege in London in May 1980.

NKOMO, JOSHUA   In April 1979 an operation was launched by Rhodesian 1st SAS Regiment (RhSAS) to assassinate the leader of ZAPU/ZIPRA, Joshua Nkomo, and to attack a ZIPRA headquarters building known as the 'Liberation Centre'. On the evening of 12 April a force of 42 officers and men of C Squadron, under the command of Major Dave Dodson, the second-in-command of RhSAS, crossed Lake Kariba in a ferry and landed in Zambia. Mounted in seven heavily armed Land Rovers, they headed for Lusaka which they reached in the early hours of the following morning. Two vehicles, under Lieutenant Rich Stannard, peeled off and headed for the Liberation Centre, a large building housing senior members of ZIPRA as well as offices and a large armoury.

At 02:55 hours the main force reached Nkomo's house. Captain Martin Pearse, who was commanding the assault group which would enter the building, was approaching the rear of the house in his vehicle when he came under fire from a sentry. He succeeded, nevertheless, in cutting through the wire fence surrounding the building and led his three men through, although one was wounded as they approached. Meanwhile, the rest of the force had engaged the ZIPRA guard force which was soon neutralized by heavy fire from the Land Rover's twin machine guns. Captain Pearse and the other two men of his assault group then proceeded to clear all the rooms in the house but found that Nkomo was nowhere to be seen.

On hearing the noise of the main assault, Lieutenant Rich Stannard launched his attack on the Liberation Centre. It was initiated by Sergeant Billy Gardner throwing a 1kg (2lb) bunker bomb charge through the window of the ZIPRA operations room, destroying it and setting it ablaze. Stannard's force then drove through the open gates of the building's compound, both vehicles opening fire with their machine guns. While the gunners continued to engage any available targets, the remainder laid explosive charges in all the offices and the armoury, as well as on 30 vehicles parked outside. Twenty minutes later, having completed their task, Lieutenant Stannard and his men departed in haste and rejoined the main force which had withdrawn and was waiting for them. Shortly afterwards the charges exploded, completely destroying the Liberation Centre and its contents.

Leaving Lusaka, which by then was the scene of complete chaos, the RhSAS withdrew and headed for Lake Kariba. Shortly afterwards the ferry appeared and the entire force crossed back safely into Rhodesia. It was subsequently discovered that Nkomo had been warned of the attack by the British, who had an agent inside Combined Operations Headquarters, and had thus stayed away from his home. Nevertheless, the operation served to help prevent any invasion by ZIPRA and the Rhodesian elections went ahead with over 60 per cent of the population taking part.

'NOAH', OPERATION On 16 August 1944, 41 men from the Belgian Independent Parachute Company (5 SAS), commanded by Major Blondeel, parachuted into the French Ardennes with the aim of discovering enemy activity in the area. The party forged a close relationship with the Maquis and thus reliable information was sent back to HQ. In addition they caused a good deal of damage to the retreating Germans. The operation ended on 13 September 1944.

'NOFILIA', OPERATION A World War II Axis airfield in North Africa which was attacked on 26 December 1941 by an SAS group, led by Lieutenant 'Jock' Lewes. The mission was unsuccessful and they only managed to destroy two enemy aircraft before they were spotted by enemy troops. Lewes was killed during an attack by an Italian aircraft as he returned to the Long Range Desert Group (LRDG) rendezvous.

NOLAN, LIEUTENANT-COLONEL TERRY – AUSTRALIAN SAS REGIMENT (SASR) Assumed command of the SASR on 1 July 1985. He was the first commanding officer to have been commissioned from the Officer Cadet School, Portsea, and the last to have seen active service in Vietnam, where he had served as a troop commander and squadron second-in-command. Nolan took over at a good time for the regiment, which had overcome manpower problems and had just reformed 2 Squadron. During the period 1986–87 new counter-terrorist training facilities were constructed comprising: a CQB (close quarter battle) complex and sniper range at Swanbourne; an urban training complex and sniper range on the Bindoon training area and an airliner mock-up at Gin Gin airfield.

One of Nolan's primary concerns was the regiment's capability of conducting offshore operations in the Bass Strait, south of Victoria. Political problems with trade unions had been experienced, but resolution of these during 1986, coupled with the introduction of Sea King helicopters in December of that year, resulted in improved training and exercises for the Offshore Installations Assault Group (OAG). He also addressed the problem of rotating the counter-terrorist role among the three Sabre Squadrons. Until then, 1 Squadron had been assigned the role permanently with a system of trickle reinforcement providing new personnel. By the time Nolan assumed command, however, a large number of men in all three squadrons had counter-terrorist experience and so he could introduce a rotational system whereby each squadron carried out the task for a period of twelve months. Consequently, at the end of 1987 2 Squadron took over the role from 1 Squadron.

On 7 January 1988 Lieutenant-Colonel Nolan relinquished command of the SASR, handing over to Lieutenant-Colonel Jim Wallace. He was later promoted to the rank of full colonel and subsequently served as Director Special Action Forces.

'NORAH', OPERATION On 12 September 1979 an operation, codenamed 'Norah', was mounted by the Rhodesian 1st SAS Regiment (RhSAS) and the Mozambique National Resistance (MNR) against a heavily defended radio and telecommunications centre on Xilvuo Mountain, which played a major role in linking FRELIMO bases throughout Mozambique. A force of 32 RhSAS and MNR commanded by Lieutenant Andrew Sanders of A Squadron was inserted and, after a two-day march, reached the area of its objective. With the help of local guides recruited by the MNR, Sanders and his men moved by night through populated areas until they reached the mountain which they scaled under cover of darkness. After making their way through the main gate and its sleeping guards, they took up their assault positions.

The attack was initiated by a 1kg (2lb) bunker bomb charge thrown into the communications centre, followed by several RPG-7 grenades which added to the destruction. During the fierce battle which ensued, two 23mm gun positions were also attacked and knocked out –

two RhSAS soldiers being slightly wounded in the process. Having caused the maximum amount of damage possible, the Rhodesians and MNR withdrew down the mountain under heavy but inaccurate fire.

Shortly after reaching a road at the bottom of the mountain, however, they were ambushed and a number of the party, including Lieutenant Sanders, became separated from the main group. As dawn broke, the patrol second-in-command, Sergeant Dave Berry, requested air support and shortly afterwards Royal Rhodesians Air Force Hunters attacked the FRELIMO follow-up forces. Some time later the main group and Lieutenant Sanders' party were picked up, but three men, Troopers Bob Jones and Paul Schofield and an MNR guerrilla, were still missing. After a day of successfully evading FRELIMO troops searching for them, they were eventually located and extracted on the afternoon of the following day.

NORTH AFRICA A young Scots Guards lieutenant by the name of David Stirling had been involved in a number of unsuccessful large-scale raids on enemy targets along the Cyrenaican coast. He understood the benefits of attacking targets behind enemy lines but felt sure the raids would have a greater chance of success if executed by small groups of men, thus using the element of surprise to its best advantage. The most critical aspect of the war in the North African desert (1940–43) was the maintenance of the supply lines. Almost all the few roads were situated near the coast and the armies relied on supply depots, airfields and ports to support them. Once an army was forced to move further away from these installations, its supply lines became longer and, as such, more vulnerable to attack.

Lieutenant Stirling knew the most effective way to reach the targets was to facilitate attacks by land, sea or air. Following the sanctioning by General Sir Claude Auchinleck, Commander-in-Chief Middle East, and Major General Sir Neil Ritchie, Auchinleck's chief-of-staff, Stirling was permitted to raise his unit, which started as L Detachment, Special Air Service Brigade, with only 65 men.

The unit got off to a disastrous start in November 1941. The aim was to attack the enemy airfield in the Gazala-Tmimi area but the men, dropped into the vicinity by parachute, were scattered on landing and failed to reach their targets. Consequently Stirling became convinced that parachute drops were far too risky for SAS missions and instead forged an alliance with the Long Range Desert Group (LRDG) who agreed to use its vehicles and drivers to transport Stirling's men to and from their targets. There followed the first successful joint SAS/LRDG operations, and in December several parties raided the airfields at Sirte, Nofilia, Agheila, Agedabia, Tamit, and 'Marble Arch' destroying some 97 enemy aircraft. The group was also requested to aid the forthcoming

Above: The **Long Range Desert Group** often carried SAS raiding units to their targets during WWII.

Left: The indefatigable **Geordie Barker.**

Below: The **buddy-buddy system** means watching each other's backs. This system is used in field operations as well as in anti-terrorist work.

Above: Candidates running over the Brecon Beacons during SAS Selection, nicknamed the **'Fan Dance'** after the highest point in the mountain range, Pen-y-Fan.

Below: The SAS anti-terrorist team will try anything during a hostage rescue situation.

Below: The first **frame charges** were home-made, and the charge required was adjusted by trial and error.

Right: A **gold-winged dagger** forged from **blood money.**

Above: The SAS ended the **Iranian Embassy siege** on 30 April 1980 in just seventeen minutes.

Left: The aftermath of an SAS assault during the **Gulf War**.

Right: An SAS man practises on a makeshift range in the jungle. He is using an **M16** with an **M203 grenade launcher** fixed underneath, one of the preferred weapons of the SAS.

Above: The **Range
Rover** has been in
service with the SAS
since 1974.

Below: The **Royal
Protection Group** receives
training from members of
the SAS at Hereford.

Right: **Resistance to
Interrogation** training is
essential to an SAS
soldier's preparation.

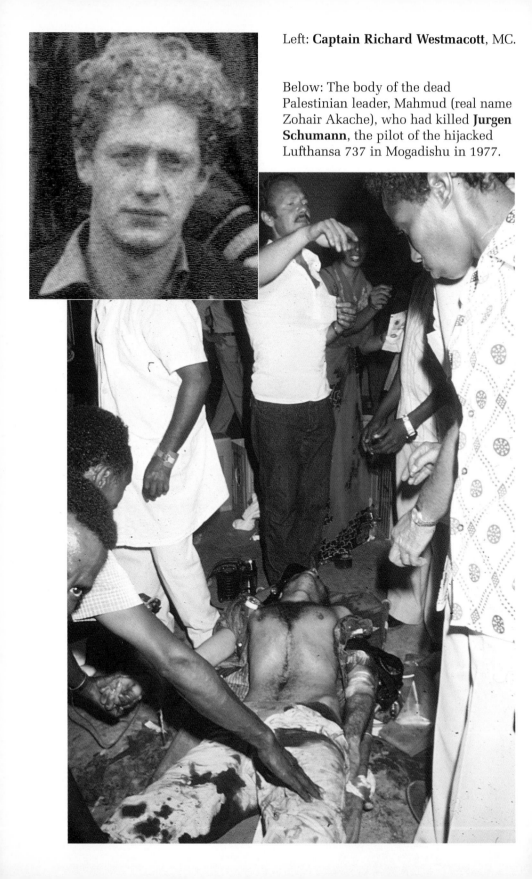

Left: **Captain Richard Westmacott**, MC.

Below: The body of the dead Palestinian leader, Mahmud (real name Zohair Akache), who had killed **Jurgen Schumann**, the pilot of the hijacked Lufthansa 737 in Mogadishu in 1977.

Eighth Army attack on Benghazi, but this operation never actually happened. Stirling was insistent that the SAS be used strategically as opposed to tactically in order to be at their most effective, although this was not always followed by Allied commanders later in the war.

The success of the SAS continued into the new year with the port and surrounding area around Benghazi being hit three times – in March, June and September. Other airfields, shipping and supply stations were also raided, including Tobruk. But by summer 1942, the German commander, General Rommel, appeared to have the upper hand by holding the Gazala Line prior to his offensive. Auchinleck felt his troops were not strong enough to launch an attack to drive the Germans back since they also held the airfield of Cyrenaica and from there were attacking British convoys as they attempted to reach Malta.

In June Stirling planned a number of raids on the Germans in addition to mounting raids on an Axis airfield on Crete. A total of 50 aircraft were destroyed by the SAS before Rommel attacked and advanced into Egypt. Undeterred, the SAS, equipped by now with its own jeeps, continued to mount attacks behind enemy lines. At Bagoush, at the end of July, all enemy aircraft were destroyed by machine gun fire whilst 40 aircraft were wiped out at Sidi Haneish.

In September 1942, in recognition of his remarkable achievements, Stirling was promoted to the rank of lieutenant-colonel and the SAS, now listed as the 1st Special Air Service Regiment, was officially placed on the roll of regiments in the British Army.

During the Battle of El Alamein in the following November, although not officially required to contribute, Stirling was determined to assist in General Montgomery's advance to Tripoli. He devised a plan which meant his men would launch a minimum of two raids a week on the stretch of land between Agheila and Tripoli, in particular concentrating on the roads being used by the retreating Germans and Italians. At the same time the Allied landings in the French North African colonies (Operation 'Torch') resulted in Axis forces retreating into Tunisia. Although the SAS had been quite successful during the Eighth Army's advance, the Tunisian countryside of scrub-covered hills and cultivated valleys was far less suited to their operations than Libya. In addition, the population was also more sympathetic to the Axis and as a result the SAS operations did not achieve the success that was expected – many men, including David Stirling, were captured.

Nevertheless, by January 1943, 1 SAS had a total of 47 officers and 532 other ranks on strength and the future of the regiment seemed secure. David Stirling's brother, Lieutenant-Colonel William Stirling, was with the British First Army in Algeria and had formed 2 SAS. By the end of the campaign in North Africa in May 1943 there was a brief time when the SAS's future was in question, but the invasion of Sicily meant its skills were in demand once more. See also Bagoush; Calvert; Stirling; Kufra; Sirte.

NORTH YEMEN   Led by Lieutenant-Colonel Johnny Cooper, an SAS veteran, two covert operations involving men from the SAS took place in the Yemen. On 26 September 1962 the ruler of North Yemen, Imam Mohammed al-Badr, was ousted by a military coup instigated by Colonel Abdullah Sallal. Sallal declared the Yemen an Arab Republic and Nasser, the president of Egypt, gave him his full backing. Badr retreated to the mountains to organize an army, while the British and French, envisaging the spread of Arab nationalism in the Gulf, planned to infiltrate North Yemen to discover the scale of Egyptian involvement before they recognized the new regime.

As second-in-command of the Omani Muscat Regiment, Cooper was chosen to lead this mission, and in June 1963 the French/SAS eight-man party met up with royalist forces near Sana. The group included three members of 22 SAS – Sergeant Dorman, Corporal Chigley and Trooper Richardson – who trained the royalist tribesmen, supplied them with weapons and gathered intelligence which confirmed Sallal's reliance on Egyptian aid. After three months, the group was ordered to leave the country, but Cooper returned to assimilate more intelligence and to arrange further air drops to the royalists. He continued to work alone in this way for a further eleven months, although he was joined by two SAS men, Cyril Weavers and David Ailey, before the air drops. Cooper spent a total of three years in North Yemen, gathering information on Egyptian forces and training royalist soldiers. All in all the Israeli Air Force completed nine air drops totally unbeknown to the Arab guerrillas.

NORTHERN IRELAND   Bringing the SAS into a country where the history of the Troubles goes back to the 1920s has since been considered a mistake. In 1968 the civil rights disturbances in Belfast resulted in a highly volatile state with emotions running high. In April 1969 the Belfast government, alarmed by the situation being fuelled by the Irish Republican Army (IRA), asked Westminster to provide military aid. In August of that year British troops were sent to the Province and were welcomed by the Catholic population of Ulster. However, the troops misused their position by raiding several Catholic areas and using unnecessary force to disperse crowds, actions which made them extremely unpopular and which culminated in the shooting of thirteen Catholic civilians on 'Bloody Sunday' in January 1972.

On a political front the Protestant Loyalists were the undoubted majority and the Catholic Nationalists, who wanted British rule to end, the minority. However, the Loyalists realized that if the British left Northern Ireland they would find themselves in the minority in a country that would become overwhelmingly Catholic. As with all religious arguments, both sides believed passionately in their cause and were quite willing to use violence to gain victory. In support, paramilitary organizations on both sides have gradually developed. The republican cause was supported by the IRA and the Irish National Liberation Army (INLA), while the Ulster Volunteer Force (UVF), the Ulster Defence Association (UDA) and the Ulster Freedom Fighters (UFF) supported the Loyalist cause.

The Province's security forces were represented by the Royal Ulster Constabulary (RUC) and the Ulster Defence Regiment (UDR), although both contained an overwhelming majority of Protestant members and have, historically, collaborated with Loyalist paramilitaries, causing an enormous amount of distrust and dislike in the Catholic communities. Despite this extremely fragile environment, the British Army and intelligence services attempt to assist the security services in the Province to keep order to the best of their ability. Unfortunately, rivalry between the different services has often occurred and it has not been possible for them to work together effectively and consistently in a way that would be beneficial to all.

When they were first sent to Northern Ireland in 1969, the SAS were able to operate more overtly than they do now. But it was not until after the Oman War in 1976 that the British Government actually announced that the SAS would have a permanent presence in Ulster. Initially this move appeared to have the desired effect, as shown by a marked decrease in the number of terrorist incidents, but this success was short lived. In the early days a great deal of the regiment's work was simply to patrol the fields of South Armagh, but as the Troubles continued their role became more defined.

In the 1970s a substantial number of successes were achieved by the regiment as a result of intense surveillance work. Following numerous ambushes many IRA and INLA terrorists were either killed or captured. The SAS also undertook cross-border raids to arrest suspects.

They continued to attract further adverse publicity with the accidental shootings of innocent civilians, even though engaging in undercover battles against such merciless and violent terrorists always carries the risk of error. Despite all the criticism, the SAS have also achieved outstanding successes in Northern Ireland by helping to instil a sense of order in the country.

NORTHERN IRELAND (NI) CELL This was set up to develop the neccessary skills for the SAS that were specifically for use in Northern Ireland. The original NI Cell was commanded by Major Tony Ball and a staff of four SAS NCOs, all of whom had been sent to the Province to gain first-hand experience from the British Army regulars. The original

NI Cell was located in the old seamstress' building at the back of the cookhouse, in what was then Bradbury Lines. It was phased out once all the squadrons had rotated through Northern Ireland and the regiment had established its own operating methods.

NORTHWEST EUROPE Leading the push through Europe, operating far ahead of the Allied lines, the SAS carried out vital long-range reconnaissance patrols. By 3 May 1945, only days before the end of the war in Europe, they had reached as far as Kiel.

NORWAY Between 1972 and 1990 the SAS travelled to Norway on an annual basis where they spent several weeks training for Arctic warfare. They also sent soldiers to the Norwegian Guerrilla Training School in Dombos. The regiment still trains in Norway but not on an annual basis.

NUI DAT Nui Dat was the base location of Australian SAS Regiment (SASR) squadrons and the 1st Australian Task Force (1 ATF) during their deployment on operations in South Vietnam from 16 June 1966 to 7 October 1971. Located in Phuoc Tuy Province, 70km (43 miles) southeast of Saigon, it was situated on a hill about 5km (3 miles) northeast of the provincial capital of Baria, on the highway known as Route 2. It was overlooked by the Nui Thi Vai and Nui Dinh mountains, which lay to the west.

The area was first occupied by the 5 Battalion Royal Australian Regiment (5 RAR) on 2 June 1966, after it had been cleared by the battalion in a joint operation with the US 173rd Airborne Brigade during the previous week. Headquarters 1 ATF moved in three days after 5 RAR, and by the end of that month it had been joined by 6 RAR, 3 Squadron SASR, which arrived on 17 June, a squadron of armoured personnel carriers, an artillery regiment, and an engineer squadron. A complete camp had to be constructed despite the worst monsoon weather for a number of years. The heavy rain turned the ground into a quagmire and filled weapon pits with water, but nevertheless the perimeter had to be wired, positions dug and sandbagged and buildings constructed.

Nui Dat was attacked on a number of occasions by the Vietcong (VC) and North Vietnamese army (NVA). In the early hours of 17 August 1966, VC mortars and recoilless rifles opened fire on 1 ATF'S area, wounding seven members of 3 Squadron and causing damage to accommodation and vehicles. In May and June rocket attacks were carried out on the base by the NVA 74th Artillery Regiment; some landed in 3 Squadron's lines wounding one man, while the others exploded harmlessly elsewhere in the 1 ATF area.

O

O'CONNOR, STAFF SERGEANT 'PADDY' Came to 22 SAS from the Irish Guards in 1966. He was posted to 24 Troop (Air Troop) G Squadron, where he became an expert on free-fall. Prior to the start of hostilities in the Falkland Islands, O'Connor was attending a course in America. He was requested to report to Delta Force where he received instructions on how to fire the Stinger missile. He later rejoined his unit in the war zone by parachuting into the sea, together with a consignment of the missiles, whereupon he became the instructor. He was tragically killed in the Falklands on 19 May 1982 when the helicopter in which he was travelling crashed during a cross-decking operation.

OFFSHORE INSTALLATIONS ASSAULT GROUP (OAG) In July 1980, the Australian SAS Regiment was directed to develop a capability for recapturing offshore oil and gas installations in the Bass Strait, in the event of their being hijacked by terrorists. Such operations were to be referred to by the code-word 'Bursa'. A specially trained force, called the Offshore Installations Assault Group (OAG) and code-named 'Nullah 1', was formed from 1 Squadron and became operational by November. It was subsequently replaced during the following year by 'Nullah 2'. The OAG included seventeen members of the Royal Australian Navy's Clearance Diving Teams, all of whom underwent the SASR Selection and basic parachute courses. Subsequently, the name of the OAG was altered to Offshore Assault Team (OAT) in 1981. In 1985, as part of the rationalization of SASR counter-terrorist designations, the code-name 'Nullah' was dispensed with and thereafter the OAT was designated as B Troop of 1 Squadron. From 1987 onwards, all three of the regiment's Sabre Squadrons assumed responsibility for the onshore and offshore counter-terrorist roles on a twelve-month rotational basis.

'O GROUP' The term 'O Group' is old British Army slang which originally meant 'Officers Group Briefing'. In SAS terms it still means much the same, but involves an all ranks briefing prior to operations.

OGS   Abbreviation for 'olive greens', a term used for standard jungle issue military clothing. Originally issued in the 1950s and early 1960s, it is still used to define lightweight plain green trousers.

OLIVER, SERGEANT 'CLIFF'   On 18 May 1972 a demolitions specialist, Sergeant Oliver of 22 SAS, together with a bomb disposal officer, Captain Robert Williams, and two members of the SBS, Lieutenant Richard Clifford and Corporal Thomas Jones, parachuted into the North Atlantic when a suspected bomb was found on the *QE2* luxury liner. It was claimed that the liner had up to six bombs on board, but this turned out to be a hoax. Staff Sergeant Cliff Oliver was senior instructor on the SAS Demolitions Wing. When the call came he was instructing students at the demolition bunker about 16km (10 miles) from Hereford. A day later he and the three others parachuted from a C-130 into rough seas, landing close to the liner where they were quickly picked up. Although they searched the liner from stem to stern, no bomb was found. The FBI later arrested the hoaxer charging him with demanding money with menaces from Cunard, the owners of the *QE2*.

OMAN   Oman was the scene of fierce fighting in the early 1970s between the SAS-backed forces of Sultan Qaboos and Communist-backed rebels. The SAS were essential to the Sultan's forces' ultimate success. See also Adoo; BATT; Dhofar; Labalaba; Mirbat.

'ONE-TIME PAD'   A form of encoding system used by the SAS and many other security organizations. The pad is a small book filled with blocks of numbers generated at random, from which the field operator can code and decode messages. The pad has an identical twin which is held by the base signaller and used in exactly the same way. The first numbers of a message indicate where to start in the pad, and the blocks of numbers are used only once, hence the name 'One-time pad'.

OP (OBSERVATION POST)   An OP is a covert site from where enemy activity can be watched and intelligence gathered. The SAS are experts in setting up OPs and remaining in them for long periods of time in the most hostile of conditions. Sometimes they are in a rural situation and are constructed from natural materials to blend in with the surroundings. At other times they may be placed in an urban area, for example in the loft space of a house or underneath a garden shed.

Wherever they are located, the rules for their construction remain the same. A site must be chosen that is not vulnerable to discovery and yet it must also afford a good view of the target position. A concealed entrance and exit are also needed. High ground, although good for visibility, is an obvious spot and one which the enemy will search, so a more unlikely place is a better choice. Once the site has been chosen, the OP can be constructed under cover of night. It can be made out of any material – waterproof sheeting, ponchos, camouflage nets, and natural or locally available materials are all useful, as long as the end product blends in with everything around it and cannot be easily seen. OPs tend to be built either in a rectangular shape, where the patrol members lie in two pairs of two facing in opposite directions, or in a star shape where each member takes up an 'arm' of the star.

As OPs are often maintained for long periods at a time – in the Falklands War one OP was maintained for 26 days – they have to contain all that is necessary for the men to be self-sufficient, particularly if it is not possible for them to be re-supplied. In addition to food, water, clothing and sleeping bags, operational gear is also stored inside the OP: weapons; radio equipment; binoculars; night sights; cameras and telescopes. This can make conditions cramped and uncomfortable, a situation often made worse by weather conditions. No sign of the men's presence can be left since it may be discovered by an enemy. Therefore even normally private functions such as urinating and defecating must be done in the OP into separate bags which are then sealed and taken away by the patrol members at the end of their operation. Other things which may not be appropriate in such a situation are smoking, cooking and the wearing of deodorant or aftershave.

Living in such close conditions it is essential that the men all get on well together. It also requires mental strength and the ability to get on with the job no matter how hard the conditions or how boring it may seem at times. However, these qualities are second nature to SAS soldiers.

OPERATIONS RESEARCH The Operations Research Cell is normally manned by two long-serving SAS soldiers, usually holding the rank of sergeant or corporal. They are tasked with finding or developing the specialist equipment the regiment requires for its operational roles. This can range from weapons, clothing and vehicles, to food and rations. Any member of the regiment may approach Ops Research and request information on a product or put forward an idea for development.

Rations have always been a bone of contention within the SAS mainly because it is difficult to satisfy the calorie requirement while providing an appetizing meal, and at the same time keeping the ration weight to a minimum. The struggle to make rations lighter, provide more energy, and have taste and texture is a continuing one for the SAS.

When Ops Research were requested to find a device that would disorientate a terrorist without harming any hostages within close proximity, they, in turn, asked the technical experts at the arms manufacturer Royal Enfield to help. Several devices were made; of these the most popular was the 'Stun grenade', but others devices such as the 'Screamer' were also developed. The 'Screamer' would emit a very loud, high-pitched scream; however, it was found to be not only too scary for the terrorists, but it was also capable of deafening the hostages and the SAS assault teams.

Those soldiers employed in Ops Research take their work seriously and over the years they have developed some quite brilliant equipment, from motorized parachutes to space-age crossbows capable of penetrating 150mm (6in) of metal at 100m (109yds).

OSBORNE, LIEUTENANT-COLONEL MIKE   Commanded 22 SAS in Malaya after the departure of Oliver Brooke. He was in the position only a short time before the command was taken over again by Lieutenant-Colonel George Lea.

'OVERBOARD', OPERATION   On 3 October 1968 a patrol of 2 Squadron Australian SAS Regiment (SASR), under Major Brian Wade, was inserted by helicopter at a location near the estuary of the Song Rai River, with the task of ambushing and capturing one of a number of Vietcong (VC) sampans which were operating on the river at night. The purpose of the operation, called 'Overboard', was to discover what the VC were transporting in the boats. Early warning groups, under Sergeants Frank Cashmore and Bernie Considine, were deployed up and down river while the main body deployed a large fishing net across the river to trap any sampan which entered the ambush area. The main body was divided into two groups, under Major Wade and Second-Lieutenant Terry Nolan respectively, and deployed on either bank of the river.

At 04:15 hours on 4 October a sampan was spotted approaching upstream from the direction of the estuary. Sailing some 10m (11yds) from the far bank on which Second-Lieutenant Nolan's group was positioned, it was crewed by two VC. As it made contact with the net the VC were ordered to halt; one dived into the river and the other was shot as he attempted to do so. On searching the boat the patrol discovered medical supplies which were subsequently extracted and returned to the squadron base at Nui Dat.

OWEN SUB-MACHINE GUN   *Specification* Calibre: 9mm; Weight: 2kg (4.21lbs); Length: 813mm (32in); Range: 200m (218yds); Rate of fire: 700 rounds; Magazine: 33-round, box; Muzzle velocity: 381m (415 yds) per second.

The Owen sub-machine gun was one of the few weapons produced by Australia during World War II and was distinctive for its top-loading magazine. Although it was used by the British SAS during the Malayan Emergency, it was mainly the Australian SAS who greatly favoured this strange-looking weapon. Despite its oddity, the Owen was a very robust weapon and ideally suited to the dirty conditions of jungle fighting.

P

'P' FOR PLENTY A phrase widely used during the SAS demolitions course. An SAS soldier will have to learn many technical formulas in order to apply the right amount of explosive to a particular type of explosive target. The 'P' for plenty is used to err on the safe side.

'PAGODA' TEAM The code-name used by the SAS to identify the anti-terrorist team in the late 1970s. The name was dropped shortly after the Iranian Embassy Siege was broken by the SAS in May 1980.

PALUDRINE CLUB Name of the regimental all ranks club of 22 SAS at Stirling Lines, derived from the name of an anti-malaria medication commonly used by the soldiers. The first club was set up in Bradbury Lines in an effort to improve the regiment's social life; it proved a tremendous success. When the new barracks were built in 1980 a more secure, purpose-built club was constructed, which retained the same name. Many famous names, especially comedians, have found themselves doing a free turn for the SAS during events at the Paludrine Club.

PARACHUTE TENT A bell tent fashioned from a parachute by securing it to an overhanging branch and pegging the parachute skirt out in a circle. Normally associated with survival.

PARACHUTING The SAS first used parachutes as a means of delivery in North Africa during World War II, albeit with little success. By the time 2 SAS were parachuting into Europe in 1944 their techniques had improved. Although parachutes were used in Malaya, tree-jumping proved very dangerous and parachuting as a delivery method was superseded by helicopters for many jungle operations.

Parachuting skills are taught to all new members of the regiment. The course involves making four low altitude 61m (200ft) static line jumps, seven normal 243m (800ft) jumps and two water jumps. Once the basics have been mastered, all SAS members will also learn HAHO (High Altitude, High Opening) techniques, as this method of insertion means that men can be dropped some 30km (18 miles) from their target.

A four-week static-line parachuting course is held at No. 1 Parachute Training School at Brize Norton, Oxfordshire. It is the last course within the Continuation training and if the candidate passes it he is awarded his 'sabre' wings and becomes a 'badged' member of the Special Air Service. Candidates from the Parachute Regiment do not have to take this course as they are already qualified in this skill. During the four weeks the soldiers have to make a total of eight jumps including a night jump, a jump from a balloon and an operational jump. These jumps are either 'clean fatigue' (no equipment), or include jumping with a bergen, which for normal parachuting is positioned below the front reserve. Once the soldier has jumped and the canopy has deployed properly, the bergen is released on a 3m (9ft) line which hangs below the feet. This ensures that the bergen hits the ground before the parachutist.

The SAS use standard British parachutes such as the PX1 Mk 4, the PX Mk 5 and the PR7 reserve which have an equipment suspension strap and integral jettison device. Once on the ground, the soldier can jettison the canopy and clear the drop-zone (DZ) immediately.

The SAS have retained their own distinctive parachute wings that were originally designed and worn in World War II.

'PARANG'   A Malaysian machete or long-bladed knife used for domestic jungle work and adopted by the SAS to replace the Army-issue golok.

'PARAQUET', OPERATION   Code-name given to the operation to recapture the island of South Georgia from the Argentinians during the Falklands War in 1982. It was also humorously known as 'Operation Paraquat' after the weed killer.

PARKA   An outer jacket used by the SAS in the 1970–80s during winter warfare operations and in cold climates. The jacket is based on an American design developed during the Korean War. It has a large hood which is trimmed with fur and an internal wire frame which allows the face to be fully covered. The parka is still in service with the British Army.

PATROL SKILLS   Patrol skills include movement, camouflage, ambush and anti-ambush drills, contact drills, and (RV) rendezvous procedures, all practised to ensure that the SAS four-man patrol can operate undetected in a hostile environment. Most SAS soldiers learn their basic patrolling skills in their original unit, especially if they come from an infantry regiment.

As most SAS patrols are made up of only four men, the commander must utilize his men to the full, placing each man within the patrol according to his abilities and individual skills. For example, he will not make the signaller or medic into the lead scout, but he will choose the demolitionist or linguist. Luckily most SAS soldiers will have more than one skill, which allows the commander greater flexibility in the structure of his patrol.

While all SAS personnel learn contact and ambush drill and RV procedures during Continuation training, no two theatres of operation are the same and a good patrol commander will insist on rehearsals prior to insertion. Likewise, once inserted the patrol must be disciplined by hard routine, obeying standard operating procedures (SOPs) to avoid detection by the enemy.

PAU A military parachute school in the southwest of France. Pau has a world-wide reputation for excellence in all forms of military parachute training. SAS soldiers, especially those in Air Troops, frequently attend the school.

PDRY People's Democratic Republic of Yemen.

PEA GREENS A light-weight uniform adopted by the SAS for the tropics and Middle East. So called because of the unusual pea-green colour of the material. The uniform was extremely smart and set the SAS apart from other units. The wearing of Pea Greens declined in the early 1980s.

PEA GREEN HOUSE In June 1965 the SAS set up its regimental headquarters in Kuching, the capital of Sarawak in Borneo. The fading colonial house had rusting wrought-iron gates bedecked with barbed wire, and was know as the Pea Green House, or PGH.

PEBBLE ISLAND Pebble Island, which is situated in the north of West Falkland, is home to a small airstrip which witnessed one of the most daring raids carried out by the SAS in the Falklands War. Previous reconnaissance had established that the Argentinians controlled the airstrip and that a number of Pucara ground attack aircraft were based there. The SAS were given their orders to destroy all the aircraft and to kill the ground crew and supporting garrison on the island, as these aircraft could have posed a major threat to the main troop landings on San Carlos Water. They were to be assisted in their task by HMS *Hermes*, *Broadsword* and also *Glamorgan*, which was to supply on-shore bombardment.

On the night of 14 May 1982 the helicopters, carrying 45 members of D Squadron, landed about 6km (4 miles) from the airstrip. The plan was that once the mortars and LAW rockets had been unloaded from the helicopters, Mountain Troop would mount the main assault on the aircraft while the other two troops were to form a reserve.

The attack on the airfield began with a heavy bombardment from HMS *Glamorgan* followed by the SAS using 81mm mortars, M203 grenade launchers, 66mm LAWS and small arms. With the Argentinians forced to take cover, the SAS moved on to the airstrip and fixed explosive charges to the aircraft. The actual assault on the airfield, which was led by Captain John Hamilton, destroyed all six Pucaras, four Turbo-Mentors and a Skyvan Transport, before the raiding party withdrew. The Argentinians were caught completely unprepared and, despite desperately returning fire, most of it missed. The only SAS injuries were slight; in fact the worst were caused by an exploding mine. It is reported that one Argentinian was killed in the firefight.

The SAS returned to the pick-up-point were they were exfiltrated by helicopter and returned to the fleet. Once back aboard HMS *Hermes*, the mission was hailed as a success. The planes had been destroyed, along with a great amount of enemy ammunition, and the Argentinians were now denied the use of the airstrip.

PEN-Y-FAN The highest point in the Brecon Beacons in Wales where the SAS carry out Selection and basic training. At 886m (2,700ft), the top of Pen-Y-Fan is a flat, barren, exposed plateau 300m (327yds) by 100m (109yds), which is used as a check-point for candidates. In winter it is extremely inhospitable with snow, rain and high winds. Attempts to reach the summit in such conditions have cost the lives of many soldiers. It is a feature that every SAS soldiers knows and few ever forget.

PERTH, BLACKHAWK HELICOPTER CRASH – AUSTRA-LIAN SAS REGIMENT (SASR) While carrying out a joint anti-terrorist exercise on board a cargo ship anchored in Perth's North Quay dock, 15 members of the SASR and 3 crew were killed and several seriously injured when two helicopters collided. The accident happened on the 15 January 1998 when six Blackhawk helicopters, flying in diamond formation, were preparing to repel the SASR men from a height of 30m (91ft) and two accidentally touched rotor blades. The first helicopter crashed to the ground and exploded in flames, killing all on board. The second crashed just seconds later killing five, but luckily the rest of those on board, including the crew, managed to escape moments before the aircraft burst into flames.

PETERHEAD PRISON On 27 September 1987 a riot erupted in D Block of Peterhead Prison in Scotland. The block held 48 prisoners, most of whom where serving long-term sentences for murder or rape. The majority of prisoners gave themselves up after a short while but a hard core of five men, holding a prison officer hostage, refused to surrender. For the next week the rioters paraded on the rooftop in full view of the world's media. The Grampian Police responded with a specialist response team; and in addition the government ordered two SAS advisors to assist. A quick review of the situation promoted the idea that the task would be best dealt with by an SAS team who were better versed in such assault tactics.

The government finally gave its consent for the SAS assault on the morning of 3 October. At around 04:00 a four-man team, armed with batons instead of sub-machine guns, made their way from a skylight across a slippery roof to the hole that had previously been made by the rioters. They dropped both stun grenades and CS gas through the hole before dropping in themselves to confront the prisoners. At the same time, back-up teams made an explosive entry through the lower floor walls and proceeded to follow up the roof assault. The hostage was first to be removed, too weak to help himself. Once on the roof, the assault team hauled him through the roof hole and carried him back to the skylight where he was lowered to safety. The prisoners, overwhelmed by CS gas and the black-clad figures, allowed themselves to be marshalled back into captivity. The SAS assault team departed from Scotland less than two hours after their arrival, having successfully completed their mission.

As a result of the Peterhead Prison riot, the government set up a specialist team to deal with such incidents; officers in this team were initially trained in Hereford.

PETTIT, SERGEANT JOHN – AUSTRALIAN SAS REGIMENT (SASR)
On 3 July 1965 Sergeant Pettit and his four-man patrol of 1 Squadron SASR crossed over the border from Sabah into Indonesian Kalimantan and headed for the Salilir River and an area to the east of the village of Baluladan. Operating under the auspices of Operation 'Claret', the patrol was to carry out an observation task and report on enemy movements on the river. It was, however, allowed to ambush any easy target within the period of the last 48 hours of its mission.

At 15:30 hours on the afternoon of 5 July a boat with six men aboard was observed travelling upstream. At 17:00 hours another boat, carrying eight Indonesians, appeared moving downstream and suddenly altered course, heading directly for the patrol. As it came within 10m (11yds) of the OP (observation post), Sergeant Pettit and his men opened fire. The enemy, who were then seen to be armed with sub-machine guns, were all either killed outright or wounded in the water. Without further ado, the patrol withdrew and returned to the Malaysian border without incident. Subsequent reports from the Border Scouts revealed that five Indonesians, including a warrant officer, had been killed in the ambush and that a further three had subsequently died of their wounds.

PFLOAG
The People's Front for the Liberation of the Occupied Arabian Gulf (PFLOAG) was a Communist-based movement which operated from the People's Democratic Republic of Yemen (PDRY),

previously known as Aden. With Soviet and Chinese assistance PFLOAG crossed the border with Oman and dominated the Jebel Massive during the early 1960s. PFLOAG absorbed the smaller existing Dhofar Liberation Front (DLF), spreading the Communist doctrine and imposing its will on the local tribes.

By 1970 the movement completely controlled the Jebel, but at the cost of isolating the many DLF followers, many of whom were systematically persecuted for their religious beliefs. Additionally PFLOAG tried hard to destroy the old tribal ways of the Jebel people by torturing the elderly who refused to deny their God and by sending the young children off to schools in the PDRY. Much of the DLF resentment had been directed against the feudal actions of the old sultan, Said bin Taimur; a coup by his more enlightened son Sultan Qaboos did much to ease the situation. Qaboos offered amnesty. This, coupled with a vigorous psychological warfare campaign carried out by the SAS, persuaded many former DLF members to leave PFLOAG and return to fight for their country. The SAS did much to cultivate these men, recruiting many into the Firqat where, due to their knowledge of PFLOAG operations and locations, they proved to be a major asset.

PFLP Popular Front for the Liberation of Palestine. See Habash, George.

'PHANTOMS' Commanded by Lieutenant-Colonel A. H. McIntosh, this remarkable organization founded by Major-General Hopkinson (who was killed while commanding the 1st Airborne Division in Italy) began secret operations early in 1940 in France, and its existence was not revealed until May 1945. The organization, made up of 150 officers and 1,250 other ranks, gathered and swiftly passed back vital information throughout World War II.

Known officially as GHQ Liaison Regiment, it adopted the name 'Phantoms' and achieved excellent results by working directly with the front line troops, keeping Army Group and Base HQ informed almost minute-by-minute of all that was happening and of the position of troops actually on the ground. Messages were sent from under the noses of the enemy by means of very small and special wireless sets invented for the purpose by Captain Peter Astbury. During the eleven months of fighting on the Western Front after D-Day, Lieutenant-Colonel McIntosh's Phantoms sent more than 70,000 of these messages from the battle areas to the headquarters of the 12th and 21st Army Groups.

In 1940 when the Phantoms came back from France after the fall of Dunkirk, sections were deployed around the coasts of England where invasion was most probable, and news of any attempted landing speedily passed on. Their headquarters were in very innocent-looking surroundings in St James's Park, London. Here were the base wireless sets through which the Phantoms worked, passing information on to GHQ. The headquarters in St James's Park also contained several lofts for the carrier-pigeons which supplemented the regiment's wireless.

Towards the end of 1940 a squadron of the regiment left Britain for Greece, and while almost all were captured they continued to transmit messages to the end.

The Phantoms suffered more casualties when they adopted a commando role, sending a squadron to join the raid on Dieppe. In November 1942 two squadrons went with the First Army to North Africa and operated throughout the Tunisian campaign, finally joining up with the Eighth Army. There they listened in to the 'wireless talk' of the German tanks, gleaning every scrap of information that was of interest, and formulating a clear picture of the battle mayhem, as well as reporting positions, casualties and strengths.

Early in 1944 the squadron, which had seen action in the Dieppe raid, was trained in parachute work. Special volunteers were called for and, after the parachute training, they joined the SAS as their 'communications', before finally being dropped with the SAS behind enemy lines. In June 1944 some of the Phantoms were parachuted into France before D-Day, while others went in with the assault troops. First news of the Normandy landings were sent back by them. By July the complete regiment was in France, deployed with the British, Canadian and American armies. This was due to an inquiry by General Eisenhower who, in the early stages of the assault on Normandy, visited the British Second Army HQ, then located near Portsmouth, and was considerably impressed by the complete intelligence picture of operations. He asked how it was done. The answer was 'Phantom patrol'. It was explained to him how the organization flashed back to England the positions of brigades and battalions in the beachhead battles. General Eisenhower immediately ordered Phantom units to work with the American formations. Likewise General Crerar (commander First Canadian Army) secured a substantial proportion of his information from the regiment, and General Patton (commander US Third Army) acknowledged their valuable assistance. Hour by hour during the Ardennes 'breakthrough' every move of German armour was reported by men who wore a small 'P' on the right shoulder.

Towards the end of the war they made known the first details of the German concentration and prisoner-of-war camps. In one last spectacular event they directed the link-up between the Russians and the American First Army, as always transmitting the news faithfully back to GHQ.

Although the unit was disbanded in 1945, Major Geoffrey Brain, a former member, organized an annual reunion, which included such prominent ex-members as the actor David Niven.

'PHANTOM', F SQUADRON F Squadron of GHQ Liaison Regiment, known as 'Phantom', was commanded by Major The Hon. J. J. 'Jakie' Astor. In early 1944 it was assigned the role of providing rear-link radio communications for the squadrons of 1 and 2 SAS Regiments deployed in France from D-Day onwards, its patrol operators communicating with the squadron base located at the headquarters of the SAS Brigade.

With a strength of 6 officers and 102 other ranks, F Squadron was organized as a headquarters and four patrols. Two patrols, under Captains Moore and McSadoine, were attached to 1 SAS and two, under Captains Hislop and Johnsen, were attached to 2 SAS. Each patrol comprised an officer and four other ranks. The two French units in the SAS Brigade, 3 and 4 French Parachute Battalions, and the Belgian Independent Parachute Company possessed their own signals units, but F Squadron provided training for them in the use of the newly developed lightweight radio sets. All F Squadron personnel were parachute-trained and during the first half of 1944 underwent training with the rest of the SAS Brigade in Scotland prior to deployment on operations with 1 and 2 SAS in June.

The signals system used for SAS communications was a duplex one using morse only, with signallers using one set to transmit and another for receiving transmissions from F Squadron's headquarters. The radio transmitter used by patrols was known as the 'Jedburgh' set. Compact and lightweight, they were carried easily by a parachutist. A shortwave crystal controlled the set, and it had sufficient range to reach England from anywhere in Europe, although much depended on the time of day when transmissions were made. For receiving messages, signallers used the MCR-1 receiver, which was a two-piece unit comprising the set itself and a power pack. Three interchangeable coil units were supplied with it, which were plugged in to its base and covered different frequency ranges.

Today, the SAS rear-link communications role is currently performed by two units of the Royal Corps of Signals: 264 SAS Signals Squadron which supports 22 SAS Regiment, and 63 SAS Signals Squadron (Volunteers) which supports 21 SAS (Artists) (Volunteers), and 23 SAS Regiments (Volunteers).

PHUOC TUY PROVINCE Located some 70km (43 miles) southeast of the South Vietnamese capital of Saigon (now Ho Chi Minh City), Phuoc Tuy Province was the area of operations for the 1st Australian Task Force (1 ATF) and the Australian SAS Regiment (SASR) squadrons deployed there from June 1966 to October 1971. To the south lies the South China Sea and to the north, east and west the provinces of Long Khanh, Binh Tuy and Bien Hoa respectively. In the southwest is the estuary of the Rung Sat River which snakes northwestwards into Bien

Hoa Province. Lined with mangrove swamps, creeks and islands, it provided good concealment and a line of communication for the Vietcong (VC) operating in the area. To the east is the Song Rai River which runs south through jungle all the way from Long Khanh Province to the coast, providing the VC with a covered route from north to south.

The provincial capital of Baria is situated in the south of the province on the junction of a number of main roads: Route 15 which leads north-west to Saigon and south to the port of Vung Tau; Route 2 which heads north to Long Khanh Province; and Route 23 which runs eastwards to the town of Xuyen Moc and Binh Tuy Province. In the west of the province lie the Nui Thi Vai and Nui Dinh hills, from which thick jungle stretches northwards to the borders with Bien Hoa and Long Khanh Provinces. In the northeast are the May Tao mountains, which run across the borders into Long Khanh and Bien Tuy Provinces, while in the south are the Long Hai hills. Together with the jungle in the west, all these upland areas provided ideal locations for the VC during the five years of 1 ATF operations in the province.

PINCKNEY, CAPTAIN PHILLIP Pinckney joined the SBS when 62 Commando was disbanded and was posted to 2 SAS in 1943. He was one of a raiding force dropped into the Brenner Pass in Italy in order to destroy a vital rail tunnel. Shortly after they had completed their mission, Pinckney was captured and subsequently executed by the Gestapo.

In many ways Pinckney was the first survival expert in the SAS; he was renowned for eating many types of insects or strange-looking plants.

'PINGED' Another word for spotting the enemy or identifying an objective: 'We had the place 'pinged!'

PINK PANTHER The first specialist Land Rover fully developed in the early 1960s to meet specific SAS requirements. The regiment decided to paint their vehicles pink as a camouflage measure after learning that an old aircraft shot down during World War II had been found in the desert burnished pink by the sand.

The 'Pinky' was a cabless, doorless long-based vehicle that held a crew of three, including the driver and front passenger, plus a rear gunner. The latter occupied a small seat fitted between two long-range fuel tanks that were self-sealing if ruptured by enemy fire, and from where a centre pivoted GPMG (general purpose machine gun) could be fired. The rear superstructure held a dropdown tailgate which was used for storing the crew's bergens and other necessary equipment. The vehicle was fitted with sand-channels which hooked on both sides of the main body, as well as two rifle boots fixed for easy access over the front wheel arches. Four banks of three smoke dischargers were fitted, two on the front bumper and two on the rear superstructure. Other additional items included spotlights, astro-navigation equipment and vehicle camouflage nets. The original Pink Panthers suffered many problems, not least the under-powered engine and weak half-shafts which had a tendency to break in the most isolated patch of desert. However, the vehicles lasted until the mid-1980s when they were replaced by the new Land Rover 110.

'PISTOL', OPERATION   Carried out by 51 men of 2 SAS who were dropped into the Alsace-Lorraine area of eastern France during the night of 15 September 1944. They were detailed to cut an enemy road and rail communication between the Rhine and Moselle Rivers. They were sectioned off into four parties and dropped blind, although one party failed to jump due to fog over the target area.

The weather conditions were appalling and the locals were pretty unfriendly because the area was near the German border and many were of German origin. However, four trains were derailed, one locomotive destroyed and one railway line cut. Some vehicles were also destroyed. Unfortunately, several SAS soldiers were caught and at least two killed by the Gestapo. The operation ended on 3 October and the remaining soldiers met up with the advancing US forces.

PLOTTER   A flat plastic sheet measuring 193 sq cm (30 sq in) that was originally used to manually convert grid references into range and bearing for artillery and mortar fire. Although plotters are still used in some countries, the system has been replaced by the 'Morzen' fire control computer, a small hand-held device that can calculate data in a fraction of the time and with far greater accuracy.

POAT, MAJOR HARRY   Poat was awarded a Military Cross for his contribution to the landings in Sicily, having first joined 1 SAS in North Africa and taken part in operations in Tunisia. In 1944 he became second-in-command of 1 SAS and his most notorious achievement was to lead A and D squadrons in Operation 'Archway' in 1945.

POINT 825   An SAS location founded by Mountain Troop of G Squadron in the Oman War. Point 825 was a defensive position in the shape of a horseshoe-type ridge, and was the scene of a mutiny by Baluchi soldiers of the Oman army. The event occurred when it was alleged a British officer, seconded to the unit, called down inaccurate mortar fire which killed the brother of a soldier who had died in similar circumstances two months earlier. The Baluchi soldiers demanded the death of the British officer, but he was saved after timely SAS intervention, which resulted in his dismissal via a brutal gauntlet of angry soldiers.

Several days after the sedition, a helicopter carrying two British seconded officers from the same unit crashed after being hit by enemy fire, just 3km (2 miles) from Point 825. SAS soldiers recovered all the bodies.

POLE BED   A form of bed used mainly in the jungle to keep a soldier off the ground. The basis of the bed is two 'A' frames which, when supported against a tree, have additional poles threaded through an SAS hammock and the ends placed over the 'A' frames. Opening the legs of the 'A' frame determines the height and security of the bed. A mosquito net and shelter sheet normally cover the bed.

'POMEGRANATE', OPERATION   As part of the Italian campaign the SAS were ordered to destroy enemy aircraft on the ground. On 12 January 1944, in an attempt to help the Anzio landings planned for 22 January, a party of six men, including Major Widdrington and Lieutenant Hughes, parachuted by night into central Italy with the purpose of raiding the German reconnaissance aircraft at San Egidio. The men successfully reached the target but were forced to split up when challenged by a German guard. Four members returned to Allied lines but Widdrington and Hughes continued with the mission. On 17 January, under cover of darkness, the two officers managed to put Lewes bombs on seven aircraft on the tarmac. Tragically, whilst making the bombs safe, one exploded, killing Widdrington and injuring Hughes. Hughes was captured and taken to a German hospital but he later effected his escape and reached Allied lines in March.

PONCHO   A form of shelter sheet with a hooded hole in the centre that covers the soldier during rainy weather. The modern day poncho, or shelter sheet, which has no hole, can be fixed above a pole bed or sleeping bag by a series of elasticised bungees to form a waterproof cover. The SAS word for this is a basha.

PONTRILAS   A small village some 19km (12 miles) to the south of Hereford where an old ammunition camp, built during World War II, has been converted into a training facility for the SAS. The content of and activities at Pontrilas are restricted. Access to the heavily guarded camp is controlled by MoD armed police.

POPSKI'S PRIVATE ARMY   During World War II various freelance armies evolved, two of which were the SAS and the Long Range Desert Group (LRDG). A Russian soldier, Vladimir Peniakoff, nicknamed 'Popski', joined a number of LRDG patrols after serving with the Libyan Arab Force. His idea was to create a small independent unit to work in conjunction with the LRDG, specializing in sabotage behind enemy lines.

As a result, 'Popski' was given charge of No. 1 Demolition Squadron in October 1942. Made up originally of 23 men all ranks, although with never more than 80 men, the unit was given the nickname 'Popski's

Private Army' by Lieutenant-Colonel Shan Hackett, co-ordinator of Special Forces. Early in 1943 the unit helped to defeat the Germans in North Africa, but it appeared that its future was rather insecure until Popski's good relationship with the Eighth Army turned things around and ensured its survival. The unit continued to serve in Italy to the end of the war, as a jeep-mounted reconnaissance and raiding force.

PORT STANLEY RAID With the Falklands War about to end, the SAS attempted one last suicidal raid on the night of 13/14 June. Wireless Ridge, a few kilometres west of Port Stanley, was being assaulted by 2 Para and in an attempt to relieve the pressure on them the SAS planned a seaborne raid on the enemy rear. It was decided that two troops from D Squadron, one from G Squadron and six men from 3 SBS would move rapidly into Port Stanley harbour, using four Rigid Raiders operated by the 1st Raiding Squadron Royal Marines. Once there, they were to destroy the massive Argentinian stores complex and set fire to the oil-storage tanks.

The Argentinians were fully prepared for a final assault by the British, and as the four Raiders appeared within range they opened fire with every weapon they had, including triple-barrelled 20mm anti-aircraft cannon depressed to their lowest trajectory. This barrage of firepower forced the Raiders to withdraw immediately to avoid loss of life. Despite their prompt action all four Raiders were badly hit and one even sunk, always considered a virtual impossibility given their design. Several of the men received injuries, although none was serious and the party returned safely. The regiment later agreed that the raid was perhaps less wise than it was adventurous.

The aim of the raid was achieved and 2 Para subsequently took Wireless Ridge. By 14 June the Argentinians, their morale broken and their position hopeless, surrendered. Mike Rose, commanding officer of 22 SAS, took the surrender, his men having contributed enormously to the British victory.

PPK, WALTHER *Specification* Calibre: 7.65mm or 9mm Short (9 × 17mm); Weight: 170g (60oz); Muzzle velocity: (at 7.65mm calibre) 280m (305yds) per second; Magazine capacity: 7-round, box.

Made by the German company Walther, the Polizei Pistole Kriminal (PPK) was originally designed for use by uniformed policemen. Easy to conceal and fairly reliable, the PPK has influenced many other gun designers, although it is not known for its stopping power. It is currently in use with many armed and police forces around the world, and is also still in use as a personal protection weapon.

PPSH-41 *Specification* Calibre: 7.62mm × 25; Weight: 1.6kg (3.64lbs); Muzzle velocity: 488m (531yds) per second; Magazine capacity: 35-round, box or 71-round, drum.

A Russian-designed sub-machine gun which was extremely popular in World War II due to its durability, accuracy and light recoil. After the war, China took up the design and the PPSh-41 became its main weapon during the Korean War. Although it was slowly phased out in the Warsaw Pact countries, some models are still in use by some rebel groups in Africa.

PRAYERS A word used to describe a daily meeting at various levels where the main points of the day's events and future instructions are given. 'Prayers' in one form or another will take place at most SAS locations irrespective of the country or location and are basically a method of updating everyone on events.

PRC 319 RADIO *Specification* Weight: 1.5kg (3.4lbs); Frequency range: 1.5 to 40MHz; Battery life: 500 hours in stand-by mode.

Most SAS patrols use the powerful Thorn EMI PRC 319 radio set which has an internal modem providing burst message capability. The PRC 319 was purpose designed for long-range covert use and is ideally suited to SAS work. The radio has many features which enable an SAS patrol signaller to assess and send messages quickly and securely. These include a transmission power far in excess of any other military radio set, a detachable electronic message unit, and 20 pre-set channels.

The PRC 319 is simple to operate and requires little instruction; it is also very robust and completely watertight, capable of withstanding the punishment SAS patrols in the field inflict on their equipment.

PRI Stands for President of the Regimental Institute. However, in most units, including the SAS, it represents a small shop which traditionally sells regimental items such as ties, belts, and plaques etc. PRIs are governed by military law as they are accountable for funds from their retail activities and income such as NAAFI rebates.

PRISONERS Much has been written about the SAS's so-called 'shoot to kill' policy. Like all regiments of the British Army they are controlled by law and operate within the law. If the number of enemy killed is high it is because the SAS are normally placed in a situation where they have little choice but to shoot first and ask questions later.

One such incident happened during the Gulf War when an Iraqi vehicle drove directly into an SAS LUP (lying-up position) mistaking it for one of its own units. The SAS lookouts spotted the vehicle, a Russian-built Gaz 69, and gave a warning to the rest of the fighting column. Remaining behind their camouflage nets, the soldiers grabbed their weapons and adopted good firing positions. Luckily, the Iraqis stopped a few metres away, not thinking that enemy troops would be so close to Baghdad. One man walked over to the nearest camouflaged vehicle while its driver walked to the front of his vehicle, opening up the bonnet to check the engine.

An SAS soldier broke cover and walked out to meet the oncoming Iraqi who was dressed in olive drab military clothing, and wearing the rank of a captain. The Iraqi officer greeted the SAS soldier at a range of 3m (3yds) before realizing he was an enemy. As he did so the SAS soldier swung up his rifle and fired. Nothing happened as the weapon had jammed. The SAS soldier then dropped to his knees clearing the line of fire for those behind him. The captain fell dead, and the camp erupted with the sound of automatic fire as everyone else joined in. The driver was hit several times before finally crumpling to the ground, also dead. The SAS then broke cover and ran towards the Iraqi vehicle only to find two more soldiers in the back. One had been fatally wounded and died an hour later, but the other was unharmed and was taken prisoner. After a swift interrogation, at which it was revealed the Iraqis were the lead element of a much larger formation, the SAS set off into the night. Hours later they contacted their HQ and a helicopter was sent to collect the prisoner and the vital information he was carrying. Other Iraqi prisoners taken by the SAS were also fairly treated, which cannot be said for those members of 'Bravo Two Zero' captured by the Iraqis.

PSYCHOLOGICAL WARFARE Psychological warfare, or 'Psy-Ops' as it is better known, is used to persuade an enemy to conform and surrender. The SAS have operated and participated in several Psy-Ops campaigns, which began during World War II in Europe, where they assisted the 'Phantoms' playing gramophone recordings of tanks in order to confuse the Germans. Likewise in Malaya, during the 1948–60 campaign, Dakota aircraft flew over the jungle dropping leaflets and safe-conduct passes. Some were fitted with loudspeakers which were used to urge members of the Malayan Races Liberation Army (MRLA) to surrender.

In 1970, after Sultan Qaboos ousted his father in Oman, the SAS operated a full-scale Psy-Ops war. This included the setting up of a radio station and the distribution of thousands of free radios to the Jebel people. Millions of leaflets, informing the rebels of the recent coup and offering them an amnesty, were dropped by Skyvan aircraft over enemy-held locations. SAS Psy-Ops teams would also distribute T-shirts and flags for the children prior to visits by the new sultan to outlying towns and villages. One SAS soldier, Corporal John Ward, who arrived in the regiment via 21 SAS, became so professional at his work that he remained in Oman to continue his Psy-Ops work.

PULK Sledge used by the SAS and other British forces to carry heavy loads across snow and ice. It is a laborious mode of transport which is pulled by attaching it to a skier's waist. Pulks are still used but, where possible, they are now towed behind snow scooters.

PUMA *Specification* Length: 16.80m (18yds); Height: 4.60m (5yds); Weight: 4,760kg (4.6 tons); Speed: 327km/h (202mph) max.

Designed in the mid-1960s to meet a French Army requirement for a new medium-lift transport helicopter, the Aerospatiale Puma was subsequently produced, in co-operation with Westland in the United Kingdom, to meet the RAF's need for an all-weather day or night tactical transport helicopter. The first flight took place on 15 April 1965 and close to 700 Pumas had been built by the time production ended in 1984. Of these, the vast majority were unarmed transports. RAF Pumas have been used extensively in Northern Ireland, Belize, the Gulf and Bosnia. In South Armagh, Northern Ireland, Puma helicopters are used exclusively to transport men and equipment to company bases on the border, since the roads are considered unsafe for troop convoys. In a troop-lift role the Puma can carry 16 fully equipped men or 20 men in light order.

PUNTA ARENAS On 20 May 1980, at the height of the Falklands War, the discovery of a crashed Sea King helicopter 16km (10 miles) south of the Chilean port of Punta Arenas caused much speculation. Many versions of the story abound, but the one most commonly accepted is as follows. The Sea King was taking a small reconnaissance party of SAS men to a point 40km (25 miles) from Rio Gallegos, an airfield in southern Argentina close to the border with Chile. The airfield was rumoured to be the main base for the Super Etendard aircraft and their Exocet missiles that were doing so much damage to ships of the British Task Force. Despite rumours that the helicopter crash-landed in bad weather, leaving the crew to find their way to the nearest British Embassy in Chile, it is also rumoured that an SAS demolitionist placed a bomb under the fuselage to destroy the helicopter.

Meanwhile, on Ascension Island, two Hercules C-130s were loaded with SAS troops from the recently arrived B Squadron. Although never confirmed, it is said that they were equipped and on their way to assault the Argentinian airfield at Rio Gallegos, a one-way mission for which those SAS men on the helicopter had been the reconnaissance team. Political intervention by the Americans, who feared that direct intrusion into Argentina would only serve to escalate the war, finally called a halt to the raid and the aircraft returned to Ascension. The remains of the Sea King were discovered and the news flashed around the world. Fearing that the element of surprise had now been lost, further such missions were aborted.

Q

Q CARS – COVERT CARS Covert cars are used by the SAS for both surveillance and assault. In Northern Ireland the SAS have a large fleet of covert cars all fitted with radios that under normal circumstances will not be found. The radio is connected to inductors, which are hidden in the roof above the driver, or in the seat headrests. The operator hears any incoming messages through an earpiece. A small presser button hidden beneath the car carpet is used for transmissions; these can be either hand or foot operated. Other refinements to the cars are cut-off switches to deactivate the tail brake lights, tracing devices, and the installation of cameras both for external and internal filming.

QABOOS, SULTAN OF OMAN Came to power in 1970 when he deposed his father in a bloodless coup. The old Sultan Said bin Taimur had hung on to power as his feudal country fell to rebellion, refusing the recommendations and offers of assistance from his British advisors. Although not a military man, the old sultan had decided to send his only son, Qaboos, to the Royal Military Academy at Sandhurst, where he became commissioned into a British regiment. His stay in England was far from wasted. With skill and the encouragement from his friends he had observed the workings of various councils and committees and familiarized himself with the workings of a modern state. Returning home, Qaboos argued for change but his father's response was to restrict his son's movements.

The situation in Oman deteriorated until 23 July 1970, when Qaboos replaced his father, aided by the young Sheikh Baraik bin Hamood. During the coup, the old sultan shot himself in the foot and was hastily bundled into an aircraft and flown to England. Qaboos took control, but the situation was far from stable. Some of the older palace guards remained loyal to his father. To ensure Qaboos' safety, four SAS soldiers trained by the counter revolutionary warfare (CRW) wing were despatched to protect him. They remained with him for some months until at last Qaboos could arrange a new trustworthy guard from his own countrymen. Within weeks of the coup SAS soldiers, part of the British Army

Training Team (BATT) began arriving in Oman. They remained there in force for five years, during which time they fought one of the bloodiest wars in SAS history, which cost the lives of fifteen men.

QATTARA DEPRESSION A geographical feature in Egypt, the Qattara Depression is 240km (149 miles) long and 120km (74 miles) wide with a salt-pan floor and steep sides which afford only a few suitable crossing points for vehicles. In 1942 this became the southern end of what the British called the El Alamein line, the northern end of which was on the North African coast. David Stirling, commander of the SAS, wanted to mount a series of raids on several forward Axis airfields, including Sidi Haneish, Bagoush, Fuka, El Daba and Sidi Barrani, and needed a forward operating base from which his parties could attacks. This was to aid the proposed offensive of the Commander-in-Chief Middle East, General Sir Claude Auchinleck. Early in July an SAS party of jeeps and trucks bearing 100 men headed south from Cairo around the edge of the Qattara Depression before reaching open desert.

A fortnight later a party was sent back to Kabrit for fresh supplies but by now the Germans had cut off the original route so the group were forced to cross the Depression. The journey was extremely difficult; nevertheless, as expected of the SAS, every vehicle successfully returned and the supplies transported to the other members of the group, who had been left behind at the forward base, 100km (62 miles) north of Qara.

QRF (QUICK REACTION FORCE) A QRF is normally used as first-line back-up in support of SAS operations, and may consist of other SAS members or be formed from a nearby military unit or police force. The role of the QRF, which is widely used in Northern Ireland, is to react immediately in support of small isolated units such as a two-man OP (observation post) or a four-man patrol who have made contact with the enemy. In such instances the QRF will seal off the area and supply stops on the routes in and out of the area of contact.

R

R & R (REST AND RECUPERATION) R & R is granted after soldiers have been working in a hostile situation or moving continually through rugged terrain. The aim of R & R is to allow the soldier to relax from a stressful combat situation, or to allow his body time to repair after a long term in the jungle. There is little R & R for the SAS; the largest concession took place during the Oman War when two or three soldiers at a time would be allowed to leave the Jebel bases and visit the main headquarters. For two days they would be well-fed, have a few beers, and take a shower. R & R is normally only associated with long-term military campaigns which are fought far from home.

R SQUADRON R Squadron is a territorial unit directly attached to 22 SAS, officered and manned by a mixture of both ex-members of 22 SAS and volunteers from civilian life. These volunteers go through the same form of Selection as regular soldiers, many having already served in the regular British Army. Members of R Squadron are highly professional and take their soldiering seriously, often training with the regular squadrons on various exercises.

The aim of the squadron is to add extra manpower support for 22 SAS. The squadron was used operationally for the first time during the Gulf War when fifteen members volunteered. They fought alongside men of the regular squadrons, showing great courage.

When one of the fighting columns was compromised by the Iraqis, they were forced into a series of 'shoot and scoot' firefights, in which seven SAS soldiers, including a member of R Squadron, became separated. With their vehicles destroyed, this group, whose number included a soldier shot in the stomach, were forced to exfiltrate on foot. After two days of dodging the enemy, the R Squadron soldier managed to slip into the rear of the Iraqis and steal a truck with which the survivors made their way to the Saudi Arabian border. Days later they were re-equipped and sent back into Iraq.

RADFAN   A highly mountainous area in the northern district of the Republic of Yemen. When Britain became involved in Aden during the 1960s, the local tribespeople contributed to many attacks on British Forces, having been trained and armed by the Egyptians. The aim of the British was to mount an advance into the Radfan mountains to appease the tribes and to try and discourage them from mining the Dhala road which was under construction. Radforce was set up to re-establish British control over the area. It included A Squadron 22 SAS which had recently arrived in the region, and which had established a base at Thumier, 50km (31 miles) from the Yemeni border. In order to capture a rocky feature code-named 'Cap Badge' overlooking Danaba, the main dissident stronghold, Radforce took part in a joint mission. On 29/30 April 1964 the approach to Danaba was to be made by 45 Commando via the Wadi Boran. At the same time 3 Troop of A Squadron would take possession of 'Cap Badge' and secure it as a drop-zone for 3 Para.

Led by Captain Robin Edwards, the SAS mission set off with a nine-man patrol. But things did not go to plan and the men were compromised before they could even reach their objective. A fierce firefight followed with two fatalities: Edwards and another man, Trooper Warburton. Two other men were wounded but the remaining members of the patrol managed to reach safety. The severed heads of Edwards and Warburton were later displayed in public in Yemen.

From concealed OPs (observation posts), the SAS teams were involved in ever-increasing action behind enemy lines in the Radfan; over the next few years, they directed air and artillery strikes against the guerrilla forces. Life in such a hostile environment was very difficult, with temperatures in the day unbearably hot whilst at night they plummeted to well below freezing. Peter de la Billière, A Squadron's commander, made the comment that conditions on the Radfan were worse than those in Borneo and proved a man's worth to the squadron. In 1967 Britain withdrew troops from Aden, and with them went the SAS.

RADFORCE   In 1962 the Soviet Union backed unrest in the Republic of Yemen which led to the overthrow of the ruling imam. The deposed ruler escaped and raised an opposition army, which was secretly aided by the British and French Governments and contained several former SAS soldiers. This was based in the neighbouring Aden Protectorate.

Yemen claimed territory in lands held by the Federation of South Arabia, and supported two resistance groups in Aden: the National Liberation Front (NLF) and the Front for the Liberation of Occupied South Yemen (FLOSY). In 1963, in response to calls for assistance from Aden, Britain intervened with military aid. The inhabitants of the mountainous Radfan area, armed and trained by the Egyptians and Yemenis, were preparing to make war on British and Federal forces. The British assembled a task force to deal with the uprising. Known as 'Radforce', it consisted of Royal Marines, the Parachute Regiment, Royal Horse Artillery, East Anglian Regiment and Aden's Federal Regular Army. It also included an SAS detachment from A Squadron.

RADIO COMMUNICATIONS HARNESS The radio communications harness, such as the CT400, is designed to permit members of an anti-terrorist team full radio communication with one another. The system can be used with the majority of radio sets currently in service and comprises the following items:

1. Electronic Ear Defender/Radio Headset:
this unit protects the wearer's ears against damage from high levels of noise, caused by gunfire and explosions at close proximity in confined spaces. At the same time, even when worn under the overhood and underhood, it will permit the wearer to hear conversation and listen to team radio traffic. The headset is connected by a lead to the Central Switching Unit. All elements of the CT400 system connect to this unit which is normally worn on the front of the body armour and also contains a press-to-talk switch activating the body-worn microphone.

2. Wrist-Worn Remote Press-to-Talk Switch:
this switch is connected by a lead to the Central Switching Unit and is worn on the wrist or on the hand inside the glove, enabling the wearer to press it against his weapon and thus activate the body-worn microphone for transmission.

3. Body-Worn Microphone:
this is a noise-cancelling device normally worn on the front of the assault body armour in the area of the neck, secured by a spring-loaded clip. In the event that a Respirator CT-12 is worn for an assault, the wearer inserts this microphone into the adapter in the spare filter canister mount on the face-piece.

4. Radio Interface and Connection Cable:
the system includes an interface which connects the CT400 to the wearer's personal radio set. This in turn is connected via a cable to the Central Switching Unit.

5. Other items of CT400 equipment also available include the following:
Team Commander's Headset: similar to the headset mentioned above, but fitted with a boom microphone. TASC Sniper's Headset: a single-earphone headset designed for use by team snipers. Fully waterproof, it incorporates a flexible boom microphone and fully adjustable headband, and is connected by cable to the wearer's personal radio.

RAID ON BENGHAZI The scene of a disastrous raid in Libya by L Detachment SAS and elements of 1st Special Service Regiment. In early September 1942 the entire force of 231 men, 45 jeeps and some 40 3-ton trucks left Kufra Oasis for the port of Benghazi. Guided by patrols of the

Long Range Desert Group (LRDG) the party advanced in three columns, losing several vehicles to mines and breakdowns en route. The columns succeeded in crossing the Great Sands Sea and reached a rendezvous in the Jebel mountains on the night of 9/10 September. Led by Major David Stirling the force moved down from the mountains towards the coastal plain area and Benghazi to coincide with an RAF bombing raid on the town. Problems caused by navigational errors meant that the SAS were delayed and it was not until 03:00 hours that the main road leading into the town was reached.

Stirling and his men then came upon a roadblock and heavy enemy fire, and so employed the SAS jeeps' twin Vickers K guns bringing counter fire to bear on the enemy positions. During the firefight several vehicles burst into flames and Stirling was eventually forced to order his men to withdraw and to go into hiding at the foot of the escarpment below the mountains. As day began to dawn the Germans located the SAS and started an air attack, which destroyed over 20 jeeps and 25 trucks, even though they were well camouflaged. By nightfall the remaining members of L Detachment withdrew to the mountains and Kufra Oasis. Six soldiers lost their lives, eighteen were wounded and five never returned. The abject failure of this operation was ultimately blamed on a breach of security.

RAKYUT   Rakyut is a small coastal town in Western Dhofar situated 35km (22 miles) from the border with the People's Democratic Republic of Yemen which, during the Oman War, proclaimed itself the capital of the liberated area. In essence, the local population had long since deserted the town which was used by the rebels as a staging area to ship military stores inland and transport them up the Wadi Khais bin Uthman to the caves of Shirshitti.

In 1974 Major General Tim Creasey, commander of the Sultan's Armed Forces (SAF), ordered the Iranian Battle Group, which was on loan from the Shah, to assault and capture Rakyut. The Iranians suffered heavy losses and the advance failed; this led to a second attempt comprising the Jebel Regiment assisted by the Firqat SAS and Firqat.

RANGE ROVER   Range Rovers were first used by the SAS when the anti-terrorist team was formed in November 1972. The government sanctioned the purchase of six Range Rovers, and a team of SAS soldiers was sent to the factory to collect them directly from the assembly line. The characteristics of the Range Rover, which at the time was only a year old, were ideally suited to its intended role; the drop down tailgate allowed for easy loading and the vehicle itself could be used in an immediate action (IA). Twenty-five years on and the Range Rover is still used by the SAS, having been adapted as a main assault delivery vehicle. Platforms and ladders attached to the Range Rovers can carry the assault personnel directly to the required height of an aircraft door or building window.

RAPID ENTRY EQUIPMENT   The SAS have a wide range of equipment designed to enable rapid entry through doors, windows and walls of buildings. Included in this range are silent hydraulic cutters and spreaders as well as a range of rams, crowbars and axes. These feature the following:

1. Manual door ram:
hand-held ram designed to force inward-opening doors by their being swung against the lock area and imparting a weight load of approximately 3 tons. It is effective against all but reinforced steel doors. Weight 7kg (16lbs).

2. Door ripper:
lightweight tool designed to force outward-opening doors, with the blade being driven between door and frame in the area of the lock. A ratchet mechanism allows the blade to be worked behind the door to provide greater force.

3. Hydraulic door ram:
designed to force reinforced inward opening doors. Supplied with three sets of claws to suit all standard widths of door from 760mm (29in) to 920mm (36in). The main ram is positioned over the lock area while the secondary ram forces the jaws into the frame. Operation of a valve activates the main ram to force the door open with a maximum force of 5 tons. An 11 ton version is also available.

RATIONS   The SAS have a variety of ration packs designed for different types of operations. The bulk of any ration pack is made up in a similar way, comprising a breakfast meal, lunch snack and main evening meal. This is supplemented by a pack containing sundry items such as tea, coffee, milk, sugar, matches and toilet paper. Variety depends mainly on the way the food is processed, ie, wet, freeze-dried, tinned or sachets. The difference between freeze dried and tinned is weight, a deciding factor when, as a member of an SAS patrol, a man may be forced to carry up to 14 days' rations. However, freeze-dried foods require a large amount of water in which to reconstitute them, making them good for the jungle but unsatisfactory for desert operations.

SAS Operations Research has put a great deal of time and effort into the development of rations with the aim of reducing weight while increasing calories. The recent progress in freeze drying has done much to improve the reconstituted quality and flavour of specialist rations.

'RAVENS ROOST'   An SAS location on the Jebel Massive during the Oman War.

RECCE   Abbreviation for carrying out a reconnaisance. SAS recce patrols, such as the one led by Captain Wight during the Falklands War, sometimes produce information that requires immediate action. Wight's four-man patrol, having established an (OP) observation post, on Beaver Ridge overlooking Port Stanley, discovered a night dispersal area for Argentinian helicopters around Mount Kent. This vital information was quickly relayed back to the fleet, which resulted in two Harrier aircraft attacking the site, destroying three enemy helicopters.

RECONDO   In 1963 Major Lawrie Clark, previously commander of 1st SAS Company, Royal Australian Regiment, introduced a series of specialist training courses in small boat handling, amphibious raiding, climbing, abseiling, and cross-country driving. He also devised the Selection tours for SAS company officers to visit units with the express intention of interviewing prospective recruits to determine the aptitude and suitability of volunteers. However, Clark's biggest innovation was the development of the Recondo Course, which was based on his experiences during Ranger training in the United States. The course lasted nineteen excruciating days and consisted of three phases, which included deployment by parachute, amphibious raiding, river crossings and movement over different types of terrain. To subject the candidates to constant levels of physical and psychological pressure, fatigue, thirst and hunger, the majority of the training was conducted at night. In order to safeguard their position in the unit, all members of 1st SAS Company were required to undergo the Recondo Course.

RED ARMY FACTION – BAADER-MEINHOF GANG   The Red Army Faction (RAF), or Baader-Meinhof gang as they later became known, ravaged Germany during the late 1960s and the mid-1970s. The Baader-Meinhof gang never seemed to have any justifiable cause for their terrorist activities other than their dislike of capitalism. They were a group of very misguided young people who let their powers of communication and intellect operate on a basis of pure destructiveness – terrorism for terrorism's own sake. The Baader-Meinhof gang was named after its two main leaders, Andreas Baader and Ulrike Meinhof. They were both educated people and came from comfortable, middle-class backgrounds. They had educated, caring parents and they attended good schools.

During the seven years of the gang's most aggressive action, twenty people were to die as a result of Baader-Meinhof terrorist activities, with scores more being injured, before their leaders were captured and imprisoned. Then, on 5 September 1977, five weeks prior to the Mogadishu hijack, Hanns-Martin Schleyer, head of the West German business confederation, was kidnapped and held to ransom. The demand was for the release of those Baader-Meinhof terrorists currently being held in the Stammheim maximum-security prison. As the West German Government wrestled with the problem, an Arab terrorist group, believed to be from the PFLP, hijacked a Lufthansa aircraft full of holiday-makers as it left Palma, Majorca. In the end, with British political support, Germany sanctioned the use of special anti-hijack teams. Among these were the SAS and the GSG9.

REDDY, TROOPER 'RIP'   Reddy was an SAS soldier from G Squadron's Air Troop who was killed in a night-time free-fall parachute drop in Oman's northern province in December 1970. He was part of a recce team whose mission was to carry out a sweep of the Wadi Rawdah, for those Iraqi insurgents who had been missed during the raid on the Musandan Peninsula. The rest of the troop landed safely and managed to carry out their task until support troops arrived by helicopter next morning. Reddy's body was discovered after he failed to report in on his radio and a search of the area revealed his parachute. It would appear that his equipment was overweight and that he had hit the ground only seconds before his parachute fully deployed.

REEVES, SERGEANT MICHAEL   On 17 September 1967 Sergeant Reeves, an SAS free-fall instructor, was watching over students at a civilian club to which he belonged. (This non-military weekend activity was common for SAS free-fallers.) The students were at the stage where they were still required to be on an extended static-line, so that after a short delay the canopy would open. However, one of the students who was jumping left the aircraft but remained attached, dangling at the end of his static-line.

Reeves ordered the pilot to increase his height (they had previously been at 760m–2,500ft), and to circle back over the drop-zone. While the pilot complied, Reeves, who had on his own free-fall parachute, climbed out of the aircraft and down the line. When he reached the candidate he held the man in a vice-like grip with his legs before cutting through the static-line. As both men fell free, Reeves activated the candidate's reserve parachute. Satisfied that the candidate would land safely, he then fell away, distancing himself before operating his own canopy which deployed just seconds before he hit the ground. Sergeant Reeves was awarded the George Medal.

'REGENT', OPERATION   Led by Captain Blondeel between 27 December 1944 and 15 January 1945, the whole Belgian Independent Parachute Company (5 SAS) was given the task of supporting the British armoured units who were attempting to prevent a German breakthrough in the Ardennes during the Battle of the Bulge. The jeep-mounted party, who operated in the St Hubert and Burl areas, were used not for reconnaissance but purely as assault troops in the wooded areas.

REID, DON Don Reid had served with the SAS and, after his service, decided to stay in Hereford. He found new adventures working in war-torn Rwanda for the aid charity Assist UK. In 1995 he was driving a truck in an aid convoy on the borders of Rwanda and Zaire. Unfortunately, the area was full of rebels, many of whom shot first and asked questions later. When his convoy came under fire, Don Reid thought it better to disappear and fled into the African bush, whereupon he went directly into survival mode. His SAS training had never left him and, by his own account, he swam rivers, crawled through jungle and ate berries for food. All the time he kept sight of the Tonga mountains, where he knew there was a charity aid post. Eventually he found a track which led him to the Oxfam house, many kilometres from where he had abandoned the truck. The news of his safe arrival was transmitted to his own aid unit Assist UK. It was a minor incident, but one that gripped the imagination of the public. One man, in hostile territory, pitting his wits against nature – moreover, he had been SAS.

REMINGTON 870 PUMP ACTION, COMBAT SHOTGUN *Specification* Calibre: 12 gauge, 70mm (2.75in); Weight: 1.6kg (3.6lbs); Ammunition types include: buckshot, birdshot, solid slug, flechette, CS, plastic baton; Magazine capacity: 7-round, tubular.

The Remington is one of the most widely manufactured shotguns in the world and is the standard shotgun used by the US Marine Corps. Its pump action and the variety of ammunition available make it ideal for counter-terrorist and security work. Combined with the Hatton round, the SAS use it for removing doors.

RENNIE, CORPORAL F.M. Member of an SAS patrol who was killed near Gorazde, Bosnia, on 6 April 1994. He had been part of a seven-man team directing air strikes on Serb positions surrounding the town. He was killed while the team was retreating back through the Serb lines.

RENNIE, MAJOR FRANK – NEW ZEALAND SAS SQUADRON
In early 1955, Major Frank Rennie of the Royal New Zealand Infantry Regiment, assumed command of the newly formed New Zealand Special Air Service (NZSAS) squadron, which was raised for service in Malaya to reinforce 22 SAS Regiment. Major Rennie commanded the squadron throughout its two-year tour of operations, from December 1955 to December 1957, after which it returned to New Zealand and disbanded. Towards the end of 1959, however, the squadron was reformed. At that time Lieutenant-Colonel Rennie was Director of Infantry and has been credited for being largely responsible for the reformation of the NZSAS, which has since remained a part of the New Zealand Army's order of battle. He eventually retired from the Army in the rank of colonel.

RESISTANCE TO INTERROGATION Understandably, one of the most frightening experiences a soldier can face is being captured and interrogated by the enemy. Members of the SAS, by the very nature of their methods of operation, are particularly vulnerable to capture. As a result, all SAS soldiers are required to undergo JSIU (Joint Services Interrogation Unit) training.

Interrogation scenarios are made as realistic as possible, although torture during training is forbidden. However, controlled applications of fear-inducing methods are used, such as white sound and the wearing of pillowcases soaked with water to give the impression of slow drowning. The rule is simple: give your name, rank and number only. The period of interrogation and isolation training lasts for 24 hours, and during this time the prisoner is constantly hooded and kept in a cold damp room.

The Geneva Convention states that every member of the armed forces, should they be captured, will only divulge his personal number, rank, full name and date of birth. The enemy, on the other hand, is unlikely to stand by the Geneva Convention, and will use any one of hundreds of known interrogation techniques to 'persuade' a prisoner to volunteer information of intelligence value. In fact, they are more likely to use the convention in an attempt to trick prisoners into collaboration, which can only be successfully avoided if the prisoner is fully aware of his rights under the convention.

A prisoner's morale, under interrogation, will be affected by his physical and mental condition. He is likely to be weak from exhausting marches, injuries or shortage of food and sleep, and feeling very vulnerable by being kept apart from his fellow prisoners. The training aims to help a prisoner to resist interrogation, but the strength of morale he shows will depend on his personal honour, integrity and discipline. He must concentrate on keeping himself physically and mentally fit, have pride in his service and unit, and strength of faith.

All SAS prisoners-of-war recognize just how imperative preserving military security is, as careless information could easily result in the capture or, at worse, the death of others. Three members of the SAS were brutally tortured by the Iraqis when captured during the Gulf War, but as we know, gave no information whatsoever, thus proving the enormous value of interrogation training.

RESPIRATOR CT-12 Developed from the S10 respirator currently in service with the British armed forces, the CT-12 has been produced to meet the requirements of units tasked with anti-terrorist operations, and is fitted with the RC670 CS filter canister. It provides protection against CS, CR and other irritant gases and aerosols. The rubber face-piece has been fitted with a high-quality speech transmitter and eyepieces with removable coated polycarbonate tinted lenses which provide protection against flash and fragments.

The second canister mount permits the fitting of an adapter into which the CT400 radio communications harness body worn microphone can be inserted. Alternatively, it can be used with a second filter canister if so required, or with a small compressed air bottle giving a short duration air supply in conditions of oxygen depletion. A voice projection unit can also be fitted to the CT-12.

RHODESIA – 'BIG BANG', OPERATION   Operation 'Big Bang' took place in Rhodesia during the period August to October 1974. By that time, the ZIPRA terrorist organization had switched tactics: instead of mounting large-scale incursions by groups of up to 100 men, which had sustained heavy casualties on each occasion, it was forming a network of cells and establishing concealed arms caches. The Rhodesian SAS C Squadron was at that time carrying out reconnaissance tasks in southwest Zambia, pinpointing ZIPRA camps. It was during one such task in August that a patrol commanded by Lieutenant Chris Schollenberg spotted a military-type vehicle and, on investigating further, discovered a terrorist camp. A further reconnaissance of the camp three weeks later revealed that the terrorists were constructing a large underground cache for weapons. Aerial surveillance on the camp and cache was maintained during the next few weeks until it was reported that the cache had been closed and concealed. At that point, it was decided to mount an operation to attack the camp and destroy the cache.

At the beginning of October, a force of approximately 40 all ranks of C Squadron moved to the southern side of the Zambesi River and established a forward tactical base which was secured by a small group of eight men. On the night of 3 October, the assault force under Captain Garth Barrett crossed the Zambesi in Zodiac inflatables and headed north. Unknown to them, however, the forward base was attacked at 02:00 hours by two ZIPRA terrorists who wounded three men; the assault force was not informed and so continued on its way. Twenty-four hours later, Captain Barrett and his men arrived at a rendezvous with Lieutenant Schollenberg who had infiltrated the area some days earlier. Schollenberg led the two assault teams to their forming-up points while three stop-groups made off towards their allocated positions.

At dawn on 5 October, Schollenberg initiated the assault and heavy fire was brought to bear on the terrorists who fled without retaliating. Nine of them died in the assault. After clearing the camp, the RhSAS turned their attention to the arms cache. On lowering themselves through a trap door, the demolitions group found a concrete-lined chamber containing a very large quantity of weapons which included AK-47 assault rifles and SKS carbines, US M-1 Garand rifles, Tokarev pistols, light machine guns, 12.7mm heavy machine guns, RPG-7 rocket-propelled grenades, 75mm recoilless rifles, ammunition, anti-tank and anti-personnel mines and explosives. After a quantity of weapons, ammunition and mines had been taken, demolition charges were laid in the cache while the rest of the force searched the camp, finding a large quantity of food as well as documents and maps. At the same time, the road leading to the camp was mined.

Having completed their task, the Rhodesians withdrew and once 500m (545yds) from the camp initiated the demolitions charges which totally destroyed the camp and cache. Making its way heavily laden with captured weapons, the force reached the Zambesi and crossed without incident. Shortly afterwards, having met up with the forward base group, it was extracted and returned to the RhSAS base at Kabrit Barracks.

It was subsequently discovered that the camp was ZIPRA's main logistics base for its operations in the Matabeleland Tribal Trust Lands. The attack was a major setback for the terrorists who did not recover from it for over six months.

RHODESIAN – (COMOPS) COMBINED OPERATIONS Adopted as a concept in 1977, Combined Operations was the nerve centre for all operations conducted by the Rhodesian armed forces during the period of unilateral independence. With its headquarters located in the heart of the Rhodesian capital of Salisbury, it co-ordinated, in close liaison with the Central Intelligence Organization (CIO), all aspects of military and police operations against the terrorist organizations of ZIPRA and ZANLA.

The Commander Combined Operations was Lieutenant-General Peter Walls, the original commander of C (Rhodesian) Squadron SAS, whose experiences in Malaya with 22 SAS Regiment were to colour much of his thinking and philosophy when conducting counter-insurgency operations in Rhodesia twenty years later.

RHODESIAN SAS – C SQUADRON AND 1ST SAS REGIMENT In November 1950 the Southern Rhodesia Far East Volunteer Unit was raised for service alongside British troops on operations against Communist Terrorists (CTs) in Malaya. Shortly afterwards, it was agreed that the unit should form part of the newly formed Malayan Scouts (SAS) commanded by Lieutenant-Colonel J.M. 'Mad Mike' Calvert. In March 1951 the unit arrived in Malaya and was designated C (Rhodesia) Squadron Malayan Scouts (SAS). A and B Squadrons were already in existence, A Squadron having been formed from volunteers from units in Malaya and B Squadron from volunteers from 21 SAS Regiment (Artists) (TA). During 1952, the Malayan Scouts were officially redesignated 22 SAS Regiment (22 SAS). Under the command of Major Peter Walls, C Squadron served in Malaya until December 1952 when it returned to Rhodesia where it was disbanded shortly afterwards.

In early 1961 C Squadron Rhodesian SAS was formed and based in Ndola, Northern Rhodesia (later Zambia), under the command of Major Courtenay Welch, as part of the Federal Army of the Central African Federation which linked Southern and Northern Rhodesia with Nyasaland. In 1963, however, the federation broke up and, with the majority of its members having decided to leave, a much reduced C Squadron moved to Southern Rhodesia, under the command of Major Dudley Coventry who had previously commanded the Independent Parachute Squadron during its attachment to 22 SAS during the Malayan Emergency.

During the subsequent war in Rhodesia from 1966 to 1980 C Squadron, commanded for much of that time by Major Brian Robinson, played a major role in mounting cross-border operations in Zambia and Mozambique, inflicting heavy losses on ZIPRA and ZANLA forces. In June 1978, having expanded to three squadrons and by then commanded by Lieutenant-Colonel Garth Barrett, the unit was redesignated 1st SAS Regiment. Two years later, however, in the aftermath of the cease-fire and the election of Robert Mugabe's ZANU party as the government of the newly created state of Zimbabwe, the Rhodesian 1st SAS Regiment was disbanded and ceased to exist.

RICHARDS, LANCE-CORPORAL MARK   A Welsh farmer who passed Selection in December 1989. He served in the Gulf War where his patrol were discovered deep inside Iraqi territory. After a fierce firefight he, along with other survivors, managed to reach the safety of the Saudi Arabian border. He was then re-inserted into Iraq for a second time. He was accidentally killed on 23 June 1992 while taking part in a live-firing jungle exercise in Belize, Central America.

RIGID RAIDER   *Specification* Length: 5.82m (6yds); Beam: 2.2m (2.3yds); Draught: 450cm (1.6ft); Weight: 360kg (800lbs); Speed: 37 knots with 140hp engine fitted.

The SAS have used the Rigid Raider assault craft on numerous operations since the 1970s, many in conjunction with the SBS. It was chosen to replace the inflatable Gemini craft and is made from glass reinforced plastic (GRP) with a steeply raked flat bow allowing the boat to be driven up shallow beaches. It also allowed faster disembarkation for the men on board. Being fitted with four lifting-points the craft can be transported by helicopter, and is powered by one or two 140 hp Johnson outboard motors with a top speed of 37 knots. It is capable of carrying nine fully-equipped men with a coxswain.

The Rigid Raider claimed to be virtually unsinkable, although one of the craft actually achieved this feat at the end of the Falklands War when 1st Raiding Squadron planned a diversionary raid on Port Stanley. All four Raiders were hit, yet only one sank, and even then not until the others had managed to pull clear of the danger.

The SAS have recently taken delivery of 16 new RTK Rigid Raiders which were specially adapted for them and which are constructed of Kevlar, giving it a hull weight of less than 300kg (135lbs). This means that a four-man patrol can carry the craft, even when it is fitted with twin 40hp motors.

RILEY, SERGEANT-MAJOR PATRICK   An original member of L Detachment who became the first sergeant-major of the SAS.

RINGMAIN   The main circuit of a demolitions set-up, which links all the charges. Most targets that require explosives need to be cut in many different locations at the same time, and in order to achieve this, a ring of detonating cord is passed from the initiator around every charge and back to the initiator. On detonation the shock waves travel both ways, and if one end should fail the other will detonate the charges.

RIP AMMUNITION   This is special 12-gauge long-range ammunition used by the SAS in their anti-terrorist role. RIP ammunition is designed to be fired from a Magnum shotgun with a 3-inch chamber and unchoked barrel. The round comprises a semi-solid slug of micronised CS gas that remains solid until penetration of a door or window is achieved, after which it breaks up and disperses into a cloud of airborne irritant which will incapacitate personnel inside. The slug will penetrate double-glazed windows, vehicle windows or bodywork at 30m (32yds) and vehicle tyres at 15m (16yds). During training the SAS use practice ammunition, which displays the same penetration capabilities as the live version but without the irritant.

RIVER CROSSING TECHNIQUES   River crossings have claimed the lives of several SAS soldiers, and for this reason river crossing is much practised. In some operational theatres, especially the jungle, it is not possible to go around or ford a major river and, in addition, rivers are normally a place of enemy ambush.

The original method was to choose the widest, slowest point, avoiding bends as they increase the current speed, and pass each man across on a secured rope or line between both banks. The first man across would have to be the strongest swimmer as he would need to secure the line on the opposite bank.

Another technique, and one more commonly used, is to waterproof all the bergens, clipping them together to form a flotation aid. This allows for all four members of the patrol to swim safely across together, and is particularly good if the patrol includes a weak swimmer, or an injured man. Although this is a safer method of river crossing, it does mean that the patrol is vulnerable should the enemy turn up at that precise moment.

ROBERTS, SERGEANT F.J. – AUSTRALIAN SAS REGIMENT

(SASR) Sergeant Fred Roberts was the commander of a twelve-man 3 Squadron patrol which was inserted on 30 October 1969 into an area 4km (2.5 miles) northwest of Nui May Tao. His task was to ambush an enemy supply route being used by Vietcong (VC) 84th Rear Services Group. The ambush was in position by the morning of the following day and at 09:40 hours a group of four VC, including two women, entered the killing area. Three were killed but the fourth, who was wounded, escaped leaving a blood trail. Their packs were found to contain food which the patrol proceeded to contaminate with a CS gas grenade before withdrawing.

By 07:00 hours on the following day the patrol was in another ambush position some 500m (545yds) away from their previous location. At 07:50 another group of four VC approached and was ambushed, all the enemy being killed in the process. Having taken the VC's weapons and packs the patrol withdrew as they heard the sounds of other enemy approaching. Sergeant Roberts requested extraction and this was carried out at 11:20 hours with the support of helicopter gunships which laid down suppressive fire on the area.

ROBINSON, MAJOR BRIAN – C SQUADRON RHODESIAN

SAS Major Brian Robinson commanded C Squadron Rhodesian SAS for the major part of the period 1966-80 that it was involved in operations against ZIPRA and ZANLA terrorists. Having served as a troop commander in the squadron, taking part in a number of the first cross-border operations, he subsequently commanded the Tracking Wing of the School of Infantry before assuming command of C Squadron in December 1972. Such were Robinson's standards that he was later credited with having turned the unit into possibly the most effective in all of southern Africa. During his tenure of command the squadron mounted a large number of cross-border operations, some of which he commanded personally from the air in a helicopter. In 1978 Major Robinson handed over C Squadron to Major Garth Barrett, subsequently being promoted to lieutenant-colonel on posting to the Combined Operations Planning Team.

ROBINSON, SERGEANT J.M. – AUSTRALIAN SAS REGI-

MENT (SASR) On 11 May 1969 Sergeant John Robinson's patrol of 3 Squadron SASR was inserted northeast of the Courtenay Rubber Plantation with the task of pinpointing Vietcong (VC) camps in the area of the border of Phuoc Tuy and Long Khanh Provinces. On the morning of 15 May it encountered a track which showed signs of recent use and later in the day Sergeant Robinson and his lead scout, Private Keith Beard, carried out a close reconnaissance of a VC camp located nearby. As they did so, they encountered five VC whom they engaged at close range, killing two. Breaking contact, Robinson and Beard rejoined the rest of the patrol which withdrew and established an LUP (lying-up position) as dusk fell.

The following morning, the patrol returned to the area of the VC camp and had just crossed the track when 30 or more enemy were seen approaching; one group was equipped with light machine guns. Unfortunately the patrol was spotted shortly afterwards and almost immediately a firefight ensued, as it was attacked by two groups of VC. Withdrawing some 100m (109yds), the patrol found itself in an enemy bunker complex but fortunately succeeded in avoiding the VC force that was coming from the direction of the original contact.

Withdrawing another 300m (327yds), the patrol established an LUP while Private Dodd established radio communications with 3 Squadron's base and requested extraction. Shortly afterwards, however, nine VC approached and Sergeant Robinson opened fire, killing one. The patrol moved out under heavy fire, Sergeant Robinson covering his men as they did so. Making its way westwards, they were forced to cross a large area of open ground, eventually taking cover in a large bomb crater. Meanwhile they could hear the VC searching for them in the jungle about 70m (76yds) away. At 13:00 hours the helicopters arrived and, after heavy suppressive fire had been laid down by the escorting gunships, a hot extraction was carried out successfully.

ROCKET LAUNCHER 3.5, RECOILLESS *Specification* Launcher length: 1,549mm (5ft); Launcher weight: 2.5kg (5.5lbs); Rocket weight: 1.8kg (4.04lbs); Effective range: 150m (163yds); Warhead: HEAT (high explosive, anti-tank).

A relic of World War II, the 3.5 Rocket launcher had been designed by the Americans for destroying tanks. The launcher is basically an aluminium tube which will unclip into two equal halves during transit. A rocket is fed into the rear of the tube, and two protruding wires are fitted to terminals on the rear outer casing. Pressing the trigger would electrically fire the rocket, either by magneto or on later models by 2 AA type batteries. The SAS used the launcher during the Aden campaign, but it was later replaced by the Carl Gustav recoilless gun, and LAW 66mm.

RODERICK, SECOND-LIEUTENANT TREVOR – AUSTRA-LIAN SAS REGIMENT (SASR) On 11 July 1965, during the Borneo Confrontation campaign, a fourteen-man patrol of 1 Squadron SASR under Roderick was inserted into an LZ (landing zone) on Sabah's border with Indonesian Kalimantan.

Its task, under the auspices of Operation 'Claret', was to ambush part of the Salilir River which was being used by Indonesian forces for the movement of troops and re-supply. En route to his ambush position, Roderick received orders to detach four men who were to carry out surveillance of enemy forces at the nearby village of Labang. Having reached the river after a march of 4,000m (2.5 miles), the remainder of the patrol took up its ambush positions. On 19 July a boat carrying a large quantity of rice and five men, one an Indonesian soldier, was observed travelling upstream. Later in the day it returned downstream and the occupants' behaviour was such that Roderick suspected that the patrol might have been spotted.

On the following day the patrol withdrew and moved to another ambush position nearer Labang, which was under observation by Sergeant Weir and his three men, who reported seeing seven Indonesian troops. The next morning the patrol observed three boats travelling upstream, each with an Indonesian soldier aboard. At 12:25 hours another boat approached the ambush killing area and, although the occupants were in civilian clothes, weapons and equipment were seen. Roderick initiated the ambush and four Indonesians were hit in the boat, and the remaining two were killed in the water as they swam towards the opposite bank.

The patrol withdrew and headed for the border. Shortly afterwards an enemy force attacked the area of the previous day's ambush site, confirming Roderick's suspicions that the patrol had been spotted earlier. An hour and a half later, the patrol heard firing from the area which they had just vacated. As Roderick and his men made for the border there were signs that the enemy were attempting to track them and at 20:00 hours that night Indonesian mortars brought down fire to the north of the patrol's LUP (lying-up position). Three days later, on 24 July, the patrol reached the border and was extracted on the following day.

ROMMEL, GENERAL ERWIN – NORTH AFRICA A distinguished officer of the German Army who, on 6 February 1941, was summoned by Hitler to lead a rescue force into North Africa in order to save the Italians. Although outranked by several Italian generals, Rommel assumed command of the Axis forces and, disregarding orders, began an offensive on 2 April. To outwit the British he used dummy tanks built on Volkswagon chassis, in reality attacking with only 50 tanks. His plan worked and Benghazi fell on 3 April. After only nine days most of the earlier British advances had been reversed and many units were evacuating to Egypt, leaving only the garrison at Tobruk defended.

Rommel pressed forward his attacks hoping to capture Tobruk, but the British continued to hold. When Rommel asked the German High Command for four more tank divisions with which he could push his way into Egypt they refused. Churchill, however, needed a victory in North Africa and despatched a convoy of much-needed supplies including 328 tanks (there had been 400 but 62 were lost, as to save time the convoy was forced to run the gauntlet, sailing through the

Mediterranean). These supplies gave the British commander, General Wavell, the means to stop Rommel's advance which he did on 14 June, but Rommel had anticipated the move and forced the British into a bottleneck at Halfaya and Hafid where the German anti-tank guns destroyed more than half the British armour. Wavell was replaced by General Sir Claude Auchinleck who, after four months of preparation, launched Operation 'Crusader' and, although the Axis forces blunted the offensive several times, by 7 December Rommel was forced to retreat.

Scarcely had Rommel retreated when he received new men and supplies, including some 50 tanks. By 5 January 1942 he was moving eastwards once again. By 25 January he had captured Benghazi, which held a significant haul of ammunition and weapons left behind by the retreating British. Once more he pressed on, overrunning the Gazala line some 64.3km (40 miles) west of Tobruk before finally taking the city on 21 June, achieving in two weeks what he had been trying to do for a year. As the British fell back into Egypt, Rommel gave chase and by 30 June he was at El Alamein, just 160km (100 miles) from Alexandria.

Lieutenant-General Montgomery then became commander of the British Eighth Army and he decided to defend Egypt and the Suez Canal at El Alamein. Rommel attacked again and again and made several small gains but in the end, low on fuel and short of ammunition and supplies, he was forced to retreat. Montgomery did not pursue the Germans but waited until his forces had built up sufficient strength and all necessary supplies were in place; only then did he launch Operation 'Lightfoot'. This began on 23 October 1942 and, with vast numerical superiority in both men and machines, began to push Rommel out of North Africa. The battles raged with the Germans and Italians trying hard to make a defensive stand against the onslaught, but to little avail, and it was not until they had passed through the Agheila bottleneck that they finally dug in. They held for two weeks before the British finally broke through. By January 1943 Rommel and his Afrika Korps were defeated.

It was against this background that the SAS were formed and operated, attacking Rommel's rear, and destroying his air force. The SAS made two abortive and costly attempts to assassinate Rommel who, for his part, refused to carry out Hitler's Commando Order, but instead treated captives as prisoners-of-war.

ROSE, LIEUTENANT-COLONEL MIKE Rose passed SAS Selection in 1967 and commanded G Squadron 24 Troop (Free-Fall). His tour as a troop commander was not notably eventful; however, he was much liked and respected by his men. He returned to the regiment in 1975 and served as squadron commander during the threatening conflict between Guatemala and Belize. He returned for a third time to command 22 SAS, leading the regiment during the Falklands War.

When he first heard of the invasion of the islands by the Argentinians, he persuaded Brigadier Julian Thompson, commander of 3 Commando Brigade, to allow the SAS a role in the Landing Task Force Group. It was his direct intervention that led to the SAS taking such an active part in the liberation of the islands. In the final stages of the war, Rose, along with a Spanish-speaking interpreter, used psychological warfare methods to persuade the Argentinians of the hopelessness of their cause. Consequently, on 14 June, Rose flew into Port Stanley by helicopter to commence talks with them. It was after these talks that Rose, together with Brigadier Peter de la Billière, accepted the Argentinian surrender which ended the war. As a mark of the man there is very strong rumour that Rose offered the Argentinian commander, Major-General Mario Menendez, a Harrier fire-power demonstration as the Argentinian troops massed around Stanley. The same rumour also claims he walked out of the building taking with him a prize statue of a horse which had reputedly been given to Menendez by a grateful government for his initial capture of the Falklands.

Rose went on to serve as brigade commander in Northern Ireland, Director of Infantry at Warminster and Director Special Forces, but his most outstanding achievement was his appointment as Commander UN Forces in Bosnia. Rose officially took over from the Belgian, Lieutenant-General Francis Briquemont, on 24 January 1994, two days after a mortar shell had killed six children in Sarajevo. Not a man to waste time, Rose quickly sought authorization for the SAS to be deployed in Bosnia. Rose planned to use them as his eyes and ears, in a similar fashion to that operated by the Phantoms during World War II. Their contribution paid immediate dividends, especially around Gorazde, where they were engaged in covert reconnaissance of Serb positions, and providing detailed assessments of the capabilities of the Serb and Muslim forces. The consequent air strikes aimed against the Serbs brought swift retaliation and shelling of the beleaguered town, and some SAS men became trapped in a bunker after being abandoned by Muslim soldiers. Rose tried everything to stop the Serb shelling, which by now was concentrated on the bunker. Yasushi Akashi, the UN special envoy, would not sanction air support, but a local cease-fire was arranged while the wounded SAS men were evacuated. One patrol member, Corporal Rennie, had been hit in the head and later died of his wounds. The other SAS soldiers, although wounded, managed to escape.

ROYAL ARMY SERVICE CORPS (RASC) 55 COMPANY   RASC

55 Company were an air re-supply unit which in conjunction with the RAF dropped vital stores to the SAS patrols operating deep in the jungle during the Malayan Emergency. The unit lost over 100 men during the campaign due to air crashes but never failed to deliver the supplies on time.

ROYAL FAMILY Protection of the Royal Family is given over to specialist police of the Royal Protection Group, yet the SAS maintain a role whereby they may be called upon to deal with a situation outside police control. In keeping with the SAS's doctrine, it is wise to let any VIP know what could be in store for them should they be kidnapped and taken hostage one day. Thus most VIPs are invited to Hereford where they will participate in hostage rescue training, leaving them with a better understanding of what can be achieved.

ROYAL PROTECTION GROUP Following the attempt to kidnap Princess Anne, the SAS became involved with the Royal Protection Group. On the night of 20 March 1974 Princess Anne and Captain Mark Phillips were driving down the Mall, accompanied by Inspector Jim Beaton. The officer was armed on this occasion, having been trained to use a 9mm Walther PPK pistol.

A white Ford Escort deliberately cut in front of the royal couple's Rolls, forcing it to stop. The driver, Ian Ball, got out and drew a gun. Beaton immediately got out and walked around the back, taking up position by the rear off-side door. No sooner had he stopped when a shot rang out, hitting him in the chest. Beaton staggered backwards, but instinctively drew his pistol and fired one shot before the weapon jammed.

After he had shot Beaton, Ball tried to open the driver's-side rear door where the princess sat. Both the princess and Captain Phillips held on to the handle, and a tug-of-war began. Ball finally managed to get hold of Princess Anne's arm and tried to pull her from the vehicle: she resisted by hanging on to her husband. When, at last the sleeve of her dress came away in Ball's hand, they managed to get the door closed once more.

Beaton then made another attempt to confront Ball, but Ball seized the advantage and demanded that the officer put down his weapon – Beaton did so. Having heard the shots, a journalist, John McConnell, arrived on the scene and challenged Ball, who produced a .22 pistol and shot McConnell in the chest. The journalist staggered away and Ball reverted to his kidnap attempt on the princess. He repeatedly threatened Beaton, pointing the pistol through the window, directly at his head. Realizing that Ball was about to shoot, Beaton put his hand up to the window in a vain attempt to protect himself. Ball shot him in the hand.

PC Michael Hills was on duty at nearby St James's Palace and also responded to the shootings. He radioed for assistance to Cannon Row police station, before confronting Ball, only to be shot in the stomach. The chauffeur of the Rolls opened his door, but Ball also shot him in the chest before he had the opportunity to take any further action. By now several more 'have-a-go merchants' had descended on the gunman. One man, Ronald Russell, who had been passing in a taxi, saw the affray and tackled Ball, successfully managing to punch him. Although Ball fired a shot at Russell, he missed and the two men were still fighting when the police arrived. Ball made a bid for freedom but was tackled by a policeman and captured.

Ten months later Commander Trestrail, Head of the Royal Protection group, visited the SAS in Hereford. This time he was not given the normal VIP demonstration, but instead he was party to a VIP three-day exercise. It soon became blatantly clear to Trestrail that the existing standards of training fell far short of what could and should be achieved. After this, the Royal Protection Group came to Hereford for training.

ROYAL ULSTER CONSTABULARY (RUC) The SAS have had a long-standing relationship with the RUC, principally with its Special Branch (SB). Although strained during the early years, the relationship between the SAS and SB grew to produce some results in the Northern Ireland conflict. The introduction of SAS Liaison Officers (LO) in the 1970s, to work directly alongside SB at the various TCG (tactical control group) headquarters allowed the regiment to control its manpower requirement.

RPG-7 *Specification* Warhead diameter: 85mm (3.3in); Length of launcher: 950mm (37in); Weight: 4kg (8.8lbs); Velocity: 300m (327yds) pe second; Effective range: 300m (327yds).

The Reaktivniy Protivotankoviy Granatomet-7 is a rocket-propelled grenade launcher that has become one of the most popular and widely used anti-armour weapons in the world. In use with former Soviet and Warsaw Pact armies, it is also in wide distribution with many Third World armies and in many of the world's hot spots.

It was introduced into service in 1962 with Soviet forces and saw action with the Egyptians in 1967 during fighting in Sinai. North Vietnamese forces used it during the street fighting in Hue in the Tet Offensive of 1968. Both sides in the Iran-Iraq and Afghan wars used RPG-7s. The RPG-7 has also proved a favourite of terrorist groups. In September 1981 German terrorists from the Red Army Faction fired an RPG at the armoured staff car which was carrying General Kroesen, Commander of US Forces in Germany. The SAS encountered the RPG-7 in the Oman War when it was widely used against them by the Adoo. An Iraqi RPG was responsible for one of the few British casualties in the Gulf War in 1991. Today the RPG-7 is being replaced by the RPG-16.

RPKAD Resemen Para Kommando Angaton Darat were an Indonesian parachute commando regiment and an elite unit. The RPKAD posed a major problem for the SAS during the Borneo campaign.

RTU Abbreviation for 'returned to unit'. If a soldier either fails Selection or is later expelled from the regiment for misbehaviour or a failure of standards, he is returned to his original unit.

RUFFIN, SERGEANT MICHAEL – AUSTRALIAN SAS REGIMENT (SASR)
Sergeant Mick Ruffin was the commander of a five-man patrol of 2 Squadron SASR which was deployed on Operation 'Silk Cord' in AO Dookie, situated southeast of Xuyen Moc in Phuoc Tuy Province, on 30 December 1968. On the third day, the patrol came across a large but unoccupied enemy bunker complex and shortly afterwards encountered a group of six Vietcong (VC) who responded very aggressively, despite losing four of their number. As the Australian patrol withdrew, it found itself moving through yet another very large unoccupied enemy base.

Sergeant Ruffin requested extraction but was refused, as all available helicopters were extracting other patrols in contact with the enemy. Unfortunately, he misheard the response and, expecting extraction, led his men to an LZ (landing zone) near to which they took up a defensive position. Fifteen minutes later, movement was observed in a nearby treeline and shortly afterwards three VC were engaged and killed at close range by the lead scout, Sergeant Fred Barclay. Three more VC opened fire but withdrew after grenades were thrown at them. Sergeant Ruffin, meanwhile, engaged the treeline with the 40mm grenade launcher on his M16 rifle. While the patrol's signaller, Private Dennis Mitchell, was trying unsuccessfully to raise contact with the squadron base, a large force of 50 VC appeared just over 100m (110yds) away and the patrol readjusted its positions to meet this new threat. At the same time, enemy mortars opened fire but fortunately proved somewhat inaccurate.

The patrol succeeded in keeping the enemy at bay despite the volume of enemy fire growing heavier. Suddenly, the enemy launched their assault under heavy covering fire from a medium machine gun and a barrage of RPG-7 grenades with groups of VC moving to both flanks. Realizing that they were about to be encircled, the patrol withdrew under extremely heavy fire and broke contact, aided by the fact that dusk was falling. The following morning Sergeant Mick Ruffin and his men were located and extracted by helicopter.

RULES OF ENGAGEMENT
The rules of engagement are there to ensure that no serviceman or woman accidentally starts a conflict. They are clear guidelines, which govern the response to any hostile action by an enemy, and what action should be taken. The purpose is to protect human life and eliminate mistakes. Due to the nature of SAS work it is sometimes difficult to estimate the exact moment when the rules of engagement should be acted upon; the shortest delay can cost lives. The rules for engagement must therefore be simple and precise.

RULES OF ENGAGEMENT (RESTRICTIVE)
Restrictive rules of engagement apply to situations such as those in Northern Ireland. They

are provided to protect the innocent in heavily populated civilian areas. These rules require a set challenge to be made before the soldier is allowed to open fire. The rules do allow for free fire in immediate life-threatening situations.

RULES OF ENGAGEMENT (WARTIME) From what is portrayed in the media, many people conclude that the SAS have a licence to kill, yet they would be very wrong. The SAS, like all other United Kingdom nationals, are answerable to the law. It is within the commander's maximum discretion that, within given geographical boundaries, SAS soldiers may fire whenever they are threatened, without warning. This applied to the SAS in several theatres of conflict, especially when they were deep behind enemy lines as they were during the Gulf War. At all other times, the rules of engagement are clearly defined.

'RUPERT' A rather deprecating term used to describe an officer, especially if he is not well regarded.

RV Abbreviation for rendezvous point, a position designated on the map or pointed out on the ground at which dispersed soldiers will meet at an arranged time. RVs are vital, especially after a contact with the enemy and where the patrol has been forced to split.

RYAN, CHRIS Pseudonym of the SAS author who wrote *The One That Got Away*, the true story of the only member of the ill-fated 'Bravo Two Zero' patrol who managed to escape to freedom during the Gulf War.

S

SA80 ASSAULT RIFLE *Specification* Calibre: 5.56mm × 45 NATO standard; Weight: 1.7kg (3.8lbs); Muzzle velocity: 940m (1,024yds) per second; Magazine capacity: 30-round, box.

The current assault rifle in service with the British Army. Made by Enfield/Royal Ordnance, it is of a 'bullpup' design. Short, accurate and well designed for urban combat, it is also equipped with a × 4 optical sight. However, it falls down on reliability, with magazines falling out unexpectedly as well as having a number of other faults. For this reason the SAS tend not to use the weapon.

S-PHONE The S-phone was a radio telephone used by the SAS during World War II particularly in northwest Europe. By comparison with earlier radios it was a lightweight, secure and compact communications system ideal for SAS teams operating behind German lines. The S-phone incorporated a homing beacon that could be detected about 20km (12.5 miles) away. This was imperative for the men on the ground who were able to link up with the aircraft dropping supplies or reinforcements.

1 SAS The first SAS operation took place on the night of the 17/18 November 1941, which is widely accepted as the official date for the formation of 1 SAS. It was intended that the operation should destroy aircraft on the German airfields at Tmimi and Gazala prior to General Auchinleck's planned offensive. Entry was by parachute, dropping 19km (12 miles) from the target, but due to high winds the SAS operation turned into a disaster, with men and equipment scattered across the desert.

2 SAS 2 SAS was formed in May 1943 under the command of Lieutenant-Colonel William Stirling, David Stirling's brother. Initially it was part of 62 Commando, which together with the SRS (Special Raiding Squadron), raided the several Greek islands under command of the 1st Airborne Division. It was later to become part of the SAS Brigade.

3 AND 4 SAS REGIMENTS In reality these French units were 2ème and 3ème Régiment de Chasseurs Parachutistes, who became 3 and 4

SAS Regiments, part of the SAS Brigade which operated from July 1944 until the end of the war. The 3 and 4 SAS Regiments were absorbed into the French Army in July 1945.

5 SAS 5 SAS began its existence as the Belgian Independent Parachute Company which was later increased to regiment size. It fought mainly with the French SAS regiments and was absorbed into the Belgian Army in July 1945.

11 SAS 11 SAS Battalion was the unit name used by a commando unit during a raid in October 1941 to assassinate General Rommel. The raid failed and 11 SAS became the 1st Parachute Battalion in September 1941.

21 SPECIAL AIR SERVICE REGIMENT (ARTISTS) (VOLUNTEERS)
Following the disbandment of the wartime units in 1945, the Special Air Service was reformed in the following year as a unit of the Territorial Army. Amalgamated with the Artists Rifles, it was designated the 21 SAS Regiment (Artists) (TA). The TA suffix was later changed to V, denoting Volunteers. The number 21 is derived from the wartime 1 and 2 SAS Regiments, but in view of the fact that at the time there was already a 12 Battalion, The Parachute Regiment (TA), the numbers were reversed to 21.

In 1950 the regiment formed M Squadron for operations in Korea, composed of volunteers with wartime experience, under Major Tony Greville-Bell. The war, though, ended before it was deployed. Instead, the squadron was sent to Malaya where it became B Squadron Malayan Scouts (SAS) which in 1952 was redesignated 22 SAS Regiment (22 SAS). Since then 21 SAS has remained a part of the British Army's order of battle. The regiment is based in the south of England with its headquarters, headquarters' squadron, training wing and two of its four Sabre Squadrons located in London; the other two Sabre Squadrons are based in locations in the south of England. The regiment recruits from civilian volunteers, some of whom have had previous military experience.

22 SAS The present SAS regular regiment is based in Hereford. The birth of the modern-day 22 SAS came about because of the Communist troubles in Malaya. In the early 1950s a British officer, Mike Calvert, who was serving in Hong Kong at the time, was instructed to appraise the Communist influence in Malaya. Calvert, a tough soldier who had commanded an SAS brigade during World War II, was the innovator of the Malayan Scouts (SAS). His basic doctrine influenced many of the SAS practices that still exist to this day, the most famous being a four-man patrol and individual SAS skills. When the Malayan Scouts became formally known as 22 SAS, Calvert instructed Major John Woodhouse to return to England and set up a structured Selection course, the basis of which still exists today.

The regiment consists of four Sabre Squadrons, A, B, D and G with a reserve R Squadron (the latter has now been renamed L Detachment). In addition to these, the unit also includes Training Squadron, 264 Signals Squadron and HQ Squadron. There are a number of smaller units such as Operations Research, Demolitions, Parachute Section, Boat Section, Army Air Corp Section and a host of sub-units responsible for the daily running and administration of such a large organization.

23 SPECIAL AIR SERVICE REGIMENT (VOLUNTEERS)   In 1959 23 SAS Regiment (23 SAS) was established as a Territorial Army unit from the Reserve Reconnaissance Unit, a joint service unit responsible for the planning and conduct of escape lines in any future war in Europe; this role was previously carried out by the wartime MI9 organization. Organized and recruited along the same lines as 21 SAS, its role during the Cold War was to support British I Corps in West Germany. Its headquarters, headquarters' squadron and training wing are located in Birmingham, while its four Sabre Squadrons are located in the Midlands, the north of England and Scotland.

Both 23 and 21 SAS receive communications support from 63 SASD Signal Squadron (Volunteers).

SPECIAL BOAT SERVICE (SBS), ROYAL MARINES (RM)   At the end of the 1940s, 1 Special Boat Section was formed by the Royal Marines Amphibious School. In 1950 2 SBS was formed from a detachment of the Amphibious School attached to the Royal Navy Rhine Squadron in West Germany. The following year saw the formation of 3 SBS, with 4 and 5 SBS being formed from the Royal Marine Force Volunteer Reserve. In addition, a further section was formed from volunteers and attached to 41 Independent Commando RM for operations in Korea. Shortly afterwards 6 SBS was formed in Malta for operations in the Mediterranean, subsequently accompanying 3 Commando Brigade during the landings at Suez in November 1956.

During the mid-1960s, 1 and 2 SBS deployed to the Far East on operations during the Borneo Confrontation, patrolling and establishing OPs (observation posts) on the rivers and coastal areas of Sabah and Sarawak. Meanwhile, 6 SBS was tasked with carrying out beach reconnaissance throughout the Arabian Gulf, being joined there by a detachment of 2 SBS.

During the early 1970s the Special Boat Company (redesignated the Special Boat Squadron in 1975) became involved in anti-terrorist operations. In 1971 SBS personnel were deployed to Northern Ireland, initially as part of the Military Reaction Force (MRF) but subsequently with 14 Intelligence and Security Unit. That year also saw two members of the SBS, together with a bomb disposal officer and a 22 SAS NCO, parachute into the Atlantic in response to a bomb threat aboard the liner *QE2*. In April 1973 an SBS protection team was again on board the *QE2* during a cruise carrying Jews from America and Europe to Israel.

In 1975 the Royal Marines were tasked with providing Britain's Maritime Counter-Terrorist Force and 1 SBS was thereafter dedicated to this role. In 1979, 5 SBS was deployed to Arbroath, Scotland, in support of Comacchio Company, the quick-reaction force for the protection of nuclear weapon sites and convoys, and for counter-terrorist operations on ships and offshore installations. Thereafter 1 SBS concentrated on operations involving ships. In 1987, 1 and 5 SBS were amalgamated and located at Poole in Dorset where they were redesignated M Squadron SBS and remained dedicated to the maritime counter-terrorist role.

In 1982, 2, 3 and 6 SBS were deployed at the start of the Falklands War, landing on the islands some three weeks before the arrival of the Task Force. SBS reconnaissance teams played a major role during the campaign, keeping enemy positions under constant observation and carrying out both close and beach reconnaissance tasks.

In 1991, elements of the Special Boat Service (redesignated as such post-1983) were deployed to Saudi Arabia during the Gulf War, carrying out Scud-hunting operations in the eastern sector of southern Iraq and attacking a major enemy line of communication. Two years later SBS personnel were deployed to Bosnia on reconnaissance tasks and remained there until 1996 as part of the British Special Forces element serving with the NATO Allied Rapid Reaction Corps.

Today the Special Boat Service, together with the three SAS regiments and two SAS signals squadrons, forms one of the elements under the command of the Directorate of Special Forces which was established in the early 1990s.

SABAH Located at the northern end of the island of Borneo, Sabah has formed part of the Federation of Malaysia since 16 September 1963. To the south it borders the northern part of Kalimantan, Indonesian Borneo. In the east, the 480km- (300 mile-) long border initially runs westwards through several islands and the estuaries of various rivers, across flat swampy terrain for some 40km (25 miles) and then into mountains inhabited by Murit tribes. It then runs through an uninhabited and virtually unexplored area known as the Gap. From there it meanders further west to the border with the Fifth Division of neighbouring Sarawak. Like the rest of Borneo, the terrain inland from the coastal areas comprises mountainous terrain covered in jungle rising to heights of 3,040m (10,000ft), with rivers and swamps in the valleys.

Sabah has a large Indonesian immigrant population and during the years of the Borneo Confrontation campaign this factor, coupled with the presence of Indonesian regular troops over the border in the northern part of Kalimantan, meant that the threat of enemy incursion was very real. Cross-border operations by SAS and infantry units, under the auspices of Operation 'Claret', were launched from Sabah with troops being inserted by helicopter into LZs (landing zones) along the border. Encounters with Indonesian forces just south of the border took place in a number of locations including Labang, Lumbis, and Nantakor. Those just inside Sabah took place at Kabu and in the area of the Long Pa Sia Bulge.

On 22 January 1964 the deepest Indonesian incursion into Sabah was tracked northeast of the village of Long Miau, just north of the Long Pa Sia Bulge, by a patrol of D Squadron 22 SAS under Sergeant Bob Creighton. Subsequently, an eighteen-man patrol of the 1st Battalion Royal Leicestershire Regiment attacked the enemy force, numbering 40 in total, which withdrew south over the border with the loss of five killed.

SABRE SQUADRON   The name given to a fighting squadron within the SAS regiments. There are four Sabre Squadrons in 22 SAS, A, B, D and G. There is also an R Squadron which is a Territorial Army reserve unit. A Squadron consists of around 60 men who are divided into four troops, and a small headquarters section. The troops are designed to operate in all terrain and environments, providing the different methods of insertion – namely, mobility, mountain, air-insertion, and boat. Each patrol within a troop is made up of four men; this unit has become the backbone of SAS soldiering. Each troop member will have an individual skill, such as medical, languages, demolitions and signals. These are the basic skills, and depending on length of service, it is not uncommon to find a troop member versed in skills of several different types.

SACRED SQUADRON (HEROS LOKOS)   This Greek unit was formed as long ago as 370 BC. Several officers of the Greek Army successfully escaped the German invasion of their country in April 1941, following which they reformed the unit. David Stirling wanted the unit to be a part of the SAS as he was convinced that their knowledge would be invaluable to his operations in the Balkans in 1942. Early in 1943 the Sacred Squadron, with 121 men, joined in the campaign in North Africa, whilst later that same year some of its members showed great bravery and heroism with the Special Boat Squadron in the Aegean Sea. Despite these various joint activities, by March 1943 most of the men had left the SAS and had returned to the control of the Greek authorities.

SAF (SULTAN'S ARMED FORCES)   The army of the Sultanate of Muscat and Oman. In 1958 the Sultan's Armed Forces (SAF) was quite small in number. It consisted of the Northern Frontier Regiment of about 450 men and detachments of the Trucial Oman Scouts. Although the soldiers were well trained and well led, they were unable to control the uprisings that broke out in the Jebel Akhdar and the Dhofar regions. The Sultan, Said bin Taimur, called on British aid. In 1958 Colonel David Smiley was appointed Chief-of-Staff to the Sultan and he helped to reorganize the SAF into a more efficient fighting force.

By 1970 there was unrest once again in Oman, but this time the guerrillas were defeated by a combination of the SAS, SAF and Firqat units. The SAF won two important victories – one at Sarfait and one at Dorra Ridge. By 1975, the war in Oman was all but over.

SAID BIN TAIMUR, SULTAN The ruler of Oman who maintained his country in a feudal state up until the mid-1970s. When his actions led to an uprising by rebellious Dhofaris, he refused to accept the advice of his British counsellors, who wanted him to let the SAS train the loyal Dhofaris as a counter-measure against the rebels. The situation became so grave that it appeared as though the rebels would take control of the entire country.

Then surprisingly, on 23 July 1970, Sultan Said bin Taimur was deposed by his son Sultan Qaboos in a bloodless coup, after which the old sultan was hastily bundled into an aircraft and flown to England.

The young Sultan Qaboos had been educated in England and then trained at Sandhurst, but on returning to Oman he had been kept almost as a prisoner by his father until he rebelled.

'SAMSON', OPERATION Between 10 August and 27 September 1944, 24 men of 3 French Parachute Battalion (3 SAS) parachuted into the area west of Limoges, southern France. Their mission was to disrupt enemy road traffic and help local Maquis forces. The operation was code-named 'Samson' and was relatively successful, destroying many German vehicles and causing about 100 enemy casualties.

'SAMWEST', OPERATION Led by Captain Le Blond, 116 men of 4 French Parachute Battalion landed in northern Brittany to establish a base near St Brieuc between 6 and 9 June 1944, with the express aim of preventing the movement of German forces from western Brittany to Normandy.

Believing that freedom and the end of the war were close, the local people warmly greeted the SAS men. However, although the local Maquis were armed, their security measures left a lot to be desired, and as a result the Germans mounted an attack on the SAS base on 12 June. The battle that followed cost the Germans many casualties, but the consequences for the SAS and the Maquis were far worse, seeing them totally scattered. As a result, the majority of the French SAS resorted to joining the 'Dingson' base.

SANGAR   This is simply a circle built of rocks. The SAS are very adept at building sangars, some of which they have lived in for several months. They can be constructed on the flat, as well as mountain tops or ridges. They offer a form of accommodation and protection not only against enemy shell fire, but also from the desert heat, when fitted with a cover. Sangars were used by the SAS in Aden and Oman, as the nature of the ground frequently did not allow the soldiers to dig defensive positions.

SARAWAK   Located on the northeast coast of the island of Borneo, the state of Sarawak forms part of the Federation of Malaysia. Divided into five administrative divisions, its capital is the city of Kuching, located in the First Division, which forms the southwestern tip of the state. Inland, along the border, the country is made up of mountain ranges of heights up to 2,432m (8,000ft), covered with dense jungle. As with the rest of Borneo, there are no roads or railways, and transportation is via the fast-flowing rivers, which act as waterways leading to the coast. Inhabited areas are within easy reach of the rivers, the population being a mix of Malay, Chinese and several indigenous races, namely Ibans, Murits, Kelabits, Kayans, Ukits and Punans.

Sarawak's unmarked border with Kalimantan is over 1,120km (700 miles) long, and during the Borneo Confrontation campaign Indonesia deployed over 1,500 irregular troops, supported by a large number of regulars and local defence force personnel, along its length. A great many possible incursion points were available for use by the Indonesians, and surveillance of the most likely routes was carried out by 22 SAS and the Guards and Gurkha Independent Parachute Companies. Once an incursion had been detected, infantry troops were deployed by helicopter to follow up.

One major incursion into Sarawak took place on 28 September 1963, when a large Indonesian force crossed the border at Balui and attacked a Gurkha and Border Scout post at the village of Long Jawi in the Third Division. Another occurred on 27 April 1965 when a battalion of RPKAD para-commandos attacked B Company, 2 Para at Plaman Mapu, in the First Division, but were beaten off with the loss of over 30 casualties.

From late 1964 onwards SAS and infantry units carried out a large number of cross-border raids from Sarawak into Kalimantan to a maximum depth of 5,450m (5,000yds) from the border. This limit was later increased to distances up to 21km (13 miles) for certain specific operations.

SARAWAK RANGERS   The unit made up of Iban trackers, from the Sarawak area of Borneo, who were employed by the British during the Malayan Emergency (1948–60). The SAS recognized the opportunity for mutual benefit from a liaison with the rangers and taught them basic military skills in return for learning the rangers' considerable tracking skills. Later the SAS were able to reap their reward when, during the campaign in Borneo between 1963 and 1966, they recruited several ex-Sarawak Rangers to fight against the Indonesians.

SARBE/TACBE   The SARBE is a small Surface to Air Rescue Beacon with a voice capability, which allows downed pilots or SAS patrols to communicate with SAR (search and rescue) aircraft. It transmits on dual distress frequencies (121.5 and 243 MHz), with voice override that is NATO standard. A new SARBE GPS locator has recently been developed, with the GPS receiver passing precise co-ordinates to searching aircraft. The TACBE (Tactical Beacon) is a similar device.

SAS BRIGADE   During the latter part of World War II, the following regiments formed the SAS Brigade:
   1 SAS under Lieutenant-Colonel R.B. Mayne.
   2 SAS under Lieutenant-Colonel B.M.F. Franks.
   3 SAS (French) under Lieutenant-Colonel J. Conan.
   4 SAS (French) under Lieutenant-Colonel P. Bourgoin.
   5 SAS (Belgian) under Lieutenant-Colonel E. Blondeel.
   In January 1944 the SAS units were formed into the SAS Brigade under the command of Brigadier R.W. McLeod. In addition to the five SAS regiments, 'F' Squadron of Phantom was also included. At the end of the war the brigade was broken up. The British 1 and 2 SAS were disbanded, 3 and 4 were absorbed into the French Army and 5 into the Belgian Army.

SAS EYES ONLY   Very much what it says. Documents marked 'SAS Eyes Only' usually contain confidential material concerning only those members in the regiment privy to such sensitive information. Most relate to SAS policy rather than some clandestine operation.

SAS REGIMENTAL PRAYER   'O Lord, Who didst call upon Thy disciples to venture all to win all men to Thee, grant that we, the chosen members of the Special Air Service Regiment may, by our works and our ways, dare all to win all, and in so doing render special service to Thee and our fellow men in all the world. Through the same Jesus Christ, Our Lord, Amen.'

SAS SMOCK   The SAS have always used some form of distinctive camouflage smock. At the end of World War II, they used the British issue parachute smock. In the early 1960s they were issued with their own distinctive slip-over type brick-coloured smock which remained in service until the mid-1970s whereupon a new purpose-designed SAS DPM (disruptive pattern material) smock came into use.

SATELLITE COMMUNICATIONS (SATCOM)   Satellite communications systems currently form part of the range of equipment used by British Special Forces. They include static, mobile and portable units, the latter weighing less than 10kg (22lbs), operating on UHF and SHF frequency bands. British forces currently use a number of Skynet 4 and 5 series satellites, which are in geosynchronous orbit, providing constant communications links worldwide. Once a transmitter/receiver has been set up and activated, it will locate and track a satellite with its dish antenna. Signals are transmitted on one frequency to the satellite which transfers it to another frequency via a transponder, boosting the signal and re-transmitting it.

'SAXIFRAGE', OPERATION   In Italy in World War II, Operation 'Saxifrage', in conjunction with Operation 'Candytuft', was intended to disrupt the railway line between Ancona and Pescara on the east Italian coast and cut off enemy supplies. Commanded by Major Roy Farran and Lieutenant Grant Hibbert, four parties from 2 SAS landed by torpedo boat on 27 October 1943 and stayed behind the enemy lines for six days. Despite atrocious weather, the groups managed to successfully cut the railway lines in several places as well as mine the coast road. At the end of the operation, all but two of the men, who were captured, were evacuated by torpedo boat.

SBLO SPECIAL BRANCH LIAISON OFFICER   The SAS provided three SBLOs for Northern Ireland, each serving a two year period. Their main task was to talent spot work for the SAS from the vast amount of intelligence gathered by TCG (tactical control group). Once an operation was initiated, the job of the liaison officer was to co-ordinate and report all activities between the regiment and Special Branch. SAS SBLOs were instrumental in fostering good relations between RUC Special Branch and the SAS.

SCHOFIELD, MAJOR, J. 'JOE'   Joe Schofield served with the SAS during the North African campaign and, despite short breaks, he remained with the regiment as Quartermaster until the late 1960s, which made him one of the longest serving members.

SCHOLLENBERG, LIEUTENANT CHRIS 'SCHULIE' – RHODESIAN SAS REGIMENT AND SELOUS SCOUTS   Schollenberg was a South African who originally enlisted in the ranks of the Rhodesian Light Infantry and rose to the rank of sergeant before being commissioned. Thereafter, he joined C Squadron Rhodesian SAS (RhSAS) with whom he soon established a reputation second to none, subsequently being awarded the Bronze Cross (BCR) and Silver Cross (SCR) of Rhodesia – the first RhSAS officer to be awarded the latter. In addition, the RhSAS also recognized his outstanding performance on operations by bestowing on him its Wings on Chest award.

At the end of his contract with the Rhodesian Army, Schollenberg returned to South Africa and civilian life but, finding the latter not to his taste, returned to Rhodesia and re-enlisted, joining the Selous Scouts as a captain. Thereafter, he specialized in conducting cross-border, two-man close reconnaissance missions, the type of mission in which he excelled and for which he became renowned.

In June 1978 Captain Schollenberg was the first to be awarded the country's highest award for gallantry, the Grand Cross of Valour (GCV) which is the equivalent of Britain's Victoria Cross. These awards recognized the large number of extremely hazardous close reconnaissance missions carried out by him deep in enemy territory outside Rhodesia's borders. The only other GCV ever awarded was to an RhSAS officer who remains anonymous to this day. The two men were Rhodesia's most highly decorated members of the armed forces, both also being the only recipients of all three of the country's gallantry decorations.

SCHOOL OF LANGUAGES – BEACONSFIELD Beaconsfield is
home to the Royal Army Education Corps School of Languages. Many SAS soldiers attend the school in order to learn a foreign language. Courses for simple languages such as German, French and Spanish etc. last about six weeks, while Arabic and Russian can take anything from three months to a year. All the courses are fairly intensive and require a good deal of homework. The school also teaches English to soldiers of friendly nations, as well as a host of non-language courses such as 'Methods of Instruction'.

SCHUMAN, SECOND-LIEUTENANT PETER – AUSTRALIAN SAS REGIMENT (SASR) The commander of a 3 Squadron SASR
patrol which was tasked with carrying out surveillance in the area to the east of the 1st Australian Task Force (1 ATF) base at Nui Dat. During the afternoon of 14 July the patrol, together with another under Sergeant Peter Healy, moved out with C Company 6th Battalion Royal Australian Regiment (6 RAR), which established an ambush that night in the area of the Suoi de Bang creek. The patrols, however, moved on and two days later separated, heading for their respective mission areas. At one point they suspected that they were being shadowed and were forced to take evasive action to shake off any enemy following them.

At 10:40 hours on 17 July, Schuman and his men detected a Vietcong (VC) camp after hearing a woman calling out. Whilst carrying out a close reconnaissance, Schuman spotted a VC taking aim at his lead scout, Private Sam Wilson, and shot him dead. The two men withdrew to rejoin the other two members of the patrol, Sergeant Jock Thorburn and

Corporal Lyn Murton. Schuman then decided to mount an attack on the camp, and the patrol moved forward under fire from the enemy who were withdrawing and eventually broke contact. On searching the camp before setting it ablaze, Schuman found documents which revealed that it had been occupied by ten VC.

The patrol withdrew 600m (654yds) and was in the process of requesting extraction when two VC approached its LUP (lying-up position). Sergeant Thorburn shot one and the other was hit three times by fire from the patrol before disappearing into the nearby jungle. Shortly afterwards, the patrol was extracted by helicopter and returned to Nui Dat.

SCHUMANN, JURGEN The pilot of a Lufthansa 737 aircraft which was hijacked in 1977. Jurgen Schumann was shot dead in front of his passengers by the terrorist leader Zohair Akache in Aden, after he had been found guilty of supplying vital information about the hijackers to the authorities. This information greatly helped the German GSG9 and British SAS to successfully assault the aircraft in Mogadishu and rescue all the remaining passengers and crew.

SCHWARZKOPF, GENERAL NORMAN Persuaded to employ the SAS during the Gulf War by General Sir Peter de la Billière. At the end of the war General Schwarzkopf personally thanked members of the SAS, and later wrote the following commendation:

Letter of Commendation for the 22d Special Air Service (SAS) Regiment

1. I wish to officially commend the 22d Special Air Service (SAS) Regiment for their totally outstanding performance of military operations during Operation 'Desert Storm'.

2. Shortly after the initiation of the strategic air campaign, it became apparent that the Coalition forces would be unable to eliminate Iraq's firing of Scud missiles from western Iraq into Israel. The continued firing of Scuds on Israel carried with it enormous unfavourable political ramifications and could, in fact, have resulted in the dismantling of the carefully crafted Coalition. Such a dismantling would have adversely affected, in ways difficult to measure, the ultimate outcome of the military campaign. It became apparent that the only way that the Coalition could succeed in reducing these Scud launches was by physically placing military forces on the ground in the vicinity of the western launch sites. At that time, the majority of available Coalition forces were committed to the forthcoming military campaign in the eastern portion of the theatre of operations.

Further, none of these forces possessed the requisite skills and abilities required to conduct such a dangerous operation. The only force deemed qualified for this critical mission was the 22 Special Air Service (SAS) Regiment.

3. From the first day they were assigned their mission until the last day of the conflict, the performance of the 22 Special Air Service (SAS) Regiment was courageous and highly professional. The area in which they were committed proved to contain far more numerous enemy forces than had been predicted by every intelligence estimate, the terrain was much more difficult than expected and the weather conditions were unseasonably brutal. Despite these hazards, in a very short period of time the 22 Special Air Service (SAS) Regiment was successful in totally denying the central corridor of western Iraq to Iraqi Scud units. The result was that the principal areas used by the Iraqis to fire Scuds on Tel Aviv were no longer available to them. They were required to move their Scud missile firing forces to the northwest portion of Iraq and from that location the firing of Scud missiles was essentially militarily ineffective.

4. When it became necessary to introduce United States Special Operations Forces into the area to attempt to close down the northwest Scud areas, the 22 Special Air Service (SAS) Regiment provided invaluable assistance to the US forces. They took every possible measure to ensure that US forces were thoroughly briefed and were able to profit from the valuable lessons that had been learned by earlier SAS deployments into Western Iraq.

I am completely convinced that, had US forces not received these thorough indoctrinations by SAS personnel, US forces would have suffered a much higher rate of casualties than was ultimately the case. Further, the SAS and US joint forces immediately merged into a combined fighting force where the synergetic effect of these fine units ultimately caused the enemy to be convinced that they were facing forces in western Iraq that were more than tenfold the size of those they were actually facing. As a result, large numbers of enemy forces that might otherwise have been deployed in the eastern theatre were tied down in western Iraq.

5. The performance of the 22 Special Air Service (SAS) Regiment during Operation 'Desert Storm' was in the highest traditions of the professional military service and in keeping with the proud history and tradition that has been established by that regiment. Please ensure that this commendation receives appropriate attention and is passed on to the unit and its members.

SCRATCHLEY, MAJOR SANDY He joined the SAS as a lieutenant in early 1942 and later took part in operations in North Africa. He was with 2 SAS in Sicily and Italy and took part in Operation 'Sleepy Lad' in 1943. He stayed on the Italian peninsula until the end of the war in 1945.

SCUD MISSILE The 11m (37ft) long Scud missile traces its ancestry back to a 1940s design for the German V-2 rocket which, with the same degree of inaccuracy, fell on London during World War II. As a Soviet client, the regime in Baghdad took deliveries of the ageing ballistic missile and improved on its range, extending the Scud-B's maximum reach of 280km (175 miles) to 624km (390 miles). The Iraqis accomplished this by cutting the fuel tank in half and welding in an extra section. Many of these modified missiles simply fell apart when fired and never reached their target. The Scud, although capable of delivering chemical and biological weapons, normally carries 662kg (1,456lbs) of conventional explosives in its warhead.

The missile can be fired from a fixed site or from the back of a mobile launch vehicle, which the Iraqis preferred. The main objective for the SAS during the Gulf War was to track down and destroy the Iraqi's Scud missiles.

SEA KING DISASTER (FALKLANDS) On 19 May 1982 at 21:30, elements of 22 SAS were being ferried by Sea King helicopter from HMS *Hermes* to the assault ship HMS *Intrepid*. The flight, which covered 800m (880yds) and took just five minutes, ended in one of the worst disasters the SAS has ever known. Upon arrival at HMS *Intrepid* the helicopter was unable to land because another helicopter which had landed a few moments before needed to have its rotor blades stowed prior to being taken below deck. The Sea King made a second circuit while it waited. When it was midway between the two ships and at a height of about 120m (400ft) something hit the rotor blades causing it to plummet into the sea with the loss of 22 lives, 18 of whom were SAS badged soldiers.

SEA KING HELICOPTER *Specification* Length: 22.15m (24yds); Height: 5.13m (5.6yds); Weight: 2,451kg (5,447lbs); Speed: 215km/h (133mph) max.

Taking its first flight on 11 March 1959, the Sikorski CH-3 Sea King helicopter set numerous records for long-distance flights. In 1969 the GKN Westland factory in Yeovil, Somerset, took on production, supplying helicopters for both Royal Navy and export customers.

Gradually GKN Westland upgraded the design by incorporating an increased payload, reducing fuel consumption and improving the reliability of the aircraft. Sea Kings are utilized by the Royal Navy for anti-submarine operations with a range of over 1,400km (868 miles), with an airborne radar for over-the-horizon cover. They are extremely versatile and in an emergency can carry 42 troops, although in more usual amphibious operations they are used to transport 28 fully equipped soldiers and can carry 1,633kg (3,629lbs) underslung loads.

During the Falklands War, Sea Kings were used to bring in SAS and SBS troops as well as 105mm Light-guns ready to engage the Argentinian defences around the town of Stanley. Tragically on 19 May 1982, 18 men of D Squadron were killed during a night-time cross-decking operation between ships of the Task Force, when the Sea King in which they were travelling hit a sea bird and crashed into the Atlantic.

SEALS US elite unit – the letters stand for 'Sea, Air and Land'. SEAL units carry out special operations work particularly connected to beach and coastal reconnaissance. They also carry out counter-insurgency work. The team that deals mainly with counter-terrorism is called SEAL Team 6 and it is part of Delta Force. It was formed in 1980 and consists of 100 of the best volunteers taken from the other SEAL teams. These men possess excellent small arms skills and are specialists in preventing terrorist attacks on oil rigs or US ships. Like many of its counterparts, SEAL Team 6 has carried out exchange training with the SAS.

SEEKINGS, SERGEANT-MAJOR REG Seekings was one of the original members of L Detachment who came from No. 7 Commando. He was a member of the first SAS operation in November 1941 and took part in many of the raids against Axis airfields in North Africa. He was a member of the Special Raiding Squadron (SRS) during the Sicilian and Italian campaigns and was awarded the Military Medal. He already had a Distinguished Conduct Medal. In October 1943 at Termoli he had a lucky escape. While he was sitting in the cab of a truck, a German shell landed in the back and killed all the occupants. In June of 1944 he was in the advance party for Operation 'Bullbasket' and was shot through the neck, the bullet just narrowly missing his spine. He now had the rank of sergeant-major. After the war he joined the Rhodesian Police force.

SEKAYAN RIVER In early 1966 three members of 2 Squadron Australian SAS Regiment NCOs, attached to B Squadron 22 SAS and commanded by Major Terry Hardy, carried out a major 'Claret' operation during the Borneo Confrontation, against an Indonesian force located at Sentas, on the Sekayan River. On 30 January B Squadron, reinforced by a platoon of the 1st Battalion Argyll and Sutherland Highlanders, departed and reached a crossing point on the Sekayan River four days later. Leaving the Argylls to guard the point and having crossed at last light, the squadron moved east along the bank of the river towards the Indonesian camp, which it was to attack at dawn the following day. Unfortunately, however, the leading troop unexpectedly came across an enemy position and shortly afterwards, as it moved uphill towards a number of huts, the Indonesians opened fire.

During the ensuing firefight, which took place at a range of only 20m (21yds), Sergeant Coleman (SASR) took cover with others behind an open wooden hut. Shortly afterwards, however, he was hit by burning phosphorus from a grenade thrown by one of B Squadron. As the battle continued, he tried unsuccessfully to extinguish the flames in a nearby stream with the assistance of two other men. While doing so, none of them noticed that the squadron had withdrawn prior to calling down an artillery fire mission. When they realized their position, and finding the only way out was the route of their original approach, the three men charged through the Indonesian camp, returning fire from several huts and coming under attack from a 12.7mm heavy machine gun from high ground behind them. Shortly afterwards they encountered a group of Indonesians attempting to follow up after B Squadron and there was another short, sharp engagement before contact was broken.

Jumping into the river, Sergeant Coleman and his two companions, Sergeant Lou Lumby and Trooper Ginge Ferguson, allowed it to carry them downstream but left it smartly after shells from the artillery fire mission, requested by Major Hardy, started landing in it. Despite the pain from the burns caused by the phosphorus, Sergeant Coleman and his two companions succeeded in making their way over difficult terrain back to the border where they reached a Gurkha patrol base.

SELECTION The SAS Selection course takes place in the Brecon Beacons. The whole course has one aim: to weed out those that are unsuitable and to push to the limit those that pass. The overall course, which was devised in 1953 by Major John Woodhouse, has changed very little over the years. More emphasis has been placed on safety after a series of deaths in the late 1970s and early 1980s. The course is long and tough. Those that pass the 'build-up to Test Week' find at the end they are faced with the 'Endurance march'. Little can prepare one for this challenge, and to succeed inside the allocated time is a fitting achievement in itself.

Continuation training lasts for fourteen weeks, at which time those candidates surviving Selection will be taught all the basics that make a good SAS soldier. These include operating as a member of a four-man patrol and learning standard operating procedures (SOPs). Specialist weapons skills and combat survival training follow. The combat and survival phase ends with an escape and evasion exercise, in which candidates are expected to avoid capture. However, irrespective of capture, all candidates undergo intensive interrogation training.

Those that pass this phase will go on to jungle training and static-line parachute training. Even then it is not finished; SAS soldiers are required to swim at least 1.6km (1 mile) fully clothed and with a full complement of equipment, and also learn to dive. Then, and only then, will the candidate be marched in to receive his beret with its coveted winged dagger. This bestows a feeling of belonging reminiscent of those warriors that have gone before and given so much.

SELOUS SCOUTS The Selous Scouts were formed in 1974 following Rhodesia's Unilateral Declaration of Independence (UDI) in November 1965. By 1973 guerrilla activity had developed into a major campaign, strengthened by the Portuguese withdrawal from neighbouring Mozambique. The Selous Scouts, named after Fredrick Selous, a close friend of the country's founder Cecil Rhodes, were originally trained as a tracker-combat unit with their prime role being one of deep penetration and intelligence gathering.

At the height of the war in 1976, the Selous Scouts, which numbered about 700 men, were under the command of Colonel Reid-Daly, a Rhodesian who had served with the SAS in Malaya. They worked in small units of four to six men who would parachute or heli-hop into the bush in hot pursuit of ZIPRA and ZANLA guerrillas. The Selous Scouts were lightly equipped, carrying mostly ammunition and water which enabled them to quickly track and close on the fleeing guerrillas. Once spotted, the Scouts would call for soldiers of C Squadron Rhodesian SAS to parachute forward of the guerrillas in order to cut them off. The Selous Scouts' methods were so effective they accounted for more guerrillas than the rest of the Rhodesian Army put together. Along with the Rhodesian SAS, the Selous Scouts were disbanded in 1980 when the Prime Minister Ian Smith handed over to Robert Mugabe's government and Rhodesia became Zimbabwe. Most of the Selous Scouts made their way into the South African Army.

SEMTEX Semtex is a Czech-manufactured RDX-based plastic explosive. Its main feature is that it contains a higher percentage of RDX than, for example, the British PE-4 plastic explosive which comprises 88 per cent RDX and 12 per cent binder/plasticiser. This means that it has a detonating velocity higher than the 8,500m (28,000ft) per second of PE-4. Semtex was originally odourless, making it difficult to detect using the normal type of explosive detection systems; in recent years, however, the manufacturers have introduced a trace element, making Semtex more easily detectable and enabling it to be traced forensically.

The explosive first entered the terrorist chain during the 1970s when Semtex H was used at a training school for terrorists in the Crimea by the Czech intelligence service and the KGB. It was also during that period that the elements of the IRA encountered it in the Lebanon's Beka'a Valley. Thereafter the Provisional IRA (PIRA) obtained considerable quantities of Semtex H from Libya but successful operations by Irish security forces, who discovered some one and a half tons, subsequently reduced the terrorists' stocks. The PIRA have since used Semtex H primarily in the manufacture of munitions such as mines, mortar bombs and rocket-propelled grenades, while using home-made explosives such as ANFO

(Ammonium Nitrate Fuel Oil) and Recrystallized Ammonium Nitrate (RAN) for bombs.

SENNYBRIDGE Sennybridge ranges in Powys are frequently used by the SAS, both for range work and during Selection. The decision to move the SAS Selection course to Sennybridge occurred in the late 1980s and was designed to cut down the amount of wasted hours travelling from Hereford to the Brecon Beacons. Sennybridge also offers some of the best live-firing ranges in the UK which are used by the SAS on a regular basis.

SFBC (Special Forces Briefing Course) The SAS run this to ensure that prospective candidates are fully aware and prepared before they attempt Special Forces Selection. It is also an opportunity for the regiment to look at prospective candidates, making sure they like what they see.

Candidates will be given a series of briefings and presentations about the role of British Special Forces in general and specifically that of the SAS. This normally starts with a briefing from Training Squadron OC, prior to being briefed on what Selection is all about and how best to prepare themselves. An example of an SFBC weekend is outlined below.

Friday evening
Briefing
TOETS
Map Reading Test
First Aid Test
Map Memory Test
Military Knowledge Test
IQ Test

Saturday
Before breakfast candidates will do an APFA (Army Physical Fitness Assessment) and a Bleep (multi-stage fitness) Test, after which they will be taken to the swimming pool where they will be required to jump from the high diving board. This to assess their initial aptitude to parachute training. During the visit to the pool they will also be required to swim 100m (109yds) in three minutes, after which they must tread water for ten minutes. All this is done in combat clothing and trainers. For the rest of the morning candidates will receive briefings on the regiment, which include not just the combat side, but also such subjects as welfare and daily living at Hereford.

In the afternoon they will be driven to a training area to the south of Hereford where they will carry out a series of fitness tests which include BFT (battle fitness test), and two CFTs (combat fitness tests). The BFT is straightforward, and the first CFT consists of running 3km (2 miles) in eighteen minutes, while the second is 12km (8 miles) in one hour and forty minutes. All these tests are done back to back. Saturday ends with a briefing on the activities of Special Forces, detailing some of their specialist roles.

Sunday

The SAS Directing Staff will run the candidates for about one and a half hours, during which time they will be required to carry other candidates. These distractions will include both the fireman's lift and baby carry, feats the candidate must undertake going both uphill and downhill. Candidates then return to barracks to watch the SAS Regimental video, which gives a rather glamorous, laid-back image of the SAS. Before dispersal around lunchtime, candidates will receive a final interview.

SHAKE-OUT A term used for rehearsals of an operation, or for the beginning of a tour in an untested theatre. The aim of a 'shake-out' is to discover and remedy any pitfalls the soldiers might encounter when conducting the actual operation.

'SHAKESPEARE', OPERATION A small detachment of 22 men of the Belgian Independent Parachute Company parachuted into the area northwest of Le Mans between 31 July and 15 August 1944. Led by Lieutenants Debefre and Limbosen, the party were given the task of harassing the retreating Germans situated to the west of Paris. Moving on foot, the Belgians only managed to come into contact with the tail of the retreating enemy forces, but were able to assist in the rescue of 150 downed Allied airmen.

SHAMAGH The shamagh is a square piece of cloth that forms an Arab headdress. The SAS have used shamaghs since their first raids into the North African desert during World War II up to and including the Gulf War. Shamaghs come in a variety of colours, some of which denote various Arab tribes or military units.

On one operation in the Middle East off the Straits of Hormuz, each SAS soldier was given six different shamaghs. The thinking behind this was simple: the assaulting Arab force was made up of several different local forces, all with a different coloured shamagh, and to avoid the SAS being mistaken for the enemy, as the different units approached their positions they would change headdress to comply with that unit. In reality, 40 SAS soldiers were all converted into Tommy Cooper lookalikes as they frequently dived into their bergens looking for the correct shamagh.

SHAPED CHARGE A shaped charge normally refers to an inverted cone-shaped explosive charge. The principle behind the charge is based on the inversion of shock waves once the explosive is initiated; this forms the explosive force into a pin-point cutting charge which, due to its stand-off, can penetrate thick steel. A shaped charge can be found in most anti-tank missiles but it is also used in SAS demolitions.

SHEEHAN, SERGEANT PETER – AUSTRALIAN SAS REGIMENT (SASR)
Sergeant Peter Sheehan was the commander of a ten-man 2 Squadron SASR patrol which was inserted on 8 October 1968 into an area 12km (7.5 miles) northeast of Xuyen Moc, near Phuoc Tuy Province's eastern border with neighbouring Binh Tuy Province. The patrol subsequently established an ambush position, its task being to intercept Vietcong (VC) re-supply groups moving through the area.

A number of VC passed through the killing area but at about 12:00 hours on 11 October three VC, two men and a woman, appeared at the left-hand end of the ambush and sat down. Sergeant Frank Cashmore attempted to shoot them with a silenced sub-machine gun but failed due to the weapon suffering a stoppage. The three VC tried to flee but almost immediately were caught in the blast of a Claymore mine fired by Corporal Terry O'Farrell: the two men were killed but the woman was captured unharmed.

The patrol was extracted shortly afterwards but ten days later returned to the same area and killed all the members of a seven-man VC group carrying supplies.

SHERMULLY 38MM HAND-HELD ROCKET
The Shermully has been in service with the British Army for many years. It is mainly used to illuminate an area during the hours of darkness. The device operates by simply removing the top and bottom caps and pulling out the safety pin; this releases a trigger lever which swings down on its own accord. The flare is then held at an angle of 45 degrees and pointed roughly in the general direction where illumination is required. Pressing the trigger lever against the rocket body instantly launches the rocket. The parachute deploys at between 200 and 300m (327yds) at which time the flare ignites. The burn time is approximately 30 seconds giving a light intensity of 80,000 candela, while the parachute descends at 3.5m (10ft) per second.

SHIRSHITTI CAVES, OMAN
Major General Creasey, Commander of the Sultan's Armed Forces (SAF), ordered the Iranian Battle Group to advance from the airbase at Manston and to secure the coastal town of Rakyut, some 27km (17 miles) to the south. The unit was also to clear the Adoo stores complex located in the caves of the Shirshitti wadi. The Iranian advance failed and with the number of casualties rising to treble figures the operation was called off.

Almost immediately a decision was taken by Creasey to re-attack using SAF, SAS and Firqat. The plan of attack was fairly simple: seize an old airstrip called Defa in order to establish a supply point, then secure the ridge that overlooked the Shirshitti depression in which the Adoo caves lay. The Jebel regiment, which had purposely been flown in from northern Oman led the advance, with the SAS and their Firqat following up. By mid-afternoon on 5 January 1975 the lead elements had managed to reach an area called Point 985, whereupon a base was established. During the night the Adoo attacked at very close range, killing four members of the SAF and severely wounding many more. At times it was difficult to establish where the Adoo fire was coming from; the SAF soldiers in the perimeter defences became extremely agitated and fired more for relief rather than in the hope of hitting a target.

Next day the force advanced down into the Shirshitti depression and by mid-morning Red Company (the leading company of the Jebel Regiment) had reached the Shirshitti wadi, whereupon the commander realized that he had moved too far south. Attached to Red Company was an SAS soldier, Lance-Corporal Thomas, who on evaluating the situation advised the company commander to stay put until the remainder of his force arrived. This advice was ignored and the lead platoons of Red Company broke cover and advanced into an area clear of bush. When they were halfway across the open ground the Adoo opened fire. Within seconds most of the platoon were dead, cut down by the ferocious Adoo firepower. The SAS men quickly grouped together for support, but even to them, as hardened soldiers, the situation was clearly out of control. The SAS party with Red Company Headquarters, in order to regain control of the situation, called in an air strike. However, such was the confusion of running bodies that the first strike mistakenly hit the company headquarters, one of the rounds striking an SAS soldier in the back. Eventually, with massive firepower supplied by artillery, mortars and Strikemaster jets, the Adoo were driven back. Amid all this carnage there were several individual acts of great courage as men braved the horrendous fire to rescue personal friends. With all the wounded and weapons recovered, a full-blown mortar barrage was called down on the battle area.

Later that day the defences at Point 985 were reinforced and it was decided to blast the Adoo out of their stronghold. For the next 48 hours the air thundered with high explosive as shell after shell rained down on the Shirshitti wadi. A bulldozer was brought up to cut a road down into the wadi on which Saladin armoured cars could travel. Once in position they were able to fire directly into the cave entrances. No further attempt to capture the caves by frontal attack was undertaken and the SAS moved out of the area on 18 January.

'SHOOT AND SCOOT' A standard operating procedure (SOP) used by the SAS, particularly in jungle warfare. Conceived by Lieutenant-Colonel John Woodhouse, it was designed to prevent heavy casualties during a surprise encounter with a hostile force, when there was no point in holding the position. It works as follows: the SAS soldiers, when attacked, would reply with a heavy barrage of fire before quickly making their individual ways to a pre-determined emergency RV (rendezvous point). In a small patrol of four men, once the lead scout has safely withdrawn, all members will rally to the patrol commander.

'SHOOT TO KILL' The supposed policy in force with the SAS in Northern Ireland, according to various conspiracy theorists. They maintain that the SAS operate death squads in order to assassinate prominent IRA terrorists, thereby acting outside of the law. No such policy exists and all SAS soldiers adhere, as much as is operationally possible, to the strict rules of engagement followed by all serving soldiers in Northern Ireland. The 'shoot to kill' stories have been propagated and stirred up to a very large extent by the propaganda machine of the IRA.

SHOULDER HOLSTER RIG Designed for covert use, the shoulder holster rig comprises a shoulder holster and double magazine carrier used to conceal a 9mm semi-automatic such as the MP5K. Manufactured in water-resistant soft leather, the harness is designed to be worn for long periods with maximum comfort. The holster and magazine carrier are fitted with loops for securing to the wearer's belt. The weapon can either be completely withdrawn or fired while still attached to the rig. The SAS favour such holsters when engaged in bodyguard work and VIP protection.

'SHOVEL' OPERATION In December 1978 Rhodesian 1st SAS Regiment was given the task, code-named Operation 'Shovel', of attacking the railway line between Beira and Moatize in northern Mozambique, by blowing a bridge which crossed a river at Mecito. The purpose of the operation was to prevent ZANLA replacing a massive arms cache located at Tete airfield which had been destroyed earlier in the month by a Rhodesian air strike.

On 15 December a patrol of twenty men, under Lieutenant McIntosh, parachuted into Mozambique and, having located the bridge, called for the 450kg (1,000lbs) of explosives required for the task to be dropped the following night. Unfortunately, however, the drop was not accurate and the containers landed some distance away, resulting in the lengthy and exhausting task of retrieving the explosives before first light. The following day, 17 December, a close reconnaissance of the bridge was carried out and during the next two nights the explosive charges were laid. This took some ingenuity as the target was considerably larger than previously thought. Nevertheless, despite the appearance of some FRELIMO militia checking the line, the task of placing the charges was completed and the patrol settled down to wait for a train.

At 21:00 hours on the night of 19 December a train appeared and Lieutenant McIntosh initiated the explosives as the engine crossed the bridge. The bridge was totally destroyed and the engine dragged several wagons into the river. The patrol followed this up by engaging the wagons still on the line with light machine guns and RPG-7s, subsequently placing explosive charges on four carriages and burying a mine back along the track. Having completed their task, Lieutenant McIntosh and his men withdrew 3km (1.8 miles) to a mountain from which they observed FRELIMO salvage operations before returning to Rhodesia.

SHRIKE A piece of demolitions equipment used to detonate electrical explosive charges. The shrike was first developed by the SAS and first came into service around 1976 and is now in service with 48 other countries. It can fire up to four charges simultaneously, at a range of up to 7.5km (4 miles).

SICILY In July and August 1943 both the Special Raiding Squadron (SRS) (1 SAS temporarily renamed) and 2 SAS were party to the Allied capture of Sicily. On 10 July, the SRS, led by Lieutenant-Colonel Paddy Mayne, first successfully assaulted Capo Murro di Porco followed by Augusta two days later. 1 SAS, with their commander Lieutenant-Colonel William Stirling were less fortunate and, of their two operations coded 'Narcissus' and 'Chestnut', only 'Narcissus' was successful. Nevertheless they did contribute significantly to Allied success on the island.

SIDI BARRANI David Stirling attempted to support an Eighth Army offensive by raiding an Axis airfield in North Africa on 12 July 1942. Commanded by Captains Warr and Schott the group decided to hit the airfield at night time, but an error over maps resulted in the raiders' inability to continue with this mission. Lieutenant Timpson, the Long Range Desert Group's (LRDG) guide, did, however, manage to shoot some enemy vehicles.

SIDI HANEISH On 26 July 1942 the SAS raided an Axis airfield in the Fuka region of North Africa. Under cover of darkness, David Stirling led fourteen jeeps, armed with Vickers K machine guns, divided into two columns of seven commanded by George Jellicoe and Paddy Mayne, on to the airfield in formation. The parked aircraft were riddled with bullets as they passed and in just a few short minutes they destroyed 40 aircraft before disappearing into the darkness. SAS casualties were small with the loss of only one man killed and two jeeps destroyed.

SIG (SPECIAL INTERROGATION GROUP) The Special Interrogation Group was made up of Germans and Palestinian Jews opposed to the Nazi Party who risked their lives by dressing themselves in German uniforms and passing themselves off as German soldiers. They even trained in German drill techniques and used German weapons. Most SIG personnel who were captured were normally shot without trial.

In one incident in 1942, two German prisoners-of-war deemed to be trustworthy, were placed in a SIG unit attached to an SAS raiding party made up mainly of Free French paratroopers. One of the prisoners was a double agent and disaster overtook the party when a company of Germans ambushed them during the raid on Derna airfield.

SIGN 'Sign' is a word used by trackers which implies tell-tale marks left behind after humans have passed through an area. Temporary signs are unavoidable marks left behind on the ground, such as disturbance of the earth, leaf and stick covering, dead insects and the disturbance of wildlife. These signs are temporary because after a short time weather and the growth of vegetation will settle the area. Permanent signs have a more lasting effect on the environment, such as cutting, breaking, dropping or leaving behind man-made objects.

The tracker has two visual ranges: 'top sign', which is generally found in vegetation above knee height – unnatural disturbance to the growing vegetation caused as a human being walks through the undergrowth. The larger the party of men the tracker is following the larger the top sign. Consequently a tracker can follow a large top sign quicker than he would when tracking an individual. 'Ground sign' is the disturbance of the actual track or path the tracker is following: young growing plants trodden down, footprints in soft soil, fallen leaves, skid-marks left by people climbing up or down hill. Again the larger the party of people being tracked the greater the ground sign.

Tracking is a skill which can be employed to improve the stealth of an SAS patrol. The awareness and interpretation of signs by the lead scout, identifying the enemy's spoor and gaining knowledge from it, forewarns the patrol of enemy activity.

SIGNALLER Communications are vital to any military unit; to the SAS it is a lifeline. All SAS operations require information to be passed between the patrol and headquarters unit, be it routine traffic or vital information about the enemy. Without communications there is no reporting, no CasEvac, no air strikes and no extraction.

The SAS signaller must learn to operate a wide variety of radios; likewise, he must also learn the art of coding and decoding messages. Morse code is still taught, but is rarely used with modern military radio equipment. The signaller normally shares his sleeping space with the patrol commander; this makes life easier as messages have to be sent at a set time, and it is normally quicker with two people. Additionally, the commander must tell the signaller what he wants to send and read any incoming messages. The latest radio set used by the regiment is the PRC

319 manufactured by Thorn EMI Electronics. It is a very powerful radio with a 50-watt output and an electronic message system. It is capable of data, voice and carrier-wave transmissions over a very wide frequency band: 1.5 to 40 MHz. The PRC 319 also has burst transmission making it almost impossible for any enemy to intercept the traffic.

The SAS signallers must also be able to operate the compact man-portable satellite communications system (SATCOM). These have been around for some time and the very latest sets are only a little larger than the PCR 319 radio. Satellite systems are extremely secure, offering communications from any point on the Earth's surface directly back to Hereford.

264 (SAS) SIGNALS SQUADRON This squadron's origins date back to 1951 when a signals troop was attached to the Malayan Scouts (SAS), which was redesignated 22 SAS Regiment (22 SAS) in the following year, for operations during the Malayan Emergency campaign. The troop remained with 22 SAS after the end of the Emergency but by 1966 SAS commitments were such that the communications support requirement was too great for a single troop. In July of that year, therefore, 264 (SAS) Signals Squadron was formed as a fully independent unit co-located with 22 SAS at the latter's base at Hereford. It is a Royal Corps of Signals unit providing radio and satellite communications support for 22 SAS for whom it operates the Communications Centre (Commcen) while also providing rear link communications for Sabre Squadrons deployed on operations. In addition, the squadron's radio technicians carry out maintenance and servicing on all communications equipment used by the regiment.

All ranks within the squadron wear the SAS beige beret with the Royal Signals badge, for which privilege they have to pass a probation course which lasts five weeks. During the first three weeks candidates are tested in physical fitness, navigation, weapon handling, shooting and signalling skills. The fourth week is devoted to physical fitness tests, all of which have to be passed before candidates are permitted to undergo the fifth and final Test Week. This comprises a number of endurance marches, carried out in four-man patrols, with radio communications being established and worked each night from patrol basha locations. Candidates who pass the course undergo parachute training. Initial service is with the squadron's Communications Troop, after which a signaller is posted to one of the squadron's four Sabre Squadron signal troops. Members of the squadron are subsequently permitted to volunteer for SAS Selection and service with 22 SAS.

Communications support for the two Territorial Army regiments, 21 SAS (V) and 23 SAS (V), is provided by a sister unit, 63 (SAS) Signals Squadron (V).

SIG SAUER P226, SEMI-AUTOMATIC PISTOL *Specification* Calibre: 9mm × 19 Parabellum; Weight: 750g (225oz); Muzzle velocity: 350m (381yds) per second; Magazine capacity: 15- or 20-round, box.

Developed by SIG in the 1980s, it combines features from the P220 and P225 models. Expensive but effective, it passed every required specification in the US joint services pistol trials. One of the best performers of the pistol world, it has now largely replaced the Browning Hi-Power within the SAS.

SILLITO, CORPORAL DAVID   During the North African campaign of World War II, Corporal Sillito, known by everyone as 'Jack' walked over 300km (180 miles) back to friendly lines after a raid on the German railway system. Corporal Sillito and a lieutenant were tasked with taking care of any German guards. As they did so the lieutenant's machine gun jammed and he died during the firefight. Sillito, pursued by the enemy, managed to escape. With no food or water, he covered the distance in a little over a week. When he was finally found by members of his own unit, he was too weak to stand.

SIMI ISLAND   On 7 October 1943 the Germans attacked the Dodecanese island of Simi which was at that time occupied by a force of 40 members of M Squadron SBS under Major Ian Lapraik. Their attempt to capture it failed, but on the following day Luftwaffe bombers carried out a series of raids during which twenty Greek civilians and two SBS soldiers were killed. One of the bombs landed on Major Lapraik's headquarters and two men, Guardsman Thomas Bishop and Corporal Sidney Greaves MM, were buried under the rubble. As others fought to rescue them, it became apparent that Private Bishop could not be freed without further debris and rubble falling on Corporal Greaves. The only solution was for Bishop's foot to be amputated and to this he very bravely and selflessly agreed.

By the light of a candle, lying on his back and working with only the minimum of instruments, an SBS medic, Sergeant Porter Darrell, carried out the operation under the guidance of an RAF medical officer, Flight-Lieutenant Leslie Ferris, who could not perform the operation himself as he was suffering from an injured wrist. It took 27 hours, despite more air raids, to free Guardsman Bishop. Unfortunately, however, he died soon afterwards from pain and shock. Sadly his death was in vain as Corporal Greaves was found to be dead on being pulled clear.

SIMPSON, LIEUTENANT GORDON 'SAM' – AUSTRALIAN SAS REGIMENT (SASR)   The commander of a six-man patrol of 2 Squadron SASR which was inserted by helicopter at 07:30 hours on 8 June 1968 in the mountainous terrain of the Nui Dinh hills in the

western area of Phuoc Tuy Province. Detailed with carrying out a raid, the patrol was relatively heavily armed: an M60 general purpose machine gun (GPMG) and three M72 66mm light anti-tank weapons (LAW) were carried in addition to the normal complement of rifles, grenades and Claymore mines. The patrol was to locate a suspected Vietcong (VC) camp believed to be in an area of approximately one square kilometre. Having found it, Simpson and his men were to attack it and capture any radios and codebooks. It was, however, believed that there were several hundred VC in the area.

The following day the patrol heard voices and other sounds 150m (163yds) away from its LUP (lying-up position). At 08:00 hours the following morning, as the patrol was moving towards the suspected location of the camp, two VC were observed passing nearby. By 13:00 hours the camp had been located and Lieutenant Simpson and his lead scout, Private Dennis Cullen, had observed fifteen VC. Simpson decided to mount an immediate attack. At 13:15 hours the assault began with Corporal Gary Lobb and Lance-Corporal Tom Kerkez opening fire with his M60 GPMG, while Simpson and the remainder of the patrol advanced into the camp, attacking bunkers with hand grenades and an M79 40mm grenade launcher. Simpson discovered the enemy radio and a quantity of documents, which he took. At that point the patrol came under fire from an RPD light machine gun and withdrew, having killed eight VC and wounded three more. Heading south, Simpson and his men requested extraction while an artillery fire mission was called down on the area of the camp. At 15:30 hours the patrol was extracted.

SIRTE One of several Axis airfields in North Africa, which were raided by the SAS during December 1941. On 8 December David Stirling and Paddy Mayne left Jalo accompanied by a unit of the Long Range Desert Group (LRDG), with the intention of attacking airfields at Tamit and Sirte. Mayne was to attack Tamit while Stirling tried to penetrate Sirte airfield. Both groups failed to breach the airfield's security perimeter and were forced to place their Lewes bombs on vehicles parked by the roadside. Stirling made a second attempt on 25 December but the same thing occurred.

'SITREP' A 'SitRep' is military abbreviation for a situation report. SAS patrols will normally call one twice a day, once in the morning and once in the evening. Any situation requiring immediate action can be sent at any time.

SIWA OASIS Situated approximately 600km (372 miles) west of Cairo, Siwa was the main base of the Long Range Desert Group (LRDG) in North Africa. It was often used by the SAS teams which were frequently transported to targets by the LRDG. In June 1942, the SAS mounted a series of raids on enemy airfields from Siwa to help a convoy of seventeen ships attempting to reach Malta. Despite the massive diversions only two of these ships got through.

SKS ASSAULT RIFLE *Specification* Calibre: 7.62mm × 39 Soviet standard; Weight: 1.7kg (3.8lbs); Muzzle velocity: 735m (800yds) per second; Magazine capacity: 10-round, box.

The Samorazyadnyi Karabin Simonova was made in the USSR and was used all over the Communist world. The predecessor to the AK-47, it was robust, reasonably accurate and easy to use. It was in use with many Communist-backed armies and guerrilla forces, but these days is hardly seen at all, except for ceremonial use. The Chinese, however, still manufacture a version of the SKS known as the Type 56 Carbine.

SKUA MOTORIZED CANOE SK120 *Specification* Length: 460cm (14ft); Weight: 36kg (80lbs) (excluding engine); Beam: 102cm (3ft); Crew: Two-man.

The Skua is a motorized canoe made by Kirton Kayaks Ltd of Devon, a company which also manufactures the Klepper canoe. Unlike the Klepper the SK120 has a moulded polyethylene skin with internal tubular aluminium skeletal frame. This makes the craft extremely robust, and with its updated 15hp engine it can now achieve 16 knots. The SAS and SBS have used motorized canoes since they were first invented in 1943.

SKYVAN *Specification* Engines: Garrett TPE331-2-201A; Turbo-props; Wingspan: 19.79m (21yds); Height: 4.60m (5yds); Weight: 3,357kg (3 tons); Speed: 325km/h (201mph); Range: 386km (239 miles).

Developed in the early 1960s, the Shorts SC7 Skyvan has proved to be one of the world's best small utility aircraft. Designed for a crew of two, the aircraft could be flown by a single pilot. Although the RAF has never purchased it, the Skyvan is in use in many countries including Oman, where between 1970 and 1976 almost all SAS locations on the Jebel Massive were supported by Skyvans, which could land on a short makeshift runway. Its name aptly describes the appearance of the Skyvan, yet the aircraft is robust and has a large carrying capacity. The rear tailgate lowers to allow access to the cargo deck.

During the Oman War the serviceable hours of the helicopters became extremely limited and the SAS were forced to build airstrips in order to maintain the supply line. Many were built by working throughout the night and while under enemy fire, and by morning the Skyvans would arrive. In fairness to the Skyvan pilots of the period, they would land on anything the SAS constructed. Equally, the Skyvan itself proved to be a major asset in winning the logistics war, without which nothing happens.

SLATER, LANCE-CORPORAL ALASTAIR MM   Al Slater was shot and killed on 2 December 1984 while confronting a member of the IRA during an operation in Fermanagh, Northern Ireland. Slater, who had joined the regiment three years earlier, having served with the Parachute Regiment, was posted to B Squadron's Air Troop were he was known as 'Mr Angry' for his impression of the radio character.

The SAS mounted an operation against the IRA when technical information indicated that several beer kegs containing 1,000kg (2,200lbs) of home-made explosive would be placed in a drainage culvert on a road leading to a local restaurant. The IRA were being continually monitored by the SAS who, due to the bomb misfiring, overheard a conversation between the bombers. When the SAS went to investigate a van parked nearby they were confronted by an IRA member called Tony MacBride. As the SAS started to question Mac-Bride, other members of the IRA opened fire from a nearby ditch, fatally wounding Al Slater. In the ensuing firefight MacBride was also killed and another IRA member, Kieran Fleming, drowned as he tried to escape by swimming the River Bannagh, which at the time was in flood. The police later arrested two more IRA members at a check-point as they tried to cross into the south.

'SLEEPY LAD', OPERATION   In an attempt to disrupt German road and rail communications between Ancona and Pescara, several groups from 2 SAS were landed by the Royal Navy on the Italian east coast on 18 December 1943. They managed to cause major damage to traffic and the railway line was severed in several places. Most of the SAS returned to friendly lines by using a local sailing boat, after the Royal Navy failed to keep to the rendezvous plan.

SLOANE, LIEUTENANT-COLONEL JOHN   Originally of the Argyll and Sutherland Highlanders, Sloane, nicknamed 'Tod', com-manded the Malayan Scouts (22 SAS) from 1951 to 1953. He insisted on a strict code of discipline and was responsible for the regiment honing its professional attitude, returning to unit anyone he thought unsuitable. This left a core of excellent soldiers who were more than capable of carrying out the demanding deep jungle operations that they were given.

'SLOT'   Another word for shooting the enemy. 'Stitched' is also used to describe the same purpose, as the bullet wounds from a sub-machine gun look like giant stitch marks.

SLR L1A1   *Specification* Calibre: 7.62mm × 51 NATO standard; Weight: 1.9kg (4.3lbs); Muzzle velocity: 840m (915yds) per second; Magazine capacity: 20-round, box.

A British version of the Belgian FN FAL which, unless specifically modified, only fires on semi-auto. This self-loading rifle has been in service with the British Armed Forces since the 1950s but has now been replaced by the SA80. Although robust, the weapon was heavy by comparison with the AR-15, which was introduced at more or less the same time. The SLR is still in service with many territorial units and other armies around the world.

SMALL, LANCE-CORPORAL GEORDIE A member of an SAS patrol in the Oman War who, while seeking to find a landmark called the Zahkir Tree during the monsoon season, made contact with the enemy. In the initial exchange of gunfire, Geordie Small was hit in the thigh, rupturing his femoral artery. Although he was treated immediately and taken to a secure area to await evacuation, he unfortunately began to haemorrhage internally and consequently died of his wounds.

'SNAPDRAGON', OPERATION On 28 May 1943 in a night-time mission a party of troopers from 2 SAS was placed on the island of Pantelleria in the Italian Mediterranean. Their aim was reconnaissance, but the team returned to the rendezvous submarine empty-handed, having achieved almost nothing, though at least they suffered no casualties.

SNIPER COMMAND AND CONTROL SYSTEM The Sniper Command and Control System is designed to give the unit commander split-second control over the members of his sniper team. The system operates via a highly secure digital telemetry radio link and comprises the following:

1. Up to eight sniper radio stations can be included in the standard system. Each comprises an UHF PRU-22 radio set powered by an integral rechargeable battery with a 9-hour life. This can be extended through the use of an external battery, which can be plugged into the radio, giving a further 24 hours of operation. Indication of a low battery is given by an amber LED display.

The PRU-22 is fitted with a target indicator button unit, which is attached to the fore end of the sniper's rifle. In addition, it also features two further red and green LED displays. Once the sniper has acquired his target and it is in the centre of his crosshairs, reticule of his telescopic sight or image intensifier, he presses his target indicator button, transmitting a constant signal to the unit commander and informing him that he has the target in his sights. Should the sniper lose the target, he releases the button and the cessation of the signal informs the commander accordingly.

While the sniper is awaiting the command to fire, the red LED display on his PRU-22 is illuminated in the 'Stand By' mode, indicating to him that the radio link with the commander's set is functioning. When he presses his Target Indicator Button the green LED illuminates, informing him that his set is transmitting properly.

2. Commander's Radio Station comprises a PRU-22 radio set which features eight pairs of red and green LED displays, each pair representing a member of the sniper team. Each illuminated red LED display shows the commander that the radio link with each respective sniper is working properly. As each sniper acquires his pre-allocated target in his sights and presses his target indicator button, the respective green LED illuminates and stays so while the target remains in the sniper's point of aim. Should a sniper lose his target, he releases his target indicator button and the appropriate green LED on the commander's set ceases to be illuminated. Once all targets are acquired, the commander can give the order to the snipers to fire at the appropriate moment over the separate team voice radio net. The PRU-22 is powered by an external battery, which will give 24 hours of operation. The radio is equipped with an amber LED display, which gives warning of low battery level.

3. VIU Touch Screen Visual Display is designed to interface with the PRU-22 and to present a graphic display of the situation. The unit is fitted with a touch screen, which features two pages of information, accommodating eight and twelve targets respectively.

The target symbols are ranged along the top of the screen and can be individually drawn by touch into the 'live' area of the screen. Likewise, the symbols representing the members of the sniper team are ranged along the bottom of the screen and can be moved on to the 'live' area and allocated targets by touch. While the snipers are in 'Stand By' mode, their individual symbols appear as grey on screen. On switching to 'On Target' mode, their symbols change to black. Similarly, the target symbols appear as grey on the screen until acquired by their respective snipers when they turn black. When all targets have been acquired by snipers who are 'On Target', a 'Totaliser' symbol on the right-hand side of the screen changes colour, notifying the commander that all targets are covered and enabling him to take a rapid decision to give the order to fire if necessary.

SNIPER TEAM The SAS anti-terrorist unit has two sniper teams which can work jointly or independently, depending on the size of the problem. They work in pairs and are normally the first to be deployed during any terrorist incident. From well-camouflaged positions the snipers will report back all terrorist movement, remaining prepared at all times to deal with any long-range situation that may present itself. Just prior to any attack by the assault teams, the snipers will indicate any terrorist targets that may be exposed. They do this by a pressing a small button on the side of their weapon which in turn triggers a small light on the team commander's display board.

Snipers often dress in a Gillie suit which provides a foliage-type camouflage, but they will frequently dress in black, identical to the assault teams, when selecting a sniper position in a building. At times the snipers cross-train for operations in the assault role.

Each sniper will have at least two rifles, one for daytime use and one fitted with a night scope. The main sniper weapons used are the British Accuracy International PM sniper rifle and the Heckler & Koch G3.

'SNOOPY', OPERATION   In September 1978 a cross-border operation, code-named 'Snoopy', was mounted by Rhodesia's 1st SAS Regiment (RhSAS) and the Rhodesian Light Infantry (RLI) against a large ZANLA base, accommodating 2,000 guerrillas in an area known as the Chimoio Circle in Mozambique. It was known that four white Rhodesians, abducted some months earlier, were being held prisoner in the base.

On 20 September the operation began with the RhSAS and RLI being landed by helicopter and finding the camp virtually abandoned. Shortly afterwards, however, a Lynx ground attack aircraft came under fire from another location 35km (22 miles) further south where a massive new base complex, measuring 30 × 40km (19 × 25 miles), was discovered. Air strikes were carried out by Royal Rhodesian Air Force Canberra bombers, Hunters and Lynx backed up by Alouette K-Car helicopter gunships. The RhSAS and RLI arrived soon afterwards, ferried by helicopter from the abandoned base, and a major battle ensued and continued throughout the day, the ZANLA guerrillas putting up a determined resistance. During the night nine FRELIMO tanks appeared but caused little trouble, departing the following morning.

During the second day of the operation, three Russian-supplied armoured personnel carriers were destroyed by air strikes, a fourth being accounted for on the following night by the RLI who killed ten FRELIMO troops. The RhSAS, meanwhile, searched for the four Rhodesian prisoners but there was no sign of them; they were later repatriated via the International Red Cross. On the third day the RhSAS and RLI withdrew, leaving a large number of ZANLA dead and the main base and peripheral camps totally destroyed.

SNOW CAVE   A shelter cut into a depth of snow of 2m (2yds) or more in thickness. This is a simple approach to Arctic survival when no other means of protection is available. It takes approximately one hour to dig into a snow drift or cornice in order to produce a cave large enough for four men. The inside roof is dome shaped to prevent the roof caving in and a well is dug just inside the doorway to draw down cold air. Lighting a candle in the cave will raise the temperature to a comfortable level. The SAS have used snow caves during Arctic exercises in Norway.

SO19/D11   The original police armed anti-terrorist team which accompanied the SAS during early terrorist operations in the 1970s were marksmen from the police D11 section. This police unit was equipped and armed in a similar manner to the SAS, and dealt with matters deemed not to require the SAS's more specialist talents. In the event of a terrorist incident, where the Home Office requested the SAS, D11 normally remained on site to assist in the handling of the situation. D11 has been replaced with the firearms section SO19 of the National Crime Unit.

SOAF (SULTAN OF OMAN'S AIR FORCE) The Air Force of Oman, abbreviated to 'SOAF' which, during the Oman War, consisted mainly of Strikemaster jets, Skyvans and Huey helicopters. It provided essential air cover to ground forces during assaults against guerrilla forces, and saved the day at the Battle of Mirbat in 1972. However, before the SAS arrived in 1970, the SOAF was not always as efficient. A lack of communication between the Sultan's Armed Forces (SAF) and the SOAF often meant that the air support would arrive long after the ground attack had finished, resulting in nearby villages being bombed instead. This did little to endear the government forces to the local civilian population. After the arrival of the SAS, communications improved and the SAS, SOAF and SAF worked more as a team, providing greater successes against the rebels.

SOE (SPECIAL OPERATIONS EXECUTIVE) This was a World War II British intelligence and espionage organization established in 1940. Most of its members were civilians, although there were some military personnel. There were SOE schools in Britain, North Africa, Italy and the Far East and by 1944 there were 7,500 SOE spies and saboteurs who were available for missions in northwest Europe. Operations behind enemy lines carried out by SOE and SAS were meant to be co-ordinated, but the SOE often saw the SAS as being under its control. SOE was also over-protective of the missions it carried out and resented the SAS forces going into areas where SOE agents were working, feeling that its operatives would be compromised. For example, the SOE had some SAS operations cancelled prior to D-Day. When the drops did take place, however, the SOE co-operated and arranged reception parties for the SAS groups.

SOUTH ARMAGH BRIGADE Peter Cleary was an IRA staff officer in the first battalion of the South Armagh Brigade who was shot while resisting arrest by the SAS on 15 April 1976. The terrorist was wanted for questioning about a series of murders and bombings, and had been on the run for a year. After mounting surveillance on his fiancées house, the SAS finally moved in to arrest him. As they waited for a helicopter to collect them and their prisoner, Cleary suddenly turned on the soldier escorting him and went for his throat. The soldier, reacting, as he thought, to save his own life started firing and only stopped when Cleary was dead, with three bullets in his chest. The soldiers involved were called to testify at an inquest, but were not identified by their real names. Despite their version of events being upheld, the whole added grist to the IRA propaganda mill that the SAS operated a shoot to kill policy.

SP TEAM Name used during the 1970s to indicate the anti-terrorist team. The 'SP' was taken from an old police call-sign allocated to the regiment, which identified their vehicles when communicating on the police network.

SPECIAL FORCES CLUB The Special Forces Club is a London-based club.

SPECIAL FORCES FLIGHTS/SQUADRONS – RAF, AAC AND RN There are two Special Forces flights within the RAF, forming part of 7 and 47 Squadrons respectively, and both dedicated to the support of Army and Royal Marine special operations units. Aircrew within both flights are trained for special operations, namely low-level deep penetration into enemy airspace and the delivery and extraction of Special Forces.

The Special Forces Flight of 7 Squadron is based at RAF Odiham in Hampshire. It is currently equipped with the UK-designated HC.2 variant of the Boeing Vertol Chinook twin rotor, heavy lift helicopter which can be fitted with four (two forward and two aft) M134 pintle-mounted mini-guns. In 2000 the flight was re-equipped with the HC.3 which will be the first special operations dedicated aircraft to be purchased by the British armed forces. The same aircraft is currently operated as the MH-47E by the US Army's 160th Aviation Battalion; better known as Task Force 160, it features a glass cockpit, terrain following forward-looking infra-red (FLIR) system, built-in fast roping brackets, and four .50 calibre Gecal mini-guns.

The Special Forces Flight of 47 Squadron is located at RAF Lyneham in Wiltshire. It is equipped with the C-130K variant (designated C.3 in the UK) of the Hercules transport, fitted with an in-flight refuelling probe, electronic counter-measure systems and chaff and flare dispensers, both the latter designed to provide a measure of defence against enemy air defence systems. The aircraft are currently being equipped with dedicated night vision goggle (NVG) compatible cockpit lighting. It is reported that four of the C-130J Hercules on order for the RAF will be for dedicated Special Forces use, being upgraded to the same specification as the MC-130E Combat Shadow operated by the special operations squadrons of the US Air Force. This aircraft has terrain-following radar and FLIR systems, NVG-compatible cockpit lighting and an integrated avionics package for long-range low-level covert operations enabling precision insertion and re-supply of Special Forces.

Finally, M Flight of the Fleet Air Arm's 848 Squadron, equipped with the Commando Mk.4 variant of the Westland Sea King helicopter, provides support for the maritime counter-terrorist role.

SPECIAL RAIDING SQUADRON (SRS) During World War II, 1 SAS was temporarily re-named as the Special Raiding Squadron, and fought under this name in Sicily and Italy in 1943.

'SPEEDWELL', OPERATION On 7 September 1943, led by Captain Phillip Pinckney and Captain Dudgeon, two seven-man teams from 2 SAS were dropped into the Spezia-Genoa area of northwest Italy, with the purpose of severing the railway lines transporting enemy reinforcements and supplies to the front. Splitting into two smaller groups, the SAS succeeded in derailing several trains and blew up many of the railway lines over the next few weeks. Nevertheless, they did encounter some misfortune; the poor weather conditions and unhealthy diet created a lot of illness amongst the men. In addition, the teams lost one of their commanding officers, Captain Dudgeon, who was shot by the Germans.

The return to Allied lines was a fragmented exercise too, some men returning after operating for 54 days, others after 73 days. One trooper, Sergeant 'Tanky' Challenor, spent 7 months behind enemy lines, including a time in an enemy hospital.

Despite these minor problems, this operation is a classic example of a World War II SAS mission, demonstrating how small groups of men could inflict severe damage on the enemy whilst remaining behind their own lines for long periods of time.

'SPENSER', OPERATION Led by Commander Bourgoin, 317 men of 4 French Parachute Battalion (4 SAS) infiltrated the area east of Bourges, central France, between 29 August and 14 September 1944. Using 54 jeeps to transport them, the plan was to inflict as much damage as possible on the Germans, as they retreated over the River Loire. The SAS took 2,500 prisoners, and 120 enemy vehicles were successfully destroyed. At the same time the SAS were instrumental in the surrender to American forces of over 20,000 German troops.

'SPIDER' Slang term used for the soldiers' quarters in the old Bradbury Lines barracks. Eight dormitories led off from the central section of the barracks building, which from the air resembled a large spider. The six outer legs were designated for sleeping accommodation while the two shorter units served as stores. The centre block housed the washroom, toilets and showers.

SPYGLASS THERMAL IMAGER The Spyglass is a hand-held thermal imager (TI) made by Pilkington Thorn Optronics. TI presents a picture of the heat patterns by day and night, generated or retained by living or inert objects. It is therefore not dependent on ambient light from stars, moonlight or artificial sources. It will also detect men and vehicles hidden by smoke or camouflage netting. The Spyglass imager is easy to operate and can be carried slung like a pair of binoculars. As TI is passive, the target will be unaware that it is being observed, and the brief burst of laser energy to assess the range may even pass unnoticed.

The Spyglass was first used on operations by the SBS when they attacked an Argentine position at Fanning Head during the Falklands War in 1982. TI was used to locate their position covering the approaches to San Carlos Bay. It was also used extensively by the SAS during the Gulf War, when they relied heavily on the Spyglass when observing the Iraqi positions prior to finding a crossing point from Saudi Arabia.

SSU (SPECIAL SUPPORT UNIT)   Also known as the HQ Mobile Support Unit, SSU acted as the armed 'active measures unit' of the RUC, working in conjunction with E4A. The personnel of this unit were trained by the SAS at their base in Hereford, but were never selected by the SAS. In fact the SAS often disapproved of the calibre of SSU operatives. It was disbanded a couple years after it was formed due to its trigger-happy tendencies.

ST MARTIN'S CHURCH   The Church of St Martin is situated on the south side of Hereford, close to Stirling Lines. The church has traditionally been used to bury those soldiers killed in the SAS since the regiment moved to Hereford. The regiment has had its own graveyard there since the mid-1970s. Additionally, in 1984 the church installed a stained-glass window depicting the regiment's battle honours, illustrating its close relationship with the SAS.

STABLE BELT, SAS   The SAS stable belt is made from dark-blue cloth with a silver-coloured, disk-type clasp. The face of the disk is embossed with the 'Winged Dagger'. The belt is worn with normal military working dress.

STATIC-LINE   A means of parachuting where the static-line attached to the parachute is clipped to a line inside the aircraft. When the soldier jumps the line is pulled out from the back of the parachute, withdrawing the canopy, which inflates due to the air-flow. When the line is at full stretch the tie, which has a low break value between the canopy and the static-line, snaps, releasing the canopy from the aircraft.

STEWART, SERGEANT ALAN – AUSTRALIAN SAS REGI-MENT (SASR)   Sergeant Alan Stewart was the commander of a six-man patrol of 2 Squadron SASR which was inserted on 10 January 1969 into an area 10km (16 miles) west of Ngai Giao, in the northwest region of Phouc Tuy Province. His task was to reconnoitre and report on Vietcong (VC) and North Vietnamese (NVA) movements in the area. Two days later the patrol observed a mixed force of some 47 VC and NVA, heavily armed with three 12.7mm calibre heavy machine guns, four 60mm light mortars, ten RPD light machine guns, RPG-7s and small arms. Among them was a tall individual over 1.8m (6ft) in height and of Caucasian appearance, accompanied by a radio operator. Artillery fire was called down by the patrol which observed over 160 enemy during the next three days, before being extracted on 14 January. This was prior to air strikes and artillery fire missions being carried out on what had transpired to be a principal movement route for VC and NVA forces.

On 22 January the patrol returned to the area and resumed its task of tracking enemy movements. Four days later it established an ambush, but confined itself to reporting back, as it was heavily outnumbered by enemy groups passing through. On 27 January the patrol was extracted again, but on the following day guided a company of the 4th Battalion Royal Australian Regiment (4 RAR) into the area. On the night of 29 January the company was attacked by 150 VC who, suffering heavy casualties, were beaten off with the help of artillery and 'Puff the Magic Dragon' Dakota gunships.

STINGER *Specification* Weight: 23kg (50lbs); Diameter: 70mm (2.75ins); Length: 150cm (60ins); Range: 4km (2.5 miles); Identification: friend or foe compatible with US/NATO. Guidance: passive IR/UV homing – fire and forget; Navigation: proportional with lead bias; Speed: Mach 1.

A portable, shoulder-fired, infra-red (IR) homing (heat-seeking) air defence guided missile, the Stinger is designed to counter high-speed, low-level, ground attack aircraft and is the only forward area air defence missile currently employed by US forces. It first became operational in the US Army in 1981; shortly after, in July 1982, several Stingers were loaned to the SAS for use in the Falklands War.

The current FIM-92C Stinger has advanced electro-optical seekers sensitive to both infra-red and ultra-violet which can effectively discriminate between target and background distractions such as flares. The Stinger is also unique in that it possesses the Target Adaptive Guidance technique, which biases missile orientation toward vulnerable parts of the aircraft and assures maximum lethal effect. This is derived from hit-to-kill accuracy, high warhead, and the impact force of the missile's kinetic energy generated by speeds of up to Mach 2. The Stinger has been proven in combat in both Afghanistan and in the Persian Gulf. In Afghanistan the basic Stinger downed over 270 Soviet aircraft (a 79 per cent combat success rate), and helped to stop air assault operations and force a Soviet withdrawal.

STIRLING, LIEUTENANT-COLONEL DAVID   Born in 1915, the founding father of the SAS. In 1940, David Stirling was a lieutenant with No. 8 Commando serving in North Africa. In the belief that a small band of dedicated men could operate successfully behind the enemy lines, he managed to present his plan to General Ritchie, who at the time was Deputy Chief-of-Staff. His idea and memorandum finally reached the Commander-in-Chief of the Middle East, General Auchinleck, and the SAS was born. As the founder of the SAS, Stirling's main strength came from his ability to select and enlist those men who had both daring and vision, one such man being Paddy Mayne.

David Stirling is quoted as saying, 'We believe, as did the ancient Greeks who originated the word "Aristocracy", that every man with the right attitude and talents, regardless of birth and riches, has a capacity in his own lifetime of reaching that status in its true sense. In fact, in our SAS context, an individual soldier might prefer to go on serving as an NCO rather than leave the regiment in order to obtain an Officer's commission. All ranks in the SAS are of "one company" in which a sense of class is both alien and ludicrous.'

He was captured in North Africa and sent to an Italian prison at Gavi, where he escaped at least four times. This caused his transfer to the notorious German prison fortress of Colditz where he waited out the rest of the war. In 1990 Stirling was knighted for his services, but sadly he died in the same year.

STIRLING, LIEUTENANT-COLONEL WILLIAM   An officer in the Scots Guards and a member of No. 62 Commando, William was the brother of David Stirling, and commander of 2 SAS. In September 1942 he was promoted to lieutenant-colonel, but by the end of the year, following its mission to Algeria, 62 Commando was disbanded. Stirling was subsequently given permission to establish a second SAS regiment, 2 SAS, which was based on the same principles as 1 SAS. William believed his men should be employed in attacking strategic targets, not just engaged in a supporting role, although his superiors were not always in agreement with his ideas. Operation 'Speedwell' in Italy and similar successful missions proved the soundness of his ideas, although senior commanders still insisted the SAS was to be employed just ahead of the front line, and not in deep-penetration. On the eve of the Allied invasion of Europe, code-named Operation 'Overlord', William Stirling ran out of patience. Supreme Headquarters Allied Expeditionary Force (SHAEF) planned to position the SAS between the enemy infantry and the German armoured reserves, just behind the beaches. Convinced that this was a suicidal move and a complete waste of his unit, Stirling resigned his position, threatening the future of 2 SAS. He was replaced by Lieutenant-Colonel Brian Franks, a discerning and popular commander, and Stirling, feeling aggrieved by the recent events, returned to Scotland.

A less charismatic character than his brother, William was nevertheless an excellent administrator and possessed a deep understanding of the true role of the SAS. With his unerring belief that the SAS was a deep-penetration unit capable of achievements totally belied by its size, William is remembered for his attempts to change the opinions of the higher echelons of the British Army, despite being somewhat overshadowed by his brother David.

STIRLING LINES   Name given to the SAS barracks in Hereford which was officially opened in 1984, when the old Bradbury Lines was renamed Stirling Lines by David Stirling himself.

STOPS   Stops' are positions taken up where the SAS wish to prevent an enemy from escaping. An example would be in Northern Ireland where terrorists are known to be arriving at an arms cache by car. It is likely that the ambush will be sprung immediately the IRA have possession of the weapons. Should the driver of the car attempt to drive off, the 'stops' should be in position to prevent it.

'STORM', OPERATION   The code-name for the plan of operations in Oman. The campaign was planned in 1970, a few months before the SAS actually became involved in the conflict. It included a 'hearts and minds' approach, with medical aid being given to civilians; it specified no indiscriminate reprisals against civilians, and emphasized intelligence gathering. It was a plan which was found to be successful, and the ideas used in 'Storm' were refined by the SAS and later applied to other conflicts.

STRIKEMASTER   Hunting/British Aerospace developed the 167 Strikemaster in 1967 from the older type Jet Provost trainer. This small ground attack aircraft, with the T-5 airframe, a larger engine, upgraded brakes and armour, was mainly built for export. The Sultan of Oman's Air Force (SOAF) used the Strikemaster in a ground support role for the Sultan's Armed Forces (SAF) and the SAS. They made a huge difference to the war in Oman, especially during the battle for Mirbat, where had it not been for the SOAF jets and the courage of the pilots the outcome would have been very different. The Strikemaster could fire twin 7.62 machine guns, 12 rockets, and carry two 100kg (220lbs) bombs.

STUN GRENADE   Royal Ordnance Enfield at the request of the SAS experimented with various devices to disorientate targets in an assault, and the one that proved most successful was the stun grenade. The device, designated G60, produces loud noise (160 Db) combined with high light output (300,000cd), without any harmful fragmentation. This is capable of stunning anyone in close proximity for a period of around

3-5 seconds when detonated, and is one of the most effective items in the anti-terrorist armoury. The effect is not dissimilar to the flashing strobes in a disco, but a million times more effective.

Also called a 'flash-bang', this efficient but non-lethal device has become essential in almost every hostage-rescue scenario. Originally developed for the regiment, it has now become a standard item in many of the world's counter-terrorist squads. It contains a mixture of magnesium powder and fulminate of mercury, which detonates once the ring is pulled and the grenade thrown. The grenade bodies are constructed with a minimum of metal parts to ensure that there is no danger of hostages being injured by fragmentation.

They were used for the first time operationally during the Mogadishu hijack in 1977 where three were thrown just prior to the assault. During the Iranian Embassy Siege in 1980 it is suspected that one of the grenades set fire to a curtain, resulting in the building being gutted by fire, although this was never proved.

SURVIVAL TRAINING The SAS take Combat and Survival training very seriously, and start the process during Selection. The reason is simple: any SAS operation involves action behind enemy lines, or in remote, unfamiliar terrain where the risk of capture and the need to survive are ever present. The subjects involved are fascinating and are all taught by both military and civilian experts. The aspects cover escape and evasion, survival and resistance to interrogation.

The course combines classroom lessons, practical outdoor instruction and a final exercise. Even if candidates avoid capture they will still have to undergo the compulsory 24-hours interrogation phase. This will involve a very realistic examination of the candidate's ability to resist questions put to him under duress. Joint Services Interrogation Unit (JSIU) carries out all SAS interrogation training.

SWANBOURNE – CAMPBELL BARRACKS Campbell Barracks at Swanbourne, on the outskirts of the Western Australia capital of Perth, has been the home of the Australian SAS since 1957, when 1st SAS Company of the Royal Australian Regiment was formed on 25 July. Initially the accommodation comprised old wooden buildings, but during the period 1967–68 a five-stage programme of building saw new accommodation and training facilities constructed for the SAS Regiment. At a total cost of A$4.2 million, the new complex provided accommodation for 500 all ranks, including accommodation for each squadron, a Warrant Officers' and Sergeants' Mess, assembly/lecture hall, swimming and diving pools and two 25m (27yd) ranges. The completed barracks was officially opened on 27 April 1968 by Mr Philip Lynch, the Minister for the Army.

SWIM-DIVING APPARATUS SAS divers have used a wide variety of diving equipment over the years, and have generally kept up to date with the latest technology. Divers are used in many roles, such as sabotage on shipping, covert entry to off-shore facilities, and underwater searches prior to VIP visits. The present diving equipment used by the SAS is the German-made Drager system, which is a lung-governed closed-circuit breathing apparatus for use with pure oxygen. This small compact unit is easily operated and maintained, giving the diver up to four hours submersion depending on the underwater activity. The Drager is ideal for covert operations as it uses a semi-closed circuit with a soda lime cartridge to provide air purification. This leaves no trace of bubbles either below water or on the surface.

SWINDELLS, CORPORAL 'DUKE' MM Originally from the Middlesex Regiment he was killed during a gun battle in the area of Jebel Akhdar on 25 November 1958. His unit was moving to assist another patrol when Corporal Swindells was hit in the chest. He was buried in a secret location in a landlocked bay close to the shoreline.

'SWORD', OPERATION This was the code-name for a sweep by the SAS deep in the Malayan jungle during the Malayan Emergency of 1948–60. The party was dropped in January 1954, but three men were killed whilst 'tree-jumping'. One man, who was injured when he hit the jungle canopy, died when he cut himself free of his harness and fell over 100m (320ft) to the ground.

SYCAMORE Helicopter used by the SAS in Oman and Borneo in the 1950s and early 1960s, for light assault and reconnaissance. Able to seat five passengers, the Sycamore had a top speed of 204km/h (126mph).

SYKES, SERGEANT FRANK – AUSTRALIAN SAS REGIMENT (SASR) On 27 June 1967, a five-man patrol of 1 Squadron SASR under Sergeant Frank Sykes was inserted 5km (3 miles) of Thua Tich, in the eastern half of Phuoc Tuy Province. Its task was to locate the headquarters of a major Vietcong (VC) unit, believed to be the 274th Regiment.

The following day the patrol discovered a grass hut with a tunnel entrance beside it and shortly afterwards came across a track. Sergeant Sykes and his lead scout were in the process of returning from reconnoitring forward when firing broke out from the remainder of the patrol in a lying-up position (LUP) nearby. The patrol broke contact and withdrew to an LUP from which it contacted 2 Squadron's headquarters by radio. Shortly afterwards it was on the move again, and having crossed a creek, moved into another LUP. Meanwhile the VC were following up, sweeping the area for the patrol. It was not long before the patrol was discovered and a fierce firefight began at a range of 25m

(27yds), with Sergeant Sykes and his men making good use of their 40mm grenade launchers to beat off the enemy attack.

Moving out swiftly and succeeding in breaking away from the VC, the patrol headed north. Establishing radio contact, it requested extraction and within a short period of time help arrived in the form of a USAF Cessna 'Bird Dog' forward observation aircraft, which brought in air strikes and helicopter gunships. Shortly afterwards the patrol was extracted by a helicopter of 9 Squadron Royal Australian Air Force, whose rotors were chopping down the secondary jungle undergrowth as the pilot, Squadron Leader Jim Cox, brought it low enough for the patrol to climb aboard.

TA Territorial Army. The SAS has two Territorial Regiments, 21 and 23 SAS, plus R Squadron.

'TAB' An SAS term for a forced march, much like the Marine term 'yomp'.

TAG, COUNTER-TERRORIST CAPABILITY – AUSTRALIAN SAS REGIMENT (SASR)

The SAS Regiment (SASR) assumed the responsibility for providing Australia's counter-terrorist capability in 1979. In February 1978 a bomb had exploded at the entrance to Sydney's Hilton Hotel, warning Australia that it could no longer consider itself out of the line of fire of terrorists. Following a six-month study of counter-terrorist forces in other countries during 1978, and the subsequent publication of a report on the subject, the Australian Government gave approval in May 1979 for the formation of a counter-terrorist team from within the SASR.

Formal authorization was given on 31 August to the commanding officer of the SASR, Lieutenant-Colonel Reg Beesley, who in turn gave responsibility for training for the new role to Guerrilla Warfare Wing, under Captain Greg Mawkes. Construction of special counter-terrorist training facilities at Swanbourne was commenced later in the year and these were completed by March 1980.

The TAG comprised a headquarters element, consisting of the commanding officer, the operations officer and two signallers, and an assault force. The latter comprised: a headquarters consisting of the commander, a signaller and driver/signaller; three assault teams, each of three men, and a ten-man sniper team. Personnel for the TAG were drawn from 1 Squadron, commanded by Major Dan McDaniel. The first TAG commander was Captain Martin Hamilton-Smith who, with Sergeant Leigh Alver, underwent training by 22 SAS in Britain in the latter part of 1979. Meanwhile 1 Squadron was reorganized, B Troop becoming the TAG and code-named 'Gauntlet 1'. It commenced training in March 1980 and was fully operational by May. In September 1980

A Troop commenced counter-terrorist training and was redesignated 'Gauntlet 2', relieving 'Gauntlet 1' in November.

In July 1980 the SASR was also tasked with developing a capability for offshore counter-terrorist operations, code-named 'Bursa', for dealing with terrorist hijackings of offshore oil or gas installations in the Bass Strait. As a result the Offshore Installations Assault Group (OAG) code-named 'Nullah 1' was formed and operational by the end of October of that year. However, the added manpower commitment caused problems for SASR and as a result seventeen clearance divers of the Royal Australian Navy were seconded to the regiment, all having passed a Selection course.

'TAILEND CHARLIE' The man who brings up the rear of a patrol in its order of march. To defend the patrol from any attacks from the rear, the man in this position constantly needs to keep watch behind him. He is usually armed with a machine gun.

TAMIT Two raiding parties, one commanded by David Stirling and the other consisting of Major Paddy Mayne, Sergeant McDonald, and Privates Bennet, White, Chesworth and Hawkins left Jalo on 24 December 1941. Once they reached Wadi Tamit the parties split up. Major Mayne lead his men to an Axis airfield where, after a short but fierce attack, 27 aircraft were destroyed.

The same airfield was raided twice by the SAS later that year. Under cover of darkness and having been dropped off by the Long Range Desert Group (LRDG) on 12 December, Major Mayne, with eight of his best men, walked on to the airfield and placed bombs on each parked aircraft. They all burst into flames but, not satisfied, Mayne wrenched the instrument panel out of one of the cockpits with his bare hands; he then burst into the officers' mess at the airfield and shot it to pieces with his machine gun. Their mission completed, and having sustained no casualties, the SAS retreated into the darkness.

Mayne returned twelve days later with five men to perform another raid, with equal success, and a further 27 aircraft were destroyed on the ground.

'TANGO', OPERATION Criticism of NATO's questionable effectiveness at apprehending war criminals resulted in an SAS operation on 10 July 1997 in Prijedor, northwest Bosnia. Their aim was to arrest two criminals, Simla Drljaca and his brother-in-law Milan Kovacevic, who had been under surveillance for some time, having been accused of setting up concentration camps around Prijedor. They were wanted for the killing of thousands of Muslims whom they had imprisoned, starved and tortured in an ethnic cleansing programme.

The operation began early in the morning when the SAS, wearing standard issue combat clothing, were transported to the target area by

US Black Hawk helicopters. The criminals had no reason to suspect the forthcoming events and went about their business as usual. Kovacevic was working in his job as a director of the local hospital when he was arrested without incident. Drljaca on the other hand, in his position as Prijedor's Chief of Police, reacted by shooting one of the arresting party in the leg. The young soldier was taken to the American Military Hospital at Tuzla where he was treated for his injuries. In the meantime the SAS returned fire, killing Drljaca outright. Two accomplices were also arrested at the scene and three more handguns were found. Kovacevic was handed over to the Criminal Tribunal authorities, who sent him to The Hague, where he was imprisoned awaiting his trial. It is expected that he will be indicted for his crimes. From start to finish the whole operation took no more than 15 minutes.

TAQA Taqa is a small coastal village midway between Salalah and Mirbat which served as an SAS base at the start of the Oman War. It was also the tribal home of the Firqat KBW. This Firqat in particular mustered more than 80 men, who were fearsome fighters. Their training prior to operations on the Jebel was undertaken by G Squadron's Mountain Troop; they proved quick learners as many had undertaken training with the Trucial Oman Scouts and had a very good knowledge of British military tactics. It was common to see the section commanders lead off giving the same hand signals that could be seen on the training areas of the Brecon Beacons. The SAS, known at the time as the British Army Training Team (BATT), lived in Taqa where they occupied a two-storey building overlooking the village square.

TARGET ATTACK Target attacks play a major role in the SAS and are normally only carried out after a careful target recce. Despite the advent of stand-off Laser Target Designators (LTD) for precision airstrikes, on-site demolitions skills are still required. All military installations, as well as civilian lines of communication and war production material, may find themselves a target during a war. SAS success in the past has been due to good intelligence coupled with security and daring.

TARGET RECCE The SAS carry out a target recce to collect as much information about the target site as possible. Prior planning will include studying maps, aerial photographs, local information, or if in battle, prisoners-of-war. A route to and from the target must be assessed, as well as the limitations needed to carry out the task and the correct equipment required for doing the job.

The following basic details will be required from any SAS patrol once they have located the target. Confirmation of the best and most secure route to and from the target. A sketch map, which covers an area of 500 sq m (600 sq yds) around the target, with north clearly indicated. This must include the name of the person who carried out the recce, giving a precise grid reference, type of target and the date. It should also show all terrain details such as woods, rivers, etc. Enemy defences, obstacles and vehicle movement should be marked, as should any possible lying-up positions (LUPs) for the target attack patrol.

A second drawing is then done showing the target details. This will include side elevations, cross sections and dimensions, as well as indicating the sort of material that will require a demolition charge, for example wood, steel, masonry, etc. A list of the type and quantity of explosives needed will be attached, as will details of any specialist demolition equipment.

Finally, security information should give an idea of the enemy's strength, disposition and alertness as well as guard changeover times, regular transport visits and the weapons positioned on site.

The SAS believe that a good target recce produces a positive target attack.

'TAURUS', OPERATION   One special operation unique to the SAS was Operation 'Taurus'. Thousands of goats and cattle were rounded up on the Jebel Massive in southern Oman and purchased by the government for food. This move was also intended to deny the enemy its regular food supply. In what has been described as an unbelievable sight, the SAS and Firqat rounded up the animals. Then, amid fighting with the enemy, and assisted by Strikemaster jets, the massive herd of animals was driven down the Jebel to the southern capital, Salalah.

TCG (TACTICAL CONTROL GROUP)   TCG units were set up in Northern Ireland to co-ordinate covert and overt police and military operations. The main aim of TCG was to combine the various sources of information available, and task the appropriate agency to carry out any subsequent operation. The Province had three TCG units positioned in Belfast, Londonderry and Armagh, each one controlled by the RUC Special Branch. Each unit also had liaison officers from CID, SAS, 14 Intelligence and Security Unit, together with brigade intelligence officers, who would answer to the senior Special Branch officer in charge of TCG. In practice the units worked extremely well, controlling both the flow of high-grade intelligence and the movement of troops on the ground, which avoided friendly forces contact. Many of the successes against the IRA in Northern Ireland can be contributed to the controls provided by TCG.

TECHNICAL SURVEILLANCE EQUIPMENT   The SAS possess a wide range of technical surveillance equipment, most of which is used by the anti-terrorist teams or for other covert operations.

1. The Video Close-In Surveillance System is fully portable and comprises a high-resolution colour monitor with VHS format video

recorder and a 430-line miniature remote head colour camera. This has a pinhole lens, with the external diameter of the camera head being just 17.5mm (.6in), with a minimum sensitivity of 5 lux. The focal length of the pinhole lens is 12.mm – in wide-angle mode it is 3mm and in telephoto 24mm (.9in). The system employs digital signal processing with automatic gain and white balance control, requiring little adjustment for changing light conditions.

2. A Flexible Endoscope comprising a 1,000mm long 5mm diameter flexible endoscope, fitted with a 2-way articulated viewing tip giving a 110 degree field of view, can be fitted to the video system.

3. Other technical equipment includes a full range of photographic equipment including cameras fitted with Databacks – on-film time, date and location data, plus a range of lenses from standard, wide angle, telephoto and zoom up to 2,000mm (78in) focal length.

'TEPID', OPERATION In October 1979 a joint operation, code-named 'Tepid', was mounted by the Rhodesian 1st SAS Regiment (RhSAS) and the Rhodesian Light Infantry (RLI). It comprised an attack by all three RhSAS squadrons and two commandos of the RLI, on a heavily defended base located in the area of Lusuto in southeastern Zambia. This was about 64km (40 miles) from Kariba, and manned by a conventional infantry battalion of ZIPRA regular troops numbering 240 in total. An initial task by two troops of C Squadron to ambush routes leading to the base ended in failure with one RhSAS trooper killed and a Lynx airborne command post aircraft, carrying C Squadron's commander Captain Bob McKenna, badly damaged by 12.7mm and 14.5mm anti-aircraft fire.

On 20 October the three RhSAS Sabre Squadrons, together with 2 and 3 Commandos of the RLI, were inserted by helicopter 3km (2 miles) to the north of their objective. They were supported by Canberra bombers which carried out an air strike at 10:00 hours. An hour later four RLI and two RhSAS mortar teams were landed by helicopter to provide support. Almost immediately, however, these came under heavy and accurate enemy mortar and 75mm recoilless rifle fire. The RhSAS squadrons took up their positions on high ground, preparing to sweep through the area of a salt pan lying between two ridges, which were to be taken by the two RLI commandos. In the event, the latter met very heavy fire on both ridges and 2 Commando suffered eight casualties while clearing trenches. An air strike by a Hunter on a 14.5mm machine gun position failed and eventually the Rhodesian attack was beaten off.

During the following night the ZIPRA battalion shelled the Rhodesian positions with 122mm rockets and mortars. However, the unit had been rattled by continual air strikes and was running short of ammunition. Under cover of darkness it withdrew and one company of 150 ZIPRA troops unknowingly passed through an RLI ambush area. Unfortunately the young RLI subaltern in command of the twenty-man ambush group decided not to take on such a large enemy force and let it pass. The following morning the RhSAS and RLI advanced into the base, which was found to be extremely well laid out with mutually supporting positions, well-camouflaged trenches with overhead cover and a field telephone system linking the battalion headquarters with each platoon. Shortly afterwards, the entire force was extracted and returned to Rhodesia.

TERMOLI Led by Lieutenant-Colonel Paddy Mayne the Special Raiding Squadron (SRS), together with the Special Service Brigade, made up of a number of Commandos, were tasked in October 1943 with the capture of the Italian Adriatic port of Termoli. The aim was to aid the Eighth Army's efforts to breach the so-called Termoli line. Given the code-name 'Devon', the mission began 3 October when 207 SRS, two commandos and their support units landed on the shore and cleared the town with ease. At noon the lead parties of the Lancashire Fusiliers and a party of 2 SAS arrived.

On the morning of 5 October the SAS was just about to re-embark when the Germans launched a huge counter-attack. Fierce fighting ensued around the cemetery and the railway, the situation only being saved by the arrival of a detachment of Royal Irish Rangers and some Canadian Sherman tanks. This was the last SRS operation in Italy.

TEST WEEK Test Week is the last and hardest week of initial SAS Selection training. It includes the 'Fan Dance' and the Endurance march.

THERMAL LANCE The Thermal Lance is designed for cutting mild steel, including objects which are underwater. The basic system consists of a 3-m (12-ft) flexible thermal lance made from Kerie cable, a single 3-litre oxygen cylinder fitted with pressure gauges, a pressure regulator, battery-powered igniter and a three-way valve which switches the system's working pressure on or off. Once ignited, the Kerie cable burns at approximately 60cm (2ft) a minute during cutting, which gives a maximum cutting time of 6 minutes. The SAS anti-terrorist team carry a back-pack portable system that weighs 4.5kg (10.5lbs), which is used for cutting during assault entry.

THESIGER, MAJOR WILFRED An explorer and adventurer fascinated by Arab culture. He was with B Squadron, 1 SAS, for a short time in late 1942 and in early 1943 during the later stages of the war in North Africa.

THIRTY-SIX HOUR PATROLS A concept developed for patrolling in the Middle East. The patrol would leave their base by night and ascend to the high ground where they would hide. By dawn they would have constructed a simple sangar for protection and camouflage, from which they would observe the surrounding area and movement. They would exfiltrate the following night. 'Thirty-six hour patrols' remained in operation until the SAS pulled out of Aden in 1967.

THOMPSON, MAJOR HARRY, MC A former Royal Highland Fusilier and commander of the final guerrilla hunts in Malaya, Thompson led a group of 37 men from D Squadron 22 SAS in the hunt for the Communist Terrorist leader Ah Hoi, known as 'Baby Killer'. In February 1958 he and his men parachuted into the swamp at Telok Anson, from where they spent 20 days tracking their target. Eventually, together with another troop led by Captain de la Billière, the terrorists' camp was surrounded and the inhabitants forced to surrender.

Following this success, Thompson was given the position of operations officer for the regiment in Borneo, but was sadly killed in a helicopter accident in May 1963.

THOMPSON SUB-MACHINE GUN *Specification* Calibre: .45mm; Weight: 2.5kg (5.63lbs); Length: 85cm (34in); Range: 300m (327yds); Rate of fire: 725 rounds per minute; Magazine: 20 round, stick/50 round, drum.

Better known as the 'Tommy gun', this weapon is associated more with American gangsters than military operations. It was widely produced during World War II and, although awkward and heavy, it proved excellent for close quarter battle. The SAS used the Thompson throughout its North African campaign and while fighting alongside the partisans in Europe.

THOMSON, TROOPER IAN 'JOCK' Trooper Thomson and Sergeant Eddie 'Geordie' Lillico were two soldiers from D Squadron 22 SAS who carried out a cross-border operation during the Borneo campaign which encountered an Indonesian ambush. On 26 February 1966, Sergeant Geordie Lillico led his six-man patrol into the area of an old Indonesian camp which was situated close to the border. This camp appeared to have been vacated some six months before, but as Trooper Thomson, who was acting as lead scout, approached the area he spotted an Indonesian soldier a few metres to his flank. The patrol had just emerged from a large clump of bamboo and had walked directly into a well-prepared Indonesian ambush.

Trooper Thomson was hit in the initial burst of fire and flung backwards into the undergrowth with a bullet in his upper thigh. Still clinging to his rifle he crash-landed next to an Indonesian soldier, whom he immediately shot. The well-concealed enemy continued their rapid fire hitting Sergeant Lillico who, as he dashed forward to help Thomson, took a bullet through the hip from a Kalashnikov assault rifle. Despite their injuries, both men continued to lay down suppressive fire whilst the remaining patrol 'bugged out'.

With the enemy all around, Sergeant Lillico, who had seen Thomson still on his feet, ordered him to return to the border and bring back the rest of the patrol. However, the bullet in Thomson's thigh had shattered the bone and he was unable to walk; he shouted to Lillico and tried desperately to join up with the sergeant. Meanwhile Sergeant Lillico started to drag himself back up the ridge, opening fire each time he saw enemy movement.

Thomson managed to avoid the enemy and, having applied a tourniquet and injected himself with morphine, he continued his struggle back towards the border. Darkness fell and gave some protection, and he settled down in the mud of a pig-hole to wait out the night. By morning of the second day Thomson had managed to cover half the distance back to the infantry camp firing single shots to attract the attention of the search party. He finally managed to make it back to the rendezvous where he was discovered by a Gurkha patrol, who had been sent to look for the missing men.

Lillico had also managed to outwit the enemy and after a while he took shelter in thick bamboo and examined his injury. Hiding under the trunk of a fallen tree he, like Thomson, waited out the night. He had lost a tremendous amount of blood and after a while he fell unconscious. When he recovered it was daylight and he heard Indonesian soldiers all around him. By this time he could hear a helicopter searching for him; however, the close proximity of the enemy deterred him from deploying his SARBE. It was only when he was absolutely certain he would not be detected that he risked using the survival radio, calling in a helicopter which managed to winch him out.

THUMIER   Name of the small village used by the SAS as a forward base 112km (70 miles) north of Aden. The site was chosen because it was flat and level, thus allowing access to aircraft in the otherwise mountainous terrain of the Radfan.

TIKKA M55 SNIPER RIFLE   *Specification* Calibre: various (.223, .243, 7mm); Weight: 1.5kg (3.27lbs); Muzzle velocity: 900m (981yds) per second; Magazine capacity: 4- or 10-round, box.

This Finnish bolt-action sniper rifle was in use with the regiment during the 1980s. It was extremely accurate up to 300m (327yds), after which the bullet had a tendency to 'fly'. The Tikka was superseded by the Accuracy International PM and the Heckler & Koch G3.

'TITANIC', OPERATION   An unsuccessful operation in World War II. In the early hours of 6 June 1944, seven members of 1 SAS were transported to an area south of Carentan in Normandy, along with a number of containers full of sand, dummy parachutists, small bombs and detonators designed to simulate small-arms fire. The purpose of this was to try and fool the Germans into believing that a full-scale airborne landing was taking place. Despite careful planning, both men and containers were widely scattered on landing and without the containers the men had no choice but to hide. On 10 July the party was surrounded and forced to surrender, three of them sustaining injuries as a result of the ensuing gun battle.

TNKU Tentara Nasional Kalimantan Utara were freedom fighters from North Borneo and Brunei who operated more as terrorists than guerrilla fighters. The organization opposed the Federation of Malaysia and was responsible for launching the Brunei revolt on 8 December 1962.

TOBIN, TROOPER TOMMY Died on 19 July 1972 due to wounds received at the Battle of Mirbat in Oman. Tobin had volunteered to go forward and give medical aid to the SAS men wounded while manning a field-gun. He was shot in the face and mortally wounded while applying medical aid to a colleague.

TOKKI RADIO A commercial walkie-talkie produced by Toshiba and used extensively for short-range conversations during the Oman War. The Tokkis were cheap to purchase and produced a much more reliable system of communications when dealing with the Firqat, who had no knowledge of operating a military radio. The Tokkis had their problems, not least the choice of only two channels, both of which became bogged down with irate voices during a contact with the enemy. It was mainly due to the lack of security when operating the Tokkis that the SAS resorted to plain language and using each others' nicknames.

'TOMBOLA', OPERATION Very successful mission carried out on 4 March 1945 by an advance party from 2 SAS, who were dropped into the area midway between Spezia and Bologna, northern Italy. The team's orders were to establish a base there, to organize the local partisans and disrupt the enemy. Included in the party was Major Roy Farran, technically a despatcher in aircraft. In addition, offensive operations were planned to coincide with US Fifth Army's expected attack in the region.

On landing, the SAS wasted little time in making contact with the partisans, establishing a base from which to work and taking steps to organize a force, ultimately consisting of 50 SAS men from 3 Squadron, local partisan units and 70 escaped Russians, all bearing arms delivered by various air drops. The force became known as the 'Battaglione Alleata'.

The force saw its first action at the end of March, when Farran led an attack on a German HQ at Albinea. In a joint action, the Russians defended the perimeter, allowing the SAS and Italians to assault the buildings. A fierce fight followed which caused Farran to retreat despite 30 Germans being killed and two buildings destroyed. In retaliation, the Germans attacked Farran's base at the beginning of April, albeit unsuccessfully. 'Alleata', the combined force, moved on to assist the Fifth Army's offensive by attacking the major route for the German retreat – Highway 12. Following these successes, the force continued to attack enemy forces, and by the time 'Tombola' ended on 24 April they had inflicted injuries on 600 enemy soldiers and taken 400 prisoners.

TONNA, SERGEANT TONY 'PANCHO' – AUSTRALIAN SAS REGIMENT (SASR)   Commander of a 3 Squadron SASR patrol inserted 2.5km (1.5 miles) south of the border between Phuoc Tuy and Long Khanh Provinces and 1km (1,000yds) east of the Courtenay Rubber Plantation on the afternoon of 31 March 1969. At 08:35 hours on the following morning the patrol observed nine Vietcong (VC) heading north along a track, and shortly afterwards established an observation post (OP) from which a large number of enemy could be heard moving through the area.

The afternoon of the following day the patrol established another OP from which four VC were observed, followed by another seventeen. On the afternoon of 5 April, having moved to another OP location 400m (436yds) further to the northeast, the patrol spotted a group of eight VC moving along a nearby track. Two of them suddenly halted while a third proceeded to head towards the OP. Private Barry Williams opened fire at close range and the Australians moved out quickly, breaking contact with the enemy soon afterwards.

Next morning, Sergeant Tonna established an ambush and within 30 minutes four VC entered the area and were killed. Having requested extraction, the patrol was lifted out by helicopter about an hour later.

TRACKING   Tracking is the ability to follow another human being. For some SAS jungle operations a skilled tracker can be an immense aid in forming a clearer picture of the enemy. The New Zealand NZSAS still emphasize tracking skills for the simple reason that a skilled tracker can be an important source of intelligence information and a major factor in a combat patrol's survivability. Various types of electronic surveillance and observation techniques have become increasingly important in recent conflicts, yet none have seriously displaced traditional tracking skills in the bush.

Tracking is probably one of the least understood of the Special Forces skills, simply because few people have a clear idea of what it is really about. One popular misconception about tracking is that the tracker follows a trail of footprints until he finally overtakes his quarry. This can happen occasionally, but more often the tracker will follow a trail left by the enemy in order to gain information – not necessarily follow the enemy until he is finally run to ground. By following various signs left by an enemy patrol, a tracker can tell how many men – or women – are in a patrol, how old the trail is, what weapons or other equipment they may be carrying, and what the patrol's purpose or possible route may be.

The modern tracker does not work in a vacuum. Before going into the bush, a tracker will find out all there is to know about whomever he will be following. This information could come from either military or even police intelligence sources. Then, once he is in the field, the tracker can either confirm existing information or modify it considerably by what he observes.

The factors which make a good tracker are, firstly, acute powers of observation and how accurately he can interpret what he sees. There was a time when tracking was becoming a lost art, but during the SAS's time in Malaya and Borneo the unit's trackers set a superb record of achievement. Likewise the Australian SAS and NZSAS used tracking techniques in Vietnam.

TRAVELLERS 'GUIDE TO HEALTH' An excellent pocket book produced by an Army colonel during the late 1960s, which became part of every SAS patrol's medic pack. It was particularly good for the patrol medics in helping diagnose the ailments of local tribespeople in their 'hearts and minds' role. The book went out of print in the mid-1970s and has not been revised.

TREE-JUMPING A technique for parachuting into the jungle devised by Captain Johnny Cooper and Alistair MacGregor of the Malayan Scouts. The idea was to land on the high jungle canopy, which would entangle with the parachute canopy, whereupon the men could release themselves and abseil down to the ground. Hence this became known as 'tree-jumping'. The first true operational jump took place in February 1959 when 54 men 'tree-jumped' into the Malayan jungle to assist those troops on the ground. Hailed as a success, the technique became accepted as a standard tactic. However, it soon became apparent that this was more dangerous than it first appeared – three men had lost their lives tree-jumping in one operation alone – and by the end of the Malayan Emergency the practice was discontinued as helicopters were increasingly being used for jungle missions.

TRUCIAL OMAN SCOUTS A battalion of Omani soldiers, trained and led by British officers and NCOs, and founded in the Trucial Oman States (now called the United Arab Emirates) in 1951. They were an extremely professional troop, strictly disciplined and with a high level of military training. Their main duties were internal security and patrolling the desert frontier. They were involved in the 1958–59 conflict in Oman and operated with the SAS in the offensive in Dhofar after 1965, and later when many of the former soldiers returned to their homes in the south and joined the Firqat.

'TRUEFORM', OPERATION On 17 August 1944, 102 soldiers of 1 and 2 SAS and the Belgian Independent Parachute Company were dropped in 25 parties on to twelve drop zones north west of Paris. The aim of the mission was to disrupt the Germans as they retreated and cause them as much damage as possible. Disappointingly, the operation suffered from a late start and, despite successfully destroying some vehicles and petrol dumps, Allied forces reached the 'Trueform' parties after only nine days.

TURNBULL, SERGEANT BOB One of the Malayan veterans who served twenty years in 22 SAS. He is best remembered for his quick reactions when he came face to face with the Communist Terrorist (CT) leader Ah Tuck, whom he shot dead. His reputation with a gun was enhanced when, in another jungle contact, he shot dead four terrorists in a single contact. He died on 1 February 1989.

UV

ULU Name used by the SAS to denote the jungle during the Malayan Emergency. Also, the name of a bar in the Garrick Hotel, Hereford, which was designed on a jungle theme and run by a former SAS Malaysian veteran, Frank Williams.

UM AL GWARIF The site of SAS headquarters and main base during the Oman War. It was positioned on the outskirts of Salalah, the southern capital, and close to the RAF airfield. The camp comprised two permanent block-type buildings, one used for the operation's room and armoury, the other as a cookhouse and bar. Accommodation for the soldiers was either in tents or Portacabins. Throughout the war SAS troops on the Jebel were re-supplied directly from Um al Gwarif. The base also served as an R & R location.

'URIC', OPERATION A major strike by Rhodesia against Mozambique, designed to cripple the latter's road and rail communications in Gaza Province, in the south of the country, and to destroy a major FRELIMO/ZANLA base at Mapai. At the beginning of September 1979 a forward administrative area was established 200km (218 miles) inside Mozambique. On 5 September, following on the heels of an air strike, a combined force from 1st SAS Regiment (RhSAS), the Rhodesian Light Infantry (RLI) and engineers was landed by helicopter near Barragem, situated 320km (198 miles) inside Mozambique and 150km (93 miles) northwest of the capital of Maputo, where it placed explosives on five road and rail bridges over a dam which supplied irrigation throughout the area. All were destroyed with the exception of a road bridge which was partially damaged.

On 6 September two bombing raids were carried out by the Royal Rhodesian Air Force on the FRELIMO/ZANLA base at Mapai within the space of 30 minutes. Shortly afterwards a combined force of 192 SAS and RLI was landed 1km (1,000yds) from the base and was soon involved in a fierce battle with FRELIMO troops and ZANLA guerrillas. They were in well-sited defensive positions equipped with twenty 37mm and 23mm anti-aircraft guns, which brought heavy fire to bear on the Canberras and Hunters supporting the assault. As the battle continued it became apparent that the force was too small and lightly equipped to succeed in overcoming such heavy defences, and during the afternoon Lieutenant-General Peter Walls, who was airborne in a Dakota command aircraft, gave the order to withdraw.

Despite the failure to take the Mapai base, however, the raid had succeeded in seriously damaging Mozambique's economy by further disrupting the country's already inefficient transport system, and damaging food production in Gaza Province which supplied most of the food for the entire country.

'US' SAS jargon for equipment that has gone unserviceable, has been broken, will not work, or is just plain useless.

US SPECIAL FORCES Also known as the Green Berets, these elite units operate in 12-man teams called A Teams. They are highly trained in various skills: airborne; medical; signalling; demolitions; languages; intelligence gathering; weapons handling; survival and engineering. US Special Forces have close links with the SAS and conduct exchange training. Colonel Charles Beckwith, a Green Beret who spent some time with the SAS, founded Delta Force, an anti-terrorist unit with many similarities to its British counterpart.

VALHALLA CLUB A private club in the old B Squadron spider accommodation which was formed in the early 1970s and named after the mythical after-world of the Vikings.

VAN DROFFELAAR, CORPORAL JOE – AUSTRALIAN SAS REGIMENT (SASR) Commander of a 3 Squadron SASR five-man patrol inserted on the morning of 20 September 1969, 7km (4 miles) northwest of Nui May Tao, in the southeastern corner of Long Khanh Province. Its task was to locate and harass the Vietcong (VC) 84th Rear Services Group which was known to be in the area. At 08:35 hours on 27 September, while approaching a track, the patrol encountered an eight-man North Vietnamese Army (NVA) patrol. Corporal Van Droffelaar and his lead scout, Private John Cuzens, killed three of the enemy while another was shot dead by Private Les Liddington. More NVA troops appeared and were engaged by Private David Fisher as the patrol withdrew using fire and movement.

Reaching the cover of jungle nearby, the signaller, Private Les Liddington, transmitted a request for a 'hot extraction'. Meanwhile, NVA troops continued to encircle the area and draw closer. Eventually, the patrol could hear the sound of the approaching helicopters, as they followed the signal from Corporal Van Droffelaar's URC 10 beacon. On seeing the lead aircraft, Van Droffelaar gave the pilot directions as to the patrol's location and two minutes later the accompanying gunships commenced laying down suppressive fire on the area. Shortly afterwards the helicopter lowered the ropes for the hot extraction and the patrol clipped themselves on with karabiners. Unfortunately, however, as the aircraft was flying clear of the area with the patrol suspended beneath it, Private David Fisher became detached from his rope and fell from a height of 30m (100ft). Despite subsequent searches of the area some hours later and during the next few days, his body was never found.

VC (VIETCONG) 'VC' was the general term for the guerrillas of the Communist-controlled National Liberation Front of South Vietnam, which was formed in December 1960. The VC were organized along three principal lines: village militias, which were recruited locally in the areas in which they would subsequently operate; regional troops recruited mainly from South Vietnamese but reinforced with individuals or groups from North Vietnam; and main force units which were normally of battalion, regimental or divisional strength – the latter being well below that of the South Vietnamese or American equivalent. VC units were well trained in guerrilla warfare, employing hit-and-run tactics, ambushing patrols and convoys, and attacking isolated outposts and villages. By the end of 1964, however, they had proved that they were also capable of taking part in conventional operations. In December of that year, 1,500 VC took part in a month-long battle near Binh Gia against 3,000 South Vietnamese troops on whom they inflicted heavy casualties.

In addition to their military units, the VC also deployed cadres whose role was the dissemination of propaganda and the indoctrination of local inhabitants in their areas. They also made extensive use of terrorism, targeting prominent leaders of local communities. In 1964 alone they were responsible for the murders of 436 government officials throughout South Vietnam, wounding a further 161 and abducting 1,131. By mid-1965, the VC reportedly controlled over 60 per cent of South Vietnam's population of twelve million people, and consisted of 40,000 cadres and 130,000 guerrillas.

In comparison, the 298 VC contacts made by the Australian SAS inflicted 492 kills, 106 possible kills, 47 wounded, 10 possible wounded and 11 captured. Of the combined 580 members of the Australian and New Zealand SAS who served in Vietnam, the casualties were one killed in action, one died of wounds, one killed in a grenade accident, two accidentally shot while on patrol, one missing during a rope extraction and one died of illness. Twenty-eight SAS soldiers received wounds serious enough to be notified.

The VC referred to the SAS units as 'Ma Rung', which translates as 'Phantoms of the Jungle'.

VENOMS A jet used by the RAF. They gave much-needed support during the Jebel Akhdar campaign.

VICKERS K MACHINE GUN *Specification* Calibre: .303mm; Weight: 21kg (46lbs); Length: 100cm (3ft 4in); Muzzle velocity: 743m (2,445ft) per second; Range: 1,828m (2,000yds).

Discovered in an aircraft hangar by David Stirling and apparently unused by the RAF, the SAS married the Vickers K to the new American jeeps to produce a formidable mobile fighting machine. The weapon was originally designed for aircraft and could fire a mixture of ball, tracer and armour-piercing ammunition. They proved their worth during the great jeep raid made by the SAS in July 1942.

VICKERS VALETTAS Name given to a British-made aircraft produced between 1947 and 1952, and which saw service until 1966. It proved a versatile and reliable aircraft and could carry 34 troops or despatch 20 parachutists, as well as carry freight or evacuate casualties. It was powered by two Bristol Hercules engines and required a crew of four. Maximum speed was around 470km/h (294mph) with a cruising speed of 272km/h (170mph), giving it a maximum range of 2,240km (1,400 miles). The SAS used the Valettas for many of their earlier 'tree-jumping' into the jungle.

VICTOR Code-name given to the training base in the United Arab Emirates which was used by the SAS prior to their move to the forward base at Al Jouf in Saudi Arabia, from where they entered Iraq during the Gulf War.

VICTOR TWO The name given to an Iraqi military control centre used, it was believed, for guiding the mobile Scud units to their targets, which an SAS mobile fighting column was given orders to destroy.

The column drove to within 1,500m (1,600yds) of the objective, where they positioned their vehicles in a fire support formation while a recce group went forward to confirm the target location. The Coalition air force had heavily bombed the Iraqi installation, which consisted of a multi-layer building complex with a microwave tower at the base, approximately 60m (200ft) in height. The camp had a wire perimeter fence with a main gate covered by a sentry position, and whilst the bombing had done damage, the station was still operating. The SAS were to totally destroy the building housing the transmission equipment together with the tower and microwave dish.

The column was under the command of a senior NCO named Billy Ratcliff (later promoted to major) who divided his force into three main assault groups. The building had one floor above ground level, with two further basement floors. All the floors were connected by a central staircase; each assault team would take one floor, clearing it of Iraqi soldiers before placing their charges. The remaining men would stay with the vehicles and act as a fire-support group.

As luck would have it the whole column managed to gain access to the camp without being detected and the plan was swiftly put into operation. Once on target the demolitions got to work, while several sentries kept watch. While they waited on the assault groups two SAS sentries heard a noise coming from a truck and went to investigate. The truck parked next to the target turned out to be a fuel tanker from which a definite mumbling noise could be heard. On opening the door they revealed two young Iraqi soldiers. When one tried to grab at his gun the SAS opened fire, killing both instantly.

Enemy fire was returned from every direction, with tremendous volume and with red and green tracer rounds flying around like little hornets, ricocheting off the ground, deflecting in every direction. The Iraqi fire was everywhere, much of it streaming across the front wall of the target compound where the demolitions teams were fitting their charges. To counter this, the vehicles acting as fire-support opened up, concentrating on protecting the demolitionists as they made good their escape. Finally, with all the explosives in place, the demolitionists fired off their grip switches, timing the explosive to detonate in one minute and thirty seconds. Now with no other alternative, the assault team made ready to exit, bursting out from the building and running for cover.

As all the men regrouped on the vehicles, a massive explosion ripped through the air, as the demolition charges went off, causing the large tower to slowly buckle before collapsing completely. At this point the enemy increased their fire, but the SAS firepower, now being delivered from the heavily armed vehicles, proved too much for the Iraqis, and the SAS managed to regroup without casualties. Once all the men were accounted for the column set a course that would lead them out into the desert where once more they would disappear into the night.

VILLA ROSSI AND VILLA CALVI SAS and Italian partisans carried out simultaneous raids on the Villa Rossi and Villa Calvi, both of which were being used as German headquarters. The aim was to shoot as many German officers as possible and set fire to the buildings, thus instilling fear into the German High Command that their headquarters were vulnerable to attack.

VOICE PROJECTION UNIT The Voice Projection Unit is a miniature amplifier unit designed for use with S-10, SF-IO and CT-12 Respirators. Powered by a standard 9-volt PP3 type battery, the unit is rapidly and easily attached to the diaphragm on the respirator face-piece. When activated by a switch, the unit projects the wearer's voice over a distance of 30m (32yds), thus enabling hostages or other personnel in the target area to hear clearly any commands being given during an assault.

WADDY, COLONEL JOHN Commander of 22 SAS in the late 1960s and early 1970s who believed that the SAS could prove invaluable in an undercover intelligence-gathering role, especially in such trouble spots as Northern Ireland. He wrote a paper on it, envisaging the future role of the regiment in counter-terrorism and how it could also work closely with the intelligence services of MI5, MI6 and Special Branch. Future events were to prove how astute he had been with his perceptions.

WADI RAWDAH In northern Oman, after the 8 December 1970 debacle on the Musandan Peninsula, the SAS were tasked to go after the Iraqi insurgents for a second time. On hearing of the military landing at Gumla, the enemy had taken refuge in a stronghold called the Wadi Rawdah. It was a natural bowl depressed within the jebel structure, a wadi with sheer rocky walls above, which towered 300m (1,000ft) even at the shortest place. On the seaward side there occurred a natural, narrow split in the rock structure, which allowed for entry and exit. The whole valley was home to a strange tribe called the Bani Shihoo, reportedly a wild and vicious people who had rarely seen a white man. Their main weapon, apart from the odd rifle, was a small axe.

The operation started on the night of 12 December 1970 with a parachute night drop carried out by two free-fall troops. This was to be the first operational free-fall drop the SAS regiment had ever undertaken. They would act as pathfinders who would hold the wadi entrance, cutting off any escape until the rest of G Squadron arrived by helicopter at first light next morning. The aircraft took off around 03:00. An hour later the men jumped from a height of 3,300m (11,000ft). During the drop Paul 'Rip' Reddy, was killed. Major Alastair Morrison, who commanded the Squadron, heard the news of Reddy's death at around 05:00 and immediately despatched the rest of his men by helicopter.

As with the surprise attack on the village of Gumla on 8 December, intelligence had got it wrong, and there was no sign of any Iraqis. Morrison left one troop in the Wadi Rawdah mainly to carry out 'hearts and minds' among the Bani Shihoo. Upon their return to base, the troop commander made a full report on the tribe. They were a strange, insular community who built small houses out of rocks that had been fashioned into uniform blocks. Many even had pitched roofs. Due to the lack of water and the rock structure of the wadi, they had carved out huge cisterns and collected rainwater. Their survival in such a inhospitable area (there was little reported sign of vegetation or animals) is a lesson to the human race in man's ability to adapt.

WALKER, CAPTAIN RODERIC RORY   An officer with D Squadron, 22 SAS, Walker took part in the assault on the Jebel Akhdar, Oman, in 1959. However, his most famous exploit was in the Indonesian capital, Jakarta. A protest against the British was taking place and a mob gathered outside the British Embassy, with the rioters throwing stones from outside the compound. Walker defied the angry crowd by marching up and down in front of the building playing his bagpipes.

WALKER, MAJOR-GENERAL WALTER   Director of Operations in Borneo, Walker was a tough veteran of both Burma and Malaya. An avid supporter of the SAS, he ordered the top-secret 'Claret' operations, to contain Indonesian and Communist incursions into Borneo. Following the success of these raids, Walker recommended an expansion of the regiment, and B Squadron was reformed. Walker was eventually replaced as Director of Operations Borneo by the SAS veteran, Major-General George Lea, during the final phase of the war. Walker was later made an honorary member of the SAS.

WALLACE, LIEUTENANT-COLONEL J.J.A. – AUSTRALIAN SAS REGIMENT (SASR)   Assumed command of the SASR on 8 January 1988. Commissioned from the Royal Military College Duntroon in 1973, he subsequently served with the regiment as a troop and squadron commander. Among other postings was a tour in 1980 as a United Nations observer in Syria and the Lebanon, and attendance of the British Army Staff College. Prior to assuming command of the SASR, he had been on the staff of the Directorate General of Army Training. On 10 December 1990 Lieutenant-Colonel Wallace handed over command to Lieutenant-Colonel Duncan Lewis.

'WALLACE', OPERATION   'Wallace' included a jeep drive by 60 men of 2 SAS in 23 vehicles led by Major Roy Farran, which landed at Rennes on 19 August 1944. The group was tasked with strengthening the existing SAS bases and establishing offensive operations against the Germans. Immediately on landing, Farran drove to the north bank of the River Loire, successfully avoiding any confrontation with German forces on the way since he wanted to delay any action until the group had reached the 'Hardy' base.

On 22 August the squadron was divided into three groups: five jeeps under the command of Captain Lee; eight under Major Farran and the remainder under the command of Lieutenant Leigh. Over the next few days the parties encountered the enemy on several occasions, one of which resulted in the death of Lieutenant Leigh. Eventually the troop joined the rest of 2 SAS, under the command of Major Grant Hibbert, at the 'Hardy' base in the Châtillon forest.

'Wallace's' most famous adventure was the attack on the German HQ in the town of Châtillon on 30 August. The local Maquis commander had been persuaded to agree to aid the SAS in the attack, but the French failed to appear on the morning of the proposed attack and Farran's men became involved in a fierce battle with the garrison and an approaching German column. He had no choice but to call off the action despite the fact that the enemy had lost 100 men, nine lorries, four cars and a motorcycle. Later that night four more jeeps were dropped by parachute, bringing the SAS's total number of vehicles to eighteen.

Dividing the vehicles into two columns of nine, Farran commanded one group himself and gave the other one to Hibbert. German forces were retreating to the Belfort Gap, the area between the Vosges mountains and the Swiss border, in an attempt to stop the Allies reaching the Rhine. The two columns of SAS troopers and vehicles set off for the Gap on 2 September entering the area between two US armies – the Third to the north and the Seventh in the south. 'Wallace' ended on 19 August when the SAS joined with the US forces. The operation's success was undisputed, save for the loss of seven lives, seven wounded, two captured and 16 jeeps destroyed. By comparison, the SAS had killed or wounded 500 enemy soldiers, destroyed 59 vehicles and derailed one train.

WALL BREACHING CANNON – 'HARVEY WALLBANGER'

The Wall Breaching Cannon is a device that eliminates the need for using high explosives as a method of entry in a hostage situation. Every wall differs and it is very difficult to judge the amount of explosive required to blow a hole without causing severe debris on the opposite side. The SAS has no second chance during any assault, thus for walls of unknown strength, more explosive than necessary is invariably used, compounding the undesired effects. The wall breaching cannon is a more suitable alternative to using high explosive.

Wall breaching in a hostage situation needs the following requirements. The device has to be instantaneous with the minimum amount of damage to walls, hostages and the assaulting team, who must be able to act at the moment of breaching. To this end the Wall Breaching Cannon, also known as the 'Harvey Wallbanger', was developed.

It is designed to direct a heavy, soft projectile with sufficient velocity to accumulate enough kinetic energy to breach a wall, then instantly dissipate the energy after breaching. A water-filled plastic container is fired by compressed air and fills this requirement very adequately. The device designed to launch the container is a muzzle-loaded smooth bore barrel. The rear of the barrel is fitted with an air reservoir separated from the main barrel by an entrapped glass disc, which ruptures by electrical detonation at a given pressure, thus presenting instantaneous pressure to the rear of the projectile. A loose piston stops any air leakage past the projectile giving good velocity at pressures between 200, 400 and 600lbs psi.

The system can be transported along with 45×25 litre (10×5 gallon) plastic containers in both helicopter or estate car with ease. A two-man team can carry it and the size allows it to pass through any standard doorway.

WALLS, GENERAL PETER   The officer in charge of Rhodesian-recruited C Squadron, Malayan Scouts, during the Malayan Emergency. After the Unilateral Declaration of Independence in Rhodesia, Walls went on to become the commander of Rhodesia's Armed Forces.

WAR CRIMES INVESTIGATION TEAM (SAS)   The SAS War Crimes Investigation Team was formed in May 1945 by Lieutenant-Colonel Brian Franks, the commanding officer of 2 SAS Regiment (2 SAS), to investigate the fate and whereabouts of 32 men missing from the unit. The latter had been deployed in October 1944 on Operation 'Loyton' in Alsace and it had been reported that they had been captured and executed by the Germans.

The small six-man team was under the command of Major Eric Barkworth, 2 SAS's intelligence officer, with WO2 (SSM) Fred 'Dusty' Rhodes as his second-in-command. At the end of May, Barkworth and his men set off from England and travelled to Germany. The team was in direct contact with the SAS headquarters at Wivenhoe, in Essex, via a radio link maintained by F Squadron Phantom. On 10 June the team eventually reached Gaggenau, where a number of bodies had already been discovered near Rotenfels concentration camp, and exhumed by French occupation forces. Some of these were identified as being those of 2 SAS personnel. Reinforced by a few more members of the regiment sent from England, the team widened its search.

In the late summer of 1945, as a result of the disbandment of the SAS, the team was seconded directly to the War Office and thereafter its radio base station was located in the offices of the Department of the Judge Advocate-General where Captain Yuri Galitzine looked after the team's affairs and provided any necessary support. In November, the team turned its attention to the Moussey area of Alsace and after lengthy and exhaustive searches uncovered a mass grave containing eight bodies which were subsequently identified as being those of 2 SAS men. Further investigations in the area uncovered the murders of further members of 2 SAS.

After six months, the team had amassed a considerable amount of information which enabled it to account for all the missing men. It was also successful in tracking down their executioners who were arrested and, having been brought to justice, were hanged at Hameln prison. The team also assisted in the investigation of other war crimes involving the executions of Allied aircrew and four women agents of the Special Operations Executive (SOE) who had been murdered in the concentration camp at Natzweiler.

WARBURTON, TROOPER J.N. An SAS soldier killed along with Captain Robin Edwards in an ill-fated operation in the Radfan region in April 1964. After their death they were decapitated and their heads displayed in North Yemen.

WARR, CAPTAIN PETER Was one of the first parachute instructors of the SAS. He joined L Detachment at Kabrit in North Africa from the British Parachute School at Manchester, after David Stirling had asked for aid. He took part in some of the earlier raids in the desert.

'WASHUP' An alternative word for de-brief.

WATER JUMP A parachute jump into water. All SAS Troops practise water jumps, but when used as a method of operational entry this is normally done by Boat Troop. The SBS are on standby to assist in the event of an oil-rig being hijacked, the type of operation that would require a water jump. A water jump differs from a land-based parachute drop inasmuch as the parachutist must disconnect from the parachute prior to hitting the water. This allows him to swim free of the parachute should it cover him on landing.

WATTS, LIEUTENANT-COLONEL JOHNNY The commander of D Squadron in 1958, he and his men were transferred from Malaya to Oman and took part in the victorious Jebel Akhdar campaign. During this time he took part in many solo reconnaissance missions so that a way could be found on to the Jebel. By 1964 he was commanding B Squadron in Borneo and by mid-1970 he was the commander of 22 SAS. During his command he was heavily involved in SAS operations in Oman; it was his report on the state of the country which led to the 'Five Fronts' Campaign which helped the new sultan, Qaboos, to win the war in Dhofar. He was also personally involved in some of the action, in particular Operation 'Jaguar', when an attack was launched on the Jebel Dhofar by the SAS and Firqat units. Unfortunately it was planned during the Muslim holy month of Ramadan and the Firqat were not keen on fighting at this time, thus threatening the whole operation. Watts threatened to withdraw all SAS aid for the units, and the Firqat, fearing for their future, gave in and took part in the offensive after all.

In 1971 he relinquished his command of the regiment, but went on to command the SAS Group and the Sultan of Oman's Armed Forces.

WEGENER, ULRICH In 1972 Ulrich Wegener was selected by the Interior Minister Hans-Dietrich Genscher as the first commander of the West German anti-terrorist unit GSG9. Wegener had worked in Genscher's office as a young officer and his capabilities were well known. In addition, Wegener had spent a great deal of time working with the FBI at their academy in Quantico, Virginia. He had trained with the Israelis, studying anti-terrorist methods and is reported to have been at Entebbe.

In 1977 he led the assault on the hijacked Lufthansa 737 aircraft at Mogadishu, were he was assisted by two members of the SAS. During the Iranian Embassy Siege in London in 1980 he acted as an advisor to the SAS. In 1979 he was promoted to brigadier-general in command of BGS West. He has since left the police to work in the private sector as a security advisor in the Middle East.

WESSEX HELICOPTER *Specification* Range: 770km (477 miles); Maximum speed: 212km/h (131mph); Crew: 3; Passengers: Up to 16; Payload: 6,150kg (6 tons); Armaments: usually none.

British helicopter used mainly for search and rescue, and as a general purpose transporter. It first saw service in 1963 and is now in the process of being phased out. A Wessex helicopter was used in the rescue of an SAS troop, in horrendous conditions, on the Fortuna Glacier in South Georgia during the Falklands War. Two other Wessex helicopters were lost on the same mission.

WESTMACOTT, CAPTAIN RICHARD On 2 May 1980 Captain Richard Westmacott was on patrol in Belfast with seven colleagues in two unmarked cars. Armed with both handguns and automatic weapons, the patrol answered a call to a house in the Antrim Road after reports of suspicious behaviour. The other vehicle approached the house from the rear whilst Westmacott's vehicle pulled up at the front and the soldiers got out. Suddenly there was an enormous barrage of gunfire and Westmacott was killed outright. Thinking the shots came from the house they had been called to, the other SAS troopers rushed inside to find nothing but a terrified middle-aged couple. Meanwhile the Army and the RUC had sealed off the area and eventually four escaped IRA terrorists surrendered. In memory of Westmacott, the door from the house was taken and is today kept at Hereford, where it is known as the Westmacott door.

The tragic events of 2 May caused the SAS to drastically rethink their tactics and today, in such a situation, the house would be put under surveillance before they would allow any direct intervention.

Nevertheless, Westmacott's death seemed to end a run of bad luck for the SAS and indeed, just three days later, they carried off the internationally famous and highly successful breaking of the Iranian Embassy Siege.

Captain Richard Westmacott was the first SAS soldier to die in Northern Ireland. He had joined the regiment from the Grenadier Guards and served as a captain in G Squadron. With curly fair hair, schoolboy looks and a love of poetry, his appearance belied his performance as a remarkably tough member of the SAS, and in recognition of his achievements he was awarded a posthumous Military Cross.

WET REP A military weather report normally required if an SAS unit is calling for helicopter or air support in an area suffering from adverse weather.

WHITE, SERGEANT P.F. – AUSTRALIAN SAS REGIMENT (SASR) In March 1966, during the Borneo campaign, Sergeant Peter White was the commander of a 2 Squadron SASR patrol tasked with escorting Major Marcus McCausland, a company commander of the 2nd Battalion 7th DEO Gurkha Rifles, on a cross-border reconnaissance for the subsequent 'Claret' operation by his company. On 17 March one of McCausland's platoons secured a crossing point on the Sungai Sekayan River, upstream from the area to be reconnoitred – the village of Sentas which was situated just over the border, directly south of the town of Tebedu in the First Division of Sarawak. Three days later the patrol crossed just before dawn and followed a creek away from the river. Moving inland they came across another creek later in the afternoon and discovered that the Indonesians were using it as a hidden trail, all the undergrowth within the creek itself having been cut away.

Shortly afterwards, the patrol encountered a local inhabitant coming up the creek. On being questioned by Major McCausland, he revealed that a group of Indonesian troops was also approaching. Without further ado Sergeant White and his patrol withdrew with some haste and made their way back to the Sungai Sekayan and the crossing point. Having crossed without incident and linked up with McCausland's platoon, the patrol headed for the border. In the meantime, the enemy had obviously found signs of its earlier presence in the area because shortly afterwards mortar bombs started landing around the crossing point.

WHITE CITY Code name for the establishment of an SAS base during the Oman War. It was Colonel Johnny Watts' suggestion to construct a airstrip in the middle of the White City firebase so that the Skyvans could alleviate the re-supply problem. As troops began arriving into the location the Firqat were sent to picket the high ground, whilst SAS men set to work constructing the airstrip. They worked all night, coming under enemy fire several times, but by dawn they were ready to receive the first aircraft. Again battle flared up. Each time a Skyvan landed the Adoo were waiting; mortar bombs began to fall and small arms attempted to shoot several aircraft down.

'WHITE-OUT'   A zero-visibility situation in a blizzard or in cloud, often experienced in Arctic conditions. It was a 'white-out' that caused the catastrophe on Fortuna Glacier in South Georgia during the Falklands War.

'WHO DARES WINS'   The famous motto of the SAS. It is alleged that it was formulated by David Stirling himself.

WILLY'S JEEP   A much-modified version of the American Willy's jeep was used by the SAS during World War II. It was light, agile and robust, ideally suited to desert conditions because of its four-wheel drive. The jeep had a top speed of 96km/h (60mph) and a range of 480km (300 miles), although this could be greatly extended by carrying additional fuel. During the North Africa campaign the SAS jeeps were normally overloaded with extra water, fuel and ammunition. The SAS also added heavy firepower in the form of 0.5in Browning heavy machine guns and Vickers K guns, the latter having been discovered sitting disused in an aircraft hangar. So equipped, the jeeps were not simply used as a means of transport but also as a weapon. On many occasions they were driven, guns blazing, directly into the enemy airfields from where they would wreak havoc on the rows of enemy aircraft. Between 1943 and 1945 the SAS used their jeeps in Europe, many of which were parachute dropped to the teams on the ground.

WINGATE-GRAY, LIEUTENANT-COLONEL MIKE   Served as second-in-command 22 SAS during the 1960s. He arrived from the Black Watch with little or no experience of the regiment, having passed Selection at the age of 42. He served in the Radfan campaign before he replaced John Woodhouse as regiment OC in January 1965, and took part in the final years of the Borneo campaign. He led the regiment's cross-border patrols in Borneo urging operations to become more aggressive, in consequence of which A, B and D Squadrons were involved in offensive cross-border patrols in the following months.

WINGED DAGGER – THE SAS BADGE   Stirling's first application for a unit badge was withheld due to the unit only being a detachment. The 'Winged Dagger', as it became known, is said to have been designed by Corporal Bob Tait, later to become Sergeant-Major Tait, MM. The sword is Excalibur, the legendary weapon of King Arthur. The two shades of blue represent the colours of Oxford and Cambridge. It received official recognition from General Auchinleck in January 1942. Cloth was chosen at the time as there were no means to forge a metal cap-badge. It has remained the same ever since.

WINGS Parachute wings in the SAS differ from those of other British airborne forces. The wings are said to have been designed from an Egyptian-style fresco admired by Lieutenant 'Jock' Lewes. They were originally worn above the left breast pocket, but since 1957 have been worn on the right shoulder. Wearing SAS wings is, for many, a source of great pride.

WINTER WARFARE OPERATIONS The Arctic is one of those theatres in which the SAS operate but say very little about. Even within the regiment, the annual trip to Norway is classed more as a skiing holiday than a military necessity. However, one would be wrong to suppose that the SAS are not well trained in Arctic warfare. They are, and to a very high standard. In addition to Norway, certain troop members are invited to attend foreign national courses, where more advanced winter warfare techniques have been developed. One such place is the German Mountain Warfare School in Mittenwald.

The squadron, committed to NATO's Northern Flank theatre, will spend three months of the year learning basic cross-country skiing and Arctic warfare tactics. This will include using the Bandvagon BV202 and BV206, a track-type covered vehicle with a trailer, designed specifically to operate in the Arctic. They are normally driven by members of Mobility Troop while the rest of the men Skijor behind. This is a method of transportation by which troops hang on to long ropes attached to the rear of the Bandvagon and are towed along. It is not as easy as one might think; one skier losing his balance can stop the whole ride, whilst the speed can cause exposed skin to freeze. Arctic survival is also taught, as the SAS will be required to stay out in long-term observation points in temperatures falling to minus 40 degrees.

The annual trip to Norway finishes with the squadron taking part in a major exercise. This may be organized with the Norwegian Army, or part of a set NATO exercise.

WIRELESS SET, NO. 11 Used by the British Army between 1935 and 1945, although its size and weight made it unsuitable for use by men on foot. The equipment, whose transceiver alone weighed 57kg (125lbs), was therefore restricted to jeep-mounted SAS operations close to the front line, as its range was only a poor 9km (12 miles)

WIRELESS SET, NO. 22 A military radio set used by the SAS in World War II, specifically in North Africa and the Mediterranean. The sender/receiver unit was quite large and weighed 7.5kg (16.5lbs), with the power unit coming in at a further 4kg (9lbs). It had a short range of some 16km (10 miles), which really was inadequate for the type of deep-penetration raids undertaken by SAS teams in World War II.

WOLSEY This was a very successful small-scale joint SAS/Phantom mission conducted in the area around Compiègne and Soissons, north-east France, between 26 August and 3 September 1944. Led by Lieutenant McDevitt, this five-man party was parachuted in to gather intelligence about enemy positions and movements in the area. The party did get some good information, particularly on an enemy convoy which was subsequently destroyed by 44 RAF Mosquito aircraft.

WOODHOUSE, LIEUTENANT-COLONEL JOHN Served with the regiment alongside David Stirling, 'Paddy' Mayne and Mike Calvert, Woodhouse was one of the regiment's most outstanding personalities and is often seen as the father of the modern SAS. He joined the British Army in 1941 as a private, after leaving public school, and was also one of the original members of the Malayan Scouts. Major Woodhouse was one of many soldiers drafted in by Mike Calvert to work in its intelligence cell in 1950, and together with Major Dare Newell began to reorganize the Scouts, training them to fight in the jungle and set up deep-penetration patrols. Refusing to accept anything but the highest level of professionalism, physical fitness and discipline, in February 1950 he led an operation in the Belum Valley of northern Malaya.

Two years later Woodhouse returned home and began to organize new SAS recruitment procedures, devising a course which formed the basis of the current SAS Selection and Continuation training at Hereford. At the end of 1954 he returned to Malaya as a squadron commander, and by 1962 was heading up 22 SAS in Borneo, which was a very popular decision within the regiment. In early 1964 he advocated the use of four-man patrols for cross-border reconnaissance work, for which he received authorization before the 'Claret' operations later that year. In October 1964 Woodhouse took part in his last operational patrol, before leaving military service in January 1965.

WRIGHT, SERGEANT DANNY – AUSTRALIAN SAS REGI-MENT (SASR) On 4 April 1971 Sergeant Danny Wright was the commander of a ten-man 2 Squadron SASR patrol inserted into an area 12km (7.5 miles) northeast of Xuyen Moc in the eastern area of Phuoc Tuy Province. Its task was to carry out an ambush at a location where Vietcong (VC) had been observed, and a bunker complex previously located by a patrol led by Second-Lieutenant Brian Jones. In addition to his ambush task, Sergeant Wright was to subsequently link up with Jones' patrol and assist in destroying the bunker.

On 8 April, having seen no enemy, Wright lifted his ambush and on the following day linked up with Jones who was accompanied by four sappers. During the afternoon the two patrols moved to the area of the bunker complex and, having established a firm base and briefed the NCOs who were second-in-command of both patrols, Wright moved forward with Jones and the warrant officer commanding the sappers. While searching the area in an arc, Sergeant Wright warned Second-Lieutenant Jones that they would soon be approaching the area in front of their patrol's position. Jones acknowledged this but continued to move forward in front of Wright, through an area of long grass and dense foliage, despite the latter's efforts to attract his attention again and stop him proceeding any further. A few seconds later a member of the patrol, unexpectedly seeing a figure with a weapon approaching through the undergrowth at close range, opened fire. Upon immediate investigation the figure proved to be Second-Lieutenant Jones.

Sergeant Wright requested emergency medical evacuation and the aircraft arrived shortly afterwards. Unfortunately, however, Second-Lieutenant Brian Jones died in the helicopter during the return flight. A subsequent inquiry completely exonerated the soldier who had opened fire, stating that Second-Lieutenant Jones should not have led the search group into the area in front of the patrol's position.

YZ

YELLOW CARD A guideline for opening fire issued to soldiers operating in Northern Ireland, so called because it is printed on yellow card. The card's general rule is that a soldier may only use firearms as a last resort, and that a challenge must be given; this challenge – 'Stop, or I shoot' – is offered three times. The Yellow Card does allow a soldier to shoot without a warning but only when there is likely to be immediate danger to life and there is no other way to prevent the danger. For example, if a member of the IRA is spotted with a rifle taking aim, or is about to detonate a bomb, and there is no other way to make an arrest, in such circumstances a soldier may shoot to kill.

YUGOSLAVIA The end of 1944 saw all Axis forces cleared from the Aegean, and the Special Boat Squadron (SBS), commanded by Lieutenant-Colonel David Sutherland, moving to Yugoslavia for further operations. In January the squadron commenced reconnaissance and raiding operations in the north of the Adriatic where the Germans held a number of islands in the Gulf of Fiume off the north coast of Yugoslavia, including Cherso, Krk, Unije, Lussin, Pag, Olib, Rab and Pasman.

During the next three months, the SBS saw some very hard fighting on several of these islands against large numbers of Italian and German troops, the latter including the seasoned veterans of XXI Mountain Corps whom the SBS had encountered during operations in the Aegean. Late March 1945, however, saw the major islands in the area cleared of enemy forces and the arrival of Allied forces at the port of Trieste, although German troops still occupied the Istrian Peninsula. The SBS was withdrawn shortly afterwards and moved to Italy for its final operations of the war.

YUKON STOVE Easily the best fire for cooking and other purposes is obtained from the Yukon Stove. If you are in one location for more than 24 hours you should certainly seriously consider the possibility of building this type of stove. It is also a secure way of providing heat and cooking.

Rocks, stones and mud are used in its construction, with the tortoise shell as the basic shape. At one side you must leave a hole for fuel and air, with another at the top as a chimney. Two further refinements are very desirable. The first is the setting of a metal box or large can into the back wall. This will provide an excellent oven. You must remember, however, that food placed in the oven will be burned unless it is separated from the metal by small sticks or stones. If twigs are used they will turn into charcoal after a day or two. You should keep them for use in de-odourizing boiled water if necessary, and other medicinal purposes. The second improvement possible is to use a large, flat rock as part of the top of the stove. It can be used as a griddle for making oatcakes, drying leaves for tea, parching grain etc. and even frying birds' eggs. The stove is constructed by the SAS during survival training.

ZAHKIR TREE   The Zahkir Tree was a prominent landmark that stood on the edge of the Shirshitti escarpment in southern Oman. It was proposed that the Sultan's Armed Forces (SAF), supported by the Firqat and SAS, should establish a base north of the Zahkir Tree at a place called Defa. Defa had been used during the Shirshitti operation and much of the fortifications remained. By 15 September 1975, the base held a company of SAF, a troop of Saladin armoured cars and several 25-pounder guns. The SAS had a whole troop in the location, but because of Ramadan the Firqat were very thin on the ground.

There was only one problem with Defa; during the Shirshitti operation the enemy had pounded the position with Soviet Katyusha rockets; now they began to rain down once more, this time from somewhere near the Zahkir Tree. As the monsoon provided a thick mist, especially in the morning, the SAS decided to silence the rocket fire by sending in a heavy patrol backed by SAF and the armoured cars.

In the early morning of 19 September thirteen SAS and two Firqats, under command of Captain Charles Delius, slipped out of Defa making their way towards the Zahkir Tree. Due to the darkness and mist the patrol found themselves on a small spur to the west of the Zahkir Tree. Delius decided to remain at the position with six men while Sergeant Rover Walker took the other six down the spur for a recce. They dropped lower into the wadi, but as dawn grew stronger and the mist became patchy, it was obvious that their tactical position was not good. Walker, a highly experienced SAS solider, moved his men and despatched Corporal Bell and one of the Firqat to proceed across the wadi bed and up the other side in search of the Zahkir Tree. Bell moved cautiously until the mist cleared and he was able to observe the landmark and take a bearing. However, as he and the Firqat moved back to rejoin the patrol they came across several sets of fresh footprints; moreover there was a very strong smell of meat hanging in the damp air.

While Walker waited for Bell to return he observed a man walking through the mist, heading roughly toward Delius's position, and quickly sent a message. Delius was still on the radio when three enemy soldiers appeared directly in front of them and a rapid exchange of fire broke out. All three enemy were cut down by the SAS but not before Lance-Corporal Small had been hit in the thigh. On hearing the shots, Walker ordered his men to make their way up the wadi, heading north for the high ground. They had just started to climb when a burst of fire signalled an all-out contact. The men dropped and wriggled forward, using the thinning mist as cover; however, the height of fire was so close it seemed as if the enemy were right on top of them. Suddenly Lance-Corporal Tony Fleming was hit badly in the back. At first Walker thought he was dead, only to see his eyes open. Dragging Fleming between them, the patrol forced itself forward, but such was the enemy fire that they eventually decided to stay put and defend as best they could. Walker explained to Delius his only option: they must stand and fight and wait to be relieved. Delius immediately called for mortar fire, but due to the mist and the fact that he did not know Walker's exact position adjustment control was difficult.

Walker's men huddled together with those who were able shooting at anything that moved, while the medics attended the wounded. The mist cleared briefly and one of the patrol shouted with relief; a line of well-dressed military soldiers was advancing towards them in open order. The SAF had arrived. Walker got to his feet and shouted, indicating their position, at which time the soldiers opened fire. Walker was hit and he went down on his knees. Another round hit him and he fell to the ground. He tried to rise, and as he did so a third round hit him. The enemy advanced to within 20m (21yds) and grenade throwing range. Still the SAS held their ground, but by now they were forced to switch to single shots as ammunition ran low. Walker, who by this time had been given morphine, shouted for Bell to take over the patrol, when suddenly an armoured car appeared coming down the slope; the enemy started to disengage.

By 09:00 the battle was over. Captain Delius rejoined his men only to find that every man in Walker's patrol had been hit.

ZEM ZEM Located south east of Tripoli in North Africa. In November 1942 David Stirling, with B Squadron, was operating in the area around Zem Zem to try to badger enemy forces as the Eighth Army advanced west after the Battle of El Alamein. At this time the SAS depot was at Benghazi, though B Squadron's forward base was situated at El Fascia. By 13 December the squadron had a total of 24 jeeps and was in place and set for action. At the same time a squadron headed by Major Paddy Mayne was operating along the road between Agheila and Bouerat.

Unfortunately for Stirling's men the area was full of enemy soldiers and hostile locals, and in a couple of days most of the patrols were captured or killed.

ZIPITS   Zipits are laced into combat boots with zips to facilitate speedier donning of the boot and easier removal.

ZIRNHELD, LIEUTENANT ANDRÉ   A popular young Free French officer who served with the SAS during its early operations in North Africa. He was in charge of one of the raids against enemy airfields in mid-June 1942 which destroyed eleven aircraft at Berka Main. In early July he was on another raid, against El Daba airfield. Due to lack of targets he had to lay ambushes on the road nearby. His final action took place on the night of 26 July 1942, when he took part in the dazzling action at Sidi Haneish airfield. Unfortunately, on the way back his three Free French SAS jeeps were attacked by Stuka aircraft and he was killed.

ZOOT SUIT   A lightweight two-piece suit, first developed by the SAS during the Malayan Emergency, which was originally made from parachute material. The Zoot Suit was used mainly to sleep in and was carried instead of a second set of clothing in order to reduce overall weight. Elastic waist and cuffs, colour green or khaki.

ZULU (TIME)   Greenwich Mean Time, used by the military worldwide to calculate timings for most operations.

Chronology

To avoid duplication this book is listed in alphabetical order and, while many entries are self-explanatory, the outline history of the Special Air Service and its family can sometimes appear mystifying and complicated. In order to rectify this, readers may find the following chronology helpful in understanding the basic historical events that have shaped the Special Air Service family. At times any combination of SAS units, from Britain, Rhodesia, Australia and New Zealand have operated together in any number of permutations. Likewise, the SAS has operated in several theatres of war during the same time-span, with the unit name being changed slightly on reformation.

1941 The Special Boat Section carried out its first raid on the night of 22 June; prior to this it had been known as Floboat section.

1941 David Stirling was given permission in July to raise the SAS from members of L Detachment. The SAS was described as a brigade; however, there was at that time no SAS Brigade, and it was a ruse to deceive the Germans.

1941 On the night of 16/17 November the SAS carried out their first raid, which was not successful.

1943 In January Lieutenant-Colonel David Stirling, founder of the regiment, was taken prisoner and later sent to Colditz Castle in Germany. Lieutenant-Colonel R.B. 'Paddy' Mayne took over command, by which time the SAS had developed considerable waterborne raiding skills. At the conclusion of the North African campaign 1 SAS was renamed SRS (Special Raiding Squadron). The Special Boat Section became the SBS (Special Boat Section) and was under the command of Lieutenant-Colonel the Earl Jellicoe. While the SBS operated in the Aegean and Adriatic, the SRS carried out commando-style raids in Sicily and Italy.

1943 The 2nd SAS Regiment was created by the founder's brother, Lieutenant-Colonel William 'Bill' Stirling.

1944 By January the SRS units, less SBS, were reformed into SAS Brigade, under the command of Brigadier R.W. McLeod. It comprised:
1 SAS Lt.-Col. R.B. Mayne, the former SAS and SRS.

2 SAS Lt.-Col. B.M.F. Franks.
3 SAS (French) Lt.-Col. J. Conan.
4 SAS (French) Lt.-Col. P. Bourgoin.
5 SAS (Belgian) Lt.-Col. E. Blondeel.
'F' Squadron from Phantom (GHQ Reconnaissance Regiment).

1945   At the end of the war in July, 1 and 2 SAS (British) were disbanded, with 3 and 4 SAS (French) going to the French Army; likewise 5 SAS went to the Belgian Army.

1945   The SAS Regimental Association was formed in November.

1947   21 SAS (Artists) TA formed under command of Lieutenant-Colonel B.M.F. Franks.

1950   2 SBS was formed from a detachment of the Amphibious School attached to the Royal Navy Rhine Squadron in West Germany.

1950   Malayan Scouts formed under the command of Lieutenant-Colonel J.M. Calvert. They were joined by volunteers from 21 SAS (Artists) TA.

1951   In March the Southern Rhodesia Far East Volunteer Unit was raised for service in Malaya. The unit was designated C (Rhodesia) Squadron Malayan Scouts (SAS). A and B Squadrons were already in existence, A Squadron having been formed from volunteers from units in Malaya and B Squadron from volunteers from 21 SAS Regiment (Artists) (TA). 264 (SAS) Signals Squadron's origins also date back to 1951 when as a signals troop they were attached to the Malayan Scouts (SAS).

1952   The Malayan Scouts were officially redesignated 22nd SAS Regiment (22 SAS).

1952   C (Rhodesia) Squadron returned to Rhodesia where it was disbanded shortly afterwards.

1955   New Zealand SAS (NZSAS) Squadron formed under Major Frank Rennie. The unit was sent to Malaya.

1957   NZSAS Squadron returned to New Zealand and was disbanded.

1957   The Australian SAS unit formed.

1958   The SAS were sent to Oman where they assaulted Jebel Akhdar.

1959   The SAS left Malaya. Settled temporarily in Malvern but were then transferred to permanent camp at Hereford the following year.

1959 The New Zealand Squadron was reformed. In May 1962 a detachment was deployed to Thailand where its two troops assisted US Army Special Forces.

1959 23 SAS (TA) formed in London, but were later transferred to Birmingham.

1962 A small team from Rhodesia was sent to train with the SAS enabling them to restart the Rhodesian SAS.

1962 Regimental Headquarters transferred from Duke's Road, Euston, to another location in London.

1963 The NZ Squadron was redesignated 1st Ranger Squadron New Zealand SAS.

1963 22 SAS were committed to Borneo.

1964 The Australian Special Air Service Regiment (SASR) was formed on 4 September.

1964 The regiment had a squadron permanently operating in Aden.

1966 In July 264 (SAS) Signals Squadron was formed as a fully independent unit located with 22 SAS in Hereford.

1966 In June an Australian SAS Squadron (SASR) was deployed to South Vietnam.

1967 The SAS withdrew from Aden.

1968 In December a detachment, designated 4 Troop, 1st Ranger Squadron NZSAS, was deployed to South Vietnam on attachment to the Australian SAS squadron based at Nui Dat in Phuoc Tuy Province.

1969 SAS troops are committed to Northern Ireland albeit in a small way; by 1971 a whole squadron was operating Province wide.

1970 The Oman War began with two squadrons leading the main assault on to the Jebel Massif.

1971 In February the New Zealand SAS withdrew from Vietnam. Subsequently, the 1st Ranger Squadron NZSAS was redesignated the 1st NZ SAS Group.

1971 The Australian SASR withdrew from Vietnam.

1974 The SAS anti-terrorist team was raised in Hereford to counter the growing international terrorist threat.

1977 Two SAS anti-terrorist team members assisted the Germans with a hijacked aircraft.

1978 1 Special Air Service Regiment (Rhodesia) officially renamed.

1980 1 Special Air Service Regiment (Rhodesia) was disbanded, many members going on to join the South African Defence Force (SADF).

1980 The SAS were called in to end the Iranian Embassy Siege.

1982 Two plus SAS squadrons were sent to the war in the Falklands, which cost the regiment 21 men.

1989 As part of a joint Anglo-American effort to defeat the drugs barons a squadron of SAS were sent to train the Colombians in anti-terrorist tactics.

1991 Three SAS squadrons were sent to fight in the Gulf War, where they operated for the full duration of the conflict deep inside Iraq.

1994 SAS soldiers were sent to Bosnia. The regiment prepared to move to its new base in Credenhill, Hereford.

Bibliography

Baker, W. D. *Dare To Win. The Story of the New Zealand Special Air Service.* Lothian Publishing Co., 1987.

Barber, Noel. *The War of the Running Dogs. The Malayan Emergency 1948–1960.* Collins, 1971.

Benyon-Tinker, W.E. *Dust Upon the Sea.* Hodder & Stoughton, 1947.

Bonds, Ray (ed) *The Vietnam War. The Illustrated History of the Conflict in South-East Asia.* Salamander Books, 1979.

Bradford, Roy & Martin Dillon. *Rogue Warrior of the SAS.* John Murray, 1987.

Cole, Barbara. *The Elite. The Story of the Rhodesian Special Air Service.* Three Knights Publishing, 1984.

Cole, Barbara. *The Elite Pictorial. Rhodesian Special Air Service.* Three Knights Publishing, 1986.

Cowles, Virginia. *The Phantom Major. The Story of David Stirling and the SAS Regiment.* Fontana Books, 1958.

Courtney G.B. *SBS in World War Two.* Grafton Books, 1985.

de la Billière, General Sir Peter. *Looking for Trouble. SAS to Gulf Command.* BCA, 1994.

Draper & Challenor. *Tanky Challenor. SAS and the Met.* Leo Cooper, 1990.

Dickens, Peter. *SAS. Secret War in South-East Asia.* Greenhill Books, 1991.

Farran, Roy. *Winged Dagger.* Arms & Armour Press, 1986.

Farran, Roy. *Operation Tombola.* Arms & Armour Press, 1986.

Generous, Kevin. *Vietnam. The Secret War.* Hamlyn/Bison, 1985.

Geraghty, Tony. *Who Dares Wins. The Special Air Service, 1950 to the Falklands.* Arms & Armour Press, 1983.

Harclerode, Peter. *PARA! Fifty Years of the Parachute Regiment.* Arms & Armour Press, 1992.

Harrison, Derrick. *These Men Are Dangerous. The Early Years of the SAS.* Blandford Press, 1988.

Hoe, Alan. *David Stirling. The Authorised Biography of the Creator of the SAS.* Little, Brown & Co., 1992.

Hoe, Alan & Eric Morris. *Re-enter the SAS. The Special Air Service and the Malayan Emergency.* Leo Cooper, 1994.

Horner, David. *Phantoms of the Jungle. A History of the Australian Special Air Service.* Allen & Unwin, 1989.

James, Harold & Denis Sheil-Small. *The Undeclared War.* New English Library, 1973.

Kemp, Anthony. *The SAS at War 1941–1945.* John Murray, 1991.

Kemp, Anthony. *The SAS. The Savage Wars of Peace, 1947 to the Present.* John Murray, 1994.

Ladd, James. *SAS Operations.* Robert Hale, 1986.

Ladd, James. *SBS. The Invisible Raiders.* Arms & Armour Press, 1983.

Ladd, James & Keith Melton. *Clandestine Warfare. Weapons and Equipment of the SOE and OSS.* Blandford Press, 1988.

Langley, Mike. *Anders Lassen VC, MC of the SAS.* New English Library, 1988.

Lassen, Suzanne. *Anders Lassen. The Story of A Dane.* Frederick Muller, 1965.

Lodwick, John. *The Filibusters.* Methuen & Co., 1947.

Lorain, Pierre. *Secret Warfare. The Arms and Techniques of the Resistance.* Orbis Publishing, 1983.

Malone, M.J. *SAS. A Pictorial History of the Australian Special Air Service 1957–1997.* Access Press, 1997.

Parker, John. *SBS. The Inside Story of the Special Boat Service.* Headline, 1997.

Pitt, Barrie. *Special Boat Squadron. The Story of the SBS in the Mediterranean.* Century Publishing, 1983.

Pocock, Tom. *Fighting General. The Public & Private Campaigns of General Sir Walter Walker.* Collins, 1973.

Ramsay, Jack. *The Soldier's Story.* Macmillan, 1996.

Seligman, Adrian. *War in the Islands. Undercover Operations in the Aegean 1942–44.* Alan Sutton Publishing, 1996.

Seymour, William. *British Special Forces.* Sidgwick & Jackson, 1985.

Smith, E.D. *Counter-Insurgency Operations: Malaya and Borneo.* Ian Allan, 1985.

Warner, Philip. *The Special Air Service.* William Kimber, 1971.

Special Acknowledgements

The author wishes to acknowledge the professional assistance rendered by the following people involved in researching this book. Without their support, in-depth knowledge and writing skills this book would not have been completed.

Peter Harclerode, who was commissioned into the Irish Guards in 1967, subsequently serving in the Middle East, the United Kingdom and Southeast Asia. In 1973 he transferred to the 2nd King Edward VIII's own Gurkha Rifles, serving with the 1st Battalion as a company commander in Brunei and Hong Kong. As a territorial Army Officer, he also served with the Special Air Service entering the defence industry before becoming an author specializing in military history, with five publications to his name.

Peter Darman worked as a research officer in the Defence Intelligence Staff, British Ministry of Defence, specializing in the armies of the Warsaw Pact and Communist China. His work included intelligence conferences in both Britain and the United States and writing classified research papers. On leaving the MoD he continued his research, concentrating on Special Forces units around the world, and specifically the British SAS. Peter has published a number of SAS books under his own name.

To Steve Collins and Debra Duckworth of P55 I owe a debt of gratitude not just for this book but for several others, and the same applies to Julie Pembridge of Gloucester for her tremendous effort in helping formulate the book.

I am also extremely grateful to all those people from Australia who have contributed to this book, in particular Cameron Hardiman who gathered the much needed information and photographs on the Australian SAS, and Benjamin Doyle-Cox who faithfully delivered them to Hereford for me. A special thanks also goes to M.J. 'Mick' Malone OAM who served with the SASR from 1967 to 1992, and who is now the current administrator of the Army Museum.

Finally, this extremely professional publication would not have been possible without the experience and skilled staff at Virgin Publishing, mentioning Lorna Russell in particular.